O(

Building MPLS-Based
Broadband Access VPNs

Kumar Reddy

Foreword by
Eli Eisenpress,
Senior Director, Software Development, Cisco Systems, Inc.

Cisco Press
800 East 96th Street
Indianapolis, IN 46240 USA

Building MPLS-Based Broadband Access VPNs

Kumar Reddy

Copyright© 2005 Cisco Systems, Inc.

Published by:
Cisco Press
800 East 96th Street
Indianapolis, IN 46240 USA

Printed in the United States of America 1 2 3 4 5 6 7 8 9 0

First Printing   November 2004

Library of Congress Cataloging-in-Publication Number: 2003101228

ISBN: 1-58705-136-2

Warning and Disclaimer

This book is designed to provide information about MPLS-based VPNs and other broadband-access VPNs. Every effort has been made to make this book as complete and as accurate as possible, but no warranty or fitness is implied.

The information is provided on an "as is" basis. The authors, Cisco Press, and Cisco Systems, Inc. shall have neither liability nor responsibility to any person or entity with respect to any loss or damages arising from the information contained in this book or from the use of the discs or programs that may accompany it.

The opinions expressed in this book belong to the author and are not necessarily those of Cisco Systems, Inc.

Feedback Information

At Cisco Press, our goal is to create in-depth technical books of the highest quality and value. Each book is crafted with care and precision, undergoing rigorous development that involves the unique expertise of members from the professional technical community.

Readers' feedback is a natural continuation of this process. If you have any comments regarding how we could improve the quality of this book, or otherwise alter it to better suit your needs, you can contact us through e-mail at feedback@ciscopress.com. Please make sure to include the book title and ISBN in your message.

We greatly appreciate your assistance.

Corporate and Government Sales

Cisco Press offers excellent discounts on this book when ordered in quantity for bulk purchases or special sales.

For more information please contact: U.S. Corporate and Government Sales 1-800-382-3419
corpsales@pearsontechgroup.com

For sales outside the U.S. please contact: International Sales international@pearsoned.com

Trademark Acknowledgments

All terms mentioned in this book that are known to be trademarks or service marks have been appropriately capitalized. Cisco Press or Cisco Systems, Inc. cannot attest to the accuracy of this information. Use of a term in this book should not be regarded as affecting the validity of any trademark or service mark.

Publisher	John Wait
Editor-in-Chief	John Kane
Executive Editor	Jim Schachterle
Cisco Representative	Anthony Wolfenden
Cisco Press Program Manager	Nannette M. Noble
Production Manager	Patrick Kanouse
Development Editor	Jill Batistick
Project Editor	Tim Wright
Copy Editor	Bill McManus
Technical Editors	Vince Mammoliti, Kali Mishra, Steve Phillips, Richard Pruss, Thomas Royce
Editorial Assistant	Tammi Barnett
Book and Cover Designer	Louisa Adair
Composition	Mark Shirar
Indexer	Brad Herriman

CISCO SYSTEMS

Corporate Headquarters
Cisco Systems, Inc.
170 West Tasman Drive
San Jose, CA 95134-1706
USA
www.cisco.com
Tel: 408 526-4000
    800 553-NETS (6387)
Fax: 408 526-4100

European Headquarters
Cisco Systems International BV
Haarlerbergpark
Haarlerbergweg 13-19
1101 CH Amsterdam
The Netherlands
www-europe.cisco.com
Tel: 31 0 20 357 1000
Fax: 31 0 20 357 1100

Americas Headquarters
Cisco Systems, Inc.
170 West Tasman Drive
San Jose, CA 95134-1706
USA
www.cisco.com
Tel: 408 526-7660
Fax: 408 527-0883

Asia Pacific Headquarters
Cisco Systems, Inc.
Capital Tower
168 Robinson Road
#22-01 to #29-01
Singapore 068912
www.cisco.com
Tel: +65 6317 7777
Fax: +65 6317 7799

Cisco Systems has more than 200 offices in the following countries and regions. Addresses, phone numbers, and fax numbers are listed on the **Cisco.com Web site at www.cisco.com/go/offices.**

Argentina • Australia • Austria • Belgium • Brazil • Bulgaria • Canada • Chile • China PRC • Colombia • Costa Rica • Croatia • Czech Republic Denmark • Dubai, UAE • Finland • France • Germany • Greece • Hong Kong SAR • Hungary • India • Indonesia • Ireland • Israel • Italy Japan • Korea • Luxembourg • Malaysia • Mexico • The Netherlands • New Zealand • Norway • Peru • Philippines • Poland • Portugal Puerto Rico • Romania • Russia • Saudi Arabia • Scotland • Singapore • Slovakia • Slovenia • South Africa • Spain • Sweden Switzerland • Taiwan • Thailand • Turkey • Ukraine • United Kingdom • United States • Venezuela • Vietnam • Zimbabwe

About the Author

Kumar Reddy is a manager of *Technical Marketing Engineering* at Cisco Systems. He has 15 years of industry experience and was involved with DSL broadband at Cisco since some of the earliest deployments in 1998. Kumar contributed to broadband technology and product evolution at Cisco and worked on major customer designs, both in the United States and internationally. Kumar's current work at Cisco focuses on technical competitive analysis for LAN switching and Access systems.

In previous roles at Cisco, Kumar was a systems engineer in France, working with service provider customers. Before joining Cisco, Kumar taught programming and networking to unsuspecting engineering students in Paris, Japan. Kumar has a degree in computer engineering from Trinity College, Dublin.

About the Technical Reviewers

Vince Mammoliti, CCIE No. 2800, is a consulting system engineer for Cisco Systems. Vince started his career after graduating from Mohawk College of Applied Arts and Technology with a computer electronics engineering technology diploma in 1987. For the last few years, he has specialized in high-speed broadband aggregation and remote access technologies, and he is currently a technical lead in the World Wide Service Provider Technology Leadership Program focusing on IP Access and Aggregation.

KP Mishra is a technical leader at Cisco Systems. His professional responsibilities include promoting advanced network technologies, technology and solution requirement analysis, and network architecture improvements with advanced technologies. During the last 20 years, he has worked in virtually every aspect of information technology, including requirement analysis, design and development of systems/networking software, managing software projects, test planning, training development, network deployment, and network architecture development.

Steve Phillips, CCIE No. 1504, has been in the networking industry for 14 years in various roles. He has worked at Cisco for eight years as a systems engineer, consulting SE, and technical marketing engineer and been implicated in several large scale network design and implementation projects for campus, large-scale IP, MPLS VPN, IP multi-cast and metro Ethernet networks. Steve gained CCIE status in July 1995.

Richard Pruss, CCIE No. 2489, is the senior manager of Edge Services Architecture Group for Cisco Internet Technology Group. His current professional interests revolve predominately around the access control, features control, network control and policy control of network services. Richard has a long history with networking technology starting 14 years ago doing humble small business networks through building South Africa's first national government owned Internet service provider to various service providers in Europe before joining Cisco to work on network design.

Thomas Royce has worked at Cisco Systems for more than three years as a technical marketing engineer with a focus in product and systems competitive activities. He has 25 years of experience in the computer industry with more than 14 years of specific focus in network communications. Tom holds degrees in engineering and management, including an ASET degree from the New Hampshire Technical Institute, a BET degree from the University of New Hampshire, and an MBA degree from Rivier College. He continues to be an active adjunct professor at UNH and provides consulting services to several universities as a member of their industrial advisory board.

Dedication

This book is dedicated to my daughters, Julia, Chloe, and Emma, and to Isabelle, my wonderful wife, who make it all worth it.

Acknowledgments

Thanks first to Stephane Lamarre, who manages to be both a boss and a good friend, for supporting me throughout this and other endeavors. He has promised to read the book and I am going to quiz him on it.

If you plan to write a book, find a group of strong and opinionated reviewers. My technical reviewers have played a huge role in transforming this work from a series of somewhat interesting parts into what I hope is a useful and interesting whole. They caught a lot of mistakes, made many useful suggestions, and challenged countless instances of muggy thinking, for which I thank them. As custom has it, all remaining errors are entirely my own.

A big "thank you" goes out to the Cisco Press team for this book. Jim Schachterle, Christopher Cleveland, Jill Batistick, Bill McManus, Tim Wright, and the rest of the team have been incredibly professional and a pleasure to work with. I couldn't have asked for a finer team.

I am lucky enough to have access to a large amount of Cisco internal reference documents that touch on the subject matter covered in this book. I have made every effort to list and credit all the documents and their authors and want to acknowledge their work and effort here.

Finally, a special recognition is due to the very talented Cisco engineers who toil night and day to create the innovation and solutions describe, in this book.

And a nod of the head also goes to those who congregate at the Friday Morning Think Tank. They know who they are and should get back to work immediately.

Contents at a Glance

Contents

Icons Used in This Book

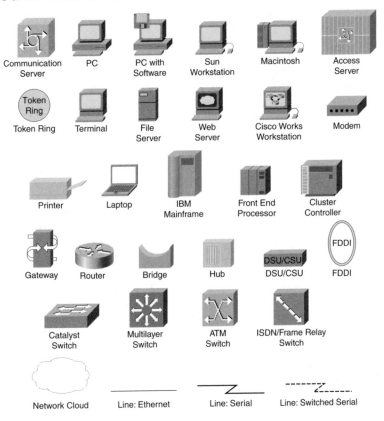

Command Syntax Conventions

The conventions used to present command syntax in this book are the same conventions used in the *Cisco IOS Command Reference*, as follows:

- **Boldface** indicates commands and keywords that are entered literally as shown. In actual configuration examples and output (not general command syntax), boldface indicates commands that are manually input by the user (such as a **show** command).

- *Italics* indicate arguments for which you supply actual values.

- Vertical bars (|) separate alternative, mutually exclusive elements.

- Square brackets ([ ]) indicate optional elements.

- Braces ({ }) contain a choice of required keywords.

- Braces within brackets ([{ }]) indicate a required choice within an optional element.

Foreword

As the Internet has evolved from an academic curiosity to a ubiquitous business tool and a popular bit of entertainment and communications gear for the home, we've seen the face of the Internet evolve by watching its applications. Starting with text-based e-mail programs and arcane file transfer commands, to basic web browsers (remember when the precursor to Netscape fit easily on a diskette?), the applications have grown in speed, power, and complexity to today's multiplayer games, video and music players, sophisticated browsers, and fancy business applications that roll entire business processes into graphical web-based business transaction systems.

Behind that color, flash, and power is an evolving system of data communications "plumbing" that's invisible to the typical user of the Internet. Although invisible, this plumbing makes it possible for information to flow over the Internet, and it has had to grow at a breakneck pace to allow the volume and complexity of the Internet's data to grow from that text-only e-mail for a few thousand users to video for millions of users.

If you've picked up this book, it's very likely you are one of those people who's interested in what is going on in the walls and the basement, how the plumbing is installed, and how things are flowing through it, even though you can't see any of it at first glance. There are large practical problems in building the Internet to carry vast amounts of data affordably, including the physical challenges of installing wiring and routers, the needs to leverage existing telephone system infrastructure, and the economic and regulatory factors. These problems have been a fascinating challenge to the data communications community and have resulted in many creative and complex solutions.

I'm part of an engineering team at Cisco Systems that builds software for a piece of gear known as aggregation equipment. That's a special-purpose router that takes many connections—for example, from home DSL users—does some interesting things with the connections, and then funnels the data up to the big Internet connection. About 1998, when the hot aggregation technology we were working with was dial-up modem connections, and the high-speed, state-of-the-art technology was ISDN, we began hearing mysterious rumblings about "remote access to MPLS." Mysterious, only because MPLS was as much of a black art to us dial-access folks as dial access was a black art to the MPLS software designers.

But, as both engineering teams learned, this was the leading edge of a very exciting link between access aggregation technologies (dial, broadband) and IP backbone VPN technologies such as MPLS. Other VPN technologies such as L2F, IPSec, and GRE were already knocking around as well. Access and VPN were important to each other because we had to combine them to build the plumbing that would fully meet the needs of home users, businesses, and the Internet service providers that were connecting them to each other and to the Internet.

To meet the needs, a bewildering array of technologies has been put in place. In many cases, the technologies are layered to provide the service that's needed with the infrastructure that's available. If the plumbing in your home's walls were like this, you might find large pipes with smaller pipes inside, entering and exiting the outer pipes almost at random according to some unwritten plumbing regulations. Amazingly, though, cold water would flow out of the cold tap and hot water out of the hot!

Kumar Reddy is one of a very small band of people who could write this book. In one corner of the communications equipment industry are the highly specialized engineers who design the equipment. Their main stock in trade is the know-how to create the hardware or software that will do its designated job. At the other end of the spectrum are the customers and equipment vendor personnel who deploy and run the equipment to provide the communications services. They know the network's design and how to install and configure the equipment to make that design a reality.

Kumar is a long-time inhabitant of the zone between these two worlds. With a deep understanding of what problems the customers are trying to solve with the communications equipment, and a detailed knowledge of what the engineers are building, he has spent years tinkering, testing, explaining, and imagining what can be done with the different parts (even some that are not yet built) for this intricate plumbing system.

In this book, Kumar weaves together his deployment and engineering knowledge and systematically leads the reader through the needs behind broadband access VPN, the technology building blocks, and how and why they are put together to solve a range of communications needs. With its comprehensive coverage of the technologies, reasons for choosing them, detailed configuration guidelines, and future trends, this book takes the mystery out of access VPN and, I hope, makes it as accessible to deploy as it is exciting for teams like mine to design.

Eli Eisenpress
Senior Director, Software Development
Cisco Systems, Inc.

Introduction

Why is there so much interest in VPNs right now? Why is broadband access growing so fast? And what do these two phenomena have in common?

This book describes a set of building blocks that you can use to build virtual private network services for broadband subscribers of almost all shapes and sizes.

Although the focus here is on MPLS, other VPN solutions are by no means forgotten; the book covers tunnels such as IPSec and L2TP in some detail and takes a detour through the technology landscape to look at the virtualization of services as well as some of the newer and more relevant developments around Layer 2 VPNs and IPv6.

There is a definite slant toward DSL as the broadband access network of choice. This is partly because it's my own background, but mostly because DSL is richer in options and more complex in regulation than other access networks. But, the problems and answers presented for DSL networks should apply equally well to cable, Ethernet, and even wireless. In fact, another book (by another person) should look at how these access technologies are converging.

One of the tenets of this book is that broadband access VPNs have different design requirements than do standard MPLS-VPN service networks. Therefore, before looking at the MPLS solution, you should understand the scale issues associated with broadband networks. Chapter 3, "VPNs in Broadband Networks," gives you that opportunity by focusing on L2TP, including AAA server load balancing, LNS groups, redundancy, session-per-tunnel limitations, and tunnel aggregation (or switching). Some of the nerd knobs become refreshingly unnecessary in an MPLS network, such as the concept of aggregating tunnels, or the need to explicitly load balance sessions across multiple LNSs. Control protocol-related features typically reappear in an MPLS-based solution. It is important that you grasp the scaling and operational problems that these networks must address to understand why a broadband access MPLS network looks the way it does.

That said, and despite the title, this book tries to adopt an open stance with regard to alternatives to MPLS and recognizes that, while MPLS is a compelling fit for broadband access, it is not the only choice.

Goals and Methods

Each chapter essentially follows a similar formula: first a discussion of the technology—how it works and what problem it tries to fix—followed by a description of how to implement the technology on Cisco products—how to make the technology work.

The purpose of the book is to help you do the following:

- Obtain a realistic understanding of large-scale broadband access network design requirements

- Recognize the impact of using MPLS and other technologies to provide access VPN services, including the advantages of quality of service, availability, and provisioning

- Understand how to use MPLS in access VPN and transport networks and deal with the unique problems of scale that such networks pose

You might want to keep this list in mind if you need to convince someone else to pay for this book.

In true Cisco Press fashion, I tend to err on the side of providing more detail rather than less. All the topologies and configurations shown in this book were tested extensively and a lot of effort was made to include as many configurations as the weight of a book would allow. When researching the various topics covered here, especially some of the more recent or esoteric ones, I would often find interesting snippets in online documentation, but not enough to do something completely useful. Looking at hundreds of lines of configuration can be less than thrilling, though, so these are relegated to the Cisco Press website: http://www.ciscopress.com/1587051362.

Who Should Read This Book?

This is not an introductory-level book, nor is it for doctoral candidates. The target readership includes network designers, planners, architects, operators, and support personnel. (Additionally, technically savvy IT executives may also benefit.) In other words, the people responsible for the support, design, and deployment of network services will find the topic, scope, and level of detail beneficial, whether they are looking at options for a new access VPN service or at migrating an existing transport infrastructure to MPLS.

The secondary audience includes the user and purchaser of access VPNs, including IT and telecom consultants and directors in small, midsize, and large enterprises, as well as network engineers and support staff.

Required Knowledge

This book is intended for a technical audience, with a level of experience ranging from intermediate to expert. A working knowledge of MPLS and broadband access is recommended; however, introductory material is included to help those who are unfamiliar with these technologies. Familiarity with Cisco IOS and Cisco routers is assumed.

How This Book Is Organized

You could read this book cover to cover, but the chapters are also designed to let you pick and choose just the material that interests you. The book does have a one-stop shop philosophy and so prepares the way for discussion of architectures by covering the protocols and technologies that networks actually use.

The book is intended to be reasonably self-sufficient, so it introduces the basics of both broadband access and label switching before tackling the union of the two. That said, a lot of background detail isn't included, so if your work, network, or interest pushes you to know more about traffic engineering, for example, you should certainly look for a specialized title. The appendix gives the full bibliography used to prepare this book, and you may find some of those references useful, too. Readers who are familiar with the introductory material should skip ahead to the parts that interest them more directly.

The book is organized into these sections:

- Chapters 2 through 4 introduce access protocols, VPNs, and MPLS.

- Chapters 5 through 8 are the core of the book and cover the architecture, configuration, and examples of use of MPLS in broadband access VPNs.

- Chapter 9 looks forward at other technologies coming soon to the access VPN near you, such as IPv6.

The details of each chapter are as follows:

- **Chapter 1, Introduction: Broadband Access and Virtual Private Networks**—This chapter introduces the players of the broadband world: PTTs, retail ISPs, and others. It also discusses different service models, which is how anyone makes money from all this technology. Finally, the chapter defines a framework that will be used to compare different VPN solutions.

- **Chapter 2: Delivering Broadband Access Today: An Access Technologies Primer**—This chapter covers the fundamentals of broadband access service architectures, highlighting the three most common protocols: PPP, bridging, and the more recent 802.1q, and looks at where the protocols are most commonly used, namely DSL, cable, and ETTx.

- **Chapter 3: VPNs in Broadband Networks**—This chapter covers the use of tunnels over IP. L2TP, IPSec, and GRE are probably the most prevalent form of VPN today. The chapter goes through each in turn, first at the protocol level and then at the configuration level, before finally comparing their suitability for broadband access using the VPN framework, which includes security capability, QoS support, and so forth.

- **Chapter 4: Introduction to MPLS**—Before getting into road-hardened discussions of large-scale broadband, this chapter reviews fundamental label-switching concepts. This is not an exhaustive explanation because this topic is addressed in other books, but it provides necessary technical grounding for readers who are unfamiliar with MPLS, focusing on the topics that become important in subsequent sections.

- **Chapter 5: Introduction to MPLS-Based Access VPN Architectures**—Tunnel-based VPNs work well between a small number of peers, but MPLS VPN becomes much more practical as the number of peers increases. Some of the main requirements of broadband access VPN are the ability to deal with complex network topologies with the least amount of provisioning, and to provide support for advanced QoS. MPLS VPN does this admirably. This chapter describes the architectures of an MPLS-based solution, explains how subscribers are mapped to VRFs, and introduces the concept of a Virtual Home Gateway.

- **Chapter 6: Wholesale MPLS-VPN Related Service Features**—In good design, detail counts, and this chapter goes into a lot of detail. For example, subscriber features and services must be VRF aware, all the way down to the av-pairs used in RADIUS profiles. Here, you get close to the implementation and go through some of the changes and permutations that can make configuring a complete VRF-aware solution a challenge.

- **Chapter 7: Implementing Network-Based Access VPNs Without MPLS**—Again, recognizing that MPLS is not mandatory and that some network designs will not or cannot use it, this chapter looks at how to use the IP tunnels covered in Chapter 2 in a network-based solution. Because the implementation reuses many of the features developed for MPLS, this is somewhat of an extended case study of how to use VRFs. The chapter discusses virtual routers—both what they are and what they aren't.

- **Chapter 8: Case Studies for Using MPLS with Broadband VPNs**—This chapter goes over two case studies at a design level (no configuration details here) and looks at the different ways to deploy network services, both with and without the MPLS-based approach to help highlight the advantages and disadvantages of each solution.

- **Chapter 9: Future Developments in Broadband Access**—Finally, this chapter looks at technologies coming soon to the broadband network near you. IPv6 is an obvious candidate and will be a motor for some big changes in broadband, just as it is in other areas of networking. In anticipation of the convergence of commercial metro and residential broadband access networks, this chapter also looks at L2VPN technologies.

- **Appendix A: References and Bibliography**—This appendix contains a list of references to help you find more information about topics that are of particular interest to you.

In this chapter, you learn about the following topics:

- Broadband Networks and Operators
- Service Models: Who Buys What
- IP Virtual Private Networks for Broadband
- A Simplified Framework for Broadband VPN

CHAPTER 1

Introduction: Broadband Access and Virtual Private Networks

After a slow start, the massive deployment of broadband is finally starting to have an aura of inevitability around it. Some statistics demonstrate how quickly this is happening. According to the DSL Forum (http://www.dslforum.org), there were 63.8 million digital subscriber line (DSL) subscribers worldwide in March 2004, 8 million of which had been added in the previous 6 months! That is a rate of over 44,000 new customers per day for DSL alone. Add in other broadband technologies, and the rate of adoption becomes truly impressive.

The broadband phenomenon is also well spread out across the world. The top five countries in terms of percentage of phone lines converted to DSL (again, DSL Forum data for 2004) are South Korea, Taiwan, Belgium, Hong Kong, and Japan. The most growth occurred in Peru and Malaysia. China, Japan, and the U.S. each had more than ten million DSL subscribers and six countries in Europe have achieved over 10 percent market penetration. DSL Forum points out that this is "half-way to mass market status."

In the broadband service market, providers using different technologies compete with one another and must often fight over the same group of potential customers and try to tempt them away from the dark ages of dial-up networking to their own particular solution. Traditional service providers use existing networks and push DSL to anyone who will have it; cable operators add data services to their video service; finally, alternate providers try to use new technology, such as Ethernet, to provide lower-cost, higher-speed services and, in doing so, hope to take a chunk of business away from everyone else.

The tool of choice in this tussle for subscribers is services. Services are how providers make their money and are also what people actually buy. Services range from the very simple, such as Internet access, through the very sophisticated, such as network-based personal video recorders. Probably the most innovative services in the market today come from the Ethernet crowd, who offer cleverly bundled content and network-based applications, such as online video recorders. But the DSL and cable operators are hot on their heels, each strenuously pushing a service typically provided by the competition. Television-over-DSL trials are underway in several European and Asian cities already and cable operators tout voice over IP (VoIP) in North America, to cite just a few examples.

A Virtual Private Network (VPN) is one particular service that has a well-established—and growing—market and has its own set of competing technologies. When designing a VPN for broadband access, several differences stand out compared to more standard VPNs:

- The number of subscribers is unlike anything seen elsewhere in IP networks.
- The devices attached to the VPN are usually very unsophisticated—and the customer premises does not necessarily have a router.
- Layers of government regulation might determine who can do what in a broadband network.

Later in the chapter, I propose a basic framework to compare different VPN solutions. Much more formal frameworks exist elsewhere, notably in Internet Engineering Task Force (IETF) drafts, but I wanted to provide something that focuses on broadband and is simple to understand. The goal behind the comparison is not so much to proclaim a "winning technology" as to offer some thoughts about what a network architect might consider when looking at different ways to solve a particular problem.

Finally, this chapter includes definitions of different types of VPNs.

But first, what is broadband? Who buys it and who sells it?

Broadband Networks and Operators

Broadband is synonymous with speed: Any network fast enough to carry voice, data, and video can use this moniker. If you have a longish memory, you will remember that ATM started life as Broadband Integrated Services Digital Network (BISDN).

A Google search for the definition of broadband ("define: broadband") returns, among many others, the following terse but precise definition, courtesy of WordNet at Princeton University (http://wordnet.princeton.edu/):

> *broadband—of or relating to or being a communications network in which the bandwidth can be divided and shared by multiple simultaneous signals (as for voice or data or video)*

In the context of this book, *broadband* means any technology that allows high-speed network access to and from a subscriber premises. The subscriber may be a person or a business.

There are a number of different technology alternatives to provide broadband access. The most common today are the following:

- DSL
- Cable
- Ethernet

More details on each different type of broadband technology are provided later in this chapter, just after the introduction of the different operators, wholesale and retail, that are active in this area.

The Players in Broadband

Although there are more stringent legal definitions, for the purposes of this book, the following are the types of broadband providers:

- **Retail provider**—Any operator that sells services to an end user, be they a residential customer or a business.

- **Wholesale provider**—Any operator that sells services to other network operators. In the context of broadband, the wholesaler is generally whoever owns the subscriber plant (wires, cables and all that sort of thing).

Looking at the flow of money is a good way to understand the different broadband players and their roles in the world. As a DSL subscriber, I receive a monthly bill from my Internet Service Provider (ISP) for high-speed Internet access. ISPs have a recognizable brand name such as AOL, Wanadoo, Earthlink, T-Online, etc. These are the retail providers. In between the subscriber and their ISP is the wholesale provider, who actually owns and operates the DSL line. Wholesale providers such as SBC, France Telecom, Telstra, and others bill their ISP customers, usually based on the size of the pipe used to deliver the DSL subscriber traffic.

NOTE	Accurate and comprehensive billing mechanisms are critical for DSL services. The retailer needs this information to bill its end users. The wholesaler likewise must bill its ISP customers. Both parties want as much data as possible in case of any dispute between them.

The separation of retail and wholesale networks means that the world of DSL looks very similar to dial-up networks, where the PTT/ILEC companies provide dial tone and ISPs sell data services on telephone lines. Just as with dial-up networks, however, DSL wholesale providers are often very strictly regulated, though there are significant regional differences in what they may and may not do. In some countries, it is not necessary to have any separation between the company that provides the copper cable (and usually the voice service that runs on it) and the company that sells data services. In other countries, the wholesaler must follow very strict rules, which may even prevent it from identifying a subscriber by name.

The different types of broadband networks are generally referred to by their physical layers: DSL, Cable, Ethernet, and so on. For the IP network, these are all just different types of access. Figure 1-1 shows how little it matters that the last mile uses a particular type of modulation on twisted pairs of copper wire. The aggregation and core network are very similar no matter what the access.

Figure 1-1 *Generic Broadband Reference Architecture*

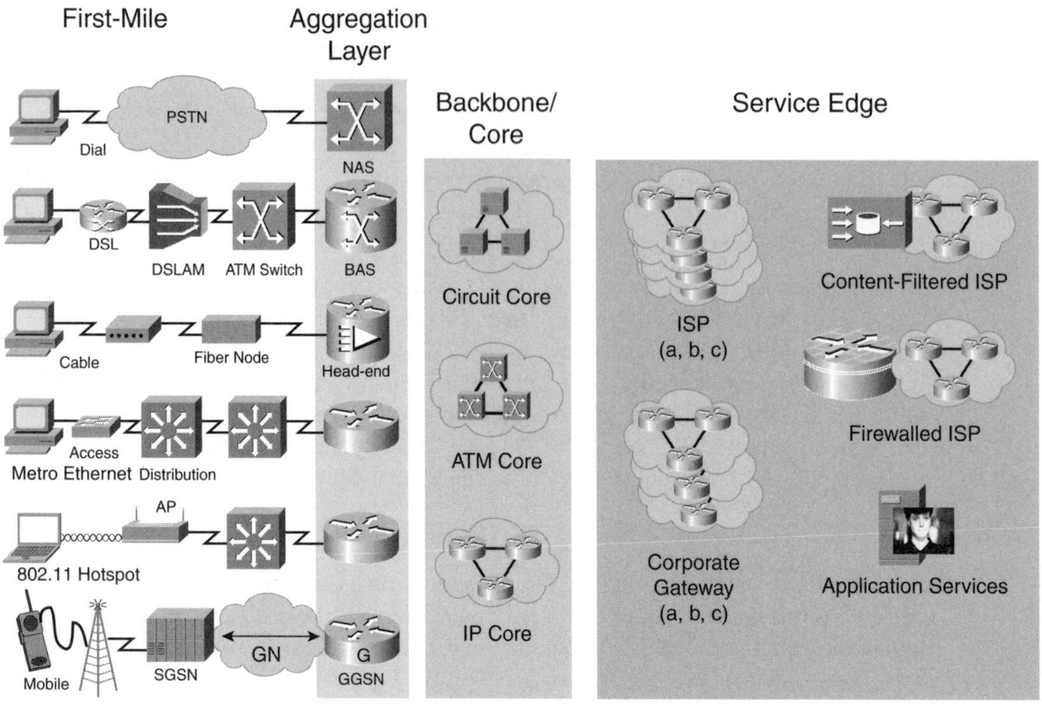

The important pieces in the broadband puzzle are the protocols that establish the conduit for IP to flow, such as PPP and bridging, which are the subject of Chapter 2, "Delivering Broadband Access Today: An Access Technologies Primer." However, the physical layers and the access networks that connect subscribers to IP devices merit brief mention here.

DSL Networks

DSL runs over copper wires and uses the traditional telephone infrastructure. Because just about everyone has a telephone in the places in the world where broadband is sold, ubiquity is the major advantage of DSL. The downside is that most telephone cabling was laid down a long time ago, with no thought at all that one day someone would want to carry something other than voice over it. As a result, especially in the U.S., there is a trade-off between reach and speed. Short loops support higher speed, but require a good-quality physical path. Long loops are more limited in their speed capability and often have additional physical impediments, such as open pairs that further reduce the signal quality.

Metropolitan-Area Networks

Metropolitan-area networks (MANs) have optical rings, which were originally laid down to carry regional data and voice traffic using SONET/SDH. Metropolitan service providers can use this infrastructure to transport Ethernet frames. Because of the cost of optical fiber, such networks really make sense only where there is a high subscriber density, such as in business districts and city centers. Consequently, there is a big interest in being able to transport Ethernet over copper.

IEEE is driving standardization efforts around Ethernet in the First Mile (EFM) for copper, fiber, and passive optical networks. (If you are interested in more details, you can look for documents from the 802.3ah Task Force at http://www.ieee802.org/3/efm/.) There is, of course, an industry alliance to compliment the push to standardization. The EFM Alliance has a useful introductory whitepaper on the topic. (See Appendix A for references.)

This discussion has only skimmed the surface, but it should be enough for you to see that the worlds of DSL and Ethernet are converging quickly.

The Role of the Access Network

Behind the First Mile network, the access network collects data traffic from the subscriber lines terminated on and transports it to the service network. The first DSL Forum reference model actually had several different service models: narrowband, BISDN, and IP; only the last of these three has seen widespread deployment. ATM is the technology of choice for the DSL access network, although there is a trend toward using Ethernet transport, at least for new deployments.

The access portion of a metro Ethernet network uses Ethernet transport and switches. An Ethernet switch maps user traffic from subscriber lines to the access network. Traffic may cross multiple layers of switches before it reaches the service network. Just like DSL, this is a Layer 2 network. You should note that there are many ways to transport Ethernet frames (over ATM, SONET/SDH, etc.) and that the term *Ethernet service* actually refers to providing a particular type of User-Network Interface (UNI). So, actual networks may look very different from the simplified reference model shown previously in Figure 1-1.

For the wholesale operator, the fundamental service offering is transport: connecting a subscriber to where they want to go, namely a service network. The service is, of course, all about IP, and the box that connects the two can be called a Broadband Remote Access Server (BRAS), a cable modem termination system (CMTS), a network provider edge (N-PE) device, or, generically, an aggregator that is found in a point of presence (POP). This is the first place that IP packets are processed and is where the Layer 3 network begins.

NOTE   *Open Access* refers to the requirement of a wholesale provider to allow a customer to connect to the service provider of its choice. Different parts of the world enforce this in different ways. One option is to open Open Access networks to competition, so that competing carriers can install and operate their own DSLAMs. Another option is to have open access at the interface between the access and service networks, implemented on the BRAS. In general, the incumbent seems to prefer the second option, while challengers like the first.

It is unusual to discuss residential broadband and VPN services in the same context, but VPNs are used to provide open access so that any residential customer can—in theory, at least—use any ISP. Some of the more interesting peculiarities of MPLS VPN in broadband networks arise from this particular scenario.

Shifting the Location of the Processing

Another tectonic shift in broadband architectures—other than the DSL- and Ethernet-based access—is that IP functionality is (slowly) migrating further toward the subscriber. There are already cases where IP processing is done on DSL Access Multiplexers (DSLAMs) or Ethernet switches in the access layer. (Looking again at Figure 1-1, this means IP is slowly drifting to the left in the diagram.) The current implementation, however, typically has the Layer 3 demarcation point at the aggregator headend, BRAS, or CMTS.

Of course, part of the broadband network is in people's homes and offices. Broadband reference models, such as the one published by DSL Forum, define the interfaces between the network and user. Typically, the customer premises equipment (CPE) is part of the retail service offering; the wholesale responsibility starts at the wall socket.

Service Models: Who Buys What

Any operator who deploys new network infrastructure needs to have a way to get its money back. No matter how exciting technical folk find any given technology, users really don't care! There must be a compelling reason for customers to switch from their current solution provider, and that compelling reason has to let the user do either something better or something new. Services are key to the success of broadband because the faster pipes down to the subscriber allow operators to imagine services that are more exciting than waiting for a modem to dial and that also give the opportunity to charge more.

To borrow some marketing jargon, you can segment the market for broadband services into two major groups: residential and business. The following sections discuss each in turn.

Business Subscribers

Businesses are the natural and intended customers for VPNs. What do businesses expect from VPNs? At a basic level, businesses expect secure, reliable connectivity for all of their applications, which increasingly includes VoIP, and for all of their people, including that pajama-wearing telecommuter in Wyoming. Translating this into networking terms, this means quality of service (QoS) is an important part of any service offering (and one thing that distinguishes MPLS as a VPN technology is the rich QoS). Finally, the service provider must offer a clear way to report on the service level agreement (SLA), so billing and accounting are an important component of the network infrastructure.

Businesses, especially the large and rich ones, pay service providers to manage large chunks of their communication infrastructure and services, such as allowing telecommuters to connect securely. This growing population already usually has broadband Internet access, so there is a strong motivation to provide a VPN service over the different access media. Architecturally, this is not very complicated, as you will see in later chapters.

Residential Subscribers

Most residential customers first move to broadband because of its faster Internet access. At this stage, the argument is usually about speed and price, and access technology can make a significant difference in both: for example, the cost advantage of Ethernet is such that a 10-Mbps service costs the same price as a 256-kbps DSL service.

After a residential subscriber is hooked, the next step for the service provider is to extract more of the subscriber's money with bouquets of services, such as the following:

- Ethernet service providers can push video, because they have a unique speed advantage over DSL. After all, most consumers won't see the benefits of a 10-Mbps Ethernet connection versus a 1-Mbps high-speed DSL service for their daily Internet access, but the difference can be used to transmit, for example, a few MPEG-4 video channels. Video is actually a complicated service because of the issues of digital rights management and licensing. However, the success of video as a telecommunications service shows in the numbers: The adoption rate for broadcast video is approximately 35 percent of subscribers. This is also a valuable way to attract new subscribers to the data offering, even if they don't actually buy it.

- Cable operators like VoIP as a residential broadband service. The attraction is obvious: It takes second-line business away from the traditional PTTs/ILEC (who are usually the purveyors of DSL, of course) and gives customers a reason to choose cable as their data-access medium. In the current, unregulated environment (at least in the U.S.), charging for VoIP service is easier than charging for video. The cable operator provides a voice gateway to the PSTN for off-net calls and uses the QoS (again) mechanisms in the Data Over Cable Service Interface Specification (DOCSIS) and IP networks to give voice packets the right level of service on its network.

IP Virtual Private Networks for Broadband

VPN service is one of the most important services available across broadband connections. VPN service is actually an unusual service because it is sold to an individual or to businesses or it is used by a network operator to connect someone else's network with its customers. Few other services cut across different populations like this. An IETF document, draft-ietf-l3vpn-requirements-00 (available online at http://www.ietf.org), has a good, general definition of a VPN:

> The term "Virtual Private Network" (VPN) refers to the communication between a set of sites, making use of a shared network infrastructure. Multiple sites of a private network may therefore communicate via the public infrastructure, in order to facilitate the operation of the private network. The logical structure of the VPN, such as topology, addressing, connectivity, reachability, and access control, is equivalent to part of or all of a conventional private network using private facilities.

The big news recently in the world of VPNs is the advent of IP, or Layer 3, VPNs. IP VPNs offer a private network that is operationally simpler for the customer and can be run on top of a shared, packet-based infrastructure. Unlike earlier VPN solutions, such as Frame Relay, X.25, or ATM, IP VPNs don't need dedicated circuits for each connection.

IP- and MPLS-based VPNs are now being used for up to 50 percent of new VPN service deployments and constitute one of the major areas of growth in today's telecom market. In the broadband arena, applications that are driving the use of VPN across higher-speed links include data applications such as file backup, but also include more sophisticated applications such as VoIP to extend intra enterprise communications to remote offices. MPLS networks, with their QoS, traffic engineering, and easy provisioning, support quick deployment of VPN services, including for broadband subscribers.

A VPN Taxonomy

VPNs can be built in different ways for different groups. The following are the different ways in which VPNs are deployed:

- **Site-to-site VPN**—A VPN that is used to connect different sites. This is the classic VPN scenario. As shown in Figure 1-2, each site has one or more CPE routers, which may be managed by a service provider (called a *managed service*) or by the enterprise whose network this is (an *unmanaged service*). The VPN can be built using a Layer 2 (for example, ATM or Frame Relay) or Layer 3 (for example, MPLS VPN) network. This term is often shortened to site VPN.

- **Telecommuter VPN**—An individual subscriber, or very small network, that connects over a third-party network to a bigger branch or campus network. This definition also includes the special case of roaming, in which the person is not in his or her usual location when connecting to the VPN. A telecommuter VPN may be one of many services available to a subscriber in a particular location.

- **Wholesale VPN**—A special case of a VPN used by a wholesale provider to transport subscriber traffic to its service provider of choice. Wholesale VPNs are transparent to end users.

- **Internet access**—This is not a VPN service, but it belongs in this list because it refers to high-speed Internet access for either consumer or business subscribers. Internet traffic may cross one or several wholesale VPNs. A VPN can be built over an Internet access connection.

Figure 1-2   *Site-to-Site VPN*

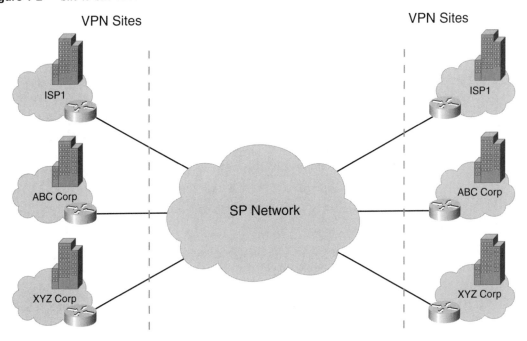

A VPN might start and end either at the customer premises or in the service provider network, as follows:

- **CPE-based VPN**—The VPN starts and ends on CPE. For example, an IPSec tunnel is initiated from one CPE router to another. The service provider network is used only to transport IP packets. RFC documents refer to this as CE-based VPN. A CPE-based VPN can be provisioned and operated either by the enterprise or by a service provider as a managed service.

- **Network-based VPN**—The VPN starts on a service provider device. It may end on either a service provider or CPE device. The most common example of a network-based VPN is Layer 2 Tunneling Protocol (L2TP), in which a tunnel is initiated on the BRAS. But it is also possible to have other network-based VPNs, such as IPSec. Privacy is an integral requirement of any VPN service, so there is an implicit assumption made here that the link between the customer and the start of the VPN is secure. This is often true in broadband networks; for example, each DSL subscriber has a different ATM permanent virtual circuit (PVC). This is also known as a PE-based VPN. A network-based VPN is always operated by a service provider.

Layer 2 and Layer 3 VPN Alternatives

VPNs can be built over Layer 2 or Layer 3 core networks. Figure 1-3 summarizes the different options for building both kinds of VPNs. The diagram is adapted from draft-ietf-l3vpn-applicability-guidelines-00 (available at http://www.ietf.org). Some terms used in Figure 1-3 merit further explanation:

- **L2oL3**—A Layer 2 VPN (L2VPN) service delivered over a Layer 3 core network. The following are the different types of Layer 2 services. L2VPNs are covered in Chapter 9, "Future Developments in Broadband Access.":

    — Virtual Private Wire Service (VPWS), a point-to-point service.

    — Virtual Private LAN Service (VPLS), a point-to-multipoint service.

- **PE-based**—A network-based VPN:

    — RFC2547–style—The VPN service is built in compliance with RFC 2547bis. MPLS VPNs are the best-known example and are covered in depth in Chapter 4, "Introduction to MPLS."

    — Virtual router–style—The VPN uses point-to-point links between virtual router instances that run on physical routers. Chapter 7, "Implementing Network-Based Access VPNs Without MPLS," goes into this in more detail.

- **CE-based**—A CPE-based VPN that uses tunnels overlaid a Layer 3 core:

    — IP Security (IPSec)—A VPN built using IPSec tunnels (covered in Chapter 3, "VPNs in Broadband Networks").

    — Generic routing encapsulation (GRE)—A VPN built using GRE tunnels (also covered in Chapter 3).

Figure 1-3   *VPN Hierarchy*

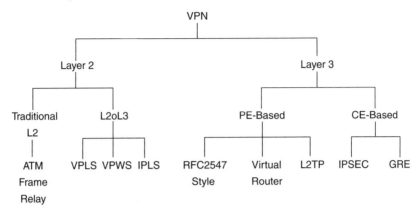

In Figure 1-3, you can see that there are two architectures for Layer 3 VPNs: the overlay model, which uses point-to-point tunnels between CPE, and the peer model, in which CPE and service provider devices have a peer relationship. (For example, they exchange IP routes.) The term *overlay* refers to the fact that one network (the customer's private one) is overlaid on top of another network (the service provider's).

Overlay VPNs

This first category of IP VPNs uses tunnels to build point-to-point connections over an IP core. The architecture is very simple: CPEs are connected to one another using tunnels that transport, usually, IP packets over the service provider network.

The common choices of encapsulation are as follows:

- **Generic Routing Encapsulation**—GRE has been around for a very long time—at least as far as networking technology goes. GRE was originally proposed to encapsulate protocols such as IPX, AppleTalk, or IP itself over a common IP network infrastructure.

- **IPSec VPN**—Today, IPSec is arguably the most common form of VPN technology used by the road warrior community at large. Businesses simply tell their roving workforce to connect to the nearest ISP to establish IP connectivity, then use an IPSec client to tunnel to their destination.

  Cisco, to take an example, moved from owning and operating a battery of AS5300 NAS servers to allow its employees to connect while traveling. There were toll and toll-free dial-up numbers throughout the world. Now, this connection while traveling is done with an IPSec-based solution. You first connect to the Internet locally, and then build an IPSec tunnel to a corporate VPN server. An army of telecommuters uses this infrastructure daily, to great satisfaction.

- **L2TP**—L2TP was designed as a tunnel mechanism for dial-up connections. It has its origins in Microsoft's PPP, which uses GRE and the Cisco Layer 2 Forwarding (L2F). L2TP cannot transport IP directly, but it is a very natural fit for any type of access that uses PPP.

  Figure 1-3 shows L2TP as a Layer 3 network–based VPN technology, because the tunnel endpoints are usually on PE routers. But in truth, it is hard to classify. L2TP is really a tunneling mechanism for a Layer 2 encapsulation, namely PPP.

You can build VPNs for broadband access using any of these tunnel solutions, and Chapter 3 looks at this process in more detail using a case study format.

The Peer Model

MPLS VPNs, which are introduced in much more detail in Chapter 4, let you build VPNs over a packet network without having to use point-to-point tunnels; instead, MPLS VPNs use a peer model, defined in RFC 2547bis as follows:

This document describes a method by which a Service Provider may use an IP backbone to provide IP VPNs (Virtual Private Networks) for its customers. This method uses a "peer model," in which the customers' edge routers ("CE routers") send their routes to the Service Provider's edge routers ("PE routers"). BGP is then used by the Service Provider to exchange the routes of a particular VPN among the PE routers that are attached to that VPN. This is done in a way which ensures that routes from different VPNs remain distinct and separate, even if two VPNs have an overlapping address space. The PE routers distribute, to the CE routers in a particular VPN, the routes from other the CE routers in that VPN. The CE routers do not peer with each other, hence there is no "overlay" visible to the VPN's routing algorithm.

In traditional overlay VPN architectures, the CE routers do peer with each other. In other words, they exchange routes directly with each other. Look out for this in Chapter 3 when you read examples of VPNs with GRE, IPSec, and L2TP. However, the CE routers do not peer with the service provider network. The RFC 2547bis model offers an alternative architecture in which enterprise and service provider routers do peer.

A common misunderstanding is that RFC 2547bis-compliant network VPNs can never use tunnels (i.e., the tunnels start and end on a PE). This is not necessarily so. As long as the router supports some way of logically separating traffic from different VPNs (which Chapter 7 looks at in more detail), then tunnels can be used.

As an example of a VPN that uses tunnels but not MPLS, draft-ietf-l3vpn-ipsec-2547-03 describes how to use IPSec with an RFC 2547 model. Figure 1-4 shows a representation of network-based VPN using tunnels, taken from draft-ietf-l3vpn-framework-00.txt. Each CE in Figure 1-4 connects over a dedicated circuit to the PE, within which there is a dedicated Virtual Forwarding Instance (VFI) for each VPN. If the tunnel supports it, packets across the core can either be multiplexed across the same tunnel, or there can be a dedicated tunnel for each VPN, which is what Figure 1-4 shows.

Figure 1-4   *Network VPN*

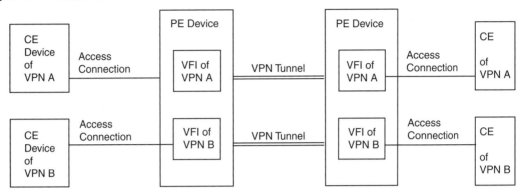

What is the attraction of MPLS VPNs for broadband access? There are really two major things to consider, which are brought out in Figure 1-5. First, IP VPNs in general, and MPLS VPNs in particular, are being deployed at ever-increasing rates, as already discussed. Service providers need a way to integrate customers on broadband links, just as they do for Layer 2 access circuits such as Frame Relay and ATM. Second, unlike tunnels, MPLS lets the service provider "be" on the data path and inject extra services at the PE router.

Figure 1-5   *Different Types of Broadband to Access an MPLS VPN*

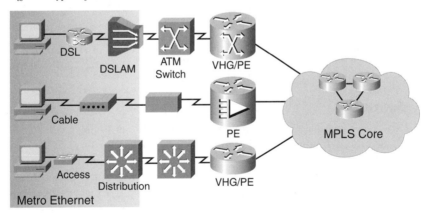

A Simplified Framework for Broadband VPN

This section uses a simple framework to compare how well a VPN technology adapts to broadband access. The qualities to look for depend, of course, on the problem you are trying to solve, so this section looks at the problem from an application perspective. (The terms site, *telecommuter*, and *wholesale* VPN were explained earlier in the chapter.)

For site VPNs, you should consider the following:

- Data confidentiality
- Efficient operation (this includes ease of provisioning)
- Efficient routing
- High availability and resiliency
- Multicast
- Quality of service
- Fragmentation

For telecommuter VPNs, you should consider the following:

- Authentication, authorization, and accounting (AAA)
- Service selection

Finally, for wholesale VPNs, you should consider the following:

- Support for any IP addressing plan
- Efficient address management
- Additional L3 services (notably QoS)

The requirements for each different type of VPN are cumulative. So, a telecommuter VPN needs everything a site VPN does, as well as authentication and service selection, and so on.

The simple framework presented here is pretty informal. Some of the attributes, such as data confidentiality, are mandatory for a VPN service; others are included to have points of comparison between different technologies (for example, fragmentation).

Data Confidentiality

A VPN is a connectivity service, of which confidentiality is a fundamental characteristic. Someone in VPN A must not be able to access traffic belonging to VPN B. However, this does not prohibit packets from two different customers from traveling on the same link. A Frame Relay network is a good example of an infrastructure in which traffic from different customers shares the same trunks, but only frames belonging to, say, Cisco are delivered on the data-link connection identifiers (DLCIs) that go to Cisco sites. Layer 3 solutions must be at least as private as the Layer 2 circuit-based networks that they are replacing. It is important to realize that this requirement does not mandate encryption.

Efficient Operation

The term *operation* refers to configuring and monitoring a running network. Operational efficiency is always going to be a subjective measurement. For a VPN, in an ideal world, when a new site is brought online, existing sites should not need any new configuration. Of course, the amount of configuration depends on the protocol and technology used. VPNs that use point-to-point circuits are generally the worst offenders in terms of number of configuration operations per node, especially in densely meshed networks.

NOTE   There is a lot of work in progress in standards bodies to simplify configuration. For example, groups are working toward adding membership discovery for Virtual Private LAN services (VPLS) and, quite independently, multipoint tunnels for IPSec and even GRE.

Monitoring is very implementation dependent. Some VPN technologies are instrumentation rich, with NetFlow statistics, good MIBs, extensive CLI counters, and debugging. Other VPN technologies are not so rich with instrumentation.

Efficient Routing

Routing over point-to-point links can create complexity in IP networks, but this has been the price to pay for connecting sites using any circuit-based architecture, be it a PVC, SVC, or IP tunnel. In fact, probably the main technical driver behind migration from traditional Layer 2 to IP VPN is that the intersite routing is outsourced to a service provider in the IP-VPN case.

For a site VPN, the network operator must correctly configure routing so that each site is reachable from the other sites. There can be a degree of routing hierarchy in many networks, with some "lesser" spoke sites configured to route traffic to a central hub, which has more complete routing information and can dispatch the data as necessary to other spoke sites. Site VPNs typically run a dynamic routing protocol between CPE.

A telecommuter VPN is an extreme example of hub and spoke, in which the spokes have a simple default route to a central hub and the hub has one route for each spoke. Unlike site VPNs, the CPE usually does not run a routing protocol.

A wholesale VPN is also a hub and spoke. Aggregation routers collect IP traffic in many points of presence and forward it to a single hand-off point, where it is delivered to the retail ISP.

The issue of hubs, spokes, and routing is covered further in Chapter 3 and Chapter 5, "Introduction to MPLS-Based Access VPN Architectures." Routing and address management are often some of the more difficult problems that arise during open access deployment. For now, it is sufficient to conclude by saying that a VPN should support alternate customer routing topologies.

High Availability and Resiliency

High availability encompasses many things, from good network design with alternate routes for traffic in case of device failure, all the way to physical redundancy on the routers themselves. The sections that follow describe the two levels of redundancy.

Device-Level Redundancy

Device-level redundancy refers to the various mechanisms that provide a failover capability on a particular device. For example, on an aggregation router, there are the following options:

- **Access cards**—Use physical line-card redundancy, either 1+1 or N+1 if available, to protect the hardware that connects to subscribers. These cards can be ATM, Ethernet, or cable HFC depending on the type of broadband network. If a card fails, the backup card takes over. Usually this can happen without sessions going down. N+1 refers to a configuration in which one dedicated redundant element backs up N active elements. 1+1 is a special case of N+1, where there is exactly one backup element to protect one active element.

- **Trunk cards**—Adding to N+1 physical redundancy, SONET APS and IP routing with Hot Standby Routing Protocol (HSRP) can both be used for trunk links that connect to the rest of the IP network. Obviously, more subscribers are affected by a trunk failure than a subscriber-facing line card.

- **Processor cards**—Advanced route processor failover mechanisms, such as Non-Stop Forwarding (NSF), Stateless Switch Over (SSO), and Route Processor Redundancy (RPR), allow secondary route processors to take over processing from the primary processors with little to no service interruption.

With exceptions that arise because of particular economic situations, router processors and trunk cards are always designed for redundancy. Note that access redundancy is more expensive to deploy extensively than redundancy on trunk cards because there are more access cards than trunks in an aggregation router.

Network-Level Redundancy

Network-level redundancy refers to mechanisms deployed in or as network protocols that offer failover capability in case a network device fails. The following list goes through three network-level redundancy mechanisms:

- **HSRP**—You can build a tunnel to a virtual IP address using HSRP. This provides a protection against device failure.

- **IP routing**—Use either dynamic routing protocols (metrics, more or less specific routes) or floating static routes to provide a backup path should the first primary go down. The time to reroute traffic is determined by how quickly the routing protocol reconverges once it detects the failure of the primary path.

- **Load balancing**—For example, use redundant tunnel endpoints for traffic load balancing during normal network operation and to provide a failover capability in case one of the routers fails. Some VPN protocols have built-in mechanisms to detect failure and hence initiate failover; others don't and must rely on routing protocols to find a new path through the network for them.

Multicast

Multicast has been an emerging phenomenon for years. However, it is now a very real requirement on enterprise networks because of e-learning and other such video-to-the-desktop applications. Finance companies use multicast extensively for stock tickers and the like. Even if not all of your customers are running multicast yet, the underlying technology used for site and telecommuter VPNs should support IP multicast, irrespective of the type of last-mile connection.

Wholesale VPN providers are more driven by residential service requirements, such as broadcast video, which can be transported over IP using multicast. Each channel of video is transmitted to a particular multicast group. When a subscriber wants to change a channel, actually moves to a different group. That is not all there is to it, by any means, but you can see that broadcast video is a big driver of multicast support.

Quality of Service

For much the same reasons that multicast is fast becoming mandatory, QoS is a big requirement for VPNs. Of course, some VPN solutions such as ATM already have excellent QoS. Corporations use QoS more and more as they converge their networks. IP Telephony is the application that often comes to mind first as needing IP QoS, but there is also a lot of critical data traffic for storage applications, for example, that need low latency between hosts for the applications to work correctly. QoS can help guarantee that low latency.

It is common to see five, seven, or more classes of service used on a campus network. With the classes go the full gamut of QoS mechanisms: multiple queues with priority queuing for low-latency traffic; schedulers to allocate bandwidth fairly or otherwise; classifiers to detect or change the class a packet belongs to; and congestion control and intelligent packet discard mechanisms.

This number of classes creates a challenge for the site and telecommuter VPN provider, who must now carry the multiservice traffic of many customers. Routers have evolved considerably in recent years to provide a QoS-rich infrastructure that is capable of moving IP packets at very high speeds, but there are still challenges, notably the fact that the number of classes a service provider can offer per customer (typically three) is lower than the number an enterprise uses internally. This creates the requirement for transposition of QoS settings from one domain to another, as a service provider checks and possibly changes classifications of the IP packets it receives from customers, possibly changes them again as packets are tunneled or label switched over the core, and, finally, possibly restores them when the packet is delivered to the customer. Even if the service provider were to have five, seven, or more classes of service in the core, that may not entirely solve the problem, because enterprises don't have a standard set of traffic classes and markings, so transposing between enterprise and service provider classes could still be necessary.

For once, the wholesale VPN gets away with doing less, at least in the short term. Until real multiservice applications drive the requirement—and this is starting to happen—large numbers of queues are not mandatory to carry Internet traffic, which is the predominant residential service today. However, broadband operators want to offer multiservice applications to their customers and have been very active in standards bodies already to define broadband infrastructure that supports QoS right across the network. If you are interested in more information, you can read DSL Forum's TR-58 and TR-59 documents (http://www.dslforum.org), by way of an example. DOCSIS standards (http://www.cablemodem.com which is the Cable Labs website) and Metro Ethernet Forum (http://www.metroethernetforum.org) standards are also available for multiservice traffic.

Fragmentation

Maximum transmission unit (MTU) debugging is a bane of the broadband operator's life. Broadband encapsulations introduce packet overhead, and VPN protocols introduce more. On Ethernet interfaces, which tend to have the smallest MTU in an end-to-end connection, this can cause problems because of badly behaved hosts. Unfortunately, an unconscionable number of systems either don't bother to discover path MTU or don't react to Internet Control Message Protocol (ICMP) notifications sent when one of their packets was discarded because it exceeded an MTU somewhere.

Servers with poor protocol stacks typically look at their local interface MTU and transmit packets up to 1500 bytes in length, in the case of Ethernet-attached devices. Of course, this packet needs to be fragmented on the first router with a smaller MTU. To compound this problem, some parts of the Internet have unnatural amounts of packets with DF bits set, so 1500-byte packets are discarded instead of being fragmented, leaving the subscriber to wonder why the application that works on their LAN does not work at all over their VPN. Troubleshooting "sometimes there, sometimes not" problems is always time consuming. Obviously, the best solution to this problem is to fix the systems that cause the problem in the first place. Failing that, workarounds in use include CPE that silently rewrites TCP MSS values to the (WAN) interface MTU, or routers that ignore the DF setting and fragment anyway.

Authentication, Authorization, and Accounting (AAA)

In the context of a VPN, a user must request access to the private network which is *authentication*. The network grants permission to the user to perform specific operations on different parts of the network, which is *authorization*. Different users can have different permissions. Finally, the network must provide billing data which is *accounting*.

Here is a look at each of these in more detail:

- **Authentication**—Site VPN connections are not dynamically authenticated, but are built between known, trusted endpoints. This is a bit of an oversimplification, but the point here is that if you can trust the site, you don't have to force each user to authenticate before joining the VPN. There are intermediate levels of security for the CPE, such as certificates or shared secrets for the routers, but site-to-site VPNs are built between known endpoints. Telecommuter VPNs authenticate the person, not the location. You can look at this the other way around if you prefer: Telecommuter VPNs involve connections from untrusted sites. Wholesale VPNs, although transparent to the end user, also authenticate the person so that the traffic can be transported to the right service provider.

NOTE   In an eloquent testimony to the pace of change in networking, wireless networking is making corporate LANs look like telecommuter VPN environments. Now, anyone with a laptop and 802.11 wireless card who comes within range can be associated to a wireless access point and essentially become part of the physical corporate network. LEAP (Lightweight Extensible Authentication Protocol), 802.1x, and so on are solutions to provide authentication and authorization (called *identity* in the LAN jargon) on Ethernet LAN ports to deal with this change in level of trust. The problem set should look familiar.

- **Authorization**—The network must determine who a user is, where he is allowed to go, and what he is allowed to do. You can enforce policy inside the network, and many enterprises do this at the application layer, where applications require specific passwords for a limited community of privileged users. This is fine for point applications, such as payroll, where the number of users is small in comparison to the overall population, but it is impractical and dangerous to control access only to servers. As a matter of good design practice, enforce policy as early as possible, because that limits how much sniffing, spoofing, and other damage a rogue user can do.

  As a general requirement for wholesale networks, subscribers on different networks need to be able to use the same name. To accommodate this requirement, names have to be network specific. The easiest way to enforce this is to append a domain qualifier so that, for example, kumar.reddy@cisco.com is not the same person as kumar.reddy@ciscopress.com. This can be done inside the network, or the subscriber can be prompted for a domain name when connects.

- **Accounting**—VPNs are a billed service, so both parties want to have as much accounting information as possible. Good VPN technology provides for this, but IP accounting, such as NetFlow, can be perfectly adequate in certain situations.

Service Selection

Service selection is not a property of a VPN, which is itself a service, but subscribers want to be able to switch between services, including the VPN. This implies a dynamic binding of subscriber to VPN. Wholesale VPNs always need to support this where open access regulation is in place. Telecommuter VPNs also need to allow service selection, for the common case in which the broadband connection doubles as the household Internet connection.

There are two common types of service selection, as illustrated in Figure 1-6 and discussed in the following list:

- **Web-based service selection**—A web page at the top of Figure 1-6 lists the services available to a particular subscriber. This is a common metaphor on today's Internet where users have personalized "My" pages (such as my.yahoo.com) with their content and services (photo pages, e-mail, etc). The web-based approach allows subscribers to manage their own subscriptions, a cost the service provider would otherwise have to bear.

- **Client-based service selection**—In the same mold as the Point-to-Point Protocol over Ethernet (PPPoE) functionality discussed in Chapter 2, host-based clients connect to different domains, each representing a service. For example, at the bottom of Figure 1-6, the user changes the domain name to connect to a different service, so joe@biggerbank.com connects to one service, but joe@gemmejobs.com connects to another.

    IPSec clients that run over an existing Internet connection are just another variation on this theme.

Support for Any IP Addressing Plan

VPNs are private networks, so it might be surprising to see addressing listed as a requirement. For any CPE-based VPN, this is a nonissue. The addressing plan used on customer sites is hidden from the core service provider network; therefore, any addressing plan can be used.

With network-based VPNs, this requirement becomes more immediate. In this case, a service provider edge router is logically part of each VPN, so the routers must have private routing tables to maintain the separation of customer address spaces on the same physical device.

Figure 1-6   *Layer 2 and Web-Based Service Selection*

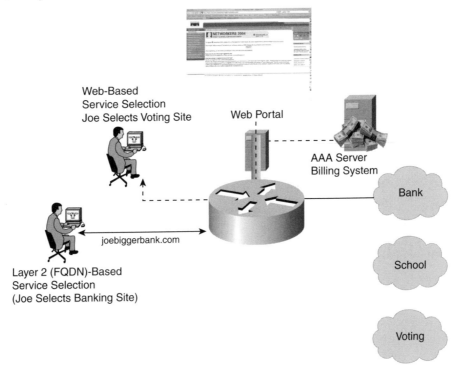

Efficient Address Assignment

To be truly operationally efficient, a wholesale VPN must support dynamic address-assignment techniques, such as DHCP and RADIUS, which are discussed in Chapter 2. The alternative, namely static allocation of customer IP addresses, is just not an option: It's too time consuming and too prone to error. A good VPN technology needs to integrate well with dynamic address-allocation mechanisms.

Additional Layer 3 Services

Wholesale providers want to offer more than simple connectivity services to their customers. Somewhat obviously, additional data services, such as web caching or network disk service, require an IP path to the subscriber. This is a challenge with many existing wholesale solutions that tunnel subscriber traffic to the retail network provider, because the service provider is essentially shut out of the IP traffic flow. Today, wholesale providers want the ability to offer additional services, so they need a VPN technology that gives them access to the data path. Network-based VPNs have this attribute.

Summary

This chapter introduced basic concepts about broadband subscriber access technologies and services, and the different types of VPN. A VPN can be built in many different ways, using either Layer 2, which you ignore or Layer 3, which you don't ignore core networks. You can build a VPN by overlaying tunnels between customer sites or by using the RFC 2547 model, which usually means that the network uses MPLS. Chapter 2 looks in much more detail at the access technologies—PPP, bridging—including how they work, what the encapsulations are, and how you configure them on a Cisco router. Then, Chapter 3 looks at different connectivity scenarios in which it makes sense to use overlay, tunnel-based VPNs.

If you want to know more, the draft-ietf-l3vpn series of documents on http://www.ietf.org are excellent sources of information. For example, draft-ietf-l3vpn-framework-00 has a more rigorous comparison between CPE- and network-based VPN alternatives.

It should be obvious that all these technology choices are for the service provider. The end user really doesn't care if the VPN is made out of tin cans strung together with wires, as long as it gets the job done. To end users, the VPN is about service, with guaranteed levels of performance (price, uptime, latency, and so forth).

In this chapter, you learn about the following topics:

- Technologies and Protocols for DSL, Cable, and Ethernet Broadband Networks
- Bridged and PPP Access Mechanisms, with an Evaluation of how well They Solve the Requirements for Broadband, Such as Quality of service, Address Assignment, Service Selection, and so on

CHAPTER 2

Delivering Broadband Access Today: An Access Technologies Primer

A VPN is a service that can carry pure data or multiservice traffic. When you design or implement a VPN for broadband access, you need to understand how the different access architectures can impact design decisions and can actually have some interesting repercussions on the VPN service itself, because of quality of service (QoS) or security trade-offs, to name but two examples.

This chapter reviews the two principal Layer 2 access architectures in use today: bridging and PPP. It looks at how each is implemented on different Layer 1 broadband media, such as digital subscriber line (DSL) and cable. Then it describes how each architecture solves some of the basic requirements of a network service, such as security, QoS support, routing, and address assignment. There are lots of permutations to go through: For example, security on a bridged cable broadband network is different from security on a bridged Ethernet broadband network, so it is worthwhile to look at each case.

If you sometimes feel lost going through all of these different scenarios, remind yourself that you are looking at how common problems are solved on different types of broadband networks. The set of problems is important, because you will want to make sure that a broadband VPN service solves it too. The major topics that are covered are as follows:

- Bridged access architectures
    - Bridging on DSL using Routed Bridge Encapsulation (RBE), including setup, routing, and address assignment
    - Bridging on cable
    - Bridging on Ethernet
    - Security for bridged access, with a look at different scenarios for DSL, cable, and Ethernet
    - Authentication and accounting for bridged access
- PPP access architectures
    - PPP over Ethernet (PPPoE), including setup, routing, and address assignment
    - PPP over ATM (PPPoA)

— PPP address assignment

— PPP authentication, accounting, and security

Bear in mind that this is a review chapter. If you are comfortable with PPP and bridging, then you can safely skip ahead to the next chapter.

Architecture 1: Bridged Access Networks

Bridged access networks are so named because they transport Ethernet frames transparently across a network. Ethernet is the most successful LAN protocol ever. It has basically replaced all other forms of Layer 2 encapsulation in enterprise networks and is arguably in the process of doing the same thing in residential networks. Not so very long ago, subscribers connected to the Internet directly from their PC using a modem. Today, home networks use Ethernet. For example, laptops have built-in Gigabit Ethernet ports, and wireless LAN is very quickly proving to be an alternative to running cables between rooms the world over. All these scenarios use Ethernet framing, and the most cost-effective broadband service will be Ethernet-centric: Ethernet ports are cheaper, Ethernet cards are cheaper, and Ethernet equipment is cheaper, too. If Ethernet is the user-to-network interface of choice, broadband access networks need some way to carry Ethernet traffic from the subscriber premises to their destination. The easiest way to do this is to simply bridge the traffic—after all, bridging was invented to connect Ethernet LAN segments together, so it should be a pretty useful way to carry Ethernet over WAN connections, too.

However, most broadband networks are not Ethernet based, so the Ethernet frames transmitted by a device on a home network must be converted to some other form before being carried over the native transport medium. For that very reason, bridging in a DSL environment is tricky, because today's DSL uses ATM as the modulation layer of choice. To carry Ethernet, you have to do a form of RFC 2684 bridging. Cable networks are easier because they can natively encapsulate Ethernet frames directly over Data Over Cable Service Interface Specification (DOCSIS). Of course, the simplest scenario of all is one where the access network is Ethernet based, using either standard Ethernet Layer 1 or some form of optical transport over longer distances.

The advantage of bridged architectures is their simplicity. The customer premises equipment (CPE) has no difficult tasks to perform, so it can be very cheap. The overall simplicity has one significant cost, however: namely security. Unless the router enforces some form of security mechanism, all bridged subscribers are in the same broadcast domain and everyone in that domain can see sensitive traffic such as ARP requests, Windows neighbor discovery packets, and so forth. This is a situation best avoided.

Although DSL, cable, and residential Ethernet networks each use radically different transport mechanisms, the issues and design considerations of bridged access are common across all the different media. The next section looks at the details of bridging in DSL networks. This is probably the most complicated scenario, because of the conversion back and forth between ATM cells. Fortunately, bridging over ATM is well standardized in RFC 2684, and the focus of the following discussion is on how bridging over ATM works on Cisco aggregation routers.

Bridging in DSL Using RFC 2684

RBE is a Cisco implementation of bridged Ethernet over ATM with a separate broadcast domain for every ATM circuit. The CPE is a simple bridge that encapsulates Ethernet frames into ATM cells using the RFC 2684 bridging standard. Figure 2-1 shows a typical RBE architecture.

Figure 2-1   *RBE Architecture*

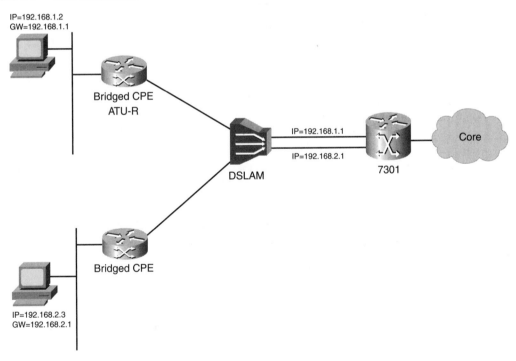

Figure 2-2 illustrates the packet encapsulations used at different points in the network.

Figure 2-2   *RBE Network Cross Section*

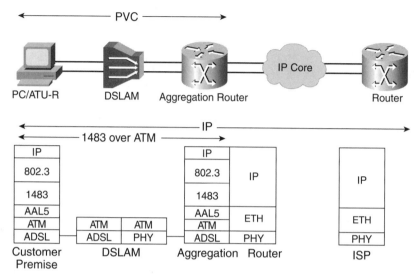

The flow of packets in Figure 2-2 works as follows:

For upstream traffic:

1 The subscriber PC is configured with the aggregation router's IP address as the default gateway. Just as on any Ethernet network, the PC sends an ARP request for the router MAC address and, once it learns it, transmits the Ethernet frame.

2 The bridged CPE encapsulates the Ethernet frame in an AAL5 bridge protocol data unit (BPDU), then segments the BPDU into ATM cells and sends it across the DSL network. Figure 2-3 shows the protocol encapsulations used at different points of the network.

3 The router reassembles the ATM cells, removes the AAL5 information and the Ethernet frame information, and routes the packet to its destination. Note how the router behaves: this is the behavior you would expect to see on a routed interface.

For downstream traffic:

1 A server sends a packet to the subscriber PC that is routed to the aggregation router.

2 The aggregation router has a static route that identifies the interface to use to reach the subscriber's IP address.

3 If necessary, the aggregator issues an ARP request to discover the subscriber PC MAC address. Then it encapsulates the Ethernet frame in an AAL5 Bridged format BPDU, segments everything into ATM cells, and transmits it.

4 The CPE reassembles the ATM cells into AAL5 PDUs, removes the AAL5 information, and transmits the frame on its Ethernet port.

5 The PC receives the data.

Figure 2-3   *Payload Format for Bridged Ethernet/802.3 PDUs (source: RFC 2684)*

LLC 0xAA-AA-03
OUI 0x00-80-C2
PID 0x00-01 or 0x00-07
PAD 0x00-00
MAC Destination Address
(Remainder of MAC Frame)
LAN FCS (if PID is 0x00-01)

For neighbor-to-neighbor traffic, note that if a subscriber PC sends a packet to another subscriber connected to the same aggregation router, the flow of packets is identical to the upstream and downstream flows described here. It is important to understand that there is no direct Layer 2 path between subscribers and that all traffic must be routed, even when subscribers' circuits are terminated on the same physical port on the router.

In Cisco IOS Software terms, the router in Figure 2-2 uses a logical point-to-point subinterface for each subscriber and treats each of these interfaces as a separate IP network. The default requirement of such a topology is, of course, to have a different IP subnet on every link. But in broadband, you have to manage very large numbers of connections, and there can be thousands of RBE subscribers connected to a single router. In such a case, IP addresses can run out very quickly. To get around this, you use unnumbered interfaces.

When using unnumbered interfaces, as in Frame Relay networks, the router no longer can know which interface to use to send traffic to a particular subscriber just by looking at the destination IP address, because no IP address space is associated with a subinterface. Additionally, to save IP address space, the subscriber IP addresses belong to the same subnet. Therefore, there must be an explicit route statement that maps the subscriber virtual circuit to its IP address. This is why Step 2 for downstream traffic mentions a route—because use of the unnumbered link.

Before learning about RBE configuration, you should understand the alternative to RBE, called *integrated routing and bridging (IRB)*, because both RBE and IRB are used (although there is less and less use of IRB). IRB is a multipoint topology in which all the subscribers are terminated on a point-to-multipoint interface. The architectural problem with IRB is that all of the subscribers are on the same Layer 2 network and are thus part of the same broadcast domain, which makes a network open both to performance degradation because of broadcast storms and to security issues. RBE is a superior, more secure implementation. For example, ARP spoofing is not possible with RBE because an ARP request for a particular address is sent only on the subinterface for that address. With IRB, the request would be flooded to all interfaces in the bridge group. RBE also prevents MAC address spoofing, again because there is a distinct subnet for each subinterface. If a hostile user tries to hijack someone else's address by injecting a gratuitous ARP packet (using their MAC and the victim's IP address), Cisco IOS will detect a subnet mismatch and generate a "Wrong Cable" error.

Note that, from a subscriber's point of view, they both look exactly the same.

Now that you understand the theory and architecture, you are ready to look at some configuration scenarios:

- Basic RBE configuration
- RBE QoS
- RBE routing
- RBE IP address assignment

These sections all get into the details of Cisco IOS commands.

RBE Configuration

RBE router configuration in Example 2-1 is straightforward.

Example 2-1 *Basic RBE Configuration*

```
interface Loopback0
 ip address 192.168.1.1 255.255.255.0
 no ip directed-broadcast
!
interface ATM0/0/0.132 point-to-point
 ip unnumbered Loopback0
 no ip directed-broadcast
 atm route-bridged ip
 pvc 1/32
  encapsulation aal5snap
!
interface ATM0/0/0.133 point-to-point
 ip unnumbered Loopback0
 no ip directed-broadcast
 atm route-bridged ip
 pvc 1/33
  encapsulation aal5snap
```

The configuration is very similar to the regular IP over ATM on a Cisco router, with only the addition of **atm route-bridge ip** to enable RBE. The subscribers' hosts must be configured to use the aggregator interface as their default gateway, in this case 192.168.1.1.

RBE Quality of Service

RBE has a full range of QoS options. Because it runs over an ATM PVC, you can fully exploit all the capabilities of the ATM layer to offer different QoS profiles to subscribers. You need to remember that ATM class of service (CoS) is applied to any and all traffic on the circuit. You can't restrict it to an individual application or destination.

Additionally, you can also use IP QoS. Cisco IOS has numerous bells and whistles that let you apply policies to combinations of application flows, IP destinations, and so forth. You can classify packets, police their rate, queue them, prioritize them—whatever it is you need to do to have different levels of service made available to user applications. You enable IP QoS by applying a **service policy** to a PVC. Example 2-2 adds a **PREMIUM** policy to output IP traffic on PVC 1/33. The **PREMIUM** policy is not included here, but is defined using standard Cisco IOS Modular QoS CLI (MQC) syntax.

Example 2-2   *RBE with IP QoS*

```
interface ATM0/0/0.133 point-to-point
 ip unnumbered Loopback0
 no ip directed-broadcast
 atm route-bridged ip
 pvc 1/33
  encapsulation aal5snap
  service-policy output PREMIUM
```

RBE supports Weighted Random Early Detection (WRED), low-latency queuing (LLQ), and policing.

RBE Routing

As previously mentioned, RBE uses unnumbered point-to-point subinterfaces with a route to each subscriber IP device. Example 2-3 shows the Cisco IOS routing commands, with the required static route for each subscriber.

Example 2-3   *RBE Static Routes*

```
! network routes
router ospf 100
redistribute static
192.168.14.0 0.0.0.255 area 0

!subscriber routes
ip route 192.168.1.2 255.255.255.255 ATM0/0/0.132
ip route 192.168.1.3 255.255.255.255 ATM0/0/0.133
```

Example 2-3 has just three lines of subscriber static routes, but imagine a configuration with 10,000 subscribers connected to the same router. If you announce all these host routes across an IP backbone, you can run into trouble with route table sizes, because each individual entry in a route table consumes memory.

Figure 2-4 shows a simple network with RBE subscribers connected to an aggregation router. Consider the flow when the subscriber PC in this network pings the server at 198.133.219.25.

Figure 2-4   *RBE Packet Flow*

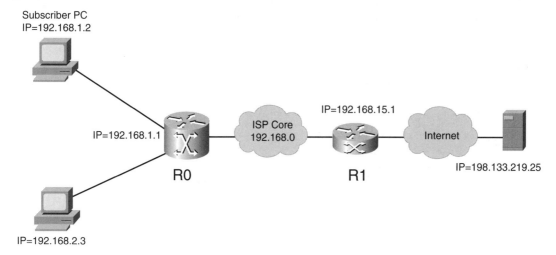

In Figure 2-4, the following happens:

1 The subscriber PC uses the aggregation router's address as the default gateway, so the ICMP ECHO request packet is sent to R0.

2 The aggregation router, R0, also has a simple default route that points to R1. R0 forwards the ICMP packet received from 192.168.1.2 to 192.168.15.1, which is the address of R1.

3 R1 forwards the packet out its egress interface across the Internet. Assuming that IP routing is functioning correctly, the ICMP packet will eventually reach its destination at 198.133.219.25.

4 Now, consider how the ICMP reply is routed back to 192.168.1.2. R1 has announced the 192.168.0.0/16 network to the Internet, so data sent to 192.168.1.2 will reach it.

5 R0 has announced /32 routes for all the RBE subscribers, so R1 will find a route entry for 192.168.1.2/32. (Of course, the next hop will be some intermediary router between R1 and R0.)

6 R1 sends the ICMP packet, which is routed to R0. R0 now looks up 192.168.1.2 in its routing table and finds the static route that points to PVC 1/32 on ATM interface 0/0/0.

Multiply this scenario by several thousand RBE interfaces on several hundred aggregation routers; throughout the 192.168.0.0 network, they quickly grow to unmanageable sizes. It is a much better design to aggregate the routes as soon as possible, and using simple a static route to Null0 is a way to do this. (Plenty of other ways exist, such as configuring OSPF to announce subnet addresses, but traffic to an interface, even Null0, is processed very quickly on a router, so performance is quite good using this method.) In the example shown in Figure 2-4, the ISP 192.168.0.0 backbone routers now need to carry only a single announcement for network 192.168.1.0/24, as indicated in Example 2-4.

Example 2-4   *RBE Static Routes on R0 with* Null0 *Route*

```
! subscriber routes
ip route 192.168.1.2 255.255.255.255 ATM0/0/0.132
ip route 192.168.1.3 255.255.255.255 ATM0/0/0.133
ip route 192.168.1.0 255.255.255.0 Null0
! default route
ip route 0.0.0.0 0.0.0.0 ATM1/0/0.100
```

Now, suppose host 192.168.1.2 sends a ping to 198.133.219.25. The following would happen:

1 On the path from 192.168.1.2 to 198.133.219.25, everything happens as before.

2 On the return path, the server at 198.133.219.25 replies with an ICMP REPLY, which finds its way to R1.

3 R1 has a route for 192.168.1.0/24 that was originally announced by R0. The ICMP REPLY packet will be forwarded to R0.

4 R0 has the same static route to PVC 0/132 on ATM interface 0/0/0.

5 Any traffic received by R0 that is for the 192.168.1.0/24 subnet, for which there is no static RBE route, will be forwarded to Null0 (i.e., dropped).

Although the use of route aggregation is well understood in large IP networks, it has not been widely used in DSL wholesale scenarios, where traffic is tunneled, not routed, to the ISP. Route aggregation is one of the challenges that reappears with IP VPNS and will be discussed further in later chapters.

In the next section, you will see how to create the subscriber routes automatically, instead of statically as in this section. Keep in mind, however, the importance of being able to aggregate as early as possible: You don't want tons of /32 routes wandering around your network.

RBE Address Assignment

You have seen RBE subscribers in all the examples so far with addresses already configured. How did they get them? How do you scale address assignment methods for broadband networks?

Because the preceding sections are all about bridging, DHCP is the logical choice for dynamic address assignment. Statically configuring all the end-station addresses obviously is impossible—the headaches this would create would completely outweigh any employment protection advantages for network operations staff.

When using DHCP on a DSL network, you have two basic options:

- Configure a DHCP server on the aggregation router. This configuration is less common, but entirely possible. You will see configuration examples of Cisco IOS DHCP servers in the "Cable CMTS" section, later in this chapter.

- Use a central DHCP server to which the aggregation router forwards DHCP requests. In this case, the router behaves as a DHCP relay agent.

To do DHCP relay, add the **ip helper-address** command to *every* subscriber interface. The **ip helper-address** command gives the address of the DHCP server, as shown in Example 2-5.

Example 2-5 *RBE Configuration with DHCP Relay*

```
interface Loopback0
 ip address 192.168.1.1 255.255.255.0
 no ip directed-broadcast
!
interface ATM0/0/0.132 point-to-point
 ip unnumbered Loopback0
 ip helper-address 192.168.2.100
 no ip directed-broadcast
 atm route-bridged ip
 pvc 1/32
  encapsulation aal5snap
```

The sequence of events when using DHCP relay is as follows:

1 When the subscriber host starts up, it broadcasts a DHCP Discover packet. This is carried in a BPDU to the aggregation router. The aggregation router recognizes this as the DHCP packet and knows that it needs to forward it to a DHCP server because of the **ip helper-address** on the subinterface. In this case, the aggregator is behaving as a DHCP relay agent.

2 The relay agent actually converts the DHCP broadcast into a unicast IP packet to the DHCP server located at 192.168.2.100. The relay agent puts its own address in the giaddr field of the DHCP packet and puts the subscriber VPI/VCI in the Option 82 field. (This data also includes the receiving interface name, so it is unique per device. The combination of the giaddr IP address and Option 82 yields a globally unique circuit ID.) You can use the global **rbe nasip** command to set the interface address the router puts in the giaddr field.

3 You can configure multiple DHCP servers by entering additional **ip helper-address** commands.

4 The DHCP server returns a DHCP Offer packet.

5 The PC chooses from the different servers that replied to its Discover message and sends a DHCP request to one of them. Remember, the PC still does not have an IP address at this point, so it broadcasts.

6 The DHCP relay agent again forwards the packet to the DHCP server. The relay agent does have an IP address, so it unicasts the packet to the server using UDP.

7 The DHCP server selects an address from an appropriate pool of IP addresses (it can use either the requesting MAC address or giaddr and Option 82 to select the scope) and returns a DHCP reply to the PC, which now has its own IP address and with it the default gateway address.

8 Crucially, the router dynamically creates a host route for the new IP address. As DHCP replies are sent by the DHCP server, the aggregation router looks at the address being assigned and creates a host route to that address using the interface on which the request was originally received. This is one of the bits of magic needed for large-scale deployment. These routes are marked as **static** in the output of the **show route** command.

You should still use the summarization technique discussed with dynamic addresses also. Announce in your favorite dynamic routing protocol the subnet of addresses that you know will be allocated to DHCP requests originating from a particular aggregation router. As new hosts connect to the network, host routes for them are created automatically as soon as they are assigned addresses. The aggregator will then have an aggregate route to make sure that packets are sent to it for the group of potential subscribers, and specific host routes for hosts that are actually active. This way you have the best of both worlds: An aggregate route is announced to peer routers, but per-subscriber routes are dynamically created as IP addresses are assigned.

More Bridged Access—Cable and DOCSIS

The worlds of cable and DSL have some major differences, but from an IP perspective they are very similar. If you ignore the many Layer 1 details on a cable headend router, the router configuration is similar to RBE, and thus many of the points already introduced for RBE also apply to cable access.

Cable modems communicate with headend routers, called CMTS, over the HFC plant using the DOCSIS standard:

> *Data is modulated and demodulated using the North American DOCSIS specifications, with downstream 6-MHz channels in the 54- to 860-MHz range and upstream ranges of 5 to 42MHz. The cable interface supports NTSC channel operation, using standard (STD), Harmonic Related Carrier (HRC), or Incremental Related Carrier (IRC) frequency plans conforming to EIA-S542.*

> *NTSC uses a 6MHz-wide modulated signal with an interlaced format of 25 frames per second and 525 lines per frame. NTSC is compatible with the Consultive Committee for*

International Radio (CCIR) Standard M.PAL, used in West Germany, England, Holland, Australia, and several other countries.

The DOCSIS radio frequency (RF) specification defines the RF communication paths between the CMTS and CMs (or CMs in STBs). The DOCSIS RF specification defines the physical, link, and network layer aspects of the communication interfaces. It includes specifications for power level, frequency, modulation, coding, multiplexing, and contention control.

This DOCSIS standard is extremely rich, but, at a very high level, provides a TDM-like system of time slots on a shared infrastructure. In the downstream direction, variable-length MPEG-4 frames carry Ethernet frames. In the upstream direction, fixed-length time slots are assigned to the cable modems by the CMTS. The downstream bandwidth is policed by the CMTS according to the QoS profile of each subscriber. Standard Ethernet 802 LLC is run on top of the DOCSIS layer. Figure 2-5 shows the encapsulation stack.

Figure 2-5 *DOCSIS Protocol Stack*

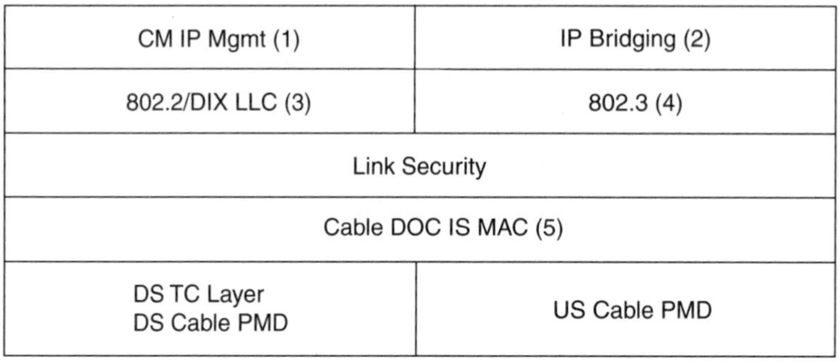

CM IP Mgmt (1)	IP Bridging (2)
802.2/DIX LLC (3)	802.3 (4)
Link Security	
Cable DOC IS MAC (5)	
DS TC Layer DS Cable PMD	US Cable PMD

1. DHCP, DNS, TFTP, TOD, CM Registration
2. IP QoS (ToS), IP Classifiers
3. MAC Management Frames, including SYNC, UCD, MAP, …
4. MAC Packet Data Frames
5. SID, …

As part of the session negotiation process, a Service Identifier, or SID, which is part of the DOCSIS Cable MAC layer, is allocated to each cable modem (CM). This is used somewhat like the ATM Circuit Identifier in DSL networks. All traffic sent to and by a given cable modem uses the same SID. The DOCSIS 1.1 specification enhances this to allow cable modems to use several SIDs, each with a different QoS profile so that voice or video can be run over the same infrastructure as data traffic. Again, the parallel with ATM PVCs is apparent.

The cable modem bridges traffic from its LAN Ethernet port over the WAN DOCSIS interface to the CMTS. Subscriber hosts see a shared-access Ethernet network. For upstream traffic, they behave just as RBE clients and need to ARP for the CMTS MAC address. The CMTS also ARPs for PC MAC addresses in the downstream case. Figure 2-6 shows the encapsulations used at different points in the network.

Figure 2-6   *DOCSIS Network Cross Section*

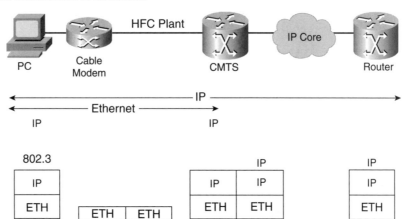

DOCSIS Cisco IOS Configuration

From a Cisco IOS perspective, there are commands specific to the cable plant (HFR) interfaces, cable-modem profiles, etc. Unlike RBE, cable interfaces are natively point to multipoint, which is less secure than point to point. The CMTS and CM have other techniques. Another difference between basic cable and RBE configuration, illustrated in Example 2-6, is the widespread use of secondary addressing (which is also supported with RBE, but is not used very much). In Example 2-6, the primary subnet is for the cable modems; the secondary subnet is for the hosts.

Example 2-6   *Basic Cable Router Interface Configuration[2]*

```
interface Cable4/0
ip address 10.1.1.1 255.255.0.0
ip address 200.1.1.1 255.255.0.0 secondary
load-interval 30
no ip directed-broadcast
cable helper-address 200.1.162.170
no keepalive
cable downstream annex B
cable downstream modulation 64qam
cable downstream interleave-depth 32
 cable downstream frequency 525000000
Cable upstream 0 power-level 0
no cable upstream 0 shutdown
Cable upstream 0 frequency 37008000
cable upstream 1 shutdown
cable upstream 2 shutdown
cable upstream 3 shutdown
cable upstream 4 shutdown
cable upstream 5 shutdown
```

Cable-modem profiles are an important component of DOCSIS networks. These profiles contain configuration instructions, such as upstream and downstream bandwidth, the number of allowed hosts per connection, etc. Example 2-7 shows four different profiles.

Example 2-7   *Cable-Modem Profiles*[3]

```
!
cable config-file platinum.cm
   service-class 1 max-upstream 128
   service-class 1 guaranteed-upstream 10
   service-class 1 max-downstream 10000
   service-class 1 max-burst 1600
   cpe max 10
   timestamp
!
cable config-file gold.cm
   service-class 1 max-upstream 64
   service-class 1 max-downstream 5000
   service-class 1 max-burst 1600
   cpe max 3
   timestamp
!
cable config-file silver.cm
   service-class 1 max-upstream 64
   service-class 1 max-downstream 1000
   service-class 1 max-burst 1600
   cpe max 1
   timestamp
!
cable config-file disable.cm
   access-denied
   service-class 1 max-upstream 1
   service-class 1 max-downstream 1
   service-class 1 max-burst 1600
   cpe max 1
   timestamp
```

Cable Address Assignment

Given that cable broadband is a bridged environment, it shouldn't be surprising to learn that DHCP is used for address assignment. There is a small quirk, though. Even though it functions as an Ethernet bridge, the cable modem also needs an IP address so that it can be managed and it can retrieve its configuration profile. Cable standards mandate the use of Trivial File Transfer Protocol (TFTP) and TOD protocols to retrieve configuration files. TFTP needs an IP address, so the modems use DHCP to get one.

Subscriber hosts also use DHCP to get their addresses. However, for security reasons, the end stations are typically on a different IP subnet than the modems.

The DHCP function on the CMTS router is quite sophisticated. You can either configure the CMTS to relay the DHCP requests to different servers, depending on whether the modem or host sends the packet, or configure different DHCP pools on the router itself—one pool for the modems, one pool for the subscribers. You can also use a mix of the two approaches.

Because of this, the Cisco IOS commands on the CMTS are a little different from RBE and you use **cable helper-address** instead of the standard **ip helper-address** command, as demonstrated in Example 2-8.

Example 2-8   *Cable Router with Multiple DHCP Relay*[4]

```
interface Cable3/0
 ip address 2.41.1.1 255.0.0.0
 no ip directed-broadcast
 no keepalive
 cable insertion-interval 500
 cable downstream annex B
 cable downstream modulation 64qam
 cable downstream interleave-depth 32
 cable downstream frequency 128025000
 no cable downstream if-output
 cable upstream 0 frequency 28000000
 cable upstream 0 power-level 0
 no cable upstream 0 fec
 no cable upstream 0 scrambler
 cable upstream 0 data-backoff 5 12
 no cable upstream 0 shutdown
 cable helper-address 1.1.1.1 cable-modem
 cable helper-address 2.2.2.2 host
```

In this example, there are two DHCP servers. The 1.1.1.1 server receives DHCP requests from cable modems. The 2.2.2.2 server receives requests from subscriber hosts. If you don't specify the [**host** | **cable-modem**] parameter, all requests are forwarded to a single server.

The **cable dhcp-giaddr** command is another powerful addition to CMTS. It modifies the giaddr field with different relay addresses, as demonstrated in Example 2-9.

Example 2-9   *Using the* **cable dhcp-giaddr** *Command*

```
interface Cable4/0
ip address 172.16.29.1 255.255.255.224 secondary
   ip address 10.1.4.1 255.255.255.0
   cable dhcp-giaddr policy
```

The **policy** parameter instructs the router to use the DHCP pool that matches the primary address for requests from the cable modems and to use the pool that matches the secondary address for host requests.

Broadband Ethernet—Ethernet to the Home/Business (ETTX)

Ethernet is still the brave new world of broadband access, and many aspects of broadband Ethernet continue to evolve as market demand and technical solutions develop.

Ethernet can be used in many different service types, which can create some confusion. An Ethernet access network may offer Layer 2 and Layer 3 VPN services as well as other IP-based services, such as Internet access. Figure 2-7 shows the hierarchy of Ethernet services.

Figure 2-7   *Ethernet Services*

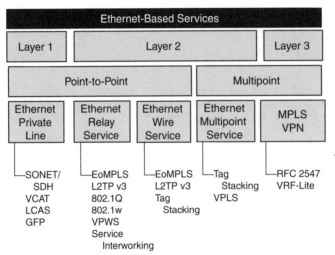

The scenario of interest here, referred to as ETTX, is when Ethernet is used as a last-mile technology for a Layer 3 service, be it Internet or VPN access. The service offering can be for small and medium-sized businesses or residential customers, but today, residential Ethernet is still confined to a metropolitan area.

Unlike DSL and cable, ETTX does not use an existing wiring plant, so it is only cost effective in places where there is an abundance of Category 5 copper cable or fiber, namely multitenant buildings or metropolitan areas. There is a lot of effort today to use Ethernet framing over copper. The next generation of high-speed DSL will, in all likelihood, be Ethernet based. Cisco had an early implementation called Long Reach Ethernet (LRE), covered in more detail in the next section.

Getting back to ETTX, a common residential Internet access architecture, as shown in Figure 2-8, uses a 24-port 10/100 switch as a CPE. Each CPE has a GE trunk port that is ultimately connected to an aggregation router. Figure 2-8 shows a typical configuration that uses switches connected together in a ring between CPE and aggregators that is used to transport Gigabit Ethernet frames.

Figure 2-8   *Residential ETTX*

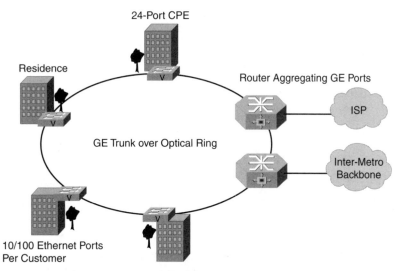

In a typical network today, there might be 10 CPE on a ring and 20 such rings per aggregator. Although sizable, the number of subscribers per aggregator is still low compared to DSL. Of course, the connection speed is many times higher. The distance from the CPE to the end station is either the standard 100 meters for Category 5 copper cable or several kilometers when using fiber. In the second case, an additional fiber-to-copper converter is required on the customer premises.

The network operation is straightforward and is identical in many ways to a switched Ethernet network in a campus. Figure 2-9 shows the by-now-familiar cross section of protocol encapsulation across the network. Frames are switched from CPE to the aggregation router across intermediary Layer 2 devices. CPE connects to 10/100 Ethernet ports, which are typically trunked over a Gigabit Ethernet port using 802.1q VLANs. The VLANs are terminated on an aggregation router (so they are switched across the access domain), which is responsible for routing traffic to its destination. As with campus networks, each VLAN runs a different IP subnet.

Figure 2-9 *802.1q Network Cross Section*

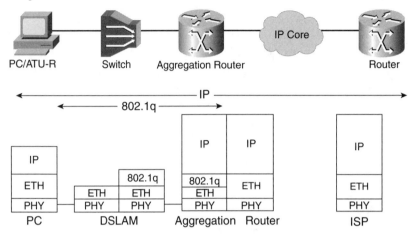

In Figure 2-9, an 802.1q header is inserted in the Ethernet header at the first switch in the access domain. Figure 2-10 shows how Ethernet frames are tagged for VLANs.

Figure 2-10 *802.1q Header*

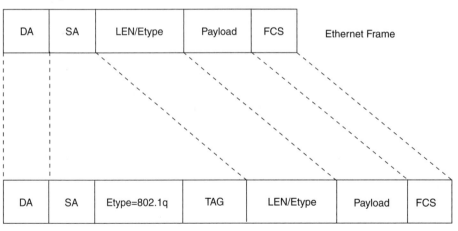

Long Reach Ethernet

Long Reach Ethernet (LRE) is another Ethernet-based solution, this time found within MxUs using copper wiring. Figure 2-11 shows a typical network architecture. Like DSL, LRE can use twisted-pair wiring.

Figure 2-11 *LRE Solution*

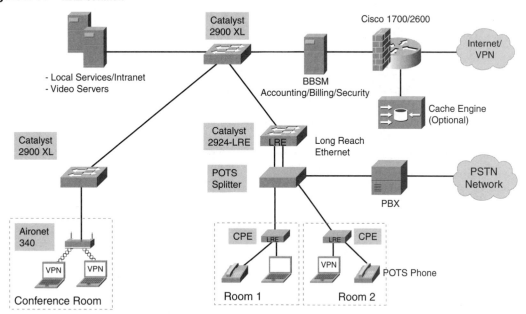

A typical LRE deployment scenario would be a hotel that wants to offer data and voice services to its guests. Because all hotels already have a telephone network, it makes sense to use this expensive infrastructure for data transmission rather than rewire. And because the data traffic is all Ethernet based, it makes no sense to use true DSL, which would require ATM. However, standard Ethernet transmission over telephony-grade wiring is not technically possible, and this is what LRE addresses. LRE uses a transcoding scheme that allows high-speed Ethernet at up to 15 Mbps to be offered across telephony-grade wiring. An LRE CPE encodes the Ethernet frame and transmits it to an LRE-capable switch.

LRE allows voice traffic to either be carried on the same wire using existing analog bandwidth, as with DSL, or to be migrated to IP. Note that LRE works with analog and digital telephones, even if DSL is also used across the same pair of wires. LRE is not widely deployed today as a consumer solution because of ongoing issues with signal interference. It is unclear whether this solution will remain cost effective given the ever-increasing success of wireless Ethernet.

ETTX Configuration

At a basic level, the ETTX configuration is identical to a campus solution. A CPE switch runs 802.1q on a Gigabit Ethernet trunk interface, with each access port in the same VLAN. In the case of Example 2-10, the CPE uses VLAN2.

Example 2-10 *ETTX CPE Configuration*

```
! CPE access port
interface GigabitEthernet0/6
switchport access vlan 2
...

! CPE trunk port
interface GigabitEthernet0/1
switchport trunk encapsulation dot1q
...
```

The Ethernet aggregator configuration has a trunk port and an IP subinterface for every VLAN, as demonstrated in Example 2-11.

Example 2-11 *ETTX Aggregator Configuration*

```
Interface GigabitEthernet1/0/0.22
encapsulation dot1Q 2
ip address 192.168.11.1 255.255.255.240
```

There are networks with a different VLAN for every subscriber, but others in which a different VLAN is used for every service. In the case of per-subscriber VLANs, there must be a scaling mechanism of some kind because the maximum number of VLANs by default is 4000. (The trick is to add a second VLAN tag, known as QinQ.) When there is a VLAN per service, all subscribers are on the same IP subnet.

ETTX Quality of Service

ETTX is often perceived to have the weakest QoS infrastructure of the three access network types under consideration. Although there is no standardized equivalent to ATM's classes (CBR, VBR, etc.) or DOCSIS, Ethernet switches do offer relatively rich QoS capabilities, such as IP- and TCP-based classification, IP DSCP or 802.1p tag-based prioritization, and sophisticated scheduling and policing. Additionally, COS-to-IP DSCP mapping can be done automatically, or COS can be set on a port basis depending on the trust that is ascribed to a user.

Cisco IOS access lists can be used for classification, so different applications or hosts can be treated differently. Even quite low-cost switches can offer multiple queues per port, which is required for multiservice applications.

As anecdotal evidence, remember that a lot of enterprises run voice over their switched infrastructure, which is a testimony to the level of QoS that Ethernet infrastructure can provide.

Apart from transporting multiservice traffic, IP QoS can also be used to help compensate for the fact that Ethernet does not offer many increments for service offerings, with jumps from 10, 100, and 1000 Mbps. Subinterfaces can be policed to lower or intermediate rates, such as 2 Mbps, 34 Mbps, and others, as demonstrated in Example 2-12. You can mark down nonconforming packets, or discard them, to enforce the particular service contract.

Example 2-12   *ETTX QoS Configuration—Policing Subscriber Interfaces*

```
policy-map option-128k
   class class-default
      police 128000 10000 10000 conform-action set-prec-transmit 0 exceed-action drop
policy-map option-512k
   class class-default
      police 512000 10000 10000 conform-action set-prec-transmit 0 exceed-action drop
policy-map option-1Meg
   class class-default
      police 1000000 10000 10000 conform-action set-prec-transmit 0 exceed-action drop
policy-map option-10Meg
   class class-default
        police 10000000 10000 10000 conform-action set-prec-transmit 0 exceed-action
drop
interface GigabitEthernet1/0/0.15
   desc VLAN connecting to customer1
    encapsulation dot1Q 15
    ip address x.x.x.x y.y.y.y
   service-policy input option-128k
   service-policy output option-128k
Interface GigabitEthernet1/0/0.88
   desc VLAN connecting to customer2
    encapsulation dot1Q 88
    ip address a.a.a.a b.b.b.b
   service-policy input option-1Meg
   service-policy output option-1Meg
```

ETTX Address Assignment

Unsurprisingly, ETTX uses DHCP for address assignment to simplify address management and distribution. If, as is common today, the network is owned and operated by a single entity, there are no new issues related to address assignment beyond those already discussed thus far in the chapter. Addresses are assigned using DHCP, and the Ethernet CPE in Figure 2-8 adds option 82 information if port identification is required. The role of the CPE is very important for security, as discussed in the next section.

Using IP addresses efficiently is just as important in ETTX networks as in any DSL or cable network. Consider the case in Figure 2-12 of an Open Access ETTX network in which each subscriber can belong to one of two ISPs, ISP A or ISP B, both of which use DHCP to assign addresses.

Figure 2-12   *Open Access Architecture for Residential Ethernet*

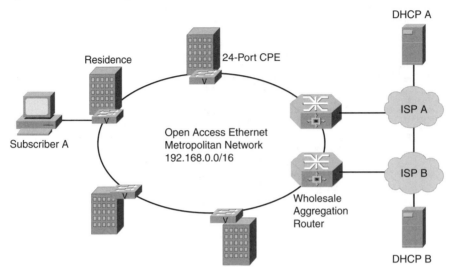

Ethernet can be delivered over point-to-point or ring topologies. Although Figure 2-12 shows just one ring, there can be multiple rings of CPE connected to every aggregation router. Each ring is terminated on a physical interface, with potentially many subinterfaces, each one corresponding to a different VLAN (and there are different policies for how VLANs are used, as previously discussed). As each VLAN corresponds to a different IP subnet, there must be as many subnets as there are VLANs. For an ISP, this can result in wasted address space.

To understand the issue of address waste, consider the following sequence of steps:

1 ISP A has 60 subscribers in the metropolitan region and wishes to use the 192.168.1.0/26 subnet.

2 Subscriber A connects on the first ring and sends a DHCP request, which is relayed to ISP A's DHCP server. VLAN20 is used.

3 The second subscriber connects, but this time in a different part of the city and on a different ring. This time, traffic is in VLAN34.

4 ISP A would like to have the same subnet for all the subscribers in this metro area, but needs a different subnet for VLAN34, or else the aggregation router could not route traffic correctly to subscribers on different subinterfaces.

The bad solution to this problem is to use a different subnet for every VLAN. Unfortunately, ISP A probably has no way of knowing how many subscribers will be on each VLAN and so would potentially need to use as many /26 subnets as there are VLANs in the network. This results in huge waste.

The solution is for the metro service provider to use unnumbered interfaces. Each subscriber has a loopback interface configured for his pool and all the VLANs are unnumbered, as demonstrated in Example 2-13.

Example 2-13 *Unnumbered Interfaces and Loopbacks for ETTX*

```
interface loopback 0
    desc ISP A
    ip address 192.168.1.1 255.255.255.0

interface loopback 1
    desc ISP B
    ip address 192.168.2.1 255.255.255.0

interface GigabitEthernet1/0/0.15
    encapsulation dot1Q 15
    ip address unnumbered loopback 1
    ip address secondary unnumbered loopback 2
Interface GigabitEthernet1/0/0.88
    encapsulation dot1Q 88
    ip address unnumbered loopback 1
    ip address secondary unnumbered loopback 2
```

NOTE   Open access is already widely deployed for DSL, but it is still a relatively new concept for ETTX networks. The architecture will continue to evolve. In Example 2-14, the addresses used by the different ISPs can't overlap, because they are terminated on the same router. You will see how to lift this restriction in Chapter 7, "Implementing Network-Based Access VPNs Without MPLS."

Security Considerations for Bridged Broadband Architectures

Security is an important part of an Internet access service, whether it is sold to residential or business customers. Security at the transport layer and application layers is beyond the scope of this work and, indeed, is independent of the type of access used. However, lower-layer security is an important part of overall network design. If the lower layers are not secure, then it is easy for an attacker to work up the stack and compromise application data such as usernames, passwords, credit card numbers, and so on.

The common Layer 2 and Layer 3 risks are as follows:

- **Address spoofing** —This category loosely encompasses all attempts to modify an end station address. It can be something as simple as changing the address on a Linux station NIC or manually changing your IP address.

ARP-based attacks are more sophisticated and, because ARP is not an inherently secure protocol, spoofing is not as difficult as it should be. These attacks involve, for example, sending an ARP reply packet with a spoofed IP address. Most routers or switches simply overwrite an IP address in their ARP table with the IP address obtained from the most recent ARP response, or may record multiple IP addresses from responses, making it easier for the attacker. Slightly more sophisticated is the use of gratuitous ARP, whereby the attacker spontaneously advertises an ARP packet with its MAC address and someone else's IP address. This is completely RFC compliant and all stations that receive the ARP packet happily install the spurious MAC/IP mapping in their ARP tables. Now, no ARP request will be sent when traffic is received for the IP destination. The use of gratuitous ARP is typically used for man-in-the-middle attacks.

As you can gather from the preceding explanation, ARP attacks are limited only to stations that are on the same broadcast domain as the offending attacker.

- **DoS attacks** — DoS attacks can be mounted in many ways. Some simple examples include using gratuitous ARPs to fill the CAM table on an Ethernet switch; using DHCP requests to exhaust IP addresses; or sending a very large number of Layer 3 flows to the default router. DoS attacks often use some form of address spoofing. DoS attacks can be very hard to prevent. Simply constantly changing Ethernet source addresses can be very effective against a switch.

  Sophisticated techniques are under development to improve network security against DoS attacks. Today's routers already have source address checking, access lists, and NetFlow statistics.

- **Broadcast traffic and OS weaknesses** — This is not really a category of network attacks, but more an observation that many host stations are inherently insecure "out of the box" and allow any neighbor machine on the same broadcast domain to browse disk contents. In remote access, the ability to broadcast is trouble.

Security in DSL Broadband Networks

RBE has two characteristics that contribute to network layer security:

- The router uses point-to-point interfaces.
- The broadcast domain is limited to a single site.

If you send a gratuitous ARP packet, the router may install it in its ARP table, but downstream traffic is always directed to the correct PVC because of the host routes used with RBE. When the router receives a packet for a host, it sends the ARP only on the PVC that matches the host route for that address. In other words, ARP is used only after the correct subscriber interface has been identified by the IP routing table. Layer 2 attacks are hard to do successfully in this case.

Even if you do successfully spoof an IP address, the host routes again make sure traffic reaches the correct destination, as described in the following step sequence:

1 Host A sends a packet with a spoofed address of 1.1.1.1 to 192.168.1.100. Its true address is 192.168.1.99.

2 The RBE router forwards the packet to 192.168.1.100.

3 On the return path, the router either routes the traffic to the correct interface for address 1.1.1.1 or drops it if no such address exists in the routing table. It is not returned to host A.

NOTE Before you conclude that this technique is a good way to send large and unsolicited streams of traffic to your neighbor, remember Unicast Reverse Path Forwarding (uRPF) checking. uRPF, if configured, will drop the packet because a router will not accept a packet if the incoming interface is different from the interface defined in the route table that reaches the packet's source address.

Security in Cable Broadband Networks

Because security has long been an issue on cable networks, the Baseline Privacy Interface was added to the DOCSIS specifications to give a secure communication channel between each cable modem and the CMTS.

Unlike RBE, the CMTS router uses a point-to-multipoint interface. Potentially, then, ARP-based attacks are possible because the CMTS sends ARP packets to all hosts on its physical interface. However, remember that the DOCSIS layer also offers protection. The cable modem can store the MAC address/SID mappings, which the network administrator can poll to troubleshoot security issues.

The **cable source-verify** command is important. It configures the CMTS to enforce address assignment by dropping packets with source addresses that it has not seen assigned by a DHCP server (using the **cable source-verify dhcp** option). For this to work properly, the DHCP server must support the DHCPLEASEQUERY message. The **cable source-verify** command prevents attacks based on theft of IP addresses (using a valid address that belongs to someone else) as well as attacks based on invented addresses (either addresses that are valid but not assigned or addresses that are made up).

Security in Ethernet Broadband Networks

Without VLANs, all subscribers in a switched network are in the same broadcast domain, which is an open invitation to trouble, because of the risks that this scenario creates (some of which were discussed earlier in this chapter). Dedicating a VLAN to each customer is, in theory, possible, but it is impractical because of the 4096 global VLAN limit in the 802.1q protocol. It is more common to configure a single VLAN per switch. This still leaves everyone on the same switch in the same broadcast domain. To solve this issue, private VLANs are used.

Private VLANs prevent traffic from a subscriber port from going to any other port on the switch, with the exception of the trunk port, which is defined as a promiscuous port. From the perspective of the subscriber, as represented in Figure 2-13, subscribers "see" a private point-to-point link to the router. The aggregating router, in turn, sees a switched Ethernet segment with multiple subscribers.

Another alternative is to use double VLAN encapsulation, called QinQ, where traffic from each subscriber's port is mapped to a different 802.1q tag, and then that frame is tagged again when it leaves the switch with a tag that uniquely identifies the switch on the Ethernet network. The aggregation router has to be smart enough to handle this double layer of VLAN tags.

Figure 2-13   *Private VLAN*

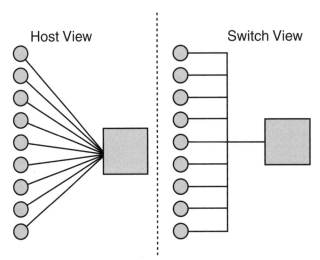

Limiting the broadcast domain stops some of the simplest attacks, but does not prevent ARP or IP address spoofing. Remember that for cable, the router enforces DHCP assignments. If a host tries to change an address, or sends a gratuitous ARP packet, the CMTS ignores it, because it was not assigned to the host by a known DHCP server. The Ethernet scenario is harder to manage because subscriber interfaces have been aggregated on the switch downstream in the network, which may not yet have the necessary mechanisms to enforce Layer 3 to Layer 2 bindings.

Port security is a useful feature that prevents the switch from allowing a MAC address learned on one port to be used on another. Port security can also allow static MAC addresses to be configured for each port. Admittedly, it is hard to scale a solution based on static addresses for a large number of subscribers without an excellent OSS system.

Ethernet switches do have an increasingly large array of tools to deal with DoS attacks. These tools include broadcast suppression, ARP throttling, route processor rate limiting, security ACLs, and so on. On good-quality switches, these features are all implemented in hardware, so they are very efficient and are well worth some extra cost.

NOTE   Identification and authorization should always be done as soon as possible in a remote-access network. There is a huge difference in effectiveness between being able to apply policies on a device where each subscriber is on a different port or Layer 2 circuit and one where this is not the case.

Currently, the 802.1x standard is emerging as a possible solution to this problem. 802.1x, which is a port-based access mechanism, works as follows:

1 The client station, or supplicant, sends a request to the switch, or authenticator, which forwards it to a RADIUS authentication server.

2 The authentication server returns a challenge to the supplicant, which must correctly respond to be granted access to the network.

3 The authenticator provides access to the LAN.

This is reminiscent of Point-to-Point Protocol (PPP) authentication and you can think of 802.1x as using a PPP-like authentication mechanism to provide port-based access control.

Authentication and Accounting in Bridged Broadband Architectures

One of the significant differences between Ethernet-based access and the PPP-based solutions is how subscribers are authenticated on the network.

With bridging, there is no authentication using a subscriber's name. This is always ideal, if you have the option, because you authenticate an individual and can then enforce policy with a fine level of granularity.

In bridged architectures, the network-access control is Layer 2 based. If you have a valid MAC address, from a valid port, you will receive a valid IP address. At no time does the user have to enter a name and password. So the user identity must always be tied back to the Layer 3 or Layer 2 addresses and, as you've just seen, these are not the most secure.

Billing is another weakness of the Ethernet solution if the service provider wants to offer a metered service. There is no standards-based way to retrieve usage statistics. Some switches have some useful data in MIBs, but some don't. On routers, if there is hardware for it, you can enable NetFlow accounting. However, NetFlow accounting on high-speed networks generates a considerable amount of data, and the OSS systems must do a lot of data crunching and cross checking between systems to work out which flow belonged to which person at a given time.

Architecture 2: Point-to-Point Protocol Networks

Dial-up access was the first remote-access mechanism and PPP was extensively enhanced to work in this environment. Because of this long deployment experience, PPP is a very mature solution that includes a rich control plane that lends itself to wholesale services. PPP is a more complex protocol than simple bridging, and this additional cost is incurred both on the client stack and on the router.

The following sections look at the variants of PPP used in broadband networks. PPPoE, by far the most prevalent variant today, involves a very simple bridging CPE. As you will see, the PPP session can be initiated from a PC. PPPoA is less common and usually (but not always) the session is initiated from a router.

PPP over Ethernet—The CPE as a Bridge

PPPoE is an interesting protocol. As the name implies, it involves a PPP session running over an Ethernet MAC layer. PPPoE is interesting because PPP was created for point-to-point interfaces, so it needed some enhancements to allow it to run on broadcast media. These enhancements included a discovery process very like the one in DHCP, which serves to establish a logical point-to-point relationship between a PPPoE client and server. All this can sometimes be confusing until you realize that PPPoE is really a superset protocol of PPP in which there is a supplementary setup protocol that runs before regular PPP starts. Cisco IOS debug output shows this really well.

Although the explanation that follows is DSL based, PPPoE is also a perfectly valid possibility for cable and ETTX networks. Figure 2-14 and the list that follows describe PPPoE operation in more detail.

Figure 2-14 *PPPoE Protocol Operation*

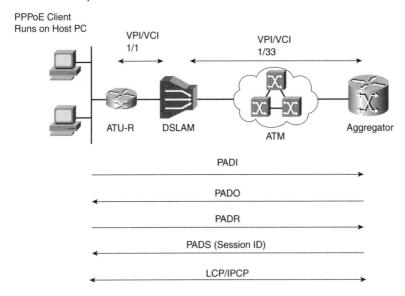

The PPPoE protocol starts before a PPP session comes up, as follows:

1 A host broadcasts an Active Discovery Initiation packet, called a PADI.

2 In theory, a number of different servers (called Access Concentrators in the RFC) can now reply with an Active Discovery Offer packet, or PADO. In the case of DSL, all the Ethernet traffic is bridged across an (point-to-point) ATM virtual circuit by the bridged CPE to a single aggregation router, which is, in fact, the PPP Access Concentrator, so it is hard to imagine a host receiving more than a single PADO on an operational network. However, it is possible. Depending on the implementation of the PPPoE stack on the client, the client may accept only the first PADO returned, or the first PADO returned with the service it wishes to connect to.

3 The host sends an Active Discovery Request (PADR) packet to a single Access Concentrator.

4 The handshake completes when the Access Concentrator sends an Active Discovery Session-confirmation (PADS) packet, which contains a session ID. In the fairly rare case where the Access Concentrator and host are on a broadcast network, this session ID establishes a logical point-to-point connection (The combination of the host MAC address and session ID is unique on the server.)

5 Standard PPP negotiation starts, with LCP and IPCP, just as for point-to-point serial connections.

6 Either side can terminate the session with an Active Discovery Terminate (PADT) packet. This is equivalent to cutting a wire because no more traffic is passed, not even to close the upper-layer PPP session.

Figure 2-15 shows the Ethernet payload for PPPoE.

Figure 2-15   *PPPoE Header (Source: RFC 2516)*

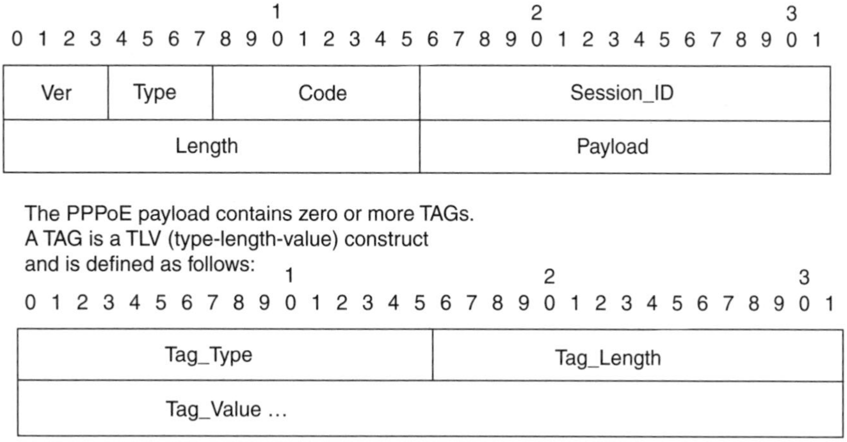

```
                         1                   2                   3
 0 1 2 3 4 5 6 7 8 9 0 1 2 3 4 5 6 7 8 9 0 1 2 3 4 5 6 7 8 9 0 1
+-------+-------+---------------+-------------------------------+
|  Ver  | Type  |     Code      |          Session_ID           |
+-------+-------+---------------+-------------------------------+
|            Length             |           Payload             |
+-------------------------------+-------------------------------+
```

The PPPoE payload contains zero or more TAGs.
A TAG is a TLV (type-length-value) construct
and is defined as follows:

```
                         1                   2                   3
 0 1 2 3 4 5 6 7 8 9 0 1 2 3 4 5 6 7 8 9 0 1 2 3 4 5 6 7 8 9 0 1
+-----------------------------------+---------------------------+
|             Tag_Type              |        Tag_Length         |
+-----------------------------------+---------------------------+
|             Tag_Value ...                                     |
+---------------------------------------------------------------+
```

Packet flow is very simple. Each subscriber is terminated on the PPP peer using a virtual-access interface. Just as with dial-up operation in Cisco IOS, these interfaces are cloned from virtual templates. All traffic is routed by the aggregation router to and from each subscriber, often referred to as *hair-pinning*. Host routes are also automatically created for each subscriber. The router treats each virtual access as a directly connected interface, and routing table entries are marked appropriately (with a letter C in a **show ip route** command). Figure 2-16 shows the packet encapsulations used at different points of a PPPoE network.

Figure 2-16   *PPPoE Network Cross Section*

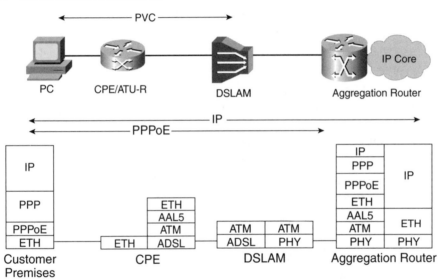

PPPoE Configuration

The PPPoE protocol runs over Ethernet frames. The host sends PPP packets in Ethernet frames, which are in turn segmented by the bridge CPE into ATM cells and sent onward over the DSL network. There are two Ethernet type values for PPPoE: 0x8863 for PPPoE discovery and 0x8864 for the actual PPPoE data sessions.

PPPoE is configured in two parts on a Cisco IOS router. The first part involves creating a PPPoE server. The second part is the standard configuration for PPP. Figure 2-17 shows the typical PPPoE architecture.

Figure 2-17   *PPPoE Architecture*

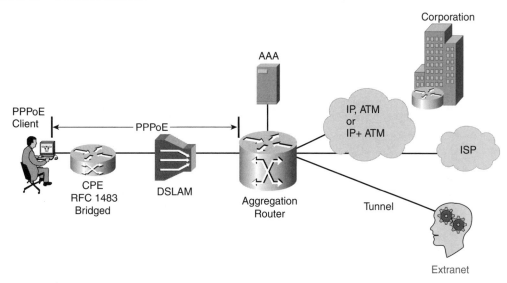

Example 2-14 demonstrates how you would configure a network such as the one shown in Figure 2-17.

Example 2-14   *PPPoE Configuration*

```
vpdn enable
! configuration for pppoe server
! interfaces for sessions will be cloned from virtual-template 1
vpdn-group 1
 accept dialin
  protocol pppoe
  virtual-template 1
! enable pppoe on this subinterface
! subscriber interface
interface ATM0/0/0.132 point-to-point
no ip directed-broadcast
pvc 1/32
 encapsulation aal5snap
 protocol pppoe

! virtual template for pppoe virtual-access interfaces
! note MTU size adjustment
interface virtual-template 1
ip unnumbered loopback0
no ip directed-broadcast
ip mtu 1492
peer default ip address pool pppoe-pool
ppp authentication pap
! pool of addresses for pppoe subscribers
ip local pool pppoe-pool 192.168.10.10 192.168.10.100
```

Example 2-15 shows the PPPoE configuration for the network in Figure 2-16 using Ethernet instead of ATM subscriber interfaces.

Example 2-15 *PPPoE Configuration*

```
vpdn-group pppoe
accept-dialin
protocol pppoe
virtual-template 1
!
interface FastEthernet2/0.2
encapsulation dot1Q 2
pppoe enable
!
interface FastEthernet2/0.3
encapsulation dot1Q 3
pppoe enable
```

NOTE Examples 2-14 and 2-15 use **vpdn-group** commands. In more recent versions of Cisco IOS, this syntax has been changed to use the newer **bba-group** commands. Chapter 6 shows how to use **bba-group**, but a lot of networks still run Cisco IOS images that have **vpdn-group**, which is why those commands are shown here and in Chapter 3, "VPNs in Broadband Networks."

PPPoE Service Selection and Discovery

Another innovation in the PPPoE protocol is the use of PADS messages to advertise services to clients. The premise behind this use is that each host potentially is subscribed to multiple network-based services and needs to choose between them or, alternatively, to discover the list of subscribed or permitted service names. Example services might include a public Internet connection, a private VPN connection, and an extranet managed by a financial institution. To switch between each service, the end customer must have some way of identifying and selecting the service in the first place. Similarly, to subscribe to a brand new service, there has to be some way to inform the customer that it exists.

It is possible to do service selection using PPPoE. To do this, the PPPoE Access Concentrator sends a list of available service names (such as Internet, VPN, SafeShopping) to the PPPoE client. The client then displays the list of services to the user, who can chose whichever one she wants to use.

From an architecture perspective, PPPoE service selection poses an interesting quandary. In the DSL reference model, only ISPs sell services to end users. Yet here is a protocol that only the wholesale providers (the Access Concentrator is a PTT device) can typically use to announce services they do not typically sell to customers they do not typically own.

That said, there is a proposal at the IETF that would allow just the PADS messages to be carried over L2TP. This would allow the ISP's network server to terminate the PPPoE protocol and manage service announcements, which is probably a more logical arrangement from a business perspective. The Cisco implementation is called PPPoE Relay.

PPP over ATM: The CPE as a Router

PPPoA was first standardized at the DSL Forum. It is commonly used, but not as widely as PPPoE. PPPoA is actually simpler than PPPoE because there is no need for any of the extensions, such as discovery.

PPPoA can be run directly from a host with an ATM NIC card. This scenario is fairly rare in operational networks because Ethernet NICs are so much cheaper. Our discussion will focus on a CPE with PPPoA.

To higher-layer protocols, a PPPoA link appears as a routed connection, with remote peer authentication and the possibility of dynamic address assignment.

PPPoA Configuration

PPPoA runs over AAL5 MUX or SNAP encapsulation. The CPE runs IP on its LAN interface and PPP as the link layer protocol on the ATM WAN interface, as shown in Figure 2-18.

Figure 2-18 *PPPoA Network Cross Section*

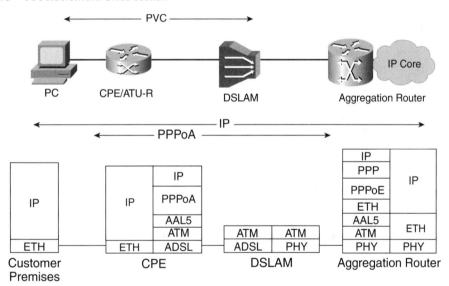

As soon as the PPP software detects that the ATM PVC is up, it tries to establish a session in classic PPP fashion. The router sends an LCP request, then changes state to authenticate and remains in this mode until either authentication succeeds or it times out. In case of timeout, the process starts over until a session is opened. This behavior can be disabled using **atm pppatm passive** but it is on by default on Cisco routers.

PPP Address Assignments

During PPP session negotiation, the client typically requests an address from the router. The router can find an address in one of several places. Either an **ip pool** is configured on the router, as in our example, or an address (or pool, for that matter) must be downloaded from a RADIUS server. (There is also the option of allowing the remote peer to keep its address, using **ip address negotiate** on the virtual template.)

The address download options are as follows:

- Download of a single address
- Download of a pool name
- Download of a pool at startup
- Use of On-Demand Address Pools

Download of a Single Address

When downloading a single address from RADIUS (using, for example, the **framed-ip-address** attribute), preference is given to downloaded attributes over parameters configured from the command line.

Example 2-16 shows how to use this attribute in a subscriber profile.

Example 2-16   Framed-IP-Address *RADIUS Profile*

```
jondoe Password = "cisco"
        Service-Type = Framed-User,
        Framed-Protocol = PPP,
        Framed-IP-Address = "192.168.11.1"
```

There are some special values for **framed-ip-address** that you should remember. If the AAA server returns a value of 255.255.255.254, that is an instruction to the router to fetch a dynamic IP address for this subscriber. In other words, the AAA server says to the router. "I want you to find a dynamic address for this subscriber." The router will probably do this using DHCP, and Example 2-17 shows the little bit of magic you need to combine DHCP and AAA.

Example 2-17   *Pools with DHCP*

```
! global command
ip dhcp-server 1.1.1.1
!
interface virtual-template 1
peer default ip address pool dhcp
```

Download of a Pool Name

In this scenario, a pool is already configured on the router and the RADIUS server just has to tell the router which one to use.

On the router, you would need the configuration in Example 2-18, with a **virtual-template** that *does not* have a pool name (or that would override the one coming from the RADIUS server) and a standard **ip address pool** .

Example 2-18 *Downloading Pool Names Router Configuration*

```
!Note no pool name
interface virtual-template 1
description PPPoE Clients
ip unnumbered loopback0
ppp authentication chap pap
ip local pool FOO 192.168.10.10 192.168.10.100
```

The corresponding AAA profile *with* a pool name would look like Example 2-19.

Example 2-19 *Downloading Pool Names RADIUS Profile*

```
janedoe Password = "cisco"
       Service-Type = Framed-User,
       Framed-Protocol = PPP,
       av-pair = "ip:addr-pool=FOO"
```

Download of a Pool at Startup

This trick is very similar to using AAA to download IP routes, in which case a Cisco IOS router can be configured to read static routing entries from an AAA server when it starts up. (The configuration is a little esoteric.)

The router is configured with a name that it uses to issue a RADIUS Access-Request at startup. The Access-Accept reply from the server includes one or more pools of IP addresses. These can be referenced in subscriber AAA profiles just as if they had been configured on the router. If a subscriber references an unknown pool, the router tries to download the complete list again. Example 2-20 shows how to activate this behavior in Cisco IOS. The router now sends an Access-Request using the name **load-pools** .

Example 2-20 *Downloading Pools Router Configuration*

```
! add this to the router configuration
aaa configuration config-username  load-pools
```

Now the RADIUS server needs a user profile that uses the same name as the router does, which is the case of the RADIUS profile in Example 2-21.

Example 2-21 *Downloading Pools RADIUS Profile*

```
nas1-pools Password = "cisco"
       Service-Type = Outbound-User,
       av-pair = "ip:pool-def#1=BAR 1921.168.11.10 192.168.11.100"
```

You can use these downloaded pools just like you do an IP address pool. Example 2-22 shows an example with a virtual-template configuration with a pool called BAR that was defined in Example 2-21.

Example 2-22 *Using Downloaded Pool Definitions*

```
interface virtual-template 2
description PPPoE Clients
ip unnumbered loopback0
peer default ip address pool BAR
ppp authentication chap pap
```

Use of On-Demand Address Pools

On-Demand Address Pools (ODAP), which is discussed in more detail in the Chapter 6, "Wholesale MPLS-VPN Related Service Features," is a powerful mechanism to allow a router to request IP pools dynamically from a DHCP server as existing ones are used.

All the techniques just described are well and good, but they let you allocate only a single host address (or pool from which a single address will be handed out to the host). What about the case of home networks with a broadband router connected to many different home computers? For that, the service provider needs other techniques, such as the following:

- **CPE PAT**—The CPE uses port address translation (PAT) to map many private host addresses to the single, public address assigned during PPP session negotiation.

- **IPCP subnet mask** —The CPE is assigned an IP subnet mask and an address during PPP session negotiation. It takes the first address of this subnet for its WAN interface and uses the rest of the pool to do network address translation (NAT) of host addresses. It is not possible to assign these addresses using DHCP, or else two links would be on the same IP subnet.

As usual, the subnet mask can either be configured on a b or in AAA. To make the IPCP subnet option work, you need to coordinate the aggregator, the CPE, and the AAA server.

Example 2-23 shows the configuration needed on the aggregation router.

Example 2-23 *IPCP Subnet Mask Router Configuration*

```
interface Virtual-Template2
ip unnumbered Loopback0
no peer default ip address
ppp authentication pap chap
ppp ipcp mask 255.255.255.240
!
```

Example 2-24 shows the configuration on the CPE, which needs to ask for the subnet mask when it brings up its PPP session.

Example 2-24 *IPCP Subnet Mask CPE Configuration*

```
!
interface Dialer 0
ppp ipcp mask request
```

Finally, Example 2-25 shows the RADIUS profile, which has a regular **framed-ip-address** , but also a subnet mask in the **framed-ip-netmask** attribute.

Example 2-25 *IPCP Subnet Mask RADIUS Profile*

```
CPE Password = "cisco"
Service-Type = Framed,
Framed-Protocol = PPP,
Framed-IP-Address=192.168.2.1
Framed-IP-netmask=255.255.255.248
```

PPP Quality of Service

There are two things to understand regarding QoS on PPP links: what type of QoS is supported and how to provision it.

One detail needs clarification at the outset: IP QoS on PPP interfaces is not as complete as on other Layer 2 interfaces. Depending on the actual router you are using, you can have classification, marking, and policing but probably not queuing. Of course, PPP runs on top of another Layer 2 interface and you can use the complete range of ATM CoS for DSL subscribers, for example. In each case (i.e., Layer 2 under PPP, or Layer 3 on the interface itself), use the classic Cisco IOS commands that were covered earlier in the chapter.

Provisioning QoS for PPP is a little different. Think first about what layer you are going to use to do the QoS and what type of QoS you need. Is it the policing at the ATM layer? Or classification at the IP layer? IP QoS commands, such as the **service-policy** command in Example 2-2, should go under the **virtual-template** on the router. ATM QoS parameters go under the PVC block. As with most things in PPP, you can provision QoS at either of these layers in a RADIUS profile.

Dynamic Bandwidth Selection (DBS) is the name of the Cisco IOS feature that lets you set a subscriber's ATM CoS profile using RADIUS. The idea behind the name is that a service provider would define different policies for subscribers: one for basic Internet access, one for VoIP, and so on. If there are different profiles predefined in RADIUS, then all the subscriber needs to do is to connect with a new username to get the new and improved QoS on his circuit. Using DBS means that the service provider operations team doesn't have to configure anything in the network as customers change back and forth between different levels of QoS.

Example 2-26 shows how to enable the DBS feature in Cisco IOS under an individual PVC, followed by Example 2-27, which gives the specific DBS RADIUS attributes.

Example 2-26 *DBS Router Configuration*

```
interface atm0/0/0.5 point-to-point
 ip address 192.168.2.1 255.255.255.0
 pvc 1/100
  dbs enable
  encapsulation aal5snap
  protocol ppp virtual-template1
```

Example 2-27 *DBS av-pairs RADIUS Profile*

```
Cisco-Avpair = "atm:peak-cell-rate=155000"
Cisco-Avpair = "atm:sustainable-cell-rate=155000"
```

The AAA parameters in Example 2-26 set the peak cell rate, which is mandatory and a sustainable cell rate. It behaves as UBR if only the PCR is given; otherwise it operates as a VRB-nrt circuit.

There is a similar set of special RADIUS attributes that let you download IP policing parameters to the aggregation router.

All in all, PPP is a little blunt when it comes to QoS support. With bridged access, there are very clear ways to map QoS policy between the IP layer and the transport layers, all of which have a good level of native QoS. The extra PPP layer blinds the access network, which cannot look into the PPP packets to know what QoS level to apply to the frames: There is no QoS marking in the PPP header and the original IP header is too deeply encapsulated to be able to look for the DSCP settings in hardware. In fact, all you are really doing with PPP QoS is prioritizing traffic on the aggregation router itself. None of the devices downstream (i.e., those between the aggregator and the subscriber) can automatically change its CoS settings if a subscriber uses a different DBS profile: This is not end-to-end QoS. Bridged access does offer, or is closer to offering, end-to-end QoS.

DSL Forum has been especially active in working on a new model that supports true multiservice traffic throughout the network, not just on the aggregation router. Interested readers should look for WT-59–related documents on the DSL Forum web site at http://www.dslforum.org.

PPP Authentication, Accounting, and Security

PPP has excellent authentication and accounting support. Millions of broadband and dial-up customers around the world use PPP for their Internet connection. The beautiful thing with PPP is that subscriber configuration can be centralized on a RADIUS server, which is a much more scalable way to run a network than to have to configure the devices independently. PPP is very well documented in other books, so the details are not going to be covered here, with the following two exceptions:

- PPP port-based authentication
- PPP security

Port-Based Authentication

Configuring a username in AAA for the CPE might seem easy to do but is in fact very awkward, because it means having a different username configured for each and every CPE. If a subscriber changes CPE, the username would have to be updated on the new device to make sure that the subscriber still gets the correct IP address. Rather than go to the pain of maintaining such a database, wouldn't life be easier if a CPE could be authenticated using the subscriber circuit ID? Happily, this is possible. The syntax on the router is **radius-server attribute nas-port format d** .

This simple statement makes the router include the circuit ID in the Radius NAS-port field. The format for ATM, which makes this value globally unique, is IP address/module/port/VPI/VCI. A corresponding format exists for Ethernet and VLANs (even QinQ) also. Obviously, the RADIUS server must support this.

PPP Security

Bridged access security is complex because it involves many subscribers who are all part of the same broadcast domain. Regardless of the actual tricks, DSL, cable, and Ethernet networks have many different bells and whistles to limit the broadcast domain as much as possible, ideally to a single subscriber.

PPP architectures just don't have this problem, because the subscriber links are actually routed interfaces and the aggregation router knows which address it assigned to whom. This removes a lot of the risk of IP and MAC layer spoofing, especially of the variety that lets one subscriber attack their neighbor *because of weaknesses in the aggregator or the broadband architecture itself.* It's important to be realistic here: suitably motivated subscribers at the other end of a PPP session *can* launch DoS and other nasty attacks. However, because the architecture provides a point-to-point link for each and every subscriber, there is inherently more security than on a network in which subscribers share the same Layer 2 segment.

You should remember the basic best practices for securing PPP connections and use CHAP authentication for the actual session itself. Also, protect the aggregation router. A PPP subscriber can still mount an attack against the default gateway. Ironically, PPP isn't as well served as Ethernet (but it doesn't have the same risks of ARP- and broadcast-based attacks), but URPF and NetFlow are also really good techniques to use in PPP architectures. A PPP-specific attack would be to launch a DoS attack against the RADIUS server by opening a gazillion sessions, or opening and closing them constantly. Cisco IOS can limit the number of sessions per connection or per MAC address, and this is a good feature to turn on. Perhaps best of all, RADIUS billing records provide a great way to track unusual usage back to an individual subscriber—even if he spoofs IP addresses and blasts a week's worth of traffic in a couple of hours, his billing record will show the volume of traffic sent over the subscriber line (ATM VC or Ethernet port).

Summary

This chapter reviewed the access technologies and protocols for DSL, cable, and Ethernet broadband networks. Even though there are major differences in the physical network, at Layers 2 and 3, they are much more similar. There are, in effect, only so many ways to connect a broadband customer, and a solution must offer efficient mechanisms for authentication, accounting, routing, and so on. Bridged access is prevalent on cable and Ethernet. PPP is more common on DSL but is used on the other two access types, because they both have an Ethernet MAC layer.

Bridged access is very simple and cost effective. It takes advantage of the fact that everyone is using Ethernet these days, and the bridged CPE is as cheap as they come. DHCP is a tried and trusted mechanism for managing addresses dynamically, and there are some enhancements in Cisco IOS that let ISPs hand out individual addresses to subscribers as they connect, but announce aggregate routes over their core networks.

PPP is very complete and lets service providers centralize customer configuration in one place. When a subscriber connects using PPP, the aggregation router authenticates using RADIUS and retrieves the subscriber's configuration from the central server. Operationally, this is a huge advantage. PPP offers many different ways to manage addresses, but they can be summarized as either allocating single addresses to individual subscribers, or allocating blocks of addresses to aggregation routers.

Security is always a concern on bridged networks and there are different solutions found on the different types of broadband-access platforms. DSL really cheats a little, and RBE treats bridged subscribers as if they were on routed, point-to-point links. The advantage to doing this is that broadcast domains are not shared across multiple subscribers. Cable has a sophisticated Layer 1, called DOCSIS, as well as enhancements on the cable modem and CMTS that address the same problems. Finally, Ethernet has a lot more security mechanisms than people usually expect, and switches offer protection that helps against spoofing and DoS attacks. PPP security is less of a major issue because there is no concept of a shared broadcast domain that works against you.

Address management and routing are really similar across all the architectures. PPP and bridging use different control protocols to allocate addresses, but once they have done so, the same guideline applies: Summarize routes early.

End-to-end QoS is much easier to achieve using a bridged architecture. Layer 2 to Layer 3 QoS mapping is well understood, and some of the broadband networks have rich native QoS capabilities—DSL because of ATM, and cable with DOCSIS. By and large, aggregation routers also allow service providers to combine this with the full gamut of Layer 3 QoS. The net result is that broadband services can carry multiservice traffic, such as Voice over IP, correctly. QoS support is a weakness of the PPP architecture. Different, even dynamic, QoS profiles are supported on the aggregation router, but end-to-end QoS across the access network is very hard to achieve.

Chapter 3 moves from the access part of the network to the service end and looks at the three major types of VPN technology used with broadband access today: GRE, IPSec, and L2TP.

In this chapter, you learn about the following topics:

- Criteria to Evaluate VPNs for Broadband Access

- Operation and Configuration of Tunnel-Based VPN Solutions, Using Three Case Studies:

    — Site VPN Using GRE Tunnels

    — Telecommuter VPN Using IPSec Tunnels

    — Infrastructure VPN Using L2TP Tunnels to Provide an Open Access Solution

- Two Limited Solutions for Open Access Without Tunnels Using NAT and Policy-Based Routing

VPNs in Broadband Networks

This chapter is really about tunnels. A lot of networks do not run MPLS, which creates a need to deliver VPN services over IP cores. These VPNs are typically built using point-to-point tunnels either between CPE routers or between provider routers.

Before taking a closer look at the world of tunnels, the chapter starts by reviewing some basic network design principles concerning tunnels and criteria to evaluate VPNs for broadband access applications for site, telecommuter, and wholesale applications.

The following sections cover the major IP-VPN tunneling solutions, namely generic routing encapsulation (GRE), IPSec, and L2TP. A case-study approach is used to look at each option, starting with a discussion of the technology used in the solution: how the protocol works, which RFCs define it, and so on. Then, you plunge into the details of the Cisco implementation, with examples of increasing sophistication that show you how to solve the problem defined by the case study under consideration. Finally, each solution is analyzed against the set of generic requirements of site, telecommuter, and wholesale VPNs.

The cases are as follows:

- Site VPN: Non-IP traffic—GRE
- Telecommuter VPN: VPN over anything—IPSec
- Infrastructure VPN: Open Access and wholesale—situations for L2TP

The same network is used for the GRE and IPSec examples, so once you understand the basic topology, you can quickly grasp what is going on in both the case studies. The focus of the L2TP case is just too different to be able to use exactly the same network, so there is a different topology.

Chapter 1, "Introduction: Broadband Access and Virtual Private Networks," introduced definitions of the various types of VPN. As a reminder, they are as follows:

- **Site-to-site VPN**—A VPN that is used to connect different sites.
- **Telecommuter VPN** —An individual subscriber, or very small network, that connects over a third-party network, such as the Internet, to its enterprise network.
- **Infrastructure VPN** —A special case of a VPN that is used by a wholesale provider to transport subscriber traffic to its service provider of choice. Internet traffic may cross one or several infrastructure VPNs.

NOTE The site-to-site solutions discussed in this chapter are all CPE based. The reason is simple: True network-based VPN solutions require support for overlapping IP address spaces. In other words, two sites, belonging to two different customers, but each using the 192.168.1.0/24 subnet, can be connected to the same edge router. To deal with this, the router needs private routing tables, which are discussed along with MPLS in Chapters 5, 6, and 7.

Tunnels, Hubs, and Spokes

It is commonly reported that tunnels are well suited to situations with a small number of peers, but do not scale well for large networks. This is sometimes, but not always, true.

If this is not always true, why is it so often cited in whitepapers and design guides? It is because of the famous N-squared problem. Consider a network with three nodes, and tunnels that connect each node to all the other nodes, giving a full-mesh topology. If you add another node to the network, each of the other networks must be configured with a new tunnel. The number of tunnels increases proportionally to the square of the number of nodes. The cost is clear. Connections, be they L2 circuits or L3 tunnels, are expensive, as are the time and talent needed to configure each and every node.

For this simple reason, most of today's VPNs use a hub-and-spoke system, similar in topology to the model used by airlines to route flights. A central node (in days past, the site with the mainframe) connects to many spokes. Traffic from one spoke to another spoke must go through a hub. The trade-off is that you get lower operational and capital costs but an increasingly complex routing topology, because the network administrator must make sure that the route tables on hub nodes correctly forward traffic from site to site, without looping (which is a fun challenge if different routing protocols are used between sites). *Full mesh* and *hub and spoke* are common terms in the VPN jargon.

A telecommuter VPN topology is always hub and spoke—there is no direct path between two telecommuter endpoints. Perhaps less obviously, infrastructure VPN topologies are also hub and spoke—the traffic is collected from all the subscribers and carried to the ISP network gateway, which is the hub. There is no direct path between subscribers; traffic must be routed through the ISP.

Internet remote-access networks are an extreme example of hub and spoke. Each subscriber represents a spoke and the network server is the hub. Again, routing over the access network is pretty straightforward because each spoke has a default route to the hub, and the hub carries a host route for the spokes. The routing requirements of each different type of VPN will be apparent in the case studies.

To Distribute or Centralize?

Which is better: a large central hub or many little hublets? Variations on this question arise frequently when designing tunnel-based networks. Tunnels must be terminated somewhere so that the IP packets they carry can be routed to their destinations. A centralized architecture terminates all the tunnels on a single device, as shown in Figure 3-1. The rationale is simple: the greater the number of nodes in a network, the greater the configuration, number of circuits, and cost. So, it is better to concentrate the tunnels on the smallest number of highly engineered machines possible.

Figure 3-1   *Centralized Architecture*

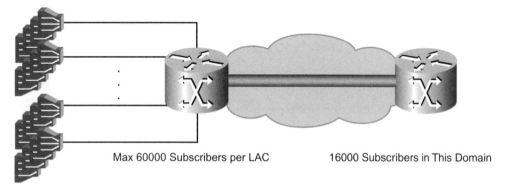

Max 60000 Subscribers per LAC   16000 Subscribers in This Domain

However, this simple formula doesn't always work in practice, because terminating tunnels has a cost, which rises with the number of tunnels, because managing the many hundreds or thousands of tunnels found on modern routers takes a lot of resources and expensive hardware. The alternative is to distribute tunnel termination across many, smaller devices, as depicted in Figure 3-2.

From an investment perspective, the network operator has the choice between the following:

- **Centralized option** —High-end routers, with dedicated hardware for encapsulation/ decapsulation, Layer 3 forwarding, and so forth
- **Decentralized option** —Simpler, lower-cost devices

As with so many network design options, there is no single best answer for every network. To understand some of the trade-offs, consider how each option works with different sizes of networks. A smaller, midrange router can terminate around 8000 subscribers, whereas a higher-end device supports over 60,000 subscribers. If there are 56,000 subscribers on the network, the decentralized option requires seven aggregation routers, whereas the centralized option needs only one aggregation router.

Figure 3-2 *Distributed Architecture*

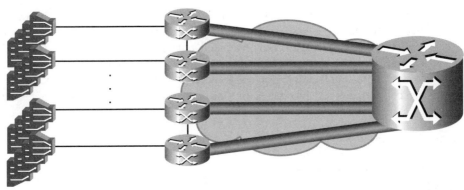

400 Subscribers per DSLAM   Max 4000 Subscribers per LAC   16000 Subscribers in This Domain

Network growth to 17000 subscribers requires adding another small LAC.

Small routers are cheaper than large ones, no matter who makes them. In fact, a single line card on a high-end system often costs more than a fully equipped small router. So, the initial capital expenditure equation often favors the multiple small routers option.

The seven aggregation devices required for the decentralized option are in all likelihood going to cost less than the single, big aggregation router required for the centralized option. Nothing is free, however, and managing seven devices will cost more in terms of network operations staff time than managing one device.

From an IP routing perspective, the difference between the centralized and distributed options is much less than is often supposed. At first glance, the distributed option (which has seven routers instead of the single central router)

- Needs more work because routing must be configured on each aggregator

- Has seven more routing peers participating in the service provider's IGP

- Creates seven summarized route announcements: 1 for 8000 subscribers (this is the best case, which assumes that all the subscriber addresses can be made contiguous and so announced in one go.)

But now put the distributed option into the context of a service provider point of presence (POP). Aggregation routers almost never connect directly to the core, because there is generally another edge router in the POP. A common scenario, shown in Figure 3-3, involves simple dynamic routing between the aggregator and the edge device, which in turn typically runs the internal Border Gateway Protocol (iBGP) across the core, and an Interior Gateway Protocol (IGP) such as IS-IS, Open Shortest Path First (OSPF), or Enhanced Interior Gateway Routing Protocol (EIGRP).

Reconsider the distributed option: The disadvantage from a routing protocol perspective is that it includes seven routers instead of one. However, the second layer of aggregation shown in Figure 3-3 means that these are "hidden" by GSR routers, which peer with the rest of the network and announce all the routes. With the centralized option, there would be a single device connected to the "GSR" routers in Figure 3-3. All of a sudden, the differences between the two options fades away.

Figure 3-3   *Broadband POP*

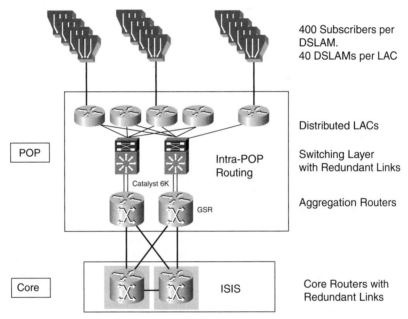

400 Subscribers per DSLAM.
40 DSLAMs per LAC

Distributed LACs

Switching Layer with Redundant Links

Aggregation Routers

Core Routers with Redundant Links

Network availability is another point that often appears on engineers' whiteboards during the centralized versus distributed debate. Availability is a valid concern that favors the high-end, redundant systems used in centralized designs.

All operators do everything possible to limit network downtime. However, they are working with many subproblems, as follows:

- For business subscribers, operators must comply with strict SLAs. Downtime is always included in these SLAs and must be minimized. In this case, it makes sense to engineer for maximum redundancy and pay more for high availability. The subscribers are paying extra for their connection, which justifies the additional cost.

Hardware redundancy protects against router problems, such as a software or line card problem. However, redundancy doesn't help with configuration errors—or a misplaced foot on a cable—which are proportionally more common.

- For residential subscribers, the issue can be quite different. Although in absolute terms operators still want to avoid downtime as much as possible, you have neither the financial penalties nor the same revenue per customer. Rather than pay for a high-end aggregator, with redundant line cards and routing engines, it may be more cost effective to design the network in such a way as to limit the cost of an outage by minimizing the number of subscribers affected per incident.

The logic of the network design approach works like this. When there is a problem with a large aggregator, tens of thousands of subscribers lose connectivity. Granted, these devices don't fail very often, but if just 10 percent of the 56,000 subscribers call the hotline, that represents a tangible and unpleasant cost for the operator. Now, consider the distributed case. If there is an identical problem with a smaller router, only 8000 subscribers are affected, which in turn lowers the load on the hotline down to a more manageable 80 callers (still assuming 10 percent of people actually call).

If there is a trend somewhere in all the various deployment architectures, it is perhaps that distributed architectures seem to work well when controlling capital outlay is crucial. If a service provider needs to get revenue flowing as fast as possible (and be profitable with it), then it is hard to argue with the economics of deploying a small box for a relatively small number of subscribers and adding routers as the money flows in. For operators whose business model allows them, or requires them, to look out further, the operational costs of many devices versus the few is often the determinant. Here, the requirement is to have machines with as much processing head room as possible. The network is built for future growth and revenue, and additional capacity is added in the form of line cards.

Access VPN Requirements Reminder

Chapter 1 discussed what to look for when choosing a VPN solution. Many of these requirements are identical to the broadband encapsulation requirements presented in Chapter 2, "Delivering Broadband Access Today: An Access Technologies Primer." As you read through the case studies for each VPN solution, the case studies will be compared to the following lists of requirements.

For site VPNs, the requirements are as follows:

- Data confidentiality
- Efficient operation (including ease of provisioning)
- Efficient routing

- High availability and resiliency
- Multicast
- Quality of service
- Fragmentation

For telecommuter VPNs, the requirements are the same as for site VPNs, plus the following:

- Authentication, authorization, and accounting
- Service selection

For wholesale VPNs, the requirements are the same as for telecommuter VPNs, plus the following:

- Support for any IP addressing plan
- Efficient address management
- Additional L3 services

Also, remember the difference between VPNs initiated at CPE (CPE-based VPNs) and VPNs initiated at service-provider devices (network-based VPNs):

- **CPE-based VPN** — The VPN starts and ends on the CPE. For example, an IPSec tunnel is initiated from one CPE router to another. The service provider network is used only to transport IP packets. Although it is not very often thought of in this way, client-based L2TP is also a form of CPE-based VPN, where the CPE is the subscriber's host.

  A client-based VPN is a special case of a CPE-based VPN. This discussion about CPE-based VPNs assumes that tunnels can only start or end on network devices. This isn't the full picture. Many companies use the same tunnel technology that is discussed here and use a PC client on one end, connected to a specialized network device (or a router) on the other end. L2TP and IPSec tunnels both are used in this way, to name just two technologies. The architecture of these client-based VPNs is really a special case of CPE-based VPNs. There are more endpoints, of course, but everything is under the control of the enterprise itself.

- **Network-based VPN** — The VPN starts on a service provider device, and may end on either a service provider or CPE device. The most common example of a network-based VPN is L2TP, where a tunnel is initiated on the broadband aggregation router. However, it is also possible to have other network-based VPNs, such as IPSec. Privacy is an integral part of a VPN service, so there is an implicit assumption that the link between the customer and the start of the VPN is secure (which means that no unauthorized person has access to the data on it, not that the data is encrypted—that's a whole other decision). This is typically true in broadband networks where, for example, each DSL subscriber has a different ATM PVC.

Case 1: A Site VPN with Non-IP Traffic—GRE

Broadband Enterprises, a company with a main headquarters and three remote satellite sites, wants to build a VPN that connects the small offices to headquarters. All the sites already have Internet access. The remote offices use cable subscriptions, and headquarters has an unmanaged Frame Relay service. The traffic is only data, with web access, but also Internetwork Packet Exchange (IPX) for some legacy servers.

The key requirement for this customer is to have a low-cost solution that supports both IP and non-IP data. The sites already have Internet access, the CPE is under the control of the end user, and the VPN topology is simple hub and spoke. If possible, the solution should reuse the existing Internet connections, for cost reasons, and build a VPN over the public Internet network.

The way the problem is presented, setting aside the IPX traffic, several good solutions are available. However, running IPX means that GRE is the obvious fit. It runs over any IP network, using tunnels to connect sites, and is not limited to IP traffic.

GRE Protocol and Operation

Generic routing encapsulation is defined in RFC 2784. The protocol is actually a little older and was first documented in RFC 1701, which appeared in 1994.

The protocol is designed to provide a very generic way of encapsulating packets of one variety in packets of another variety. Figure 3-4 shows the encapsulation stack.

Figure 3-4 *GRE Encapsulation*

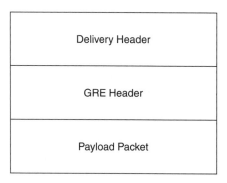

The GRE header is very simple (RFC 2784), as you can see in Figure 3-5.

Figure 3-5 *GRE Header*

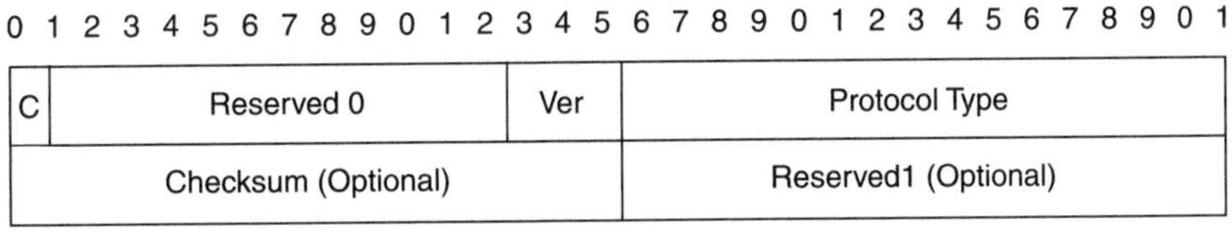

```
0 1 2 3 4 5 6 7 8 9 0 1 2 3 4 5 6 7 8 9 0 1 2 3 4 5 6 7 8 9 0 1
```

C	Reserved 0	Ver	Protocol Type
	Checksum (Optional)		Reserved1 (Optional)

The simplest possible expression of this header is a simple Protocol Type field. All the preceding fields are typically 0, and the subsequent ones can be omitted. You can find freeware implementations that work only with the first two octets, but all four should be supported. This conciseness and simplicity allows GRE to be implemented in hardware on high-end systems.

NOTE   Retrofitting tunnels on such machines can often be problematic because they introduce extra length and processing on processors optimized to work with a 20-octet IP header and forward at OC-48 and OC-192 rates. Indeed, one of the ongoing challenges in the area of router design is knowing what to encode in application-specific integrated circuits (ASICs) and microcode for line-rate forwarding. Designers often need to leave themselves spare hardware cycles to be able to add new protocols and features after the hardware has shipped.

Interestingly enough, the original RFC (RFC 1701) had a more complicated header, as shown in Figure 3-6.

Figure 3-6 *RFC 1701 GRE Header*

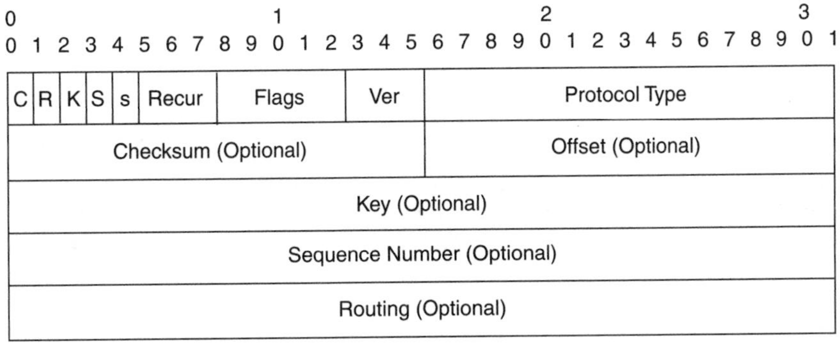

```
0                   1                   2                   3
0 1 2 3 4 5 6 7 8 9 0 1 2 3 4 5 6 7 8 9 0 1 2 3 4 5 6 7 8 9 0 1
```

C	R	K	S	s	Recur	Flags	Ver	Protocol Type
	Checksum (Optional)							Offset (Optional)
	Key (Optional)							
	Sequence Number (Optional)							
	Routing (Optional)							

The various bits at the start of the packet indicated whether the optional fields were present. The Key field was for authentication; the Sequence Number field was to detect out-of-order packets; and the Routing field was for source routing. IP already has a way to number packets and to do source routing, if they are required, so there was not much point duplicating these in the GRE layer. A different RFC, RFC 2890, now specifies the optional Key and Sequence extensions. The 16-bit Key field is used to identify flows within a tunnel.

To manage backward compatibility, RFC 2784 states that the first 5 bits of the Reserved0 field (the ones that match the R|K|S|s bits of the older format) must be zero unless RFC 1701 is supported. The Version field is always zero (except if PPTP is transported, in which case it is set to 1). To detect the version in use, you can assume that if any of the first 5 bits is a non-zero value, the sender is using the RFC 1701 format. If the receiver supports this, well and good; if not, the packet is simply discarded.

The Protocol Type field uses the same values as the IEEE Ethernet Type field, so our example IPX payload has a Protocol Type value of 0x08137. The delivery header would be the standard IP header, with a protocol number 47 to indicate a GRE packet.

GRE Configuration

GRE is very easy to configure. Define each tunnel endpoint as a Cisco IOS interface, with a globally routable tunnel source address that will be used as the source IP in the Delivery header, and a globally routable tunnel destination, which is the other end of the tunnel.

Before looking at the router configuration files, a word about the basic network topology used in the examples. So that it's easier to replicate the configurations (or just try them), the topology shown in Figure 3-7 simulates Internet connections between the different sites with the router called INET-r. The 10.0.0.0 subnet is used to represent public addresses. This same network will be used for all the GRE and IPSec examples.

Figure 3-7   *Example Network Internet Connections*

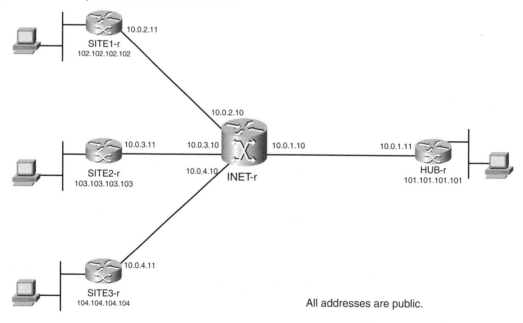

The VPN is overlaid on this network using GRE tunnels as shown in Figure 3-8. The IP addresses in Figure 3-8 are all private, VPN addresses. Each site has a WAN interface (192.168.x.x) and a LAN interface (for example 13.13.13.13). The LANs are actually simulated using loopback interfaces—again, to try to make it easier to replicate this configuration using a small number of routers.

Figure 3-8   *GRE Topology for CPE-Based Site-to-Site VPN*

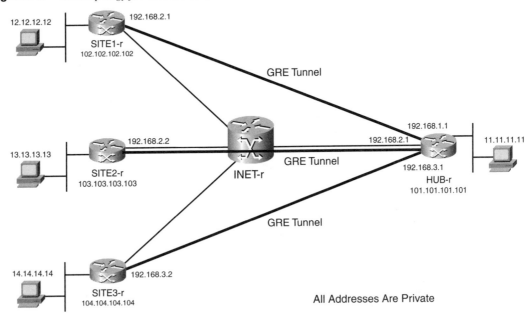

Example 3-1 is the configuration file of the hub router. The site 1 CPE, called SITE1-r, is shown in Example 3-2. Examples 3-3 and 3-4 give the configurations for sites 2 and 3, respectively.

NOTE   The examples throughout the book are extracts from the complete configurations, which are posted at http://www.ciscopress/1587051362 and available for download.

Example 3-1   *HUB-r Router Configuration*

```
interface Loopback0
 ip address 101.101.101.101 255.255.255.255
!
interface Loopback1
 description Enterprise Internal interface to be advertised to all sites
 ip address 11.11.11.11 255.255.255.255
!
```

continues

Example 3-1 *HUB-r Router Configuration (Continued)*

```
interface Tunnel0
 description VPN to Site1
 ip address 192.168.1.1 255.255.255.252
 tunnel source Serial0/0
 tunnel destination 10.0.2.11
!
interface Tunnel1
 description VPN to SITE2-r
 ip address 192.168.2.1 255.255.255.252
 tunnel source Serial0/0
 tunnel destination 10.0.3.11
!
interface Tunnel2
 description VPN to SITE3-r
 ip address 192.168.3.1 255.255.255.252
 tunnel source Serial0/0
 tunnel destination 10.0.4.11
!
interface Serial0/0
 description HUB-r Internet connection
 ip address 10.0.1.11 255.255.255.0
!
router ospf 302
 log-adjacency-changes
 network 11.11.11.11 0.0.0.0 area 0
 network 192.168.1.0 0.0.0.3 area 0
 network 192.168.2.0 0.0.0.3 area 0
 network 192.168.3.0 0.0.0.3 area 0!
ip route 0.0.0.0 0.0.0.0 Serial0/0
```

As previously stated, configuring GRE is very easy. Create a tunnel interface for each peer. On HUB-r in Example 3-1, there is a tunnel to reach every single spoke, so you see interfaces Tunnel0, Tunnel1, and Tunnel2. Under each tunnel interface, you specify the source and destination addresses you want the router to use to carry the GRE packets using the **tunnel source** and **tunnel destination** commands.

Taking interface Tunnel1 as an example, the private address on this interface (i.e., the one that is part of the VPN) is 192.168.2.1. To send packets to and from this interface, the router uses an IP source address of 10.0.1.11 (the address of Serial0/0) and a destination address of 10.0.4.11 (the address of the WAN interface on SITE2-r). There must be a route to reach the destination address configured on the GRE tunnel interfaces.

The routing configuration in Example 3-1 has two sections. OSPF runs across the GRE tunnels, announcing the private, VPN routes, namely 11.11.11.11/32 and 192.168.x.0/28. Remember, 11.11.11.11 represents the enterprise LAN interface. It should be reachable only from a VPN source address (you can try this out). The second routing section has a static default route through Serial0/0. This is for the public, Internet-facing addresses (the 10.0.0.0/24 address space in this topology).

Example 3-2 shows the configuration on the first spoke route, SITE1-r. Look for the addresses on interface Tunnel0 to be on the same 192.168.1.0/24 subnet as interface Tunnel0 on HUB-r. There is no need for the actual interface names on each router to match—it's just a coincidence that they do so here.

Example 3-2   *SITE1-r Router Configuration*

```
interface Loopback0
 ip address 102.102.102.102 255.255.255.255
!
interface Loopback1
 description Enterprise internal interface to be reachable by all sites
 ip address 12.12.12.12 255.255.255.255
!
interface Tunnel0
 description VPN to HUB
 ip address 192.168.1.2 255.255.255.252
 tunnel source Serial0/0
 tunnel destination 10.0.1.11
!
interface Serial0/0
 description SITE1-r Internet connection
 ip address 10.0.2.11 255.255.255.0
!
router ospf 302
 log-adjacency-changes
 network 12.12.12.12 0.0.0.0 area 0
 network 192.168.1.0 0.0.0.3 area 0
!
ip route 0.0.0.0 0.0.0.0 Serial0/0
```

Examples 3-3 and 3-4 are included to complete the picture. The configuration is functionally identical to the SITE1-r router of Example 3-2. Again, the Internet is simulated here with the 10/8 network.

Example 3-3   *SITE2-r Router Configuration*

```
interface Loopback0
 ip address 103.103.103.103 255.255.255.255
!
interface Loopback1
 description Enterprise internal interface to be reachable by all sites
 ip address 13.13.13.13 255.255.255.255
!
interface Tunnel0
 description VPN to HUB
 ip address 192.168.2.2 255.255.255.252
 tunnel source Serial0/0
 tunnel destination 10.0.1.11
!
interface Serial0/0
 description SITE2-r Internet connection
```

continues

Example 3-3   *SITE2-r Router Configuration (Continued)*

```
ip address 10.0.3.11 255.255.255.0
!
router ospf 302
 log-adjacency-changes
 network 13.13.13.13 0.0.0.0 area 0
 network 192.168.2.0 0.0.0.3 area 0
!
ip route 0.0.0.0 0.0.0.0 Serial0/0
```

Example 3-4   *SITE3-r Router Configuration*

```
interface Loopback0
 ip address 104.104.104.104 255.255.255.255
!
interface Loopback1
 description Enterprise internal interface to be reachable by all sites
 ip address 14.14.14.14 255.255.255.255
!
interface Tunnel0
 description VPN to HUB
 ip address 192.168.3.2 255.255.255.252
 tunnel source Serial0/0
 tunnel destination 10.0.1.11
!
interface Serial0/0
 description SITE3-r Internet connection
 ip address 10.0.4.11 255.255.255.0
!
router ospf 302
 log-adjacency-changes
 network 14.14.14.14 0.0.0.0 area 0
 network 192.168.3.0 0.0.0.3 area 0
!
ip route 0.0.0.0 0.0.0.0 Serial0/0
```

The following are some key points to notice about the spoke configurations in Examples 3-2 through 3-4:

- The Loopback1 networks represent internal subnets that are reachable only by sites in the same VPN. This is an easy way to simulate networks in a lab environment. Hereafter these subnets are referred to as spoke LANs.

- Each router has a default route through interface Serial0, which is what you would expect to find in a scenario where each site has an Internet connection. The tunnel endpoints are part of the VPN and so use 192.168.x.0/30 addresses. These are used in the payload IP header. The globally routable GRE delivery header source and destination addresses are the respective Serial0/0 addresses at either end of the tunnel (which use the 10.0.0.0 subnet).

- The Loopback0 addresses are used for routing protocol IDs.
- Use **ip ospf network broadcast** on the tunnel interface; otherwise, OSPF gets confused about the interface type and will not form full adjacencies with the site routers.
- Although none of the routers uses a distance-vector routing protocol, if you do use one, turn off split horizon for RIP and EIGRP; otherwise, routes learned from one site will not be advertised back out the tunnel interface to the others.

Now you need to figure out if all the routers are doing what they are supposed to. A good first step is to check that all the interfaces are up. Because tunnels are logical interfaces, the underlying physical interface must be up also. Example 3-5 lists the interesting portion of the output of a **show ip interface brief command** on SITE2-r.

Example 3-5   **show ip interface brief** *on SITE2-r*

```
SITE2-r#show ip interface brief
Interface            IP-Address      OK? Method Status        Protocol
Serial0/0            10.0.3.11       YES manual up            up
Tunnel0              192.168.2.2     YES manual up            up
```

If the interfaces are up, a simple test to see if the VPN is working is to ping between sites using the "internal" loopback addresses, as shown in Example 3-6.

Example 3-6   *ping Between VPN Addresses*

```
SITE2-r#ping
Protocol [ip]:
Target IP address: 12.12.12.12
Repeat count [5]:
Datagram size [100]:
Timeout in seconds [2]:
Extended commands [n]: y
Source address or interface: 13.13.13.13
Type of service [0]:
Set DF bit in IP header? [no]:
Validate reply data? [no]:
Data pattern [0xABCD]:
Loose, Strict, Record, Timestamp, Verbose[none]:
Sweep range of sizes [n]:
Type escape sequence to abort.
Sending 5, 100-byte ICMP Echos to 12.12.12.12, timeout is 2 seconds:
Packet sent with a source address of 13.13.13.13
```

Network 12.12.12.12/32, which is the spoke LAN on SITE1-r, is reachable through the VPN, as the route tables in Example 3-9 show, so everything is working as planned. (The example even uses the Site2-r spoke LAN source address.) The VPN routers are exchanged using OSPF, so look for entries marked **O** in the output of the **show ip route** command in Example 3-7.

By following the structure of the routes, you can see that all the ping packets in Example 3-6, which go from SITE1-r to SITE2-r, are actually forwarded through the hub router, HUB-r.

Example 3-7   **show ip route** *on SITE2-r*

```
SITE2-r#show ip route
Codes: C - connected, S - static, I - IGRP, R - RIP, M - mobile, B - BGP
       D - EIGRP, EX - EIGRP external, O - OSPF, IA - OSPF inter area
       N1 - OSPF NSSA external type 1, N2 - OSPF NSSA external type 2
       E1 - OSPF external type 1, E2 - OSPF external type 2, E - EGP
       i - IS-IS, L1 - IS-IS level-1, L2 - IS-IS level-2, ia - IS-IS inter area
       * - candidate default, U - per-user static route, o - ODR
       P - periodic downloaded static route
Gateway of last resort is 0.0.0.0 to network 0.0.0.0
     103.0.0.0/32 is subnetted, 1 subnets
C       103.103.103.103 is directly connected, Loopback0
     10.0.0.0/24 is subnetted, 1 subnets
C       10.0.3.0 is directly connected, Serial0/0
     11.0.0.0/32 is subnetted, 1 subnets
O       11.11.11.11 [110/11112] via 192.168.2.1, 00:02:04, Tunnel0
     12.0.0.0/32 is subnetted, 1 subnets
O       12.12.12.12 [110/22223] via 192.168.2.1, 00:02:04, Tunnel0
     192.168.1.0/30 is subnetted, 1 subnets
O       192.168.1.0 [110/22222] via 192.168.2.1, 00:02:04, Tunnel0
     13.0.0.0/32 is subnetted, 1 subnets
C       13.13.13.13 is directly connected, Loopback1
     192.168.2.0/30 is subnetted, 1 subnets
C       192.168.2.0 is directly connected, Tunnel0
     14.0.0.0/32 is subnetted, 1 subnets
O       14.14.14.14 [110/22223] via 192.168.2.1, 00:02:05, Tunnel0
     192.168.3.0/30 is subnetted, 1 subnets
O       192.168.3.0 [110/22222] via 192.168.2.1, 00:02:05, Tunnel0
S*   0.0.0.0/0 is directly connected, Serial0/0
```

As you would expect, all the VPN routes in Example 3-7 are reachable only through the **Tunnel0** interface.

Example 3-8 shows the routing table on the hub.

Example 3-8   **show ip route** *on HUB-r*

```
HUB-r#show ip route
Codes: C - connected, S - static, I - IGRP, R - RIP, M - mobile, B - BGP
       D - EIGRP, EX - EIGRP external, O - OSPF, IA - OSPF inter area
       N1 - OSPF NSSA external type 1, N2 - OSPF NSSA external type 2
       E1 - OSPF external type 1, E2 - OSPF external type 2, E - EGP
       i - IS-IS, L1 - IS-IS level-1, L2 - IS-IS level-2, ia - IS-IS inter area
       * - candidate default, U - per-user static route, o - ODR
       P - periodic downloaded static route
Gateway of last resort is 0.0.0.0 to network 0.0.0.0
     101.0.0.0/32 is subnetted, 1 subnets
C       101.101.101.101 is directly connected, Loopback0
     10.0.0.0/24 is subnetted, 1 subnets
```

Example 3-8   show ip route *on HUB-r (Continued)*

```
C       10.0.1.0 is directly connected, Serial0/0
        11.0.0.0/32 is subnetted, 1 subnets
C       11.11.11.11 is directly connected, Loopback1
        12.0.0.0/32 is subnetted, 1 subnets
O       12.12.12.12 [110/11112] via 192.168.1.2, 00:02:41, Tunnel0
        192.168.1.0/30 is subnetted, 1 subnets
C       192.168.1.0 is directly connected, Tunnel0
        13.0.0.0/32 is subnetted, 1 subnets
O       13.13.13.13 [110/11112] via 192.168.2.2, 00:02:41, Tunnel1
        192.168.2.0/30 is subnetted, 1 subnets
C       192.168.2.0 is directly connected, Tunnel1
        14.0.0.0/32 is subnetted, 1 subnets
O       14.14.14.14 [110/11112] via 192.168.3.2, 00:02:42, Tunnel2
        192.168.3.0/30 is subnetted, 1 subnets
C       192.168.3.0 is directly connected, Tunnel2
S*  0.0.0.0/0 is directly connected, Serial0/0
```

On the hub router, VPN routes are again exchanged using OSPF, so they are marked with the letter **O** in the Cisco IOS routing table. Note that unlike the site routers, Example 3-8 shows that there is a different tunnel interface used to reach every site. Cisco IOS treats GRE tunnels as it does any physical interface. This makes it very easy to run routing protocols across the point-to-point VPN interfaces, as was done in the example with OSPF, and to carry non-IP traffic. This is not true of all the tunneling technologies covered in this chapter.

The original design requirements for this network included IPX connectivity. You do this as you would on any "regular" Cisco IOS interface. IPX is added to the SITE2-r router in Example 3-9.

Example 3-9   *IPX Routing on SITE2-r*

```
ipx routing 2222.2222.2222

!
interface Tunnel0
 description VPN to HUB
 ip address 192.168.2.2 255.255.255.252
 ipx network 2222
 tunnel source Serial0/0
 tunnel destination 10.0.1.11
```

There are two new commands in Example 3-9. First, the **ipx routing** command enables IPX and sets a pseudo-mac address. (Cisco IOS creates one randomly if no IEEE interface is available.) Second, the **ipx network 2222** command configures a network address on the GRE tunnel interface. Use the **show ipx interface** and **show ipx route** commands to check this very simple configuration. The **show ipx interface** output should show that IPX is enabled on the **Tunnel0** interface, and the **show ipx route** command displays the IPX routing table. On SITE2-r, it would have just one line for **Tunnel0** .

The next step is to add the corresponding IPX configuration to the hub router. Example 3-10 shows the commands to add to HUB-r.

Example 3-10 *HUB-r IPX Command Configlet*

```
ipx routing 1111.2222.3333
!
interface Tunnel1
 description VPN to SITE2-r
 ip address 192.168.2.1 255.255.255.252
 ipx network 2222
 tunnel source Serial0/0
 tunnel destination 10.0.3.11
!
```

Finally, Example 3-11 checks that everything works by testing connectivity with an IPX ping from SITE2-r to HUB-r.

Example 3-11 *IPX pings Between Site and Hub*

```
SITE2-r#ping ipx
Target IPX address: 2222.1111.2222.3333
Repeat count [5]:
Datagram size [100]:
Timeout in seconds [2]:
Verbose [n]:
Type escape sequence to abort.
Sending 5, 100-byte IPX Novell Echoes to 2222.1111.2222.3333, timeout is 2 seconds:
!!!!!
Success rate is 100 percent (5/5), round-trip min/avg/max = 64/98/168 ms
```

In all the GRE examples shown so far in this chapter, there is nothing in the configuration files that shows that the network uses a broadband cable connection. In fact, Broadband Enterprises decided to use a router that connects to the cable modem over the Ethernet port, not an integrated cable-modem router. There are reasons for doing it this way:

- In line with the earlier definition of a CPE-based VPN, all the routers are assumed to be completely under the control of the enterprise. This is unlikely to be true of a cable router delivered by a cable service provider.

- Later examples use encryption and other advanced features that need the extra processing power of a full router.

- The external cable-modem solution is more general purpose. There are fewer routed cable modems available.

Although the scenarios don't use it, the integrated cable-modem router configuration is shown in Example 3-12, for reference. You might find it useful for cases in which you do want to configure GRE over a Cisco IOS cable modem router. You can see that the GRE-related portion is identical to the spoke routers in Examples 3-2 through 3-4.

Example 3-12 *uBR Cable Modem Router Configuration*

```
interface Tunnel0
ip address 192.168.1.2 255.255.255.252
tunnel source Ethernet0
tunnel destination 10.0.1.11
!
! Internal LAN interface
interface Ethernet0
 ip address 12.12.12.12 255.255.255.0
 ip rip send version 2
 ip rip receive version 2
 no ip route-cache
 no ip mroute-cache
!
!
interface cable-modem0
 ip rip send version 2
 ip rip receive version 2
 no ip route-cache
 no ip mroute-cache
 no cable-modem compliant bridge
!
router rip
version 2
passive-interface Tunnel0
network 10.0.0.0
network 12.0.0.0
no auto-summary
!
```

A key difference with the cable modem router in Example 3-12 is that the WAN interface IP address (on interface cable-modem0) is dynamic, being assigned by the cable provider with the Dynamic Host Configuration Protocol (DHCP). This is not exactly convenient if you have to specify the address at the remote end of the tunnel. If you can't find a provider who issues static IP addresses, then you must use some other routable address, which is why the 12.0.0.0 subnet is advertised with RIP in Example 3-12.

GRE Design Considerations

GRE is a classic tunnel-based architecture, with the attendant disadvantages:

- All site-to-site traffic is routed through a central hub. If there is a lot of high-speed, intersite traffic, the hub becomes a bottleneck.

- The size of the hub router configuration grows with the number of sites. There are five lines of text per site. This is not an issue with the small VPN in the example, but it can be prohibitive in a large VPN. A workaround is to introduce some hierarchy in the design to limit the number of tunnels terminated on a single hub. For example, connect odd-numbered sites to one hub, and even-numbered sites to another hub.

How does GRE fare as a VPN solution for broadband access? Referring to the requirements for site VPNs from the section, "Access VPN Requirements Reminder," consider the following protocol and implementation considerations:

- **Confidentiality** —GRE offers neither strong security nor strong authentication. There are some interesting websites devoted to spoofing GRE to gain access to enterprise networks. If security is a concern, pure GRE is not an optimal solution to build a VPN over a shared infrastructure. However, GRE does satisfy the basic need of a VPN to preserve data confidentiality between customers. In the previous examples, short of a malicious misconfiguration, no way exists for one customer's data to end up on someone else's network.

- **Efficient operation** —GRE is easy to configure and operate for anyone already conversant in Cisco IOS syntax. In a minimum configuration, only the commands for endpoint addresses are new. The standard IP WAN **show** and **debug** commands for interfaces and routing are available. Of great importance for any operations staff, the concepts and protocol are simple. There is very little that is VPN specific to go wrong. Apart from the issue with configuration file length, GRE operation is straightforward. This is a great advantage.

- **Efficient routing** —Unless a full mesh is used, all tunnel-based solutions do badly here, and GRE is no exception. Routing from site to site is inefficient because it must go through the hub. The customer in the example has the added operational overhead of making sure the routing protocols are properly configured for hub and spoke. Of course, if most of the network traffic is destined for the hub anyway, then this may not be a huge issue. This issue becomes more acute as the number of sites and hubs increases and whenever "exceptions" are made to the simple design rules (for example, by connecting two sites directly). It should be obvious that many of the same routing design challenges exist here as when running IP over point-to-point ATM or Frame Relay circuits.

- **High availability and resiliency** —There are no hooks in GRE to help provide any form of resiliency. For example, the protocol has no control channel to detect peer failure. If one end of the tunnel goes down, say because of a problem on the interface card, there is no way for the remote end to detect this. You can see this happening in Example 3-13. The tunnel interface itself is shut down. (This could be because of an operator error, for example.) There are no **debug** commands turned on, and what you see on the SITE2-r router are log messages that relate to an interface changing state to down. The **show ip interface brief** command in Example 3-13 confirms that the tunnel is, in fact, down.

Example 3-13 *Tunnel Failure at SITE2*

```
SITE2-r(config)#interface tunnel0
SITE2-r(config-if)#shutdown

02:53:16: %OSPF-5-ADJCHG: Process 302, Nbr 101.101.101.101 on Tunnel0 from FULL to
DOWN, Neighbor Down: Interface down or detachend
02:53:18: %LINK-5-CHANGED: Interface Tunnel0, changed state to administratively down
02:53:19: %LINEPROTO-5-UPDOWN: Line protocol on Interface Tunnel0, changed state to
down
02:53:19: %SYS-5-CONFIG_I: Configured from console by console
SITE2-r#
SITE2-r#show ip interface brief
Interface              IP-Address       OK? Method Status                Protocol
Serial0/0              10.0.3.11        YES NVRAM  up                    up
Loopback0              103.103.103.103  YES NVRAM  up                    up
Loopback1              13.13.13.13      YES NVRAM  up                    up
Tunnel0                192.168.2.2      YES manual administratively down down
```

Moving across to the other end of the tunnel on HUB-r, Example 3-14 shows the tunnel interface as up in the output of **show ip interface brief.** In other words, there is no mechanism in the GRE protocol that lets one endpoint know when the other end of the tunnel is unreachable.

Example 3-14 *Tunnel Still Up on HUB-r*

```
HUB-r#show ip interface brief
Interface              IP-Address       OK? Method Status    Protocol
Serial0/0              10.0.1.11        YES NVRAM  up        up
Loopback0              101.101.101.101  YES NVRAM  up        up
Loopback1              11.11.11.11      YES NVRAM  up        up
Tunnel0                192.168.1.1      YES manual up        up
Tunnel1                192.168.2.1      YES manual up        up
Tunnel2                192.168.3.1      YES manual up        up
HUB-r#
02:55:32: %OSPF-5-ADJCHG: Process 302, Nbr 103.103.103.103 on Tunnel1 from FULL to
DOWN, Neighbor Down: Dead timer expired
HUB-r#
```

In Example 3-14, you can see a log message (look for the **OSPF-5-ADJCHG** message) from the OSPF process, which detects that the remote peer is unavailable because Hello packets no longer make it through the tunnel. The solution to this problem is to create backup paths for the tunnels. If there were another path between HUB-r and SITE1-r, OSPF would select it as a route and both routers could now use it.

A backup router can also be used to load balance traffic across hubs, so that the backup for SITE1 and SITE2 can be the primary for SITE3 and SITE4. This is more economical in terms of hardware, even if it means that each site must correctly identify its primary hub. Figure 3-9 shows a relatively simple case in which SITE1 and SITE2 have their primary connection on HUB1-r and their backup on HUB2-r, but SITE3 does just the opposite. This architecture provides load balancing, because traffic will be balanced between hubs (a little unevenly in the example, because there are only three sites). This architecture also provides redundancy, because traffic continues to flow even if one of the hub routers fails.

Figure 3-9 *Secondary Hub*

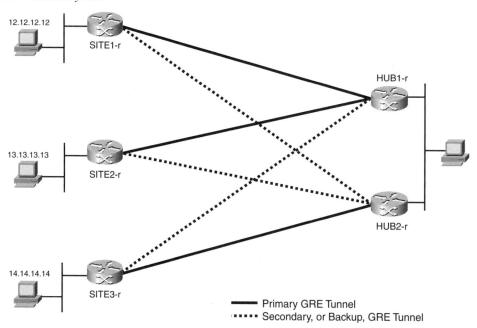

Continuing the discussion of protocol and implementation considerations, we have the following:

- **Multicast** —The Cisco IOS GRE implementation is fully compatible with IP multicast. It is one of the most significant advantages of this solution compared to others, notably IPSec.

- **Quality of service** —QoS on tunnels is a complicated business. Ideally, the network's QoS policy is respected over the WAN. This requires two things to happen:

  — LAN QoS policy must be mapped to WAN policy.

— The WAN must support the QOS policies.

As with all tunnels, you need to be sure that you are applying QoS based on the right policy: For example, do you want to mark using the payload or tunnel header? For GRE packets, by default, IP TOS settings are automatically copied from the payload to the delivery header, allowing a network administrator to apply the same policy to a tunneled packet that is applied to its payload.

Queuing on tunnels is harder to understand than marking. Without congestion, FIFO packet delivery is the norm on an interface. This is quite normal, but often requires explanation. Level 3 queuing interacts intimately with level 2 queues in the interface drivers. IP packets are queued only when they arrive too quickly for the lower-level driver to transmit them. This back pressure from layer 2 is required for Cisco IOS to turn on fancy queuing algorithms, such as Class-Based Weighted Fair Queuing (CBWFQ). Without the back pressure, packets are sent in the order they were received (i.e., FIFO). In Cisco IOS, tunnel interfaces have no hardware-related bandwidth limitation, and thus never congest in this way. You have to be a little creative to do fancy queuing on tunnels (for example, by using the Hierarchical Policy feature). Hierarchical policing allows classification and policing to be applied directly on the tunnel interface and for the IP queuing to be applied on the underlying physical interface.

An alternative approach is to congest the tunnel interface by shaping it. If traffic arrives at a higher rate than the shaper is allowed to send, IP packets form a queue and, once again, fancy queuing is possible.

All that said and done, GRE can support IP multiservice applications. Again, the network connecting the sites together must support IP multiservice applications also to have true end-to-end QoS.

- **Fragmentation** —GRE does not introduce a huge overhead: a 4-octet protocol header and another 20 octets for the deliver packet (IP) header. On an Ethernet interface, the MTU would be 1476 octets (1500–24). Over PPPoE, this goes down to 1450 octets. Some freeware implementations default to 1450 bytes, just in case. The default MTU can be overridden on tunnel interfaces (which is useful in the case where the packets have the DF bit set but need to be fragmented anyway).

To summarize, GRE is a straightforward protocol, with a simple configuration and operation paradigm. This is a significant advantage in a live network.

Case 2: VPN over Anything—IPSec

Broadband Enterprises has grown and acquired a financial services company, with a large and mobile sales force. The VPN must adapt to support this new population and to better protect customer data from interception. Thankfully, the IPX protocol was retired from service after the acquisition.

The key driver behind the network design is the need for confidentiality: The company has financial data and an insecure underlying infrastructure. That, coupled with the fact that the sales force will be connecting remotely, points very strongly to a solution using IPSec. The architecture of the VPN is identical to the previous case, with point-to-point tunnels between the CPE routers and a central hub to provide a site VPN network.

IPSec provides a very complete security service, and it is beyond the scope of this book to go into all the details. The next section covers the key concepts you need to know to understand the protocol; the following section, "IPSec Configuration," shows how to configure an IPSec-based VPN. To make life easier, the IPSec examples in this section use the same network addresses and routers as in the GRE examples.

IPSec Protocol and Operation

IPSec is defined in the following RFC documents:

- RFC 2401: Security Architecture for the Internet Protocol
- RFC 2402: IP Authentication Header
- RFC 2403: The Use of HMAC-MD5-96 Within ESP and AH
- RFC 2404: The Use of HMAC-SHA-1-96 Within ESP and AH
- RFC 2405: The ESP DES-CBC Cipher Algorithm With Explicit IV
- RFC 2406: IP Encapsulating Security Payload (ESP)
- RFC 2407: The Internet IP Security Domain of Interpretation for ISAKMP
- RFC 2408: Internet Security Association and Key Management Protocol (ISAKMP)
- RFC 2409: The Internet Key Exchange (IKE)

IPSec was originally conceived to provide secure transport over IP networks. The framework is very complete and includes strong authentication (AH) and encryption (EH) protocols and ciphers, key exchange mechanisms, and more. Much work has gone into allowing peers to interoperate by negotiating capabilities and keys.

NOTE   Data encryption algorithms are notoriously CPU intensive, which, combined with the complexity of managing certificates, has delayed the deployment of IPSec as a pervasive layer of security on all IP networks. IPSec is deployed as a form of IP VPN because it provides strong security, which notably allows a VPN to be built over the Internet (although IPSec can be deployed over private IP networks too).

A security association (SA) is a contract between peers that defines the specific encryption and authentication algorithms they will use with each other. The Security Parameters Index (SPI) field in Figure 3-10, when combined with the destination IP address, uniquely identifies the SA for the packet. An SA is negotiated when an IPSec session is initiated.

Figure 3-10   *IPSec ESP Header*

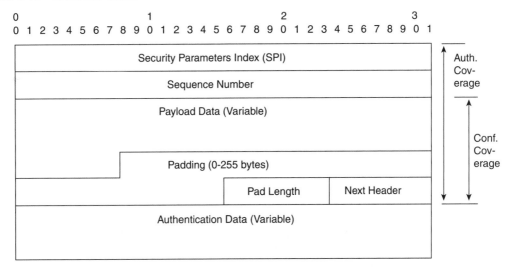

The following are the key points to understand about the IPSec protocol:

- The AH and ESP headers
- Key exchange using IKE
- Tunnel and transport modes

AH and ESP Headers for Authentication and Encryption

IPSec offers two services: authentication and encryption. It is possible to use each service separately or both together, as follows:

- **Authentication** —Offers nonrepudiatable authentication between two parties. Uses the IPSec Authentication Header (AH), which carries a hash, calculated over the payload. Supported algorithms include MD5 and SHA.

- **Encryption** —Offers encrypted communication between two parties. The payload is encrypted using a wide variety of supported algorithms, including DES, Triple-DES (3DES), Blowfish, etc. Note that data encrypted with public-key cryptography is presumed to be just as tamper proof as data authentication. The hash algorithms are computationally faster, though.

If used in combination, the AH header precedes the ESP header.

Key Exchange with IKE

IPSec requires a lot of negotiation to bring up a session, so much so that there is a separate control channel protocol, called IKE, used to negotiate the SA between peers and exchange keys (to be more precise, exchange key material).

IKE is used not only during tunnel setup. During confidential data exchange, the session keys used to protect unidirectional traffic need to be changed regularly. The negotiation for this is also performed with IKE.

IKE traffic is encrypted and in fact has its own SA. Most of the parameters are fixed and are as follows:

- 56-bit DES for encryption
- MD5 or SHA hashing
- RSA (public key) signatures or preshared keys

IPSec Tunnel and Transport Mode Encapsulations

There are two ways to encapsulate IPSec packets. The first, called tunnel mode, shown in Figure 3-11, encrypts an entire IP packet, including the header. A new IP header is generated for the encrypted packet.

Figure 3-11 *IPSec Tunnel Mode Stack*

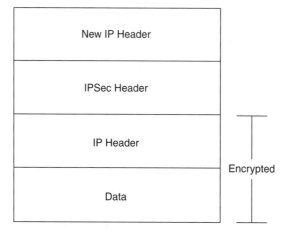

Tunnel mode adds a 20-octet overload with the new IP header. To reduce issues with packet size and fragmentation, a second mode was defined, called transport mode, which is shown in Figure 3-12.

Figure 3-12 *IPSec Transport Mode Stack*

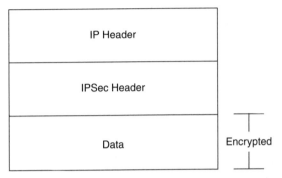

Transport mode is always used when using IPSec to encrypt GRE packets. Figure 3-13 shows how.

Figure 3-13 *GRE and IPSec Encapsulation Stack*

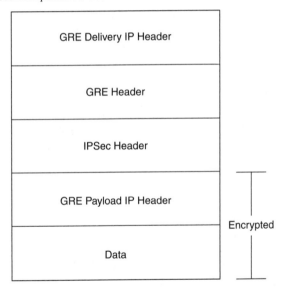

IPSec Configuration

There is a lot more to IPSec than you will see here, but there are three basic parts to the configuration.

The first basic part is the IKE policy. IKE negotiates its own SA with the remote peer, so it too needs a policy. The **crypto isakmp policy** command defines the type of authentication, the IP address of the remote peer, and the shared secret used to protect the IKE exchanges, as indicated in Example 3-15.

Example 3-15 *IKE Policy Settings*

```
crypto isakmp policy 1
 authentication pre-share
crypto isakmp key secret address 10.0.3.11
```

As usual, default values don't appear in the configuration. This policy uses 768 bits of key material (which corresponds to a **group 1** command). Using **group 2** increases this to 1024 bits. The hash algorithm is SHA. The lifetime defaults to 1 day, which is not ideal for a real deployment, but fine for the purposes of an example.

The key is **secret** and must be the same on the remote peer, 10.0.1.11. To use public keys, the routers need to consult a trusted third party, called a certificate authority (CA), which functions rather like a phone book. Each router starts by generating a private/public key pair. The private key is written in a protected area of NVRAM and the public key is registered, along with the router's name, with the CA. somerouter.cisco.com's public key is then available for any peer to look up (the phone book analogy) and use to send data that can be decrypted only by using the corresponding private key.

NOTE   CAs have scale advantages in an enterprise environment because they avoid the need to define shared keys for every possible IPSec session. However, CAs are rare in the wider world of the Internet, possibly because people tend to use different CAs.

The second basic part of the IPSec configuration is the IPSec policy. IPSec is configured as a policy using a crypto map. The role of the crypto map is to define the remote peer, the encryption and authentication algorithms (called transforms) that this router will accept to set up an SA and the interesting traffic to be encrypted. As in so much of Cisco IOS, interesting traffic is defined using standard access-lists: If a packet matches an access-list entry, then whatever IPSec policy is defined in the crypto map is applied to the packet.

Example 3-16 defines a transform-set, called ONE, that uses MD5 for AH and 56-bit DES for ESP. The **crypto map** in Example 3-21 uses the **ONE** transform-set.

Example 3-16 *IPSec Transform-Set*

```
crypto ipsec transform-set ONE ah-md5-hmac esp-des
```

The crypto map in Example 3-17 brings all the different pieces together. In the example, the remote peer is 10.0.1.11. The SA lifetime is 3 minutes and the transform-set is called **ONE**. Finally, the crypto map is applied to all traffic that matches access-list 101.

Example 3-17 *IPSec Crypto Map*

```
crypto map VPN 1 ipsec-isakmp
 set peer 10.0.3.11
 set security-association lifetime seconds 180
 set transform-set ONE
 match address 101
```

The final step is to apply the crypto map on the outgoing interface, as in Example 3-18. When packets enter or leave the Serial0 interface on this router, they are compared against access-list 101 (which is given in Example 3-19). If there is a match, the packets are encrypted using DES and then go through MD5 authentication checksum calculation. The result is encapsulated in an IPSec packet with AH and ESP headers and sent to its destination.

Example 3-18 *Interface with Crypto Map*

```
interface Serial0
 ip address 10.0.2.11 255.255.255.0
 no ip mroute-cache
 no fair-queue
 crypto map VPN
```

The last basic part is the traffic policy. Example 3-19 defines the flows to encrypt with an access control list (ACL). The ACL in Example 3-19 is applied in the crypto map in Example 3-18.

Example 3-19 *ACL to Encrypt Matching Traffic*

```
access-list 101 permit ip 60.60.60.0 0.0.0.255 50.50.50.0 0.0.0.255
```

Remember to let IPSec traffic through any existing access-lists. IKE runs on port udp/500 and IPSec uses IP Protocol values of 50 and 51.

IPSec Configuration Examples

This section presents two simple configuration examples. The first example sets up an encrypted session between two sites. The second brings GRE back into the picture to get a complete working VPN solution.

Simple Site-to-Site IPSec

To establish a simple IPSec session between SITE1-r and SITE2-r, you enter the corresponding entries for IKE, IPSec, and traffic policies on both routers. Example 3-20 gives the configuration highlights for SITE1-r, one of the endpoints, and Example 3-21 gives the configuration of SITE2-r, the other endpoint. Once again, the full configuration files are available on the ciscopress.com website. As a reminder, you are using the same topology as was used for the GRE example.

Look out for the configuration of the IPSec components already discussed, namely the IKE policy (**crypto isakmp policy**), the transform-set, and the IPSec policy (**crypto map VPN**) itself. Also, check that the interesting traffic defined in access-list 101 matches only traffic belonging to the VPN (the site LANs introduced in the GRE example earlier in the chapter).

Example 3-20 *SITE1-r Simple IPSec Configuration*

```
crypto isakmp policy 1
 authentication pre-share
crypto isakmp key secret address 10.0.3.11
!
!
crypto ipsec transform-set ONE ah-md5-hmac esp-des
!
crypto map VPN 1 ipsec-isakmp
 set peer 10.0.3.11
 set security-association lifetime seconds 180
 set transform-set ONE
 match address 101
!
interface Loopback0
 ip address 102.102.102.102 255.255.255.255
!
interface Loopback1
 description Enterprise internal interface to be reachable by all sites
 ip address 12.12.12.12 255.255.255.255
!
interface Serial0/0
 description SITE1-r Internet connection
 ip address 10.0.2.11 255.255.255.0
 crypto map VPN
!
ip route 0.0.0.0 0.0.0.0 Serial0/0
!
access-list 101 permit ip host 12.12.12.12 host 13.13.13.13
!
```

Example 3-21 *SITE2-r Simple IPSec Configuration*

```
crypto isakmp policy 1
 authentication pre-share
crypto isakmp key secret address 10.0.2.11
!
!
crypto ipsec transform-set ONE ah-md5-hmac esp-des
```

Example 3-21   *SITE2-r Simple IPSec Configuration (Continued)*

```
!
crypto map VPN 1 ipsec-isakmp
 set peer 10.0.2.11
 set security-association lifetime seconds 180
 set transform-set ONE
 match address 101
!
interface Loopback0
 ip address 103.103.103.103 255.255.255.255
!
interface Loopback1
 description Enterprise internal interface to be reachable by all sites
 ip address 13.13.13.13 255.255.255.255
!
interface Serial0/0
 description SITE2-r Internet connection
 ip address 10.0.3.11 255.255.255.0
 crypto map VPN
!
ip route 0.0.0.0 0.0.0.0 Serial0/0
access-list 101 permit ip host 13.13.13.13 host 12.12.12.12
```

The access-list in Example 3-21 encrypts traffic from 13.13.13.13 to 12.12.12.12. (Remember, these loopback addresses represent LANs on each site.) Check that traffic can go between the VPN sites by using an extend **ping**, as indicated in Example 3-22.

Example 3-22   *pings over IPSec Session*

```
SITE2-r#ping
Protocol [ip]:
Target IP address: 12.12.12.12
Repeat count [5]:
Datagram size [100]:
Timeout in seconds [2]:
Extended commands [n]: y
Source address or interface: 13.13.13.13
Type of service [0]:
Set DF bit in IP header? [no]:
Validate reply data? [no]:
Data pattern [0xABCD]:
Loose, Strict, Record, Timestamp, Verbose[none]:
Sweep range of sizes [n]:
Type escape sequence to abort.
Sending 5, 100-byte ICMP Echos to 12.12.12.12, timeout is 2 seconds:
Packet sent with a source address of 13.13.13.13
..!!!
Success rate is 60 percent (3/5), round-trip min/avg/max = 128/142/160 ms
SITE2-r#ping
Protocol [ip]:
Target IP address: 12.12.12.12
Repeat count [5]:
```

continues

Example 3-22 *pings over IPSec Session (Continued)*

```
Datagram size [100]:
Timeout in seconds [2]:
Extended commands [n]: y
Source address or interface: 13.13.13.13
Type of service [0]:
Set DF bit in IP header? [no]:
Validate reply data? [no]:
Data pattern [0xABCD]:
Loose, Strict, Record, Timestamp, Verbose[none]:
Sweep range of sizes [n]:
Type escape sequence to abort.
Sending 5, 100-byte ICMP Echos to 12.12.12.12, timeout is 2 seconds:
Packet sent with a source address of 13.13.13.13
!!!!!
Success rate is 100 percent (5/5), round-trip min/avg/max = 108/124/128 ms
```

An SA is created when there is data on the router that matches a security policy. No traffic has been sent across the VPN before the first **ping** of Example 3-22, so no SA exists and they have to be negotiated. Thus, some packets are lost while the SAs are established between the peers. The second **ping** is run immediately afterward and all the packets are successfully received because the SAs already exist.

So far, you have established that data can go between the SITE1-r and SITE2-r routers. You have not yet proved that the data is being encrypted. You need to be careful of this: A lot of IPSec configurations appear to work very well, but the right packets are not actually encrypted! You can check that this is not the case in this example with the **show crypto ipsec sa** command, as shown in Example 3-23. The output of the command has counters that increment when packets are encrypted, decrypted, and so forth by the IPSec process on the router. The output is quite long (and is not all included), but the relevant lines are highlighted in Example 3-23.

Example 3-23 **show crypto ipsec sa** *Output*

```
SITE2-r#show crypto ipsec sa
interface: Serial0/0
    Crypto map tag: VPN, local addr. 10.0.3.11
   protected vrf:
   local   ident (addr/mask/prot/port): (13.13.13.13/255.255.255.255/0/0)
   remote ident (addr/mask/prot/port): (12.12.12.12/255.255.255.255/0/0)
   current_peer: 10.0.2.11:500
     PERMIT, flags={origin_is_acl,}
    #pkts encaps: 8, #pkts encrypt: 8, #pkts digest 8
    #pkts decaps: 8, #pkts decrypt: 8, #pkts verify 8
    #pkts compressed: 0, #pkts decompressed: 0
    #pkts not compressed: 0, #pkts compr. failed: 0
    #pkts not decompressed: 0, #pkts decompress failed: 0
    #send errors 2, #recv errors 0
     local crypto endpt.: 10.0.3.11, remote crypto endpt.: 10.0.2.11
     path mtu 1500, media mtu 1500
     current outbound spi: 4375B67C
```

Encrypted GRE

You may have noticed that there were no routing protocols used across the sites in Examples 3-20 and 3-21. The reason for that is both well known and awkward. IPSec doesn't support IP multicast. The RFC was written to support unicast traffic. For that and other reasons, IPSec is often combined with GRE traffic to provide a complete VPN solution where the routing protocols run over GRE, and the GRE packets are encrypted with IPSec.

Before looking at the configuration, consider the network design again and what needs to be tunneled by GRE and what must be encrypted with IPSec. The 11.11.11.0, 12.12.12.0, 13.13.13.0, and 14.14.14.0 networks are obviously part of the VPN. However, so are the GRE tunnel interfaces, which use the 192.168.X.1 and 192.168.X.2 scheme. Finally, the routing protocols use the Loopback0 addresses of 101.101.101.101, 102.102.102.102, etc. Figure 3-8 shows all of these private addresses. The GRE delivery headers use the public 10/8 addresses shown in Figure 3-7. The IPSec ACLs must match traffic between all of these addresses, so that VPN traffic is encrypted. There is a choice between encrypting everything that flows between SITE and HUB routers, or being more granular and just encrypting packets that carry the GRE protocol. Both work.

Figure 3-14 shows how the GRE tunnel is encrypted inside the IPSec tunnel, with the relevant IP addresses used by each tunnel.

Figure 3-14   *GRE and IPSec Topology Between SITE2-r and HUB-r*

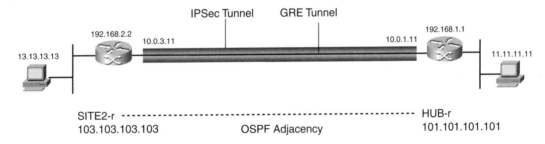

Internal GRE tunnel from 192.168.2.2 to 192.168.1.1
encrypted in external IPSec tunnel between 10.0.3.11 and 10.0.1.11.
Routing peers are 103.103.103.103 and 101.101.101.101.

Example 3-24 lists portions of the configuration files of the SITE2-r spoke router. The IPSec configuration is structurally identical to what you saw in Example 3-23, but ACL 101 matches all GRE traffic between the VPN addresses, so all GRE packets are encrypted as planned. (This can be checked using **show crypto ipsec** commands, though.) Because the router uses an IPSec and GRE solution, SITE2-r has its **Tunnel0** interface again and the IPSec crypto map is applied on this interface. OSPF also runs over the GRE interface (because of the **network 192.168.2.0 0.0.0.3** statement in the **router ospf** command block).

Example 3-24 *SITE2-r Configuration*

```
crypto isakmp policy 1
 authentication pre-share
crypto isakmp key secret address 10.0.1.11
!
!
crypto ipsec transform-set ONE ah-md5-hmac esp-des
!
crypto map VPN 1 ipsec-isakmp
 set peer 10.0.1.11
 set security-association lifetime seconds 600
 set transform-set ONE
 match address 101
!
interface Loopback0
 ip address 103.103.103.103 255.255.255.255
!
interface Loopback1
 description Enterprise internal interface to be reachable by all sites
 ip address 13.13.13.13 255.255.255.255
!
interface Tunnel0
 description VPN to HUB
 ip address 192.168.2.2 255.255.255.252
 tunnel source Serial0/0
 tunnel destination 10.0.1.11
 crypto map VPN
!
interface Serial0/0
 description SITE2-r Internet connection
 ip address 10.0.3.11 255.255.255.0
 crypto map VPN
!
router ospf 302
 log-adjacency-changes
 network 13.13.13.13 0.0.0.0 area 0
 network 192.168.2.0 0.0.0.3 area 0
!
ip route 0.0.0.0 0.0.0.0 Serial0/0
!
access-list 101 permit gre host 10.0.3.11 host 10.0.1.11
```

Example 3-25 gives the HUB-r configuration extract. The GRE and OSPF configuration is the what you would expect to find on a GRE hub router: There is one tunnel interface that connects to each remote site, and OSPF runs over each of them. The hub router IPSec configuration is a little different from the configuration of the spokes.

As already mentioned, each spoke router has a crypto map with the IP address of the remote end of the IPSec tunnel, which makes sense on a spoke because you know the single hub address you want to connect to. However, on the hub, spelling out the addresses of each and every remote site in a different crypto map would be very painful. Wouldn't it be better to have a way to just instruct the router to accept all incoming tunnels that know a specified secret and use the appropriate transform set? This is exactly what HUB-r is configured to do in Example 3-25. You should notice straight away that the crypto map in Example 3-25 has no IP addresses configured under it (and it uses the **dynamic** key word), but there is a wildcard address associated with the shared secret with the **crypto isakmp key secret address 0.0.0.0 0.0.0.0** command. Such a configuration is known as a *dynamic crypto map*.

Example 3-25 *HUB-r Configuration*

```
crypto isakmp key secret address 0.0.0.0 0.0.0.0
!
crypto ipsec transform-set ONE ah-md5-hmac esp-des
!
crypto dynamic-map VPN 1
 set transform-set ONE
!
crypto map HUB-VPN 1 ipsec-isakmp dynamic VPN
!
interface Loopback0
 ip address 101.101.101.101 255.255.255.255
!
interface Loopback1
 description Enterprise Internal interface to be advertised to all sites
 ip address 11.11.11.11 255.255.255.255
!
interface Tunnel0
 description VPN to Site1
 ip address 192.168.1.1 255.255.255.252
 tunnel source Serial0/0
 tunnel destination 10.0.2.11
 crypto map HUB-VPN
!
interface Tunnel1
 description VPN to SITE2-r
 ip address 192.168.2.1 255.255.255.252
 tunnel source Serial0/0
 tunnel destination 10.0.3.11
 crypto map HUB-VPN
!
interface Tunnel2
 description VPN to SITE3-r
 ip address 192.168.3.1 255.255.255.252
 tunnel source Serial0/0
 tunnel destination 10.0.4.11
 crypto map HUB-VPN
!
interface Serial0/0
 description HUB-r Internet connection
```

continues

Example 3-25   *HUB-r Configuration (Continued)*

```
ip address 10.0.1.11 255.255.255.0
crypto map HUB-VPN
!
router ospf 302
 log-adjacency-changes
 network 11.11.11.11 0.0.0.0 area 0
 network 192.168.1.0 0.0.0.3 area 0
 network 192.168.2.0 0.0.0.3 area 0
 network 192.168.3.0 0.0.0.3 area 0
!
ip route 0.0.0.0 0.0.0.0 Serial0/0
!
access-list 101 permit gre host 10.0.1.11 host 10.0.3.11
```

NOTE   If you plan to check this configuration, it's a good idea to start simple and add things to a working configuration. For example, once you have GRE running between hub and spokes, encrypt just one of the tunnels and see if everything still works. Then you can move to wildcard addressing on the hub before you bring the other spokes online.

To check that GRE packets are encrypted, use an extended ping between two VPN addresses. Use **show crypto ipsec sa** before and after and look at the encrypt and decrypts counters. There's a lot going on in Example 3-26. One hundred packets are sent from SITE1-r to SITE2-r. The counters are shown on HUB-r for the crypto map on the **Tunnel1** interface (to SITE2-r) and the **Tunnel0** interface (to SITE1-r) before and after the ping. The counters increase by more than 100 packets, but remember that the OSPF processes are exchanging Hello messages, which also generate encrypted traffic.

Example 3-26   *Encrypted ping from SITE1 to SITE2, with* **counter output**

```
HUB-r#show crypto ipsec sa interface Tunnel1
interface: Tunnel1
    Crypto map tag: HUB-VPN, local addr. 10.0.1.11
   protected vrf:
   local  ident (addr/mask/prot/port): (10.0.1.11/255.255.255.255/47/0)
   remote ident (addr/mask/prot/port): (10.0.2.11/255.255.255.255/47/0)
   current_peer: 10.0.2.11:500
     PERMIT, flags={}
    #pkts encaps: 19, #pkts encrypt: 19, #pkts digest 19
    #pkts decaps: 18, #pkts decrypt: 18, #pkts verify 18
    #pkts compressed: 0, #pkts decompressed: 0
    #pkts not compressed: 0, #pkts compr. failed: 0
    #pkts not decompressed: 0, #pkts decompress failed: 0
    #send errors 0, #recv errors 0
     local crypto endpt.: 10.0.1.11, remote crypto endpt.: 10.0.2.11
     path mtu 1514, media mtu 1514
     current outbound spi: 45D0B233
```

Example 3-26 *Encrypted ping from SITE1 to SITE2, with* **counter output (Continued)**

```
HUB-r#show crypto ipsec sa interface Tunnel0
interface: Tunnel0
    Crypto map tag: HUB-VPN, local addr. 10.0.1.11
    protected vrf:
    local  ident (addr/mask/prot/port): (10.0.1.11/255.255.255.255/47/0)
    remote ident (addr/mask/prot/port): (10.0.2.11/255.255.255.255/47/0)
    current_peer: 10.0.2.11:500
      PERMIT, flags={}
     #pkts encaps: 20, #pkts encrypt: 20, #pkts digest 20
     #pkts decaps: 18, #pkts decrypt: 18, #pkts verify 18
     #pkts compressed: 0, #pkts decompressed: 0
     #pkts not compressed: 0, #pkts compr. failed: 0
     #pkts not decompressed: 0, #pkts decompress failed: 0
     #send errors 0, #recv errors 0
      local crypto endpt.: 10.0.1.11, remote crypto endpt.: 10.0.2.11
      path mtu 1514, media mtu 1514
      current outbound spi: 45D0B233
HUB-r#ping
Protocol [ip]:
Target IP address: 13.13.13.13
Repeat count [5]: 100
Datagram size [100]:
Timeout in seconds [2]:
Extended commands [n]: y
Source address or interface: 11.11.11.11
Type of service [0]:
Set DF bit in IP header? [no]:
Validate reply data? [no]:
Data pattern [0xABCD]:
Loose, Strict, Record, Timestamp, Verbose[none]:
Sweep range of sizes [n]:
Type escape sequence to abort.
Sending 100, 100-byte ICMP Echos to 13.13.13.13, timeout is 2 seconds:
Packet sent with a source address of 11.11.11.11
!!!!!!!!!!!!!!!!!!!!!!!!!!!!!!!!!!!!!!!!!!!!!!!!!!!!!!!!!!!!!!!!!!!!!!!
!!!!!!!!!!!!!!!!!!!!!!!!!!!!!!!!!!
Success rate is 100 percent (100/100), round-trip min/avg/max = 112/139/188 ms
HUB-r#show crypto ipsec sa interface Tunnel1

interface: Tunnel1
    Crypto map tag: HUB-VPN, local addr. 10.0.1.11
    protected vrf:
    local  ident (addr/mask/prot/port): (10.0.1.11/255.255.255.255/47/0)
    remote ident (addr/mask/prot/port): (10.0.2.11/255.255.255.255/47/0)
    current_peer: 10.0.2.11:500
      PERMIT, flags={}
     #pkts encaps: 129, #pkts encrypt: 129, #pkts digest 129
     #pkts decaps: 127, #pkts decrypt: 127, #pkts verify 127
     #pkts compressed: 0, #pkts decompressed: 0
     #pkts not compressed: 0, #pkts compr. failed: 0
```

continues

Example 3-26 *Encrypted ping from SITE1 to SITE2, with* **counter output (Continued)**

```
      #pkts not decompressed: 0, #pkts decompress failed: 0
      #send errors 0, #recv errors 0
       local crypto endpt.: 10.0.1.11, remote crypto endpt.: 10.0.2.11
       path mtu 1514, media mtu 1514
       current outbound spi: 45D0B233

HUB-r#show crypto ipsec sa interface Tunnel0
interface: Tunnel0
   Crypto map tag: HUB-VPN, local addr. 10.0.1.11
   protected vrf:
   local  ident (addr/mask/prot/port): (10.0.1.11/255.255.255.255/47/0)
   remote ident (addr/mask/prot/port): (10.0.2.11/255.255.255.255/47/0)
   current_peer: 10.0.2.11:500
     PERMIT, flags={}
    #pkts encaps: 129, #pkts encrypt: 129, #pkts digest 129
    #pkts decaps: 127, #pkts decrypt: 127, #pkts verify 127
    #pkts compressed: 0, #pkts decompressed: 0
    #pkts not compressed: 0, #pkts compr. failed: 0
    #pkts not decompressed: 0, #pkts decompress failed: 0
    #send errors 0, #recv errors 0
     local crypto endpt.: 10.0.1.11, remote crypto endpt.: 10.0.2.11
     path mtu 1514, media mtu 1514
     current outbound spi: 45D0B233
```

A **ping** using non-VPN addresses, such as the 10.0.X.0 subnet, should *not* increase the counters. You can verify this, as shown in Example 3-27, with the same combination of **show crypto ipsec** and extended **ping** commands.

Example 3-27 *Unencrypted ping Between CPE with* **counter output**

```
SITE2-r#show crypto ipsec sa
interface: Tunnel0
   Crypto map tag: VPN, local addr. 10.0.3.11
   protected vrf:
   local  ident (addr/mask/prot/port): (10.0.3.11/255.255.255.255/47/0)
   remote ident (addr/mask/prot/port): (10.0.1.11/255.255.255.255/47/0)
   current_peer: 10.0.1.11:500
     PERMIT, flags={origin_is_acl,}
    #pkts encaps: 54, #pkts encrypt: 54, #pkts digest 54
    #pkts decaps: 55, #pkts decrypt: 55, #pkts verify 55
    #pkts compressed: 0, #pkts decompressed: 0
    #pkts not compressed: 0, #pkts compr. failed: 0
    #pkts not decompressed: 0, #pkts decompress failed: 0
    #send errors 1, #recv errors 0
SITE2-r#ping
Protocol [ip]:
Target IP address: 10.0.1.11
Repeat count [5]: 100
Datagram size [100]:
Timeout in seconds [2]:
Extended commands [n]: y
```

Example 3-27 *Unencrypted ping Between CPE with* **counter output** **(Continued)**

```
Source address or interface: 10.0.3.11
Type of service [0]:
Set DF bit in IP header? [no]:
Validate reply data? [no]:
Data pattern [0xABCD]:
Loose, Strict, Record, Timestamp, Verbose[none]:
Sweep range of sizes [n]:
Type escape sequence to abort.
Sending 100, 100-byte ICMP Echos to 10.0.1.11, timeout is 2 seconds:
Packet sent with a source address of 10.0.3.11
!!!!!!!!!!!!!!!!!!!!!!!!!!!!!!!!!!!!!!!!!!!!!!!!!!!!!!!!!!!!!!!!!!!!!!!!
!!!!!!!!!!!!!!!!!!!!!!!!!!!!!!!!!!
Success rate is 100 percent (100/100), round-trip min/avg/max = 28/46/60 ms
SITE2-r#sh cry ipsec sa
interface: Tunnel0
    Crypto map tag: VPN, local addr. 10.0.3.11
   protected vrf:
   local  ident (addr/mask/prot/port): (10.0.3.11/255.255.255.255/47/0)
   remote ident (addr/mask/prot/port): (10.0.1.11/255.255.255.255/47/0)
   current_peer: 10.0.1.11:500
     PERMIT, flags={origin_is_acl,}
    #pkts encaps: 59, #pkts encrypt: 59, #pkts digest 59
    #pkts decaps: 59, #pkts decrypt: 59, #pkts verify 59
    #pkts compressed: 0, #pkts decompressed: 0
    #pkts not compressed: 0, #pkts compr. failed: 0
    #pkts not decompressed: 0, #pkts decompress failed: 0
    #send errors 1, #recv errors 0
```

Dynamic Multicast VPN

The standard hub-and-spoke approach has a variety of problems:

- The network administrator must configure the hub device every time a spoke is added.

- Consequently, the hub configuration file becomes very large, with more than five lines of text per spoke (not including any changes to the routing protocol or access-lists that might also be required).

- Spoke-to-spoke traffic is encrypted and decrypted twice. Example 3-26 shows this explicitly. Each ICMP packet from SITE1-r to SITE2-r is decrypted on **Tunnel0** then encrypted on **Tunnel1.** (Now you know why the output for both tunnels was included.) This is CPU intensive.

- There is an IPSec **crypto map** and GRE **Tunnel** interface for every peer, aggravating both of the first two problems.

Meet TED

The standard IPSec implementation also has an *N*-squared scalability limitation because there has to be a crypto map statement for every peer. Tunnel Endpoint Discovery (TED) is a enhancement to solve this.

TED works by sending probes to peers whenever the first packet matches an ACL statement that would result in encryption. If there is no SA for the remote peer, the router sends a TED probe to the destination of that packet to discover the remote IPSec peer (which is not necessarily the same thing). The IPSec peer returns its own TED probe, so revealing its own IP address. IPSec negotiation then proceeds normally.

Only wildcard preshared keys can be used with TED, with an IP address of 0.0.0.0 in the crypto map (so any peer can build an IPSec tunnel to the router). TED is useful if the remote IPSec peer's address is unknown.

Dynamic Multipoint VPN (DMVPN) is a relatively recent addition to Cisco IOS that is specifically designed to reduce the configuration overhead of an IPSec and GRE VPN solution. DMVPN uses dynamic IPSec crypto maps, multipoint GRE (mGRE), and Next-Hop Resolution Protocol (NHRP) so that a spoke has to maintain a tunnel only to the hub, and other tunnels are created dynamically *between* spokes when there is traffic that needs to go from site to site. DMVPN really simplifies IPSec VPN operation and makes the overall solution quite compelling. Figure 3-15 shows the principal of DMVPN in the example network topology.

Figure 3-15 *DMVPN Architecture*

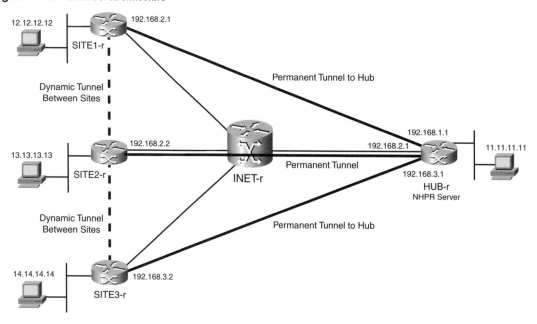

Each spoke in Figure 3-15 has a single tunnel to the hub, but the hub has only a single mGRE multipoint tunnel interface, which connects to all the spokes. It works like this:

Each spoke has a permanent IPSec tunnel to the hub, not to the other spokes within the network. Each spoke registers as clients of the NHRP server.

When a spoke needs to send a packet to a destination (private) subnet on another spoke, it queries the NHRP server for the real (outside) address of the destination (target) spoke.

After the originating spoke learns the peer address of the target spoke, it can initiate a dynamic IPSec tunnel to the target spoke.

The spoke-to-spoke tunnel is built over the multipoint GRE (mGRE) interface.

The spoke-to-spoke links are established on demand whenever there is traffic between the spokes. Thereafter, packets are able to bypass the hub and use the spoke-to-spoke tunnel.

The following definitions apply to the rule set:

- ***NHRP**—A client and server protocol where the hub is the server and the spokes are the clients. The hub maintains an NHRP database of the public interface addresses of each spoke. Each spoke registers its real address when it boots and queries the NHRP database for real addresses of the destination spokes in order to build direct tunnels.*

- ***mGRE Tunnel Interface**—Allows a single GRE interface to support multiple IPSec tunnels and simplifies the size and complexity of the configuration.*

Comparing Layer 3 VPN with Frame Relay, for example, you can see that the problem of provisioning circuits as the number of sites increases is not new. In Frame Relay, multipoint interfaces were introduced to reduce the configuration on hub routers, and the same principle is used in mGRE.

Returning to the original hub configuration, in Example 3-25 you saw that there was a separate tunnel subinterface for each and every remote site. The generic configlet to configure this is given in Example 3-28, using the addressing plan from the example network topology that has been used throughout the chapter. To configure the tunnel to the fourth site, replace the letter N in Example 3-28 with the number 4. If there are 100 sites, there need to be 100 of the configuration blocks of Example 3-28.

The configurations and diagrams that concern DMVPN in this section are derived from the Cisco whitepaper, "Dynamic Multipoint IPSec VPNs (Using Multipoint GRE/NHRP to Scale IPSec VPNs)" on http://www.cisco.com/en/US/tech/tk583/tk372/ technologies_white_paper09186a008018983e.shtml.

Example 3-28 *Generic Hub Configlet to Connect to Spoke Sites*

```
! Tunnel to SPOKE N
interface TunnelN
 description VPN to Site N
 ip address 192.168.N.1 255.255.255.252
 tunnel source Serial0/0
```

The mGRE equivalent is given in Example 3-29 and you need only one of them to connect to all the spokes. The mGRE configuration is much shorter than the standard GRE equivalent.

Example 3-29 *mGRE Multipoint Interface*

```
! HUB multipoint interface
interface Tunnel100
 description VPN to all sites
 ip address 192.168.1.1 255.255.255.0
 tunnel source Ethernet0
 tunnel mode gre multipoint
 tunnel key 200
```

Getting back to the network configuration, Example 3-30 shows how to use DMVPN on the HUB-r router. Note the change of dynamic routing protocol from OSPF to EIGRP. (This is done only to show you how to correctly configure a non-link-state protocol over mGRE.)

Example 3-30 *DMVPN HUB Configuration*

```
crypto isakmp policy 1
 authentication pre-share
crypto isakmp key secret address 0.0.0.0 0.0.0.0
!
!
crypto ipsec transform-set ONE ah-md5-hmac esp-des
!
crypto ipsec profile MVPN
 set transform-set ONE
!
interface Loopback0
 ip address 101.101.101.101 255.255.255.255
!
interface Loopback1
 description Enterprise Internal interface to be advertised to all sites
 ip address 11.11.11.11 255.255.255.255
!
interface Tunnel0
 description VPN to all Sites
 ip address 192.168.1.1 255.255.255.0
 no ip redirects
 ip nhrp map multicast dynamic
 ip nhrp network-id 1007
 ip nhrp holdtime 600
 ip nhrp server-only
 no ip split-horizon eigrp 302
 tunnel source Ethernet0/0
 tunnel mode gre multipoint
 tunnel key 200
 tunnel protection ipsec profile MVPN
!
interface Ethernet0/0
 description HUB-r Internet connection
 ip address 10.0.1.11 255.255.255.0
!
```

Example 3-30 *DMVPN HUB Configuration (Continued)*

```
router eigrp 302
 network 11.11.11.11 0.0.0.0
 network 192.168.1.0
 no auto-summary
!
ip route 0.0.0.0 0.0.0.0 Ethernet0/0
```

There are several new components to explain in Example 3-30:

- **Multipoint tunnels** —The **tunnel mode gre multipoint** command creates a multipoint interface, as already shown in Example 3-29.

- **Tunnel protection** —Previous examples used access-lists to encrypt GRE traffic between routers. Because the source/destination pair of the ACL always matches the source/ destination of the GRE packets themselves, it should be possible for the router to work this out automatically, which is exactly what the **tunnel protect** command does. In this case, all GRE traffic is encrypted using **crypto ipsec profile MPVN**. Doing it this way is particularly useful on multipoint interfaces, when there are many GRE tunnels to encrypt.

- **NHRP**—The hub is configured as an NHRP server. Clients register with the server and then request next-hop router IP addresses as they need to forward packets.

- **EIGRP**—The routing protocol now sees a point-to-multipoint interface, so split horizon must be disabled or else the hub will not advertise routes from one spoke to another.

A spoke configuration extract is shown in Example 3-31. Each spoke is an NHRP client, with the server defined to be on the HUB. An NHRP map statement is included to reach the Next Hop Server (NHS) server address.

Example 3-31 *DMVPN Spoke Configlet*

```
crypto ipsec profile MVPN
 set transform-set ONE
!
interface Tunnel0
 description VPN to HUB
 ip address 192.168.1.2 255.255.255.0
 no ip redirects
 ip nhrp map 192.168.1.1 10.0.1.11
 ip nhrp map multicast 10.0.1.11
 ip nhrp network-id 1007
 ip nhrp nhs 192.168.1.1
 no ip split-horizon
 tunnel source Ethernet0/0
 tunnel mode gre multipoint
 tunnel key 200
 tunnel protection ipsec profile MVPN
!
```

DMVPN greatly simplifies overall VPN provisioning and is more efficient. It also avoids the double-encryption problem. As already stated, DMVPN is a recent addition to Cisco IOS, so time will tell how well it works in live networks.

IPSec for Remote Access

All the previous examples have shown, with increasing sophistication, how to use IPSec to build a site VPN. One of the strengths of IPSec is that you can use it for remote access over the Internet, one of the main requirements in this chapter's case study.

The main change in dealing with remote access is that incoming subscribers must be authenticated against a corporate user database. Cisco IOS uses a lot of the same semantics as with standard PPP-based access: There is a concept of a subscriber connection, with authentication and authorization, and RADIUS is the AAA protocol of choice. With several small extensions, Cisco IOS allows the integration of the familiar remote-access components on the router so that, once authenticated, the client can receive an IP address, DNS server, and so forth.

The IPSec operation is the same as previous site-VPN cases, except that the client is now (probably) some software stack on an end system, not a router. There is no question of defining preshared keys on the router, and all client authentication is performed against an external RADIUS database.

The significant changes to the HUB-r configuration to support remote-access IPSec tunnels are shown in Example 3-31. Although this is not shown, the router must have an address pool called RAPOOL as well as a radius server configuration. Address pools were introduced in Chapter 2, "Delivering Broadband Access Today: An Access Technologies Primer." You can see that there are some new keywords in the **crypto maps** in Example 3-32. These serve to tell the router's IPSec process that the tunnel's security credentials need to be authenticated using AAA and that the client's IP address needs to be allocated by the router.

Example 3-32   *IPSec Remote-Access Configlet*

```
aaa new-model
!
! Authorize with RADIUS
aaa accounting login USERLIST group radius
aaa authorization network IKE group radius
!
! Define pool of IP addresses for IPSec sessions
! local configuration for DNS, WINS, domain can be
! included here, in which case IKE list would
! also define "local"
crypto isakmp client configuration address-pool local RAPOOL
!
! link IKE and IPSec connections to RADIUS
! and configure router to issue IP addresses to clients
crypto map RAVPN client authentication list USERLIST
crypto map RAVPN isakmp authorization list IKE
crypto map RAVPN client configuration address initiate
crypto map RAVPN client configuration address respondcrypto map RAVPN 1 ipsec-isakmp
dynamic VPN
```

There are IPSec-specific, RADIUS, vendor-specific attributes (VSAs) that let you completely manage the subscriber's IPSec connection, including DNS server, WINS server, tunnel type, password preshared key, address pool name, and even ACL definitions.

IPSec Design Considerations

After all those examples, it's time to evaluate IPSec as a broadband VPN solution. IPSec is another point-to-point tunnel technology, so many of the technical arguments are identical to those in GRE, as already discussed in the section, "GRE Design Considerations." For the purposes of completeness, the IPSec solution is presumed to include both IPSec and GRE. Once again, the evaluation of IPSec is going to be based on the criteria introduced at the beginning of this chapter. As a reminder, they follow.

For site VPNs, the requirements are as follows:

- Data confidentiality
- Efficient operation (including ease of provisioning)
- Efficient routing
- High availability and resiliency
- Multicast
- Quality of service
- Fragmentation

For telecommuter VPNs, the requirements are the same as for site VPNs, plus the following:

- Authentication, authorization, and accounting
- Service selection

For wholesale VPNs, the requirements are the same as for telecommuter VPNs, plus the following:

- Support for any IP addressing plan
- Efficient address management
- Additional L3 services

In addition, keep in mind these important criteria:

- **Confidentiality** —Obviously, given its origins and purpose, IPSec offers excellent security, so much so that it can and is used to establish private communication over shared public infrastructure.

- **Efficient operation** — IPSec is fundamentally a point-to-point VPN solution, with the same operational challenges experienced with GRE. Recent improvements such as DMVPN, mGRE, and TED are intended to address the provisioning complexity. Without them, configuration can still be cumbersome, and network management system (NMS) tools are invaluable to provision large point-to-point VPNs.

  Additionally, the encryption process is CPU intensive, so either faster CPUs or extra, if not dedicated, hardware is mandatory for good performance on VPN platforms.

- **Efficient routing** — IPSec by itself lacks support for IP multicast. To route between sites, use encrypted GRE. The DMVPN solution offers an interesting permutation because the tunnels are built dynamically between sites. The challenge here is not so much architectural as hardware related. Small sites often have small routers, which do not have the performance to manage the multiple IPSec sessions that are created by DMVPN when sites communicate with each other. If this were rare, then the problem may not be significant. If not, a hardware upgrade might be in order.

- **High availability and resiliency** — IPSec behaves like GRE in terms of architecture, but IPSec has the added advantage of being able to detect peer failure, thanks to IKE keepalives. However, when you combine IPSec and GRE, you still need to use IP routing to switch from one VPN tunnel to another, because GRE will not be able to detect a WAN connectivity problem, even if IPSec can (the two processes don't talk to each other, so the IPSec SAs can all go down, but the GRE tunnel will still stay up and all traffic sent on the interface will be lost.)

- **Multicast** — Again, IPSec does not natively support multicast, so a VPN solution must also rely on GRE. This is important not only for routing, but also for video traffic.

- **Quality of service** — IPSec data, being transported in IP packets, can be marked, classified, queued, and so forth using standard QoS mechanisms throughout the IP core network. However, if you contrast the crypto maps with GRE subinterfaces, you can see that IPSec does not have any form of interface for its endpoints. Because of the way QoS is implemented in Cisco IOS, this means that QoS policy must be applied at another layer, either on the underlying physical interface or on GRE tunnel interfaces before encryption. You can use the **qos-preclassify** command introduced in the section titled "GRE Design Considerations" to apply policy based on the QoS settings of the payload packet (before it is encapsulated for tunneling).

- **Fragmentation** — Fragmentation is not a strong point for the IPSec solution because there are two layers of protocol encapsulation. Protocol overhead can add 60 bytes, compounding the broadband MTU problem. The solutions are the same as for GRE, but with a smaller starting value of MTU if both GRE and IPSec are used to encapsulate data. Cisco IOS has knobs to control whether IPSec packets must be fragmented before or after encryption, using the **crypto ipsec fragmentation** command. The **crypto ipsec df-bit** command is another useful command to control how the router treats the DF bit.

  Note that IPSec works for telecommuter situations too.

- **AAA**—Example 3-31 showed that Cisco IOS implementations allow good integration between IPSec and RADIUS. This is an enormous step up from pure GRE. IKE configuration and user configuration may be local or in AAA.

- **Service selection** —There are no hooks in IPSec to do service selection. Today's end-user experience when using an IPSec client is pretty simple: A pop-up window is used to select one of a list of preconfigured destinations. The only way to go to a different destination is for the client to disconnect from the current destination and to build a tunnel to the appropriate IPSec endpoint. Adding new destinations means that a configuration file needs to be updated on routers and clients, which adds administrative overhead.

To conclude, IPSec is a good, widely deployed solution for CPE-based VPNs of all kinds, despite the performance, packet overhead, and potentially cumbersome configuration, which is addressed by the DMVPN solution.

Case 3: L2TP—For Open Access

Broadband Enterprises sees a new business opportunity in the residential Ethernet market, selling high-speed Internet access to subscribers. Regulation forces the company to allow consumers the choice of ISP, each of which wants complete control over its customers in terms of pricing, billing, service offerings, and so forth.

From a VPN perspective, this is a clear case of an infrastructure VPN—where a wholesale provider uses VPN technology to connect a customer to their retailer of choice. Service selection and network-based VPN operation are important factors, as are billing and the need to support overlapping address spaces. Given these constraints, the network designers at Broadband Enterprises decide to use L2TP.

L2TP Protocol and Operation

L2TP was submitted to the IETF to unify two proprietary remote-access protocols: the Microsoft Point-to-Point Tunneling Protocol (PPTP) and the Cisco Layer 2 Forwarding Protocol (L2F Protocol). Both of these protocols had their origin in dial networks and were developed to tunnel subscriber PPP sessions to an ISP or a corporate home gateway over an IP network. The L2TP protocol is defined in RFC 2661.

L2TP is not often thought of as a VPN, but it supports private addressing, runs over an IP infrastructure, and connects subscribers to someone else's network—matching every common definition of a VPN. The difference is that L2TP is really a Layer 2 VPN technology. Unlike GRE and IPSec, which natively transport IP packets, L2TP carries only PPP frames, as shown in Figure 3-16. L2TP and PPP have a very symbiotic relationship and L2TP relies on the PPP layer to manage subscriber AAA.

The L2TP standard introduces two network components (quoting from RFC 2661, found in its entirety at http://www.ietf.org/rfc/rfc2661.txt):

L2TP Access Concentrator (LAC)

A node that acts as one side of an L2TP tunnel endpoint and is a peer to the L2TP Network Server (LNS). The LAC sits between an LNS and a remote system and forwards packets to and from each. Packets sent from the LAC to the LNS requires tunneling with the L2TP protocol as defined in this document.

L2TP Network Server (LNS)

A node that acts as one side of an L2TP tunnel endpoint and is a peer to the L2TP Access Concentrator (LAC). The LNS is the logical termination point of a PPP session that is being tunneled from the remote system by the LAC.

RFC 2661 also gives a very elegant summary of how the protocol works:

Session

L2TP is connection-oriented. The LNS and LAC maintain state for each Call that is initiated or answered by an LAC. An L2TP Session is created between the LAC and LNS when an end-to-end PPP connection is established between a Remote System and the LNS. Datagrams related to the PPP connection are sent over the Tunnel between the LAC and LNS. There is a one to one relationship between established L2TP Sessions and their associated Calls.

Tunnel

A Tunnel exists between a[n] LAC-LNS pair. The Tunnel consists of a Control Connection and zero or more L2TP Sessions. The Tunnel carries encapsulated PPP datagrams and Control Messages between the LAC and the LNS.

Figure 3-16   *L2TP Protocol Stack (Source: RFC 2661)*

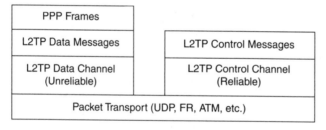

Figure 3-17 shows how the control and data channels are (usually, but not exclusively) carried over UDP datagrams, using port 1701. The data channel is unreliable, but L2TP guarantees delivery of control messages, so the RFC specifies the sequence numbers, sliding windows, retransmission algorithms, etc. that are needed to provide a reliable transport channel. It is a little reminiscent of TCP.

Figure 3-17   *L2TP Message Header (Source: RFC 2661)*

0										1										2										3	
0	1	2	3	4	5	6	7	8	9	0	1	2	3	4	5	6	7	8	9	0	1	2	3	4	5	6	7	8	9	0	1

T	L	X	X	S	X	O	P	X	X	X	X	Ver	Length (Optional)
Tunnel ID													Session ID
Ns (Optional)													Nr (Optional)
Offset Size (Optional)													Offset Pad... (Optional)

Control and data packets share a common header, as shown in Figure 3-17. The first bit identifies whether the message is control (1) or data (0). The Version field is always 2; 1 is reserved for L2F, which also uses the same UDP port number. The Tunnel ID is a multiplexer field that allows multiple tunnels to run between the same LAC and LNS. The Session ID is a field used to identify the (PPP) session within the tunnel, so it allows multiple sessions to be carried in the same tunnel. Both of these fields have values of local significance only; that is, the value used by the LAC can be different from that used by the LNS to refer to the same PPP session, or tunnel. When the LAC needs to refer to a particular session, say to tear it down, it uses the value defined by the LNS in the control message.

The actual control message—the RFC specifies 15 different types—is placed behind the common header. The content of each message varies according to the type of each message. For example, Start-Control-Connection-Request (SCCRQ), which is used for control setup, can include a host name and a CHAP authentication challenge. Incoming-Call-Request (ICRQ), used for session setup, can have a session ID and call bearer type. Both SCCRQ and ICRQ have other fields, too.

It is easier to understand how the protocol works by looking at some examples of tunnel and session setup. This is done in the following sections.

L2TP Tunnel Setup

The first step is to establish the control channel. The sequence is as follows:

1 Initiator sends SCCRQ

2 Responder sends SCCRP

3 Initiator sends SCCCN

Either side can initiate the control channel, which is bidirectional. Usually the LAC starts the process, when it receives a PPP call with a domain name that matches an L2TP tunnel definition. The simplified end-to-end authentication sequence is shown in Figure 3-18.

Figure 3-18 *PPP and L2TP Setup Sequence*

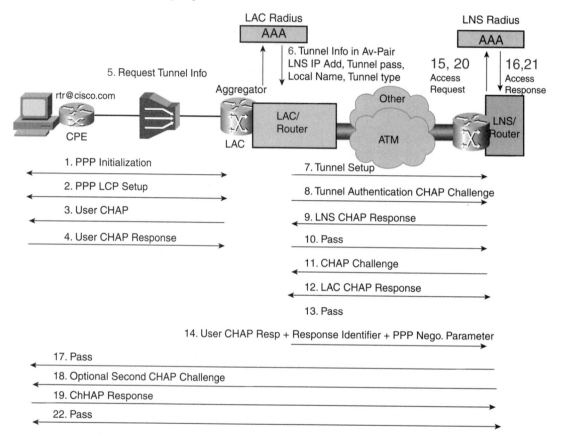

SCCRQ/SCCRP exchanges contain information for CHAP authentication, tunnel ID, host name, and vendor name. Examples 3-33 and 3-34 show Cisco IOS debug output for tunnel setup on the LAC and LNS, respectively. The SCCRx messages are clearly visible in the output, for example in line 8. An *I* signifies an incoming message (Example 3-33, line 8), and an *O* means an outgoing message (Example 3-33, line 5). The LAC is using a tunnel ID of 4 (Example 3-33, line 13); the LNS chooses 1 (Example 3-34, line 6). The debug messages in Example 3-33 also clearly show each peer changing states from the initial idle state to wait-ctl-reply (line 6) and then to established (line 14) when the tunnel is set up.

Example 3-33 *LAC Debug Output for Tunnel Setup (Line Numbers Added for Reference)*

```
1 Tnl/Cl 2/1 L2TP: Session FS enabled
2 Tnl/Cl 2/1 L2TP: Session state change from idle to wait-for-tunnel
3 As3 2/1 L2TP: Create session
4 Tnl 2 L2TP: SM State idle
5 Tnl 2 L2TP: O SCCRQ
6 Tnl 2 L2TP: Tunnel state change from idle to wait-ctl-reply
```

Example 3-33 *LAC Debug Output for Tunnel Setup (Line Numbers Added for Reference) (Continued)*

```
7 Tnl 2 L2TP: SM State wait-ctl-reply
8 Tnl 2 L2TP: I SCCRP from lns
9 Tnl 2 L2TP: Got a challenge from remote peer, lns
10 Tnl 2 L2TP: Got a response from remote peer, lns
11 Tnl 2 L2TP: Tunnel Authentication success
12 Tnl 2 L2TP: Tunnel state change from wait-ctl-reply to established
13 Tnl 2 L2TP: O SCCCN to lns tnlid 4
14 Tnl 2 L2TP: SM State established
```

Example 3-34 *LNS Debug Output for Tunnel Setup (Line Numbers Added for Reference)*

```
1 L2TP: I SCCRQ from lac tnl 1
2 Tnl 4 L2TP: New tunnel created for remote sp_lac, address 172.22.66.23
3 Tnl 4 L2TP: Got a challenge in SCCRQ, sp_lac
4 Tnl 4 L2TP: O SCCRP to sp_lac tnlid 1
5 Tnl 4 L2TP: Tunnel state change from idle to wait-ctl-reply
6 Tnl 4 L2TP: I SCCCN from sp_lac tnl 1
7 Tnl 4 L2TP: Got a Challenge Response in SCCCN from lac
8 Tnl 4 L2TP: Tunnel Authentication success
9 Tnl 4 L2TP: Tunnel state change from wait-ctl-reply to established
10 Tnl 4 L2TP: SM State established
```

L2TP Session Setup

Once the tunnel exists, the LAC and LNS can establish PPP sessions between them. Session establishment involves a three-way handshake and is similar to what you have seen for the control channel.

  1 LAC sends ICRQ.

  2 LNS replies with ICRP.

  3 LAC replies with ICRP.

  4 LAC sends ICCN.

The ICRQ/ICRP messages contain the session ID, information about bearer capabilities, calling and called number (for dialup), and proxy LCP and authentication LCPs. Link Configuration Protocol (LCP) is part of PPP, and these last two fields are needed for the case when the LAC performs LCP authentication with the calling party to discover its identity. This information is forwarded to the LNS, which can either accept and initiate the session or force a renegotiation with the caller. (Remember that the incoming PPP session is terminated on the LNS.)

Example 3-35 shows debug information for the LNS. Line numbers are again added for clarity. **Tnl 4/1** in lines 2 through 8 shows that this is the Session 1 in Tunnel 4, the same one as in Example 3-34. On line 1, the LNS received an ICRQ message, to which it replied on line 5, with an ICRP. Lines 3, 6, and 8 show the state transitions from idle, to wait-for-tunnel, to wait-connect, and finally to established when the PPP session is connected between the client to the PPP server on the LNS.[3]

Example 3-35   *LNS Debug Output for Session Setup (Line Numbers Added for Reference)*

```
1 Tnl 4 L2TP: I ICRQ from sp_lac tnl 1
2 Tnl/Cl 4/1 L2TP: Session FS enabled
3 Tnl/Cl 4/1 L2TP: Session state change from idle to wait-for-tunnel
4 Tnl/Cl 4/1 L2TP: New session created
5 Tnl/Cl 4/1 L2TP: O ICRP to sp_lac 1/1
6 Tnl/Cl 4/1 L2TP: Session state change from wait-for-tunnel to wait-connect
7 Tnl/Cl 4/1 L2TP: I ICCN from sp_lac tnl 1, cl 1
8 Tnl/Cl 4/1 L2TP: Session state change from wait-connect to established
```

Note how well L2TP is designed to carry a large numbers of sessions. Once the sessions are set up, there is no state information exchanged for each call in the tunnel. The amount of control message needed to transport two calls is the same as for 2000 calls in the same tunnel. An L2TP Hello message does exist, but it is for the tunnel, not to the sessions within it.

L2TP Configuration

In Cisco IOS, L2TP is configured either using **vpdn-group** s on the device or with RADIUS attributes. **Virtual-templates** , which should be familiar because they are used for PPP, are used on both LAC and LNS, as are the typical **aaa** and RADIUS **server-group** statements that go with remote-access authentication. More complete examples are given in Examples 3-38 and 3-40, but for now look at the new commands in Example 3-36.

Example 3-36   *LAC **vpdn-group** (Line Numbers Added for Reference)*

```
1 vpdn-group ISP4A
2  request-dialin
3   protocol l2tp
4   domain isp4a.com
5  initiate-to ip 10.1.1.141
6  local name ISP4A
7  l2tp tunnel password 7 104D000A0618
```

The following list describes the commands in Example 3-36. The entire **vpdn-group** creates an LAC tunnel definition for L2TP.

- **initiate-to ip 10.1.1.141** —The LAC will initiate a tunnel to the LNS at IP address 10.1.1.141 (line 5).

- **domain isp4a.com** —This VPDN definition is used whenever a PPP session authenticates with domain isp4a.com (line 4).

- **l2tp tunnel password** —The tunnel has a shared password for L2TP authentication purposes (line 7).

- **local name ISP4A** —The LAC will identify itself with this name (line 6).

- **request-dialin** —The **-dialin** suffix on line 2 can be confusing, but this refers to the fact that PPP clients are calling the LAC, not the other way around (which is a different feature, called L2TP dialout).

At the other end, the LNS definition, shown in Example 3-37, terminates tunnels.

Example 3-37 *LNS* **vpdn-group** *(Line Numbers Added for Reference)*

```
1 vpdn-group ISP4A
2  accept-dialin
3   protocol l2tp
4   virtual-template 1
5  terminate-from hostname ISP4A
6  local name TO-ISP4A
7  l2tp tunnel password 7 01100F175804
```

Take a look at the following details of Example 3-37 to see how to configure the LNS:

- **accept-dialin** —Tells the VPDN process to accept incoming sessions (line 2).

- **virtual-template** —Uses **virtual-template 1** as the template for PPP sessions (line 4).

- **terminate-from** —There is no matching domain name on the LNS, but the **terminate-from** keyword on line 5 allows this **vpdn-group** to match the LAC **local name** on line 6 of Example 3-36. By coordinating tunnel names in this way, a different LNS **vpdn-group** can be configured for different domain names.

- **local name** —The LNS uses the name TO-ISP4A to identify itself (line 6).

There are many other options possible with L2TP configuration, such as controlling window sizes and establishing precloned virtual-access interfaces (which are not discussed here). If you omit the **terminate-from** instruction, then the **vpdn-group** becomes a catchall for all domains. If you have lots of LACs and they are all set up in the same way, you can have a single **vpdn-group** on the LNS.

Putting all the pieces together, Example 3-38 shows an LAC configuration file. There are two tunnels available to reach the same LNS: ISP42A, with a **vpdn-group** in the LAC configuration file, and ISP42B, with a tunnel definition downloaded from RADIUS. Each tunnel is for a separate domain—there is no load balancing. In Example 3-38, subscribers connect on VCs 0/42 and 0/43. The service provider runs IP over an ATM network to connect to its ISP customers. ISP42A is reached over VC 4/105 and ISP42B is reached over 4/101.

The network topology is given in Figure 3-19 and shows the two tunnels between the LAC and LNS, and the ATM VCs and IP addressing used on each path.

Figure 3-19 *L2TP Example Topology*

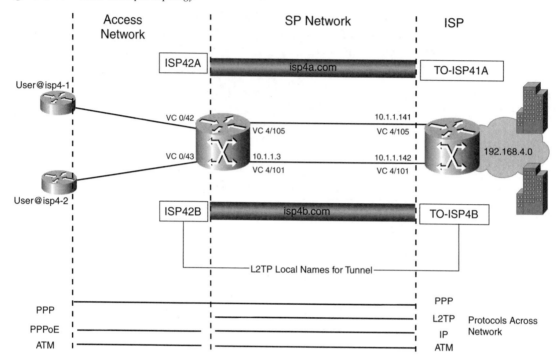

Example 3-38 *LAC Configuration Example*

```
!
aaa new-model
aaa authentication login default local group radius
aaa authentication ppp default group radius local
aaa authorization network default group radius local
aaa accounting network default start-stop group radius
aaa nas port extended
enable password cisco
!
username cisco password 0 cisco
username ISP4A password 0 cisco
vpdn enable
!
vpdn-group 1
 accept-dialin
  protocol pppoe
  virtual-template 1
 pppoe limit per-mac 10
 pppoe limit per-vc 10
!
vpdn-group ISP4A
```

Example 3-38 *LAC Configuration Example (Continued)*

```
request-dialin
 protocol l2tp
 domain isp4a.com
initiate-to ip 10.1.1.141
local name ISP4A
l2tp tunnel password 7 104D000A0618
!
!
interface Loopback0
 ip address 100.1.1.3 255.255.255.255
 no ip directed-broadcast
!
interface Loopback1
 ip address 10.1.1.3 255.255.255.255
 no ip directed-broadcast
!
 interface Loopback2
 ip address 10.1.1.4 255.255.255.255
 no ip directed-broadcast
!
interface ATM0/0/0
 no ip address
 no ip directed-broadcast
 no ip mroute-cache
 no atm ilmi-keepalive
!
interface ATM0/0/0.42 point-to-point
 description PC3 PPPoE
 no ip directed-broadcast
 no ip mroute-cache
 pvc 1/42
  encapsulation aal5snap
  protocol pppoe
 !

 !
!
interface ATM0/0/0.4101 point-to-point
 description PVC 4/101 to ISP4-2
 ip unnumbered Loopback1
 no ip directed-broadcast
 pvc 4/101
  encapsulation aal5mux ip
 !

interface Ethernet0/0/0
 description Management LAN
 ip address 192.168.2.3 255.255.255.0
 no ip directed-broadcast
!
```

continues

Example 3-38 *LAC Configuration Example (Continued)*

```
interface Virtual-Template1
 ip unnumbered Loopback0
 no ip directed-broadcast
 ip mtu 1492
 ip mroute-cache
ppp authentication pap chap
!
router ospf 1
 network 10.1.1.0 0.0.0.255 area 0
!
!
radius-server host 192.168.2.55 auth-port 1645 acct-port 1646
radius-server host 192.168.2.56 auth-port 1812 acct-port 1813 key cisco
radius-server key cisco
```

The configuration in Example 3-38 includes the Cisco IOS LAC components covered previously in Example 3-36. The following are some noteworthy points:

- The LAC runs OSPF, which is how it learns the route to reach the LNS at 10.1.1.141. Because this is an LAC, there is no need to announce subscriber routes. (The LNS has this responsibility—it is where the subscriber sessions terminate.)

- There is no need to allocate IP addresses to the PPP subscribers on an LAC, so there is no address pool configuration on the **virtual-template** .

- There are two radius servers configured on the LAC. The LAC uses the first one at 192.168.2.55, until and unless it receives no response from this server, in which case it starts using the backup server at 192.168.2.56.

- There are two **vpdn-groups** on the LAC in Example 3-38. The first, called **vpdn-group 1**, is for PPPoE session termination. The second, called **vpdn-group ISP4A** , is for L2TP. You need to terminate the PPPoE protocol on the LAC, even if the PPP session is tunneled on to an LNS.

One common option commonly used is to centralize L2TP endpoint definitions in RADIUS; Example 3-39 gives the RADIUS profile to build the L2TP tunnel for domain ISP42B.

Example 3-39 *LAC RADIUS Definition to Reach LNS ISP42B*

```
# L2TP  to ISP42 : VANILLA
isp42b.com Password = "cisco"
        av-pair = "vpdn:l2tp-tunnel-password=cisco",
        av-pair = "vpdn:ip-addresses=10.1.1.142",
        av-pair = "vpdn:tunnel-type=l2tp",
        av-pair = "vpdn:tunnel-id=ISP42B"
```

The way to create a tunnel definition in RADIUS is to define a "user" that matches the domain of the tunnel, in this case isp42b.com. The RADIUS profile has attributes, whose names are self explanatory, to list the LNS address, tunnel password, name, and type. The first time that a PPP session with a username that ends in isp42b.com connects, the LAC sends a RADIUS ACCESS-REQUEST packet using isp42b as the username. If the profile is configured in the RADIUS database, the server sends an ACCESS-ACCESS packet with the profile shown in Example 3-39. The LAC uses this information to build the tunnel to 10.1.1.142.

The LNS doesn't need to know whether the LAC tunnel definition was in RADIUS or local to the router: Its configuration is the same in both cases.

An LNS configuration can also be in RADIUS. It is a more recent addition to Cisco IOS, so it is not as widely used as the LAC. Also, from a design perspective, an LNS typically has only a single (or a very small number) domain to terminate, so the advantages of centralizing the configuration are fewer.

The LNS configuration to terminate both tunnels for ISP42A and ISP42B is shown Example 3-40.

Example 3-40 *ISP42 LNS Configuration Example*

```
!
hostname isp4-2
!
aaa new-model
aaa authentication login default local group radius
aaa authentication ppp default group radius local
enable password cisco
!
username cisco password 0 cisco
username ISP42B password 0 cisco
username TO-ISP42B password 0 cisco
username ISP4A password 0 cisco
username TO-ISP4A password 0 cisco
!
vpdn enable
!
vpdn-group ISP42B
 accept-dialin
  protocol l2tp
  virtual-template 1
 terminate-from hostname ISP42B
 local name TO-ISP42B
 l2tp tunnel password 7 030752180500
!
vpdn-group ISP4A
 accept-dialin
  protocol l2tp
  virtual-template 1
 terminate-from hostname ISP4A
 local name TO-ISP4A
 l2tp tunnel password 7 01100F175804
!
!
!
interface Loopback0
 ip address 100.1.1.142 255.255.255.255
```

continues

Example 3-40 *ISP42 LNS Configuration Example (Continued)*

```
 no ip directed-broadcast
 !
 interface Loopback1
  ip address 10.1.1.142 255.255.255.255
  no ip directed-broadcast
 !
  interface Loopback2
  ip address 10.1.1.141 255.255.255.255
  no ip directed-broadcast


 !
 interface ATM4/0
  no ip address
  no ip directed-broadcast
  no ip mroute-cache
  no atm ilmi-keepalive
 !
 interface ATM4/0.4101 point-to-point
  description ISP4-2 pvc 4/101 from NP3
  ip unnumbered Loopback1
  no ip directed-broadcast
  pvc 4/101
   encapsulation aal5mux ip
  !
  interface ATM4/0.4105 point-to-point
  description ISP4-1 pvc 4/105 from NP3
  ip unnumbered Loopback2
  no ip directed-broadcast
  pvc 4/105
   encapsulation aal5mux ip
 !
 interface Virtual-Template1
  ip unnumbered Loopback0
  no ip directed-broadcast
  peer default ip address pool default
  ppp authentication pap chap
 !
 router eigrp 100
  redistribute connected
  redistribute static
  network 192.168.4.0
 !
 router ospf 1
  network 10.1.1.0 0.0.0.255 area 0
 ip local pool default 192.168.41.1 192.168.41.10


 !
 radius-server host 10.1.2.56 auth-port 1812 acct-port 1816
 radius-server key cisco
 !
 !
 end
```

Here are some key points to note about the LNS configuration in Example 3-40:

- All subscriber definitions are authenticated using AAA, so there are no username/passwords on the LNS itself, but this is, of course, possible.

- Unlike the LAC, there is just one RADIUS server on the LNS.

- The LNS is responsible for assigning IP addresses to subscribers. In Example 3-40, a local pool called **default** is used. The alternate address allocation strategies were discussed in Chapter 2.

- OSPF runs between the LNS and LAC, so the LNS address 10.1.1.42 is reachable when the LAC tries to build a tunnel to it.

- EIGRP runs on the core-facing interfaces of the LNS. Notice how static and connected addresses are redistributed directly into EIGRP. It would be better practice to announce an aggregate route instead of the host routes (which is what this router will do). This was covered in a lot more detail in Chapter 2.

Scaling L2TP Networks

From the very first, L2TP networks have supported large numbers of subscribers and devices. Load-balancing and redundancy techniques play an integral part in allowing L2TP to do this successfully. This section looks at the two components that enable proper load balancing:

- **Data plane** —L2TP LNS load balancing and redundancy
- **Control plane** —AAA load balancing and redundancy

A Brief History of the IDB

Not long ago, Cisco IOS supported a maximum of only 300 interfaces of any type. Associated with each interface was a software structure called an Interface Descriptor Block (IDB), which contained all the vital information for an interface, such as IP address, interface, MAC addresses, MTU lengths, and various other information that other protocols need to use the interface. Each of these IDBs required memory, so there had to be some limit on their number, and 300 interfaces seemed to be plenty. However, first dialup and then broadband changed router requirements permanently. Today's high-end, leased-line aggregators routinely terminate several thousand interfaces, so the 300 limit was doomed without remote access anyway, but this was the driver for interface scaling.

The first step in a long and little-told saga of relentless engineering effort was to separate the information needed for the Layer 2 interface from the Layer 3 information found in the IDB and create a new descriptor, called a software IDB. A physical interface requires one hardware IDB and one software IDB. Logical interfaces, which include, for example, tunnels, Frame Relay subinterfaces, and PPP virtual access, require software IDBs, which consume less memory, meaning there can be more of them. Logical interfaces are associated with at least one physical interface, so the number of IDBs used for *N* logical interfaces, or subinterfaces, is 1+*N*. Other modifications included tweaking software routines to remove loops run across all router interfaces, optimizing control-plane processing so that large numbers of sessions could come up in a short amount of time, and making sure data-plane forwarding wouldn't starve bandwidth from control-plane processing and more.

Most recently, on some Cisco routers, PPP sessions do not even create virtual-access interfaces at all. These subvirtual-access interfaces can be seen with the **show vtemplate** command on high-end routers.

From a user point of view, all this is invisible, of course. But the PPP session count has been scaled by a factor of 213 in just a few years (from 300 to 64,000).

Data Plane: L2TP LNS Redundancy and Load Balancing

Enabling redundancy is as easy as configuring the LAC with a list of LNS endpoints. If the tunnel to the primary address fails, the LAC builds a new one to the next address. Example 3-41 shows a RADIUS profile for a domain isp42c.com, for which there are three different LNS definitions.

Example 3-41 *Redundant LNS Defined on LAC—AAA Version*

```
isp42c.com Password = "cisco" Service-Type = Outbound
        Tunnel-Type = :1:L2TP,
        Tunnel-Medium-Type = :1:IP,
        Tunnel-Server-Endpoint = :1:"10.1.1.143",

        Tunnel-Preference = :1:0,
        Tunnel-Password = :1:"cisco"

        Tunnel-Type = :2:L2TP,
        Tunnel-Medium-Type = :2:IP,
        Tunnel-Server-Endpoint = :2:"10.1.1.144",

        Tunnel-Preference = :2:1,
        Tunnel-Password = :2:"cisco"

        Tunnel-Type = :3:L2TP,
        Tunnel-Medium-Type = :3:IP,
        Tunnel-Server-Endpoint = :3:"10.1.1.145",

        Tunnel-Preference = :3:2,
        Tunnel-Password = :3:"cisco"
```

The Tunnel-Server-Endpoint and Tunnel-Preference attributes in Example 3-41 do all the magic to create a redundant configuration:

- **Tunnel-Server-Endpoint** —IP address of LNS. Note that each LNS definition has a different IP address.

- **Tunnel-Preference** — Sets the relative preference of a tunnel. Sessions are load balanced across tunnels with the same preference value.

NOTE   Example 3-41 uses IETF av-pairs, whereas the other examples earlier in the chapter used Cisco vendor-specific attributes (VSAs). In Example 3-40, the first number that appears after the equal sign is the tag value; as quoted from RFC 2868 (Tunnel-Type description): "The Tag field is one octet in length and is intended to provide a means of grouping attributes in the same packet that refer to the same tunnel. Valid values for this field are 0x01 through 0x1F inclusive. If the Tag field is unused, it MUST be zero (0x00)."

Now that there are three potential LNS destinations for isp42.com, how does the LAC know to reroute sessions in case of failure? L2TP failure detection is done at the protocol level, using a Hello message. This message allows tunnel endpoints to distinguish periods of inactivity (Hellos received) from a tunnel down condition (no Hellos). When a period goes by without a Hello message, the L2TP endpoint deduces that some failure has occurred and that it can tear down the tunnel and create a new one to a new L2TP destination.

By the way, a tunnel is not always torn down because of a catastrophic event. For example, quiescent tunnels (defined as a tunnel with no sessions—the **l2tp tunnel nosession-limit** command controls the amount of time L2TP waits before timing out an empty tunnel) are removed during the normal course of L2TP operation. The L2TP protocol even has a StopCCN message, which also allows forced tunnel tear down (i.e., one where there are still sessions running inside).

In any case, when a tunnel goes down, or is torn down, the PPP sessions inside the tunnel are brought down too and must be renegotiated whenever a new tunnel starts. This is an important point: L2TP failover is not transparent to PPP sessions.

Load balancing is the logical step after redundancy; Example 3-42 shows an LAC configured to load balance PPP sessions across multiple LNSs.

Example 3-42 *Load Balancing Across Multiple LNSs*

```
isp42d.com Password = "cisco" Service-Type = Outbound
        Tunnel-Type = :1:L2TP,
        Tunnel-Medium-Type = :1:IP,
        Tunnel-Server-Endpoint = :1:"10.1.1.143",
        Tunnel-Assignment-Id = :1:"isp42",
        Tunnel-Preference = :1:1,
        Tunnel-Password = :1:"cisco"

        Tunnel-Type = :2:L2TP,
        Tunnel-Medium-Type = :2:IP,
        Tunnel-Server-Endpoint = :2:"10.1.1.144",
        Tunnel-Assignment-Id = :2:"isp42",
```

continues

Example 3-42 *Load Balancing Across Multiple LNSs (Continued)*

```
            Tunnel-Preference = :2:1,
            Tunnel-Password = :2:"cisco"

            Tunnel-Type = :3:L2TP,
            Tunnel-Medium-Type = :3:IP,
            Tunnel-Server-Endpoint = :3:"10.1.1.145",
            Tunnel-Assignment-Id = :3:"isp42",
            Tunnel-Preference = :3:1,
            Tunnel-Password = :3:"cisco"
```

Once again, the LAC in Example 3-42 gets a list of addresses from RADIUS when the first subscriber for the isp42d.com domain connects. Because the Tunnel-Preference value is identical for each LNS, the LAC load balances sessions across 10.1.1.143, 10.1.1.144, and 10.1.1.145. There is no special configuration required on the LNS.

L2TP load balancing and redundancy is statically configured. In practice, network designers must plan carefully to contend with the limits on the number of tunnels a device can handle, and on the number of sessions the device can put in those tunnels. To see why, consider Example 3-42 again. Imagine that the LAC can process 32,000 sessions, 24,000 of which will be in the isp43d.com domain. There are three LNSs in the isp43d domain, so each needs a maximum capacity of 8000 sessions to accommodate the peak load of 24,000 sessions. Now imagine that one of the LNSs in the domain fails. The remaining two need to be able to terminate 12,000 subscribers each. (Yes, Cisco IOS should evenly distribute the sessions previously on the failed LNS.)

An inconvenience with the static load-balancing configuration of L2TP is that every time an LNS is added to, or removed from, the network, not only does the capacity picture change, but several LAC configurations might need to be updated, depending on the load-balancing scheme in use. (The opposite is not true. Adding a new LAC to the network has no effect on the configuration of the LNS, presuming, of course, that there is enough bandwidth to process the new calls.)

Finally, remember that tunnel failover isn't enough to provide end-to-end redundancy. On the subscriber-facing side, the LAC terminates Layer 2 circuits, which cannot be rerouted dynamically if the LAC device becomes inoperative. Because of this, device and line-card redundancy is fundamental on an LAC. The LNS is much simpler to deal with.

In summary, L2TP has a good level of support for failover and load balancing, but the design and then configuration can be tricky. Thankfully, LAC configuration can be stored on a central RADIUS server, greatly minimizing the scope of intervention if a change to the network occurs. This point leads nicely to the next section, which discusses the control plane.

Control Plane: AAA Redundancy and Load Balancing

One of the most important things to qualify on routers with very high capacity is control-plane scalability. With tens of thousands of subscribers connected to a single router, the time needed to bring up all the sessions can be the most significant part of the network recovery time. After all, the only thing that matters to the customers is the total time to restore their connectivity. The previous section looked at scaling the data plane by load balancing user traffic across multiple destinations. The final piece is to make sure that AAA queries don't slow everything down again.

For both speed and reliability, RADIUS requests can be load balanced across multiple servers, as follows:

- **Client load balancing** —Multiple addresses are configured on the client in RADIUS server-groups. Using round-robin or random lookups, the RADIUS client (i.e., the router) load balances requests across individual servers.

- **Server load balancing** —A single IP address is configured on the client, but a network load-balancing engine, such as a Cat6500 Server Load Balancing (SLB) card, sits between the client and servers. It is easier to add or change servers, because the physical IP addresses are all hidden between the SLB's virtual address. You also have a much wider choice of load-balancing algorithms this way, but at the cost of some extra hardware.

Independent of the type of load balancing is the consideration that the router software must be capable of processing several hundred calls per second to restore service in a timely fashion when numerous subscribers share the same device.

L2TP Tunnel Switching

Sometimes tunnels and sessions appear to be similar to ATM virtual paths and virtual circuits. It may be tempting to want to switch tunnels between LAC and LNS, for a variety of reasons. In fact, this is rarely needed. L2TP scales well, because the behavior of the core is uncorrelated to the number of subscriber sessions transported across it. For the core routers, it is all IP traffic, and whether the tunnels carry millions of subscribers or ten does not matter.

That said, networks do use L2TP tunnel switching. One potential reason for tunnel switching is if the number of LACs is so large that, perhaps because of device limitations, an ISP's LNS cannot terminate tunnels from each LAC.

An L2TP tunnel switch either multiplexes traffic from two or more ingress tunnels to a single egress tunnel or demultiplexes traffic from an ingress tunnel to multiple egress tunnels. The following text considers each of these cases in turn.

Fan-in Tunnel Switch

Sessions from many ingress tunnels are forwarded out a single egress tunnel, as shown in Figure 3-20. The purpose of doing this is to allow the wholesale provider to deploy a single LAC device in a region, perhaps sparsely populated, and forward all sessions on a single egress tunnel. At some other point in the network, namely the fan-in tunnel switch, a new tunnel must be created for each L2TP domain so that the ISP terminates only sessions from its own customers.

Figure 3-20 *Second L2TP Example Topology*

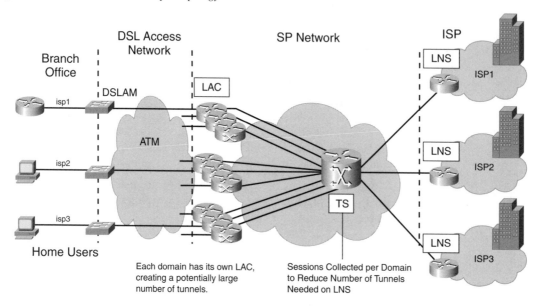

Each domain has its own LAC, creating a potentially large number of tunnels.

Sessions Collected per Domain to Reduce Number of Tunnels Needed on LNS

Fan-out Tunnel Switch

The ingress tunnel carries sessions belonging to many different domains. The fan-out tunnel switch forwards each session to a tunnel unique to its domain, as shown in Figure 3-21. The purpose here is to reduce the number of tunnels terminated on the ISP LNS.

Tunnel switching moves, not solves, the problem of scalability. Think again of the undercapacity LNS scenario that prompted deployment of a switch. Now, the tunnel switch itself is the bottleneck, because it has its own session limits. How so? Well, in both of the preceding scenarios, the domain name is used to map sessions between tunnels. The domain name is buried inside the PPP session, and the tunnel switch must negotiate LCP with the LAC to get at the name. Thus, session limits still apply. Of course, you can have a higher-capacity central tunnel switch, but the problem of scalability is being solved by additional hardware, not through network design.

Figure 3-21   *Third L2TP Example Topology*

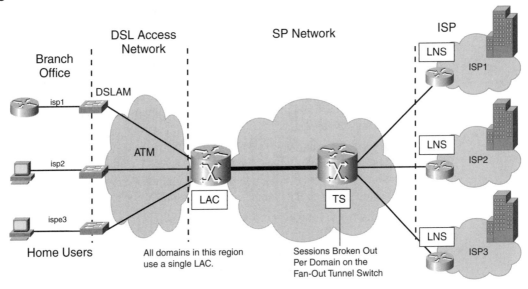

In reality, "tunnel switching" is usually a misnomer. "Session switching" would be a more accurate description. That said, tunnel switching is deployed in operational networks. The Cisco IOS feature name is VPDN Multihop. Examples of tunnel switch configurations are provided on the ciscopress.com website and for fan-in configurations for LAC, tunnel switch, and LNS, respectively.

L2TP Design Considerations

Just as was done with the previous solutions, take a look at how L2TP performs as a VPN solution:

- **Confidentiality** — The L2TP protocol has authentication mechanisms as part of tunnel and session negotiation, even if they are not impervious to man-in-the-middle attacks. In general, L2TP is excellent over private network infrastructure, but can be insufficient to protect sensitive data over shared networks. IPSec can be used to encrypt L2TP packets.

- **Efficient operation** — L2TP is very operationally efficient, as benefits its heritage in service provider dialup networking. All of the subscriber configuration and most of the network device configuration can be stored in a single point of configuration (RADIUS database). Many L2TP devices even have MIBs that allow tunnel utilization statistics to be monitored. AAA records are also generated for tunnel start/stop events, which allows operators to monitor their traffic utilization very closely over time. For the LAC and LNS devices themselves, the configuration scalability problems have received a lot more attention than for other VPN technologies. For example, the entire router configuration for an L2TP network with 32,000 subscribers can be done with as little as a few hundred lines of Cisco IOS commands.

- **Efficient routing** —L2TP and IP operate like the proverbial ships in the night. (Remember the protocol name used to be Layer 2 Forwarding.) There is no routing on the LAC, and tunnel endpoints do not have Cisco IOS interfaces. PPP sessions, however, do have Cisco IOS interfaces, and routing protocols can run over virtual-access interfaces as well as announce these interfaces to other routing peers. From a topology perspective, L2TP imposes strict hub and spoke.

- **High availability and resiliency** —The L2TP protocol control channel offers a scalable way to load balance tunnels and provide failover capability. Currently, most implementations do not fail over PPP sessions, which must be renegotiated. For that reason, call setup rate is an integral part of overall availability.

- **Multicast** —Cisco IOS supports multicast over PPP subinterfaces. L2TP does not change this.

- **Quality of service** —IP TOS settings can be mapped to the outer L2TP packet headers to allow QoS policy to be preserved across the WAN. However, virtual-access interfaces only support FIFO queuing.

- **Fragmentation** —L2TP has no effect on session MTU. To understand why, remember that it is a network-based VPN solution and the tunnel layer doesn't start until the LAC starts. There are still plenty of MTU issues on networks that use PPP over L2TP, but they have nothing to do with the tunnel overhead, which is invisible to the PPP client.

  It is true that the L2TP layer does add packet overhead in the core, but MTU values are often much bigger (POS interfaces are widespread) or can be fixed in the unlikely case that there is a problem.

- **AAA**—All L2TP implementations offer excellent integration with AAA.

For the first time in this chapter, wholesale requirements need to be considered, as follows:

- **Support any IP addressing plan** —L2TP is compliant with this requirement. The LNS can allocate any address it wants to the PPP client: It is transparent to the service provider network.

- **Efficient address management** —Again, the L2TP solution is compliant. The full gamut of PPP mechanisms using RADIUS and even DHCP is available to download individual or ranges of addresses to subscribers.

- **Additional L3 services** —All the reasons that make L2TP so wonderful as a wholesale solution make it a poor choice for offering services to the subscriber. Recall that this issue is for the transport provider to try to extract extra revenue from the broadband subscriber for more than just fast Internet access. Well, L2TP builds a Layer 2 pipe between subscriber and ISP—the Layer 3 wholesale network is completely invisible. To offer any form of service, or even to let the subscriber select a service, the PPP session must be terminated in the wholesale network so as to have an IP path to talk to the customer.

Other Open Access Solutions

Are tunnels the only way to provide a VPN service? In a word: no. IPSec and GRE are a very good fit for CPE-based solutions, but less so for network-based architectures because of the requirement to have private routing tables for L3 VPN.

PPP and L2TP work very well for wholesale, but again less well as a CPE solution because the cost of implementing the L2TP/PPP protocols, with their associated state machines and so forth, isn't justified by the benefits when compared with something more straightforward, such as bridged access.

There is no one size fits all solution here: Different technologies solve different problems better than others.

Open access deserves further discussion. Of the technologies considered in this chapter, only L2TP fits the bill but with the important caveat that the end station must support PPP. This is easy enough with PCs, but set-top boxes, televisions, and other household appliances are finding their way onto home networks. PPP on a refrigerator may be some time away, so it is useful to skim over some other solutions for open access for bridged or routed clients, such as:

- Network Address Translation (NAT)
- Policy-based routing

Open Access with Network Address Translation

Sometimes service providers want to manage their own IP domain. Reasons for this might include the following:

- The service provider offers access to local content as part of a base package, but Internet access is an additional service. This scenario is referred to as a *walled garden* (the content is unavailable unless you are inside the walls) and is only accessible to subscribers.

- A wholesale provider wants to offer services to its ISP customers, such as content server hosting. These services are now shared, so they must be accessible by customers from multiple networks.

One design option is for the subscribers and services to use private IP addresses on the entire service provider network. A single NAT router connects the network to the Internet and translates addresses between the private and public domains. The two main advantages of this solution are as follows:

- **Simple address management** —There is no danger of running out of address space.
- **Centralized NAT router** —NAT is a useful function, but it is CPU intensive. Unfortunately, it is annoyingly hard to code in hardware. For NAT to work correctly, all IP addresses must be translated between private and public domains. But many applications embed the host IP addresses in their protocol exchanges, so NAT routers must look very deeply into packet payload to find and change these addresses. Centralizing the NAT function mitigates the performance impact by keeping NAT off the other routers.

There is a disadvantage that is unique to open access. The NAT router topology just described manages a single public and a single private address space. Open access, however, requires you to translate subscriber addresses to *multiple* public address spaces, each corresponding to different ISPs. This is hard to do because, by the time a packet reaches the egress NAT router, there is no information available that identifies the subscriber: All the router sees is an IP packet with a source and destination address pair. The only option is to use different address pools for customers of different ISPs (this is actually done in practice), in which case packets destined to ISP A, for example, can be routed to a NAT router that manages the address translation for that ISP, and packets for ISP B can be translated on a different NAT router. In any case, address management is no longer simple.

The Cisco Service Selection Gateway software actually solves this problem of multiple NAT address spaces, but you need some external way to determine VPN membership—you can't tell by looking at an IP packet.

Open Access with Policy-Based Routing

Some wholesale providers don't manage any IP addresses at all, but instead make (or ask) their retail provider partners assign public addresses. The wholesaler then deploys route policies throughout its network to establish different Internet route paths for subscribers depending on their source address (which indirectly tells what ISP they are going to).

Like the NAT-based open access scenario, routing and address management are difficult. The ISP receives DHCP requests for addresses, which are assigned on a first-come, first-served basis, without looking at where on the network the subscriber will be. The wholesale provider has to carry the routes for all of these addresses and, in the worst-case scenario, could find it very hard to aggregate them sensibly.

Security and scalability are two other open issues with this design. The switches and routers closest to the subscriber have to enforce security policy and prevent people from sending traffic where they are not allowed to. Just stopping address spoofing is a headache. It is also hard to claim that this is a scalable design if all the subscriber routes must be carried in core routing tables.

Summary

The first conclusion that comes to mind after this look at different VPN technologies is that there is no one size fits all solution. GRE, IPSec, and L2TP each have their uses. GRE and IPSec are good solutions for CPE-based VPN services. L2TP is a network-based VPN ideally suited for providing open access.

Can any one protocol replace the others in their own solution space? In theory, it is possible, but because of both implementation and protocol limitations, L2TP is an awkward fit for a CPE-based solution: Why impose the complexity of the PPP and L2TP state machines if there is another way? Similarly, IPSec and GRE introduce encapsulation overhead and lack many of the controls that go with PPP and AAA that combine to make L2TP such a good fit for wholesale.

Open access is an area with the most unaddressed weaknesses, as follows:

- L2TP is the only solution that works. Neither GRE nor IPSec implementations support open access because IP addresses cannot overlap in the same device. (Actually, there is a way to do this, by leveraging the private VRF forwarding tables originally defined for MPLS-VPN, which will be introduced in the next chapter.) The L2TP architecture also requires a PPP client, which is not always possible.

- Load balancing and redundancy must be manually provisioned in L2TP. There is no way to dynamically signal a new peer.

- An L2TP carrier cannot introduce new services, such as selling to the ISP community with web hosting, video distribution, or selling content to the end users. Transport is the only service possible.

- L2TP may not require state on core routers but it, or more exactly PPP, does create state on the LAC and LNS. You generally need a more powerful router to terminate 8000 sessions than you do to route traffic from 8000 PCs. This creates additional cost for the ISP.

- The realities of limited sessions per device and limited sessions per tunnel lead to considerable tunnel engineering, examples of which include load-balancing sessions across tunnels, load-balancing tunnels across LNS, switching sessions from one tunnel to another, etc. The closer the network gets to these per-device limits, the more complex it is to manage.

- MPLS is already the convergence technology of choice, either because of an ATM-to-IP migration or because of IP-based services. For this highly pragmatic reason, it quite simply may make more sense to use MPLS VPN for the broadband network if it has been deployed everywhere else already.

MPLS-based VPNs are going to help solve a lot of these problems.

In this chapter, you learn about the following topics:

- The Definition of MPLS, Including Forwarding and Encapsulation
- Traffic Engineering
- MPLS-TE Cisco IOS Configuration
- Layer 3 VPN Services
- MPLS QoS

CHAPTER 4

Introduction to MPLS

This chapter introduces Multiprotocol Label Switching (MPLS) technology and lays the foundation for subsequent discussion on the use of MPLS-based services in Chapters 5, 6, and 7. These services were developed for leased-line applications (so-called *VRF-aware applications*), but this book applies them in a broadband context.

NOTE If you are already familiar with MPLS, you may safely skip this chapter.

The following are the three primary texts used as reference for this chapter:

- "MPLS Architecture Overview," by Jay Kumaraswamy—Cisco Networkers Presentation. It is available at www.cisco.com.
- "Deploying MPLS for Traffic Engineering," by Eric Osborne—Cisco Networkers Presentation. It is available at http://www.cisco.com.
- "Advanced Topics in MPLS-TE Deployment" (white paper). It is available at http://www.cisco.com.

Many of the figures in this chapter are adapted from the Cisco Networkers Presentations referenced in the preceding list, as are the Cisco IOS examples for Traffic Engineering (TE). Appendix A lists additional excellent reference works that discuss MPLS in great detail.

Definition of MPLS

MPLS is defined in a set of IETF documents, as follows:

- "Multiprotocol Label Switching Architecture" (RFC 3031)
- "MPLS Label Stack Encoding" (RFC 3032)
- "MPLS Using LDP and ATM VC Switching" (RFC 3035)
- "LDP Specification" (RFC 3036)
- "LDP Applicability" (RFC 3037)

NOTE   The IETF MPLS website has a complete listing of RFCs. You can access this site at http://www.ietf.org.

Tag (later called *label*) switching was first proposed as a way to move IP packets more quickly than was possible with everyday routing and routers. The hope at the time was to have a device that would be as fast as an ATM switch (which uses fixed-length labels) with the same functionality as an IP router (which uses variable-length prefix matching).

It soon became apparent, however, that any increase in speed was very slight. What really allowed MPLS to come of age as an infrastructure is that it could provide new IP services: Virtual Private Networks (VPNs) and Traffic Engineering (TE).

The best known of these proposals were Ipsilon Technology's IP Switching and Cisco Systems' Tag Switching; however, IBM, Toshiba, and others also had implementations that addressed the same problem. As so often happens, an IETF MPLS standard unified several competing proposals from different vendors.

Today, there are over 140 networks running MPLS, including commercial VPN services in both the United States and Europe. Like any technology, MPLS is not intended to solve all the problems for all the people (something that can be quickly forgotten when attending industry conferences), but it has been a huge success by any measure.

More recently, MPLS has also been proposed as the core technology for service providers to integrate, or converge, their disparate networks. A carrier today might have a Frame Relay network for data VPN services, a huge voice infrastructure for voice services, an IP network for Internet access services, and so on. The promise is that a single MPLS network will be able to offer either the same services as the different networks it would replace (such as IP VPN, Internet access, Layer 2 VPNs, and, one day, voice) or transport for these networks across a common, converged backbone.

NOTE   Those with long memories will remember that ATM was also promised as a multiservice convergence solution, so time will tell how well MPLS fares.

Viewed topically, MPLS may look a little like ATM. There are circuits and circuit identifiers, but for variable-length packets, not small fixed-length cells. This similarity has not escaped notice, and the MPLS marketplace is an interesting mix of ATM and IP vendors, competing for business and actively participating in different standards bodies.

The rest of this section looks at how labels are used for forwarding, how labels are exchanged, and how packet encapsulation is used in MPLS.

The final sections in the chapter cover how labels are applied in TE and VPN applications, finishing with a discussion of MPLS quality of service (QoS).

IP and MPLS Packet Forwarding

In a normal routing scenario, when a router needs to forward a packet, it finds the outgoing interface by looking for a matching IP address prefix in the routing table.

The actual interface used for forwarding corresponds to the shortest path to the IP destination, as defined by the routing policy. Other administrative policies, such as QoS and security, may affect the choice of interface. This collection of criteria used for forwarding decisions is more generally referred to as a Forward Equivalency Class (FEC). The classification of a packet to FEC is done on each router along the IP path and happens independently of the other routers in the network.

MPLS decouples packet forwarding from the information in the IP header. An MPLS router forwards packets based on fixed-length labels instead of matching on a variable-length IP address prefix. The label is a sort of shortcut for an FEC classification that has already happened. Where the label comes from is discussed later in this section, but for now, it is enough to say that the labels are calculated based on the topology information in the IP routing table. RFC 3031 puts it like this:

> *In MPLS, the assignment of a particular packet to a particular FEC is done just once, as the packet enters the network. The FEC to which the packet is assigned is encoded as a short fixed length value known as a "label". When a packet is forwarded to its next hop, the label is sent along with it; that is, the packets are "labeled" before they are forwarded....*
>
> *In the MPLS forwarding paradigm, once a packet is assigned to a FEC, no further header analysis is done by subsequent routers; all forwarding is driven by the labels.*

Before looking at this in more detail, you need to understand some definitions:

- **Label switch router (LSR)**—A router that switches based on labels. The original Cisco terminology was P-router (P for provider). An LSR swaps labels. Unlike a traditional router, an LSR does not have to calculate where to forward a packet based on the IP packet header (which is a simplified way of saying it does not do FEC classification when it receives a packet). An LSR uses the incoming label to find the outgoing interface (and label).

- **Edge LSR**—A router that is on the edge of an MPLS network. The Cisco term, which is still very widely used, is provider edge (PE) router. The edge LSR adds and removes labels from packets. This process is more formally called *imposition* and *disposition* (and also *pushing* and *popping*, because labels are said to go on a stack). The IETF (LSR) and Cisco terms (PE) are used interchangeably throughout the book.

A packet is processed by each hop as follows:

- At the edge of the network, as shown in Figure 4-1, LSR A classifies a packet in an FEC and assigns (or imposes) label 17 to the packet. A label is of local significance on that interface just like an ATM VPI/VCI or a Frame Relay DLCI.

- In the core, LSRs, such as LSR C and LSR B, swap label values. LSR A removes the old label, 17 in the example shown in Figure 4-1, and imposes the new one, 22. The values of the ingress label and interface are used to find the values of the egress label and interface, which will be clearer in Figure 4-4 later in this chapter.

- LSR B, as the second-to-last hop in the MPLS network, removes the outermost label from the label stack, which is called penultimate hop popping (PHP). So, packets arrive at LSR D without any label, and standard IP routing is used to forward the packet. The process of removing a label is also called *disposition*.

- Once the label is removed, the packet is forwarded using standard IP routing.

Figure 4-1   *MPLS Network Taxonomy*

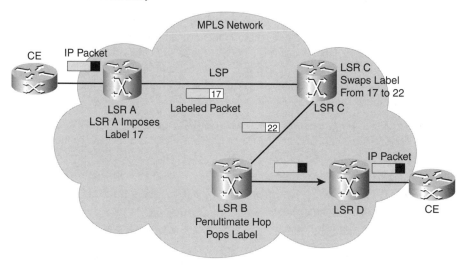

The end-to-end path through the network is called a label-switched path (LSP). Labels are assigned using a specific protocol, called Label Distribution Protocol (LDP).

Now the difference with standard IP forwarding should be clearer. FEC classification is done when a packet enters the MPLS network, not at every hop. An LSR needs to look only at the packet's label to know which outgoing interface to use. There can be different labels on an LSR for the same IP destination. Saying the same thing in a different way, there can be multiple LSPs for the same destination.

A key point to understand is that the control plane is identical in both the IP and MPLS cases. LSRs use IP routing protocols to build routing tables, just as routers do. An LSR then goes the extra step of assigning labels for each destination in the routing table and advertising the label/ FEC mapping to adjacent LSRs. ATM switches can also be LSRs. They run IP routing protocols, just as a router LSR does, but label switch cells instead of packets.

What is missing from this description is how label information is propagated around the network. How does LSR A in Figure 4-1 know what label to use? MPLS networks use a variety of signaling protocols to distribute labels. Before you look at this in more detail, you first need to understand MPLS encapsulation, which is discussed in the following section.

MPLS Encapsulation

MPLS uses a shim header, shown in Figure 4-2 and defined in RFC 3032, which is inserted between the Layer 2 and Layer 3 headers. Encapsulation stacks are defined in different RFCs for Ethernet, ATM, PPP, and other media, as shown in Figure 4-3.

Figure 4-2   *MPLS Shim Header*

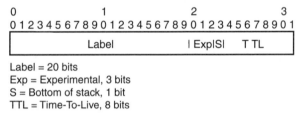

Label = 20 bits
Exp = Experimental, 3 bits
S = Bottom of stack, 1 bit
TTL = Time-To-Live, 8 bits

Figure 4-3   *MPLS Header Insertion*

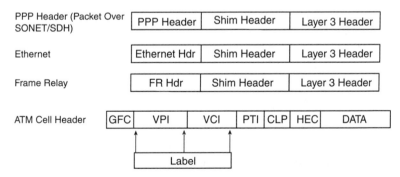

The MPLS header is very simple, as you can see in Figure 4-2. The label itself defines a flat, 20-bit address space. The EXP bits are defined as experimental, but are in fact used for QoS. MPLS QoS is explained in more detail in the "MPLS QoS" section of this chapter. The S bit is set on the lowest label when there is more than one label on a packet, which is called a *stack*. The TTL is analogous to the IP TTL.

Many MPLS applications, such as TE or Fast Reroute, involve multiple layers, or stacks, of labels. However, the LSR forwards on the basis of the top, or outer, label values only and never looks at the inner ones.

Label Distribution

As already mentioned, LSRs use the IP control plane to calculate paths through the MPLS network. However, they need a way to tell each peer what label to use for each FEC. A variety of protocols are used to do this. MPLS uses LDP between adjacent peers. Applications use other protocols for label distribution; for example, VPNs use MP-BGP, and Traffic Engineering uses RSVP.

LDP Operation

LDP packets contain FEC/label mappings. An LSR uses an label/FEC mapping to tell its neighbors "If you want me to send a packet to this destination, use this label," as shown in Figure 4-4.

Figure 4-4   *MPLS Label Distribution*

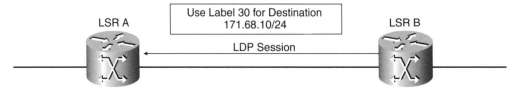

In I/F	In Lab	Address Prefix	Out I/F	Out Lab
6	44	171.68.10	1	30
...	...	...	...	...

In I/F	In Lab	Address Prefix	Out I/F	Out Lab
0	30	171.68.10	1	-
...	...	...	...	...

Once all the labels have been exchanged, the LSR has everything it needs to forward. LDP operates in the following way:

1 LDP uses a UDP-based neighbor discovery process and creates a TCP-based session for each peer.

2 LDP neighbors negotiate session parameters in the same way as they do before they bring up the session.

3 Once the routing table converges, an LSR generates a label for every destination it knows about. In Figure 4-4, both LSRs have routes to 171.68.10/24.

4 The labels are announced to the LDP peers. Referring back to the example in Figure 4-4, LSR B will use LDP to tell LSR A to use label 30 when sending packets to the 171.68.10/24 network. LSR A advertises label 44 for the same prefix to its neighbors. LSR A puts the label-mapping information in its Label Forwarding Information Base (LFIB). If there are multiple labels available for the same FEC, the LSR uses the best match and would thus prefer the label for 171.68.10/24 over the label for 171.16/16 to reach the destination 171.68.10.1.

5 In Figure 4-4, when LSR A receives a packet on interface 6, with a label value of 44, it looks in the LFIB and finds that it must send the packet on interface 1 with a label value of 30.

6 When LSR B in Figure 4-4 receives a packet with a label value of 30 on interface 0, it has no label for the destination in the LFIB (it is the penultimate hop), so it pops the label and sends the packet on interface 1. Neither LSR looks at the destination IP address.

Something special happened in Step 6. LSR B removed the label before forwarding. In MPLS, the penultimate hop (i.e., the second-to-last router in the MPLS network) behaves like this. The egress edge LSR in the network signals to its neighbors that it is the last router in the MPLS domain for an FEC. (It uses sends a special label value in LDP, called Implicit Null label to do this.) Therefore, any upstream LSRs will know that they are the penultimate hop and so must pop the label before sending.

Labels are generated per FEC. On certain networks, there can be multiple destinations that are reachable across the same physical link. To save label space, a single aggregate label can be used to bind multiple FECs. You will see this, for example, on an Ethernet segment.

The timing of label distribution and whether peers will listen depend on the following factors, which are configurable options in Cisco IOS:

- **Ordered delivery**—The LSR advertises a label only if it either is the egress LSR for the FEC or has already received for the FEC a label from its neighbor.

- **Independent delivery**—The LSR sends labels for its routes as soon as possible, without waiting to receive a label from downstream.

- **Unsolicited delivery**—Labels are sent to upstream peers whether they ask for them or not. This is the default in packet networks. (*Downstream* means closer to the destination; *upstream* means further from the destination.)

- **On-demand delivery**—The LSR sends a label only when asked for it by its upstream neighbor. Looking from source to destination, labels are requested as the packet flows downstream, hence the name. On-demand delivery potentially preserves label space because labels are not created unless a route to a given destination is actually used. On-demand delivery is the default in ATM networks.

- **Liberal retention mode**—The LSR retains all labels received from all neighbors. If paths need to change, this can improve convergence time.

- **Conservative retention mode**—To save memory, the LSR retains labels from a neighbor only if it is a next hop for the FEC.

Traffic Engineering

Traffic Engineering (TE) is one of the oldest arts in networking. It involves calculating and configuring paths through a network so as to use bandwidth efficiently. This strategy started in voice networks many years ago after engineers noticed that traffic load varied during the day. This insight coincided with the still-pertinent revelation that networks are expensive and need to use bandwidth in a cost-effective way. In circuit-switched networks, TE is automated and is done using offline tools. The results are downloaded to the switches and provide deterministic paths for different destinations.

In IP networks, there are several major reasons to engineer traffic:

- **Link congestion**—A well-known issue in IP networks is that IGP best paths may be overutilized while alternate paths are either underutilized or not utilized at all.

  For example, in Figure 4-5, the link between C and D is never used to forward traffic from A to E. All the packets go through B, which is the path with fewer hops (or the least path cost). An IGP can be prompted to use a path with more hops by including bandwidth as one of the link metrics for SPF calculation, but this is an approximate science and one that has no notion of congestion. TE asks a different question: What is the best path to a destination with X Mbps free?

- **Load balancing**—The common example given to explain the requirement for TE is a network with three transatlantic links, each with a different capacity. Again, standard IP routing only allows a very blunt solution, in which traffic is load balanced equally across each path. Traffic cannot be balanced across unequal paths. (The IGP will ignore the alternate routes because they are longer.) In Figure 4-6, data between A and F can be equally load balanced across the top and bottom paths, but this does not take into account the different link sizes between B and D and between C and D. The {10, 40} notation at the top of Figure 4-6 means that there are two segments on the path: The first has a link bandwidth of 10 Mbps, the second a bandwidth of 40 Mbps.

- **Link protection**—If there is a path or device failure along the primary LSP, routing protocols have to rerun the full SPF calculation before traffic can be forwarded again. This can take several seconds. Figure 4-7 shows this scenario, with failure on a primary link.

Figure 4-5   *Fish Problem*

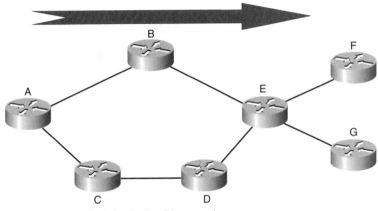

All traffic from A to F and A to G flows across Path A - B - E.

Path A - C - D - E is unused.

Figure 4-6   *Load-Balancing Problem*

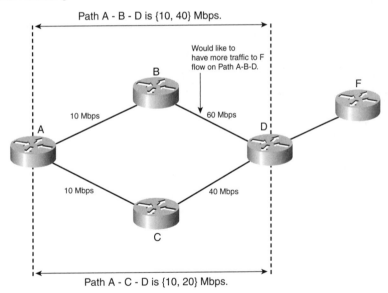

Path A - B - D is {10, 40} Mbps.

Would like to have more traffic to F flow on Path A-B-D.

Path A - C - D is {10, 20} Mbps.

Figure 4-7   *Link Protection Problem*

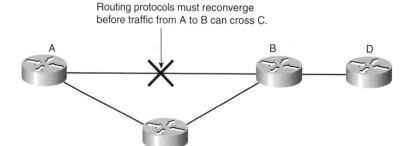

MPLS TE gives network operators a way to solve the problems described in Figures 4-5 through 4-7. TE involves building an LSP called a *tunnel* through the MPLS core. Any packet injected into the start of the tunnel (called the *headend*) will always be forwarded along the same path before popping out the other end. Unlike IP strict source routing, which can also provide a determinate path through the network, TE reserves bandwidth for the tunnel on each LSR.

The operation is as follows and is illustrated in Figure 4-8:

1   Routers run a link-state routing protocol, which also includes an extension that uses reservable link bandwidth as a metric. TE requires link-state routing so that each LSR can have a complete network topology as the basis for calculating the best path for a tunnel. Both IS-IS and OSPF have the necessary extensions for TE.

2   Router A in Figure 4-8, the tunnel headend, runs a modified form of SPF, called Constrained Shortest Path First (CSPF) and determines the best path to G based on available bandwidth. In Figure 4-8, Router A wants a path with 40 Mbps available. Router A uses CSPF and finds the path to be A – C – D – E – G. (The links through B are slow and congested.) As link utilization conditions change, the CSPF algorithm may give different results for the same destination, but that's the whole point.

3   The headend uses RSVP to build the tunnels. The headend sends a PATH message to the far end of the tunnel, represented in Figure 4-8. The RSVP message follows the intended path of the tunnel defined by CSPF.

4   Each LSR along the path checks whether it could allocate the requested bandwidth to the tunnel and updates the RSVP payload accordingly.

5   The remote endpoint sends an RSVP RESV message back along the tunnel path.

6   When it receives the RESV message, each LSR along the path reserves the bandwidth and allocates a label for the tunnel. The label data is communicated to the upstream LSR in the RSVP message, which is represented in Figure 4-8.

7 A tunnel path still needs to be included in the routing tables before a router can use them. You can do this with simple static routes on the headend router, or by announcing it through the IGP as a directly connected path. Policy routing is a third option. Note that TE does not do this final step for you automatically.

8 The tunnel is ready for use. The new topology is shown in Figure 4-9, with the label values used at each hop on the LSP.

Figure 4-8   *RSVP Tunnel Setup*

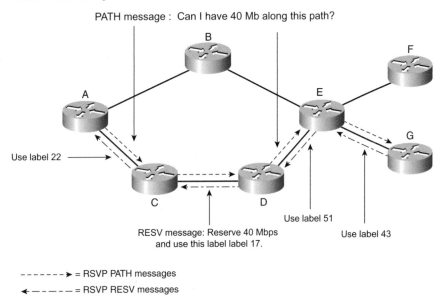

Figure 4-9   *40-Mbps Tunnel Established*

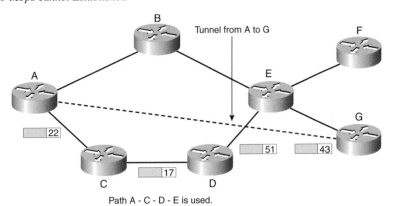

MPLS TE helps solve the three problems listed previously, as follows:

- **Link congestion**—This is the most obvious one. Network administrators can build tunnels across less-utilized paths and route traffic along them. Figure 4-9 shows that the traffic will now flow on the previously unused A – C – D – E path. With less traffic on them, previously congested paths become (hopefully) decongested.

- **Load balancing**—This is fixed thanks to an improvement in the TE implementation, which has 16 hash buckets for paths to a single destination. These buckets are allocated according to bandwidth, thus providing a proportional load-balancing capability. Figure 4-10 shows that two tunnels now exist between A and F. Router A sees that each tunnel has a different bandwidth and load balances traffic to A accordingly.

- **Link protection**—More recently, new knobs have been added to MPLS TE that allow backup paths to be defined. You can preconfigure a backup LSP at any point along the tunnel path, which the traffic will use if a link failure occurs on the protected LSR. The trick behind this is that the backup LSR imposes a new label that corresponds to the backup LSP along a different path. Just as with a normal tunnel, the label is popped at the penultimate LSR, thereby revealing the original label, which allows the packet to be threaded back into the original LSP. Figure 4-11 shows an example. A backup tunnel from A – C – B protects the A – B link. When it fails, packets use this alternate LSP.

Figure 4-10 *Tunnel Load Balancing*

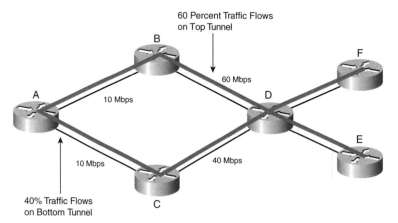

Figure 4-11   *Link Protection*

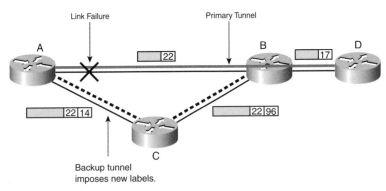

MPLS-TE Cisco IOS Configuration

MPLS-TE tunnels are easy to configure, even if there are many parameters you can tweak to control behavior.

Example 4-1 shows the global and per-interface commands for switches along the tunnel path, including the tail.

Example 4-1   *MPLS-TE Tunnel Midpoints*

```
!Enable TE globally
mpls traffic-eng tunnels

!Enable TE on all relevant interfaces
interface POS4/1/1
   ...
  mpls traffic-eng tunnels
  ip rsvp bandwidth 10000 10000

! TE compatible OSPF
router ospf 100
  mpls traffic-eng router-id Loopback0
  mpls traffic-eng area 0
```

The **ip rsvp** command in Example 4-1 reserves a total amount of bandwidth on this interface for all MPLS-TE tunnels. The values used may vary from one interface to another. As PATH messages arrive, this pool of bandwidth is consumed. However, these interface reservations are static. If there is not enough, or too much, bandwidth on the interface for the actual traffic, the network administrator has to manually reconfigure the **rsvp** statements all along the tunnel path. The **autobandwidth** option dynamically adjusts tunnel bandwidth by monitoring traffic and establishing a new LSP if necessary. This is very desirable for dynamic sizing and resizing of the network based on traffic pattern changes.

In addition to the global and interface commands in Example 4-1, the headend needs a tunnel interface, as shown in Example 4-2. The **tunnel mpls traffic-eng autoroute** option in Example 4-2 tells the router to automatically add the tunnel to the routing table as a directly connected interface. CSPF will run to find the path to 10.1.1.1.

Example 4-2 *MPLS-TE Headend*

```
interface Tunnel0
  ip unnumbered Loopback0
  tunnel mode mpls traffic-eng
  tunnel source Loopback0
  tunnel destination 10.1.1.1
  tunnel mpls traffic-eng autoroute
  tunnel mpls traffic-eng path-option 10 dynamic
```

You can see from Examples 4-1 and 4-2 that MPLS-TE tunnels are bidirectional. The tunnel starting from the router in Example 4-2 is a one-way path. The tail router has no tunnel LSP back, but one could, of course, be configured.

Layer 3 VPN Services (RFC 2547)

Layer 3 VPN is without doubt the MPLS application that has caused the most ink to flow. RFC 2547 proposes a peer architecture in which customer edge (CE) routers exchange routes with service provider edge routers (universally called PE, for provider edge). Unlike a Frame Relay or ATM VPN service, there are no point-to-point connections between customer sites.

Figure 4-12 shows an MPLS-VPN reference architecture, with two different VPNs. Customer sites have a CE router that connects to service provider PE routers. PE devices are connected by LSRs. A single PE can peer with CEs that belong to different customers, as is the case for PE A. To provide backup routes, a CE can also peer with different PEs that belong to the same, or even to different, service providers. Sites in a VPN can communicate only with other sites in the same VPN. Standard IP traffic runs over the CE-PE link, so this link cannot be shared with other customer traffic. (By the way, that is a very important point: The CE and PE do not exchange labels, or labeled packets.) This is identical to existing Layer 2 VPN networks, so an MPLS-VPN service requires no architecture change to the customer's network.

Even though each site has just one link into the service provider cloud, thanks to the MPLS-VPN architecture, there can be a full-mesh connectivity between the sites. In fact, the intersite IP topology can be of arbitrary complexity. MPLS-VPN implementations default to full mesh and must be constrained to provide a more hierarchical connectivity model, such as hub and spoke.

Figure 4-12   *MPLS-VPN Reference Architecture*

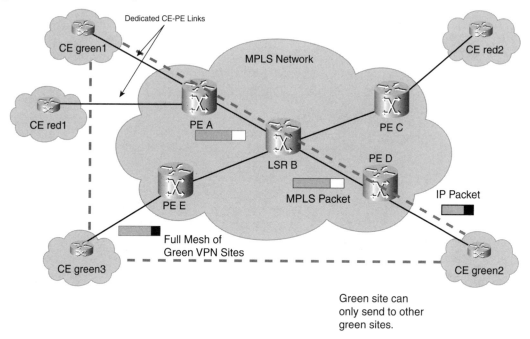

The MPLS-VPN model makes it easier to route between CEs, compared to the costly approach of using dedicated WAN connections between sites and the relative difficulty of routing effectively over such point-to-point networks.

For CEs to communicate, the service provider needs to exchange (private and possibly overlapping) customer IP routes and carry packets to those routes across its network. MPLS provides a solution that supports customer address-space independence using a forwarding mechanism that uses a two-label hierarchy in which the inner label identifies the VPN and the outer label identifies the destination PE device. RFC 2547 mandates the use of the Border Gateway Protocol (BGP) to exchange prefixes and labels between PE devices and introduces some new attributes to provide this functionality.

Speaking of BGP, how are customer routes advertised in an MPLS-VPN network? Figure 4-13 shows that several different routing protocols are used. The following sequence explains the operation behind Figure 4-13.

Figure 4-13 *Routing in an MPLS VPN Network*

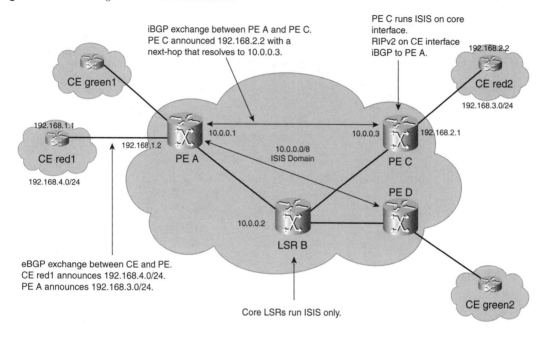

1 CE red1 advertises the 192.168.4.0/24 prefix to PE A. A CE can use static or dynamic routing (RIP, eBGP, or OSPF) to exchange routes with a PE. CE red1 runs eBGP. CE green2 uses RIPv2.

2 PE A imports the prefixes announced by the CE into the route table for this VPN. If other interfaces on the same PE belong to the same VPN, routes are announced to the local peers. Each VPN has its own routing table.

3 PE A uses iBGP to announce reachability for each of its attached customer sites. In Figure 4-13, PE A has one iBGP session with PE C for the red VPN and another with PE D for the green VPN. PE C imports the routes into the routing table used for the red VPN, and PE D imports the routes for the green VPN. The PEs are in a full iBGP mesh and each can run many different VPNs.

4 PE C announces the 192.168.4.0 route to CE red2 using RIPv2. A **show ip route** command on CE red2 will show 192.168.4.0/24 with a next hop of 192.168.2.1, which is the address of PE C. Similarly, CE red1 has an entry for 192.168.3.0 with a next hop of 192.168.1.2. PE A's routing table for the red VPN has an entry for 192.168.4.0 through 192.168.1.1 and another entry for 191.168.3.0 with a next hop that points to PE C. This is where the MPLS-VPN magic occurs. PE C announces itself as the next hop for the 192.168.3.0 route. Because this is a BGP route, PE A will use another lookup to find the route and, this time, the next hop will be 10.0.0.2, which is the LSR.

5 When traffic must go between sites, the CE forwards IP packets to the PE as it would to any other router. Figure 4-14 shows a packet going from CE green1 to CE green2, following this sequence:

  a. PE A identifies the next hop (PE D) for this packet as a BGP neighbor.

  b. PE A first imposes a label, 22, that will identify the VPN routing table to PE D. This label was advertised by the neighbor, PE D, during the exchange of BGP prefixes, which happened some time before the preceding step.

  c. The packet must now travel across the MPLS network, so PE A imposes another label, 96, that identifies the next-hop LSR on the IGP path to PE D. This label was advertised by the downstream LSR (LSR B) from 10.0.0.2.

  d. Each LSR in the core swaps labels and forwards the packet as normal toward PE D. The penultimate hop pops the outer label. In Figure 4-14, there is only one hop to the egress LSR, so LSR B removes the outer label.

  e. PE D uses the remaining label, 22, to identify which VPN routing table to use for the packet, and then pops the label from the packet.

  f. PE D does an IP lookup in the VPN routing table to find the outgoing interface and then forwards the IP packet to CE green2, which will route it to its destination.

Figure 4-14 *Packet Flow in MPLS-VPN Network*

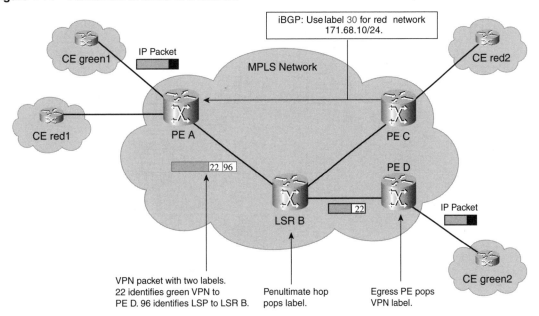

It is very important to understand that the LSRs have no visibility of the VPN traffic. They forward labeled traffic along LSPs established by whatever routing protocol is running in the service provider core. Of course, this IGP can be completely different from the IGPs running on the CE-PE links.

MPLS-VPN Attributes

Defining an MPLS VPN is harder than you might expect. For the longest time, the Cisco IOS implementation had no single number or string that would define a VPN in a network. Fortunately, a VPN ID has since been introduced to address this problem.

Note that every VPN on a Cisco router has the following attributes:

- Dedicated interfaces, which can be logical or physical
- Dedicated routing table
- A local name and, optionally, a numeric ID
- Rules that determine how VPN routes are advertised to peer routers

Route reachability within an MPLS VPN is established through the selective import of BGP routes. Several new extended attributes have been added to BGP in accordance with the specifications in RFC 2547. Figure 4-15 shows how PEs exchange these attributes.

Figure 4-15 *iBGP Attribute Exchange*

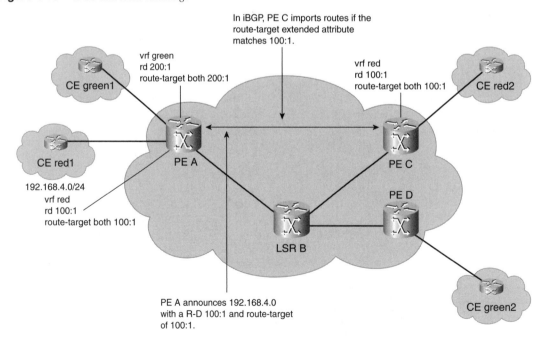

The following are the most important BGP attributes:

- **route-target**—Each PE defines a numeric value, called a route-target, that is associated to all the routes it exports to its BGP peers. PEs also define another value used to filter incoming routes. In order for a route to be accepted, the route-target export value must match the import value at the receiving device. Note that the import and export values do not have to match, which allows topologies other than full mesh to be defined. The route-targets are carried in BGP updates. In Figure 4-15, PE A uses 100:1 for both export and import route-targets. PE C uses the same values, so routes from the red VPN sites will be exchanged between these two routers.

- **route-distinguisher**—A BGP attribute that is appended to private routes to make them globally unique. Consider a case in which two networks each use the 10.0.0.0/24 prefix and connect to the same service provider PE. The PE uses different virtual routing tables because the prefixes belong to different customers, so there is no conflict in address space when importing the routes into the service provider network. Now every PE that connects to a CE in the customer's VPN must receive reachability information for the 10.0.0.0/24 prefix. The PE announces the route to all its PE peers, but only those with the same VPN and matching route-target import it. The route-distinguisher (RD) is included in the routing exchange to make sure that each BGP peer treats the prefixes as belonging to different networks. Returning to Figure 4-15, the red VPN uses an RD of 100:1; the green VPN is configured for 200:1. Although not necessary, having the same RD throughout a VPN is better, for operational simplicity.

MPLS-VPNs require private routing tables in each VPN so that they can peer with the CEs in the different domains. In Cisco jargon, these are called *VRFs*, as shown in Figure 4-16, and the standard routing table is called the *global routing table*. In the example given that described the operation of Figure 4-13, the VPN routing tables referenced in the text are VRFs.

VRFs are populated by routing processes associated with each VPN. Note that in other implementations, separate processes run in each VPN, but Cisco IOS does a mix of both. BGP, for example, is a single process across the whole router, but there are independent OSPF processes for each VPN. LFIBs are populated using information from VRFs.

Even though each VPN on a PE router has its very own VRF, no VRFs are required on CE routers. (There is an optional exception to this called, rather unimaginatively, multi-VRF CE, but the basic RFC 2547 scenario requires no such thing.)

Figure 4-16 *VRFs*

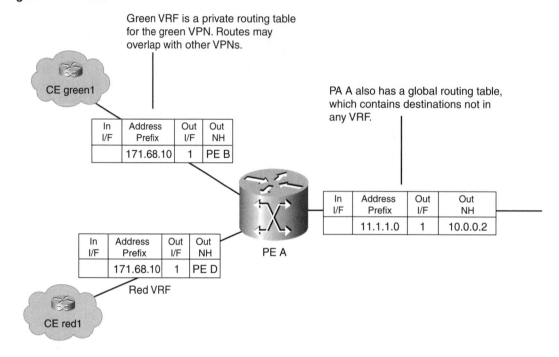

MPLS-VPN Cisco IOS Configuration

This section gives the extracts necessary to deploy a simple MPLS VPN. Example 4-3 is the configuration of a PE. The underlying network topology is the same as used in the examples in Chapter 3.

Example 4-3 *MPLS-VPN PE Configuration*

```
! Define a VRF for the VPN with route-target and r-ds
! R-T 101:1 is used for both import and export
ip vrf RED
 rd 101:1
 route-target both 101:1
interface Loopback0
 ip address 12.0.0.3 255.255.255.255
 no ip directed-broadcast

! Add each CE-PE link to the VRF
! Remember the IP address must be added after the VRF name
interface Ethernet1/0/0
 ip vrf forwarding RED
 ip address 11.1.4.1 255.255.255.255
 no ip directed-broadcast
```

Example 4-3   *MPLS-VPN PE Configuration (Continued)*

```
! Core facing links
interface FastEthernet0/0/0
 ip address 192.168.1.3 255.255.255.0
 tag-switching ip
 no ip directed-broadcast
 full-duplex
 no cdp enable

! Configure iBGP to the 2 remote PEs
router bgp 101
 neighbor 12.0.0.1 remote-as 101
 neighbor 12.0.0.1 update-source Loopback0
 neighbor 12.0.0.2 remote-as 101
 neighbor 12.0.0.2 update-source Loopback0
 !
 address-family ipv4 vrf RED
 redistribute connected
 redistribute static
 no auto-summary
 no synchronization
 exit-address-family
 !
 address-family vpnv4
 neighbor 12.0.0.1 activate
 neighbor 12.0.0.1 send-community extended
 neighbor 12.0.0.2 activate
 neighbor 12.0.0.2 send-community extended
 exit-address-family
 !
```

Example 4-3 shows the first PE configuration. There are three basic sections. The first global command sets up a VRF for the VPN, with some name, route-distinguisher, and route-target values. Then, every CE-PE link needs to be added to the VRF. There is no VRF on core-facing links, which simply do label switching. The final section is iBGP, which in this example established two sessions to peers at 12.0.0.1 and 12.0.0.2. Each VPN has its own **address-family** configuration, where you can configure which networks to announce and so forth. The **VPNv4 address-family** establishes the peers as being MPLS-VPN savvy, so BGP peers understand the necessary extended communities.

Example 4-4 gives the LSR configuration, which, as you can see, is very straightforward.

Example 4-4   *MPLS LSR Configuration*

```
! Core facing links
interface FastEthernet1/0/1
 ip address 192.168.1.4 255.255.255.0
 tag-switching ip
 no ip directed-broadcast
 full-duplex
 no cdp enable
```

continues

Example 4-4 *MPLS LSR Configuration (Continued)*

```
interface FastEthernet2/0/1
ip address 192.168.4.2 255.255.255.0
tag-switching ip
no ip directed-broadcast
full-duplex
no cdp enable
```

Example 4-5 gives the PE Configuration at the other side of the network.

Example 4-5 *MPLS-VPN Egress PE Configuration*

```
! Route-target and RD values must match. VRF names don't have to
! but better if it does
ip vrf RED
 rd 101:1
 route-target both 101:1

interface Loopback0
 ip address 12.0.0.1 255.255.255.255
 no ip directed-broadcast

! egress CE-PE link
interface Ethernet1/0/0
 ip vrf forwarding RED
 ip address 11.2.4.1 255.255.255.255
 no ip directed-broadcast

! Core facing links
interface FastEthernet0/0/0
 ip address 192.168.4.1 255.255.255.0
 tag-switching ip
 no ip directed-broadcast
 full-duplex
 no cdp enable


router bgp 101
 neighbor 12.0.0.2 remote-as 101
 neighbor 12.0.0.2 update-source Loopback0
 neighbor 12.0.0.3 remote-as 101
 neighbor 12.0.0.3 update-source Loopback0
 !
 address-family ipv4 vrf RED
 redistribute connected
 redistribute static
 no auto-summary
 no synchronization
 exit-address-family
 !
 address-family vpnv4
 neighbor 12.0.0.2 activate
 neighbor 12.0.0.2 send-community extended
```

Example 4-5   *MPLS-VPN Egress PE Configuration (Continued)*

```
neighbor 12.0.0.3 activate
neighbor 12.0.0.3 send-community extended
exit-address-family
!
```

NOTE   **ping**, **telnet**, and **traceroute** have VRF options so that they can be used between PEs. Why don't the standard commands work? Remember that a VRF represents an entirely private routing space. Commands issued from the Cisco IOS command line use the global routing table. On a PE, this means that all the LSRs are reachable, but no device in a VPN address space is. Therefore, these commands need a new parameter to tell the router which VPN to originate a **ping** in, for example. Of course, a **ping** within a VRF, or from any CE, will not see any LSR, because those are in a different address space. This makes sense enough in theory, but can take some getting used to in practice.

MPLS-VPN architecture provides full-mesh configuration by default. In other words, a PE forwards traffic directly to its destination. It turns out that some enterprise networks need to change this behavior. A common reason is a security policy that requires all sites in a certain area to forward traffic through a regional hub, which might have some expensive virus-checking package for e-mail, or perhaps needs to do NAT on traffic between sites. Whatever the reason, MPLS VPNs can be deployed as hub-and-spoke topologies by using route-targets.

If a spoke imports routes only from a hub, then traffic will in turn flow through the hub to get somewhere else. (Remember, PEs forward to BGP next hops.) Because a hub must know all the routes, it imports from all spokes. Spokes must never import from each other. This scenario is shown in Figure 4-17, with correct use of route-targets.

Figure 4-17 *Hub-and-Spoke Topology*

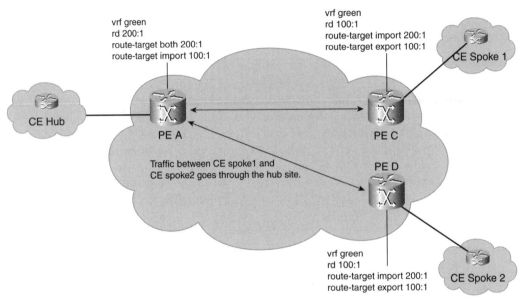

Examples 4-6 through 4-8 show how to configure the route-targets to match the figure.

Example 4-6 *PE A – Hub*

```
!Hub imports from Spokes
vrf green
rd 200:1
route-target both 200:1
route-target import 100:1
```

Example 4-7 *PE B – Spoke*

```
!All spokes import from Hub
vrf greenrd 100:1route-target import 200:1route-target export 100:1
```

Example 4-8 *PE C – Spoke*

```
!And export to Hub
vrf greenrd 100:1route-target import 200:1route-target export 100:1
```

Although the details will not be provided here, route-targets are also used to build extranets. An extranet is a VPN with limited reachability of destinations inside other VPNs.

MPLS QoS

One of the principle virtues of MPLS in a broadband environment is its ready support for quality of service. MPLS QoS is distinct from IP QoS models, so it is good to understand how these models are mapped from IP to MPLS domains and back again. Therefore, this section concentrates on classification and assumes that link efficiency, shaping, and all the other QoS mechanisms "just work" in an MPLS network.

QoS in MPLS Packet Headers

Recall that the MPLS packet header has a 3-bit EXP field, which indicates the class of traffic to which a packet belongs. In QoS terms, this is called the *per-hop behavior* (PHB) and is applied by each hop crossed by the packet, as the name implies. Each hop may define a different PHB for each traffic class.

The EXP field has the happy property of being exactly the same length as the IP precedence (PREC) field. Therefore, mapping an IP precedence to the MPLS domain is very straightforward: You simply copy the three IP PREC bits to the EXP field. However, there are two complications to this otherwise simple picture. The following sections discuss each in turn.

Complication 1: DSCP

The DiffServ model uses 6 bits of the IP TOS field to define DiffServ Code Points (DSCPs), which distinguish how packets are to be treated by the network (their class). DiffServ is defined in RFC 2474 ("Definition of the Differentiated Services Field [DS Field] in the IPv4 and IPv6 Headers") and RFC 2475 ("An Architecture for Differentiated Services").

RFC 2474 defines two PHBs:

- **Default**—A simple best-effort class, with a DSCP value of 000000. Packets with no defined DSCP are mapped to the default class for best-effort service.

- **Class Selector**—Provides for backward compatibility with 3-bit IP PREC classes. Basically, it defines a DCSP of *XXX*000, where *XXX* represent the PREC bits.

The two most significant PHBs are Assured Forwarding (AF) and Expedited Forwarding (EF).

RFC 2597 defines Assured Forwarding as follows:

The AF PHB group provides delivery of IP packets in four independently forwarded AF classes. Within each AF class, an IP packet can be assigned one of three different levels of drop precedence.

This gives a total of 12 different permutations of DSCP values out of the total 63 possible in the IP TOS field.

Classes are commonly written as AF*ny*, where *n* is the class and *y* is the drop probability within the class. AF11 has a lower drop probability (so a better service) than AF13, for example.

It is up to the network administrators to define which AF classes they want to use for different traffic types and to configure the routers to allocate resources appropriately, which means using things like WRED for drop probability and CBWFQ for bandwidth allocation. Public networks sometimes publish their DSCP mappings on the Internet.

RFC 2598 defines Expedited Forwarding. EF offers a leased-line type of service, with strict guarantees for latency, jitter, packet delivery, and so forth.

NOTE   After the preceding and rather long digression, how are DSCP values to be mapped to MPLS? The simplest way is to use the same model as for IP PREC. For many networks, this is sufficient, because they only have three to five traffic classes anyway. MPLS vendors often have some suggestions, such as AF31 ≥ EXP 3, but there is no actual standard to follow. Each administrator is free to come up with whichever mapping works best for their applications.

Complication 2: ATM

The second big exception concerns ATM. There is an MPLS shim header for ATM MPLS networks, shown in Figure 4-3, where the label is carried in the VPI/VCI fields, leaving no room for EXP bits. The solution is to use different LSPs for each class of service. A gold service would have one set of labels, and each LSR would prioritize that traffic over cells with bronze-labeled cells.

Tunnels and Pipes

In a world already rich in acronyms and definitions, MPLS QoS adds a few of its own! You'll see one of the main reasons for this has it roots in penultimate hop popping (PHP), as discussed in the following list:

- Because of PHP, the last LSR on an LSP does not see the MPLS EXP field, so how does it know which class to use?

- Should the IP TOS value change if the MPLS EXP changed as the packet crossed the network, perhaps because the packet was reclassified as out-of-class due to a source sending too fast for the traffic contract?

Fortunately, MPLS support for DiffServ (notably in RFC 3270, "Multi-Protocol Label Switching [MPLS] Support of Differentiated Services") adds different models to account for the various places that labels can be popped and how to relay marking information between domains. First, the following list qualifies the different kinds of LSPs used with the DiffServ model:

- **E-LSP**— An LSP where the PHB is defined by the EXP field only.

- **L-LSP**— An LSP where the PHB is defined by both the EXP and Label fields. ATM MPLS networks use L-LSPs (with no EXP). The rationale behind the added complexity of L-LSPs is that they offer more than the eight PHBs possible with the 3-bit EXP field.

- **Uniform Tunnel mode**—Any changes to a packet's DSCP are permanent, as shown in Figure 4-18 and discussed in the following list:

    1 A packet arrives at LSR A with a DSCP setting of 3. The switch policy determines that the appropriate EXP value for this class is also 3.

    2 The packet is forwarded across the core toward its destination.

    3 LSR B reclassifies the packet into another class and sets the EXP to 4.

    4 LSR C, the penultimate LSR, pops the MPLS label and sets the TOS value to 4, to match the change in the MPLS core. If there is a label stack, then the changes *are* propagated to the inner EXP field and the next label would have its EXP set to 4.

    5 LSR E receives an IP packet with DSCP setting of 4.

- **Pipe Tunnel mode**—Unlike Uniform Tunnel mode, changes to DSCP are not permanent, as shown in Figure 4-19 and discussed in the following list:

    1 A packet arrives at LSR A with a DSCP setting of 3. The switch policy determines that the appropriate EXP value for this class is also 3.

    2 The packet is forwarded across the core toward its destination.

    3 LSR B reclassifies the packet into another class and sets the EXP to 4.

    4 When LSR D transmits the packet, the DSCP setting is still 3. However, if there is a stack of MPLS labels, the changes *are* propagated to the inner EXP field. But, even in this case, the IP settings are never modified.

    There is a subtlety with Pipe Tunnel mode, which is shown in Figure 4-19. LSR D ordinarily does not see the EXP values because of PHP on C. However, it needs to in a Pipe Tunnel so that it can apply the correct PHB for the packet. To reconcile this conflicting state of affairs, the egress LSR uses a concept called *Explicit Null*, which causes the penultimate-hop router to no longer pop the outer label when forwarding frames to its upstream neighbor. Explicit Null labels are not needed if the egress LSR is going to receive a label anyway (which happens with MPLS VPN, which uses two labels, and even if the outer label is popped, the PE always receives a labeled packet).

- **Short Pipe Tunnel mode**—The egress LSR also uses the IP TOS to apply PHB.

Figure 4-18 *Uniform Tunnel Mode*

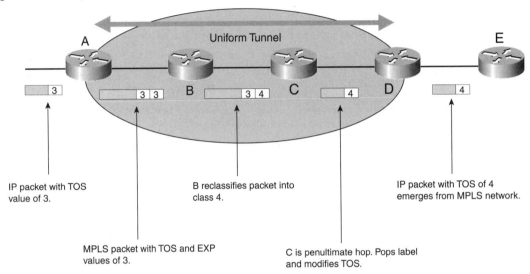

IP packet with TOS value of 3.

B reclassifies packet into class 4.

IP packet with TOS of 4 emerges from MPLS network.

MPLS packet with TOS and EXP values of 3.

C is penultimate hop. Pops label and modifies TOS.

Figure 4-19 *Pipe Tunnel Mode*

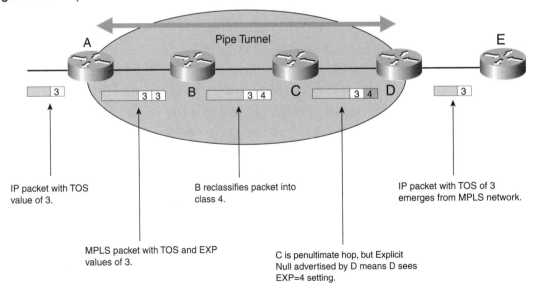

IP packet with TOS value of 3.

B reclassifies packet into class 4.

IP packet with TOS of 3 emerges from MPLS network.

MPLS packet with TOS and EXP values of 3.

C is penultimate hop, but Explicit Null advertised by D means D sees EXP=4 setting.

DiffServ-Aware Traffic Engineering

If TE can guarantee bandwidth on links, is there need to worry about QoS anymore? Well, think about what would happen if voice and data traffic were to use the same network. With the description given previously in this chapter, there is no way to build tunnels that assign bandwidth for different classes of traffic. LSRs reserve a single pool on an interface and share this between all the tunneled packets.

DiffServ-aware TE (DS-TE) adds the concept of classes to TE. Simply put, LSRs now advertise pools of bandwidth per class type and the RSVP process is modified to check that adding a new tunnel does not affect tunnels in other classes.

DS-TE, just like regular TE, is a control plane reservation mechanism. You still need to use queuing and discard mechanisms to enforce the traffic classes on the data plane.

Summary

This chapter is by no means an exhaustive discussion of MPLS. There are entire library shelves dedicated to the topic. However, it does give an overview of what goes on in an MPLS network, especially the use and distribution of labels and how to use them to build TE tunnels and VPNs.

Note that a big advantage of MPLS is the interoperability with IP services, as shown here with quality of service. The EXP bits allow the same QoS policies to be applied to MPLS packets as are applied to IP packets. Chapter 5 looks at how VPN services are offered on broadband interfaces.

In this chapter, you learn about the following topics:

- Architecture Overview of MPLS VPN in Broadband Networks

- The Role of the PE and How to Map Subscribers to VRFs

- Introduction to Virtual Home Gateways and Multi-VRF CE

- Detailed Examples of Configuration and Monitoring for Three Different PE
  Deployment Scenarios: Direct Termination, Two-Box Solution, and Multi-VRF CE

CHAPTER 5

Introduction to MPLS-Based Access VPN Architectures

This chapter gets into the central topic of this book: MPLS-VPN architectures for broadband and why they look the way they do. The chapter is divided into roughly two different sections. The first looks at how the different types of broadband traffic are mapped to an MPLS VPN, and the side effects of connecting potentially many hundreds of thousands of subscribers to a PE. There are two main design options: direct termination and two-box solutions. Direct termination is the typical design for bridged access. PPP architectures are more complex, as usual, and can use either. To make things more digestible, this chapter avoids mentioning any features developed specifically for these architectures. The idea is to take what exists and see how far it can go.

In the second section, the chapter moves from the abstract to the concrete and shows Cisco IOS configurations and monitoring commands for Virtual Home Gateways, whether they use direct termination or two-box solutions. A complete solution involves more than is shown in this chapter: The configurations are deliberately simple. Chapter 6, "Wholesale MPLS-VPN Related Service Features," goes into the full details of VRF-aware features, especially regarding how to integrate RADIUS and DHCP into the solution.

Architecture Overview of an MPLS-Based Access VPN

An MPLS PE is the point at which the private customer network and the service provider network meet. At a very basic level, a broadband MPLS PE links subscribers who connect over a variety of different access networks to an MPLS network. Figure 5-1 gives some idea of the sheer number of different types of broadband domains that exist.

From a protocol perspective, the PE in Figure 5-1 takes IP traffic from the different access encapsulations, such as PPP, and inserts it into an MPLS VPN. This is a significant and fundamental point. For the PE, broadband access is just a different collection of slightly exotic Layer 2 interfaces. The rest of the MPLS network neither knows nor cares that IP traffic traversed a Routed Bridge Encapsulation (RBE) interface, for example.

Figure 5-1 *Broadband Access to MPLS Network*

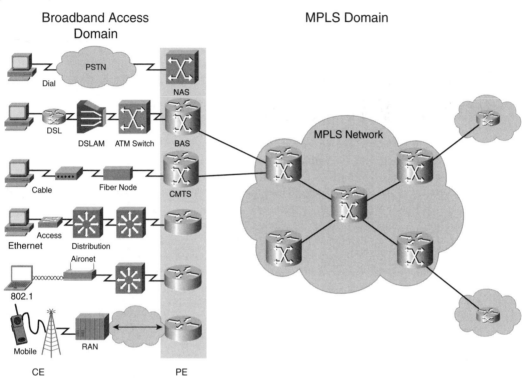

Although there are some important implementation-related details, there are no architecture-level changes to the MPLS-VPN model itself. For example, there are no specific LSPs required to carry broadband traffic, so special labels and new signaling protocols are not required. (There are quite enough of those already.) MPLS TE and QoS work just as before.

What do things look like for broadband subscribers? Well, the fact that a VPN service is delivered over an MPLS network is more or less irrelevant to end users. However, the service provider does see a difference: The network it uses to deliver VPN services is now based on Layer 3. Mapping policy to subscriber traffic is that much easier, to cite one example, because the service provider's routers can look directly at subscriber packets at the network edge, instead of simply tunneling data blindly.

If life continues as before for the MPLS core and other PEs, what does change? Simply put, the PE has to do a lot more work.

The rest of this section looks at the additional work a PE must take on, first generally, then for DSL, cable, and Ethernet broadband access. Then, the Virtual Home Gateway is introduced, with usage scenarios for cable and DSL.

The Role of the PE

Figure 5-2 shows broadband access in slightly more detail for the different types of VPN. As you can see, with the DSL and cable broadband topologies, there is no mandatory external CE device. The function can be part of the client. This has some interesting side effects, because many MPLS-VPN designs assume there is some Layer 3 intelligence at the remote site for either QoS or routing purposes. This is not necessarily true in the case of broadband networks, so this is another source of extra work for the PE, which now has to make up for the lack of CE at the far end of the broadband link.

Figure 5-2   *Broadband Access Topologies—Where's the CE?*

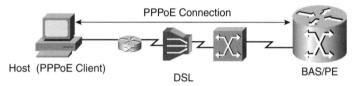

Host (PPPoE Client)   DSL   BAS/PE

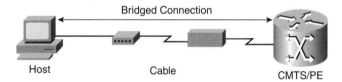

Host   Cable   CMTS/PE

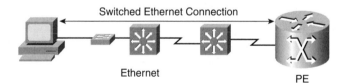

Ethernet   PE

Of course, CPE is still deployed on the customer premises in some situations:

- Site VPN connections use a classic MPLS-VPN topology, with fully fledged routers as CE.

- Residential broadband routers fall somewhere in between. They can typically run a routing protocol (often something as simple as RIP), even if they are most often configured to simply forward to a default route. These devices do not have any support for IP QoS or for other, more advanced features such as DHCP relay. Furthermore, unlike a standard CE, they are often not managed by the service provider. For this reason, they are, at best, very limited CE.

- With Ethernet, there are two very different scenarios. The first involves using a very simple Layer 2 switch as CPE. In this case, there is no external CE router. However, and this is the second case, an increasing number of switches have considerable Layer 3 intelligence and can be considered as a CE device, complete with routing protocols and Layer 3 ACLs.

The first problem to solve is how to map subscribers to VPNs. Subscriber interfaces must be configured to be part of some VRF to belong to a VPN. With the notable exception of PPP, this is done by adding the VRF name to the Cisco IOS interface configuration for the subscriber access line. PPP is more flexible, because the virtual private dial-up network (VPDN) domain name can be mapped to the subscriber VRF, with the result that the VPN binding can be completely dynamic. This can be a significant operational advantage and should be considered when deciding on the type of access protocol to use.

Mapping Cable Subscribers to VRFs

Cable is something of an interesting case. The bare-bones configuration is simply to map a cable subinterface to a VRF. That way, all the subscribers behind a cable router CPE are in the same VPN. Traffic from hosts can reach other destinations on the VPN but cannot, of course, reach the service provider network, which is in a different address space. However, recall from Chapter 2, "Delivering Broadband Access Today: An Access Technologies Primer," that cable networks make extensive use of secondary addressing to separate the management and customer networks. Cable modems are on a different subnet from subscriber devices and need to communicate with TFTP and TOD servers as part of the boot process. Simply putting the whole interface into a customer VPN breaks this reachability.

The solution is to use an MPLS extranet topology, which leaks routes from management subnets into each customer VPN. That way, the cable modems can still reach the provisioning servers. The details of this solution involve having a management VRF that exports routes with a certain route-target value. All interfaces that connect to the DHCP and other management servers are in this VRF. All other VRFs on the PE import and export routes from the management network by matching on the route-targets used in the management VRF. That way, all the servers are reachable from the subscriber interfaces, and the cable modems can get their addresses and configuration files.

Now that there is a solution for the cable modems themselves, static interface configuration is fine when all the subscriber traffic goes to the same ISP, but this is not always the case. In multiservice applications, video traffic might be in a different VPN. Or, different PCs in the same household might need to connect to different ISPs. In a DOCSIS 1.0–compliant network, there is no way to map different devices connected to the same cable router CPE, using the same SID, to different VPNs, except by using some form of addressing-based solution.

Using the SFIDs that are part of the DOCSIS 1.1 specification, it is possible to have multiple VPNs on the same cable interface. The idea is that the cable modem also has MPLS-VPN configuration information and sends traffic belonging to different VPNs with different flow IDs.

The cable modem termination system (CMTS)/PE is almost unchanged from a static configuration: It still uses the VRF-per-subinterface model. For the PE, the SFID provides a private L2 link, very like 802.1q or ATM PVCs.

Service flows were created for QoS profiles, so some overloading of configuration parameters is required to apply this to MPLS VPN. To start with, there must be a different DOCSIS configuration file for each cable modem. Each one of these files defines classifiers that map traffic to flow IDs. The classifiers themselves match on the source MAC addresses of CPE. Once it has classified traffic, the cable modem sends the VPN membership information using the MPLS-VPN Route-Distinguisher (RD) value in the vendor-specific portion of the DOCSIS Flow ID. The parameter is called the VPN Route Distinguisher.

The CMTS/PE looks at the DOCSIS frame to find the SFID, then looks at the RD value to identify the appropriate subinterface on which to receive the packet. Figure 5-3 shows this in operation.

Figure 5-3   *SFID to MPLS*

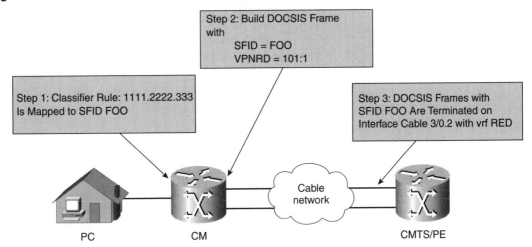

Architecturally, service flow mapping is a partial extension of the VPN to the CPE device. Unlike other variations on the theme, however, the following is true:

- There is no signaling on the PE-CE link: The cable-modem VPN memberships are part of its DOCSIS configuration file.

- There are no private addressing tables on the cable modem, so there is only a single address space.

In conclusion, although it is possible to deploy a somewhat dynamic cable solution, the provisioning is nontrivial because the cable modem must match MAC source addresses to SFIDs in the (rare) cases in which all the devices on the network on the customer premises are not on the same VPN.

Mapping Ethernet Subscribers to VRFs

Today, cable CPEs are nearly always dedicated to a single user or home. However, Ethernet deployments, especially in metro environments, involve CPEs that are shared between multiple customers. The classic example is a multitenant office building, with a 100-Mps Ethernet connection in the basement. The switch CPE delivers 10-Mbps ports to different customers, with each port being potentially connected to different networks, and hence must connect to different VPNs. In contrast to the cable SFID scenario, here the architecture requires VPN integrity to be preserved on the CPE because of the following:

- Each customer network needs a separate address space.

- The native Ethernet security model is such that strong Layer 3 separation can greatly help reduce security risks.

There are two solutions to this problem. The first involves putting each port into a separate VLAN and Layer 2 switching the VLAN to a PE device upstream, which maps the VLANs to VRFs. In the case of the first solution, the network between CE and PE is purely Layer 2. The second solution is to extend the VRFs to the CE. This solution provides separate address spaces and routing tables per VPN on the CPE itself, as shown in Figure 5-4. The difference in the two solutions is in the way packets are mapped from subscriber to trunk ports. With the first solution, they are bridged: All subscribers in a VLAN are on the same broadcast domain. With the second solution, IP is running on the CE and the packets are routed to the trunk VLANs.

Figure 5-4   *Multi-VRF CE*

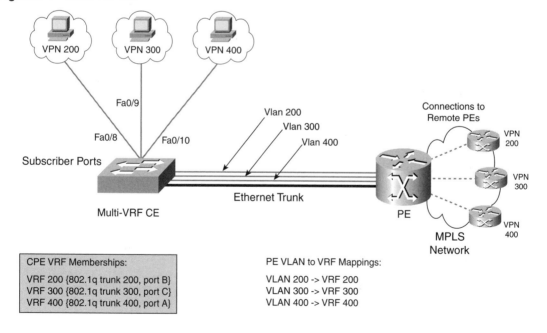

CPE VRF Memberships:

VRF 200 {802.1q trunk 200, port B}
VRF 300 {802.1q trunk 300, port C}
VRF 400 {802.1q trunk 400, port A}

PE VLAN to VRF Mappings:

VLAN 200 -> VRF 200
VLAN 300 -> VRF 300
VLAN 400 -> VRF 400

Referring again to Figure 5-4, there are no LSPs on the CE-PE link, nor is there any signaling used between these devices, and the CE has a dedicated PE-facing Layer 2 link for each VPN. The CE VRF contains both a LAN port for customer traffic and the WAN interface.

Tracing the ports in Figure 5-4 shows VRF membership clearly. Taking VPN 300 as an example, note the following:

- On the CPE, port Fa0/9 is dedicated to a site. This port is in VLAN 300.

- In the multi-VRF CE configuration used here, traffic from port Fa0/9, and any other ports in the same VPN, is 802.1q encapsulated and routed to the PE, which is the default router. In the more traditional switched architecture, traffic from port Fa0/9 would be Layer 2 forwarded to the PE, which would be the default router for the subscriber link. In both cases, the CE-PE link uses 802.1q.

- On the PE, interface Fa0/0.2 runs 802.1q encapsulation, terminates VLAN 300, and is in VRF 300.

This allows for the traffic from the subscriber port to be connected to the rest of the 300 VPN sites.

One important point to keep in mind is that this is a Layer 3 service. The end user is *not* buying a transparent Layer 2 connection between two Ethernet ports, but *is* buying an IP-VPN service, delivered over an Ethernet last-mile connection. In this case, the choice of last-mile technology is made by the service provider and is probably related to the equipment cost, bandwidth, availability of optical loops, and so forth. A lot of VPN collateral relating to Ethernet does in fact describe Layer 2 VPNs, so this distinction is important.

Unfortunately, this simple concept can go by different names, the most common being Multi-VRF CE or VRF-lite. This book uses *Multi-VRF CE* to mean something that relates to CPE only and *VRF-lite* as a more general term referring to the use of VRFs without an MPLS core. Chapter 7, "Implementing Network-Based Access VPNs Without MPLS," looks at other VRF-lite deployments.

Mapping DSL Subscribers to VRFs

DSL has three major access architectures. The first two are simple, the third one less so. The following sections discuss each in turn.

Routed Interfaces

The first architecture involves terminating routed RFC 2684–encapsulated packets. This is a classic MPLS-VPN configuration, where each subinterface is part of a VRF. Unlike the cable scenario, there is no issue with secondary addresses, because the site really must connect to the rest of the VPN and to nowhere else. If, say, a PC at a site sends a DHCP request to a remote server, the CE router plays the role of the DHCP relay agent and the request travels back and forth across the MPLS cloud just the same as any other UDP/IP packet.

Routed Bridge Encapsulation

Recall that RBE-encapsulated interfaces behave just like routed interfaces. To place an RBE interface in an MPLS VPN, you just need to configure a VRF name on the subinterface. In practice, RBE configurations often use unnumbered IP interfaces on the provider side to save IP address space (this was discussed in Chapter 2.) Unnumbered interfaces work just fine as long as the loopback interface is part of the same VRF.

PPP

PPP is the most complex scenario of all, because it is so well endowed with control protocols. The basic configuration involves terminating a PPP session in a VRF on a PE. The VRF name goes on the virtual-template interface on the PE and all sessions are put into the same VPN. Placing a VRF name on the virtual-template interface is analogous to putting a VRF name directly on an RBE or Ethernet interface, and is a form of static provisioning. There are certain limitations to this approach. If a subscriber wants to change VPN, the VRF name on the virtual-template interfaces must be manually updated. And, in the very likely scenario that different subscribers want to connect to different VPNs, each PPP session must be configured to use different virtual-templates.

In a regular L2TP architecture, VPN selection is dynamic. The subscriber's VPDN domain name is nothing more than a key that selects a VPN tunnel (that uses the L2TP protocol). Why not have the same flexibility with an MPLS-based VPN and allow the subscriber to select his VPN using domain names? Well, it is certainly possible. However, the implementation is not straightforward: You can no longer put the VRF name under the virtual-template, because this defeats the purpose of using the domain name as a selector. Cisco IOS does not allow you to dynamically select which **virtual-template** is used to terminate a particular PPP session based on the domain name. (Actually, there is a way to do this, using a structure called templates, which are covered in Chapter 6.) Yes, you can have up to hundreds of **virtual-templates**, each in a different VRF, and then statically map subscriber lines to the right template. With ranges and VC-auto provisioning, this is quite easy to do. But it's static.

There are two ways to do dynamic VPN selection. You can either use a Virtual Home Gateway (VHG) or use Cisco IOS virtual profiles. The next two sections look at the VHG option. Virtual-profiles require AAA and are covered in Chapter 6.

Virtual Home Gateway

A VHG is a PE router that is used for broadband access. In Cisco literature, the term VHG is used to mean any PE that terminates broadband encapsulations. The name is derived from the fact that a service provider who deploys a VHG no longer needs dedicated Customer Home Gateways, which were a feature of dial environments.

VHGs can either terminate broadband sessions directly into VRFs, or be divided across two different devices. There is a technical reason for using a two-box solution as opposed to a single device, the reasons for which are explained a bit later in this section. From a terminology standpoint, the terms *VHG* and *two-box architecture* are occasionally used interchangeably in this discussion.

To understand why a two-box solution may make sense, consider the network shown in Figure 5-5. VPNs 100, 200, and 300 are on PE1, but VPNs 400, 500, and 600 are on PE2. With static binding, such an arrangement requires the service provider to connect all the Layer 2 links from subscribers in VPN 200, for example, to PE1, and all the links from subscribers in VPN 400 to PE2. However, with dynamic binding, a subscriber physically connected to PE1 might suddenly want to join VPN 500. The service provider now has two choices—either somehow move the Layer 2 link to PE2, or allow VPN 500 to be instantiated (created) dynamically on PE1. There is no easy way to move the Layer 2 connections, so the service provider has to use the second option, which is shown in Figure 5-6.

NOTE	Of course, there are ways to provision Layer 2 circuits dynamically, which could in theory solve the problem without instantiating VRFs on new PEs, but it is very hard. As you know, ATM networks can run PNNI, with switched virtual circuits (SVCs) between DSLAMs and aggregation routers. But you would still need some way for the subscriber's choice of VPN to be mapped to a new NSAP address on a different device. (Only a committee would suggest running SVCs from the subscriber's PC—don't try that at home.) Even Ethernet does not have an obvious solution. If subscriber traffic is mapped to a different VLAN on the CE switch, you still need to configure the network to switch this to PE2. Once again, there is no obvious way for the subscriber's choice of VPN to be detected at the Ethernet layer.

Figure 5-5 *Divide and Conquer*

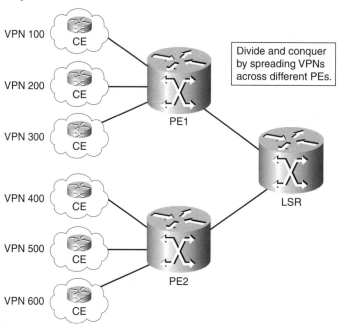

Compared to the alternatives, dynamic instantiation is looking attractive. Unfortunately, there is no way to create VRFs dynamically in Cisco IOS. A VRF, including name, route-target, RD, and so forth, must be configured using the CLI. This is usually a good thing because VPN membership is a static thing and network designers would not necessarily want to have lots of PEs joining and leaving VPNs, with the impact that would have on BGP stability. But it does mean that an interface can be bound to a VRF only if that VRF has been completely configured beforehand. There are only two ways to solve this. Either every broadband PE is part of every VRF in the service provider network or a divide-and-conquer method is used.

The disadvantage of running every VRF on every broadband PE should be fairly obvious: It is wasteful. Figure 5-7 shows PE1 with six different VPNs, but with no subscribers in the VPNs 400, 500, and 600. PE1 is needlessly importing routes from all the PEs that connect to these VPNs—just in case a subscriber connects to one of those VPNs.

Figure 5-6   *Dynamic Binding: Before and After*

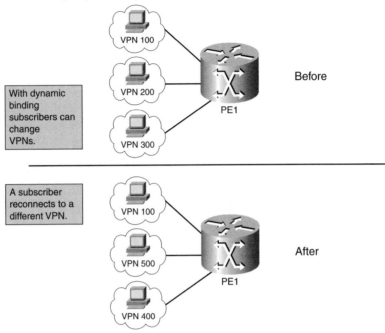

Figure 5-7   *PE with Unused VPNs*

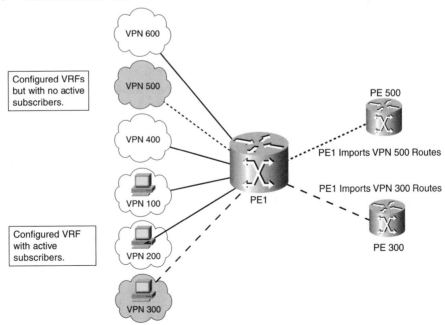

The other approach, shown in Figure 5-8, is to use a two-box VHG architecture. The first device terminates the access protocol and forwards IP traffic to the right PE for the subscriber's VPN.

Figure 5-8 *Two-Box Virtual Home Gateway*

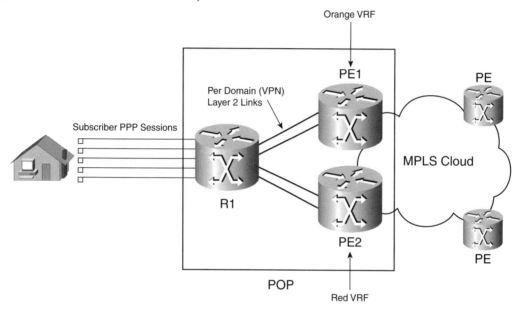

The following call flow (in reference to Figure 5-8) helps explain the operation:

1. Subscriber jane@orange.com starts a PPP session.

2. The PPP session is terminated on R1.

3. R1 forwards IP traffic to PE1.

4. joe@red.com connects.

5. The PPP session is again terminated on R1.

6. R1 forwards IP traffic to PE2.

In summary, a VHG aggregates subscriber sessions on one device, which forwards them over a per-domain link to the right PE.

A VHG solution has the following properties:

• VHG can find the right PE dynamically.

• VPN integrity is preserved.

• VPN usage is linked using the domain qualifier.

If there are different VPNs running on different PEs, as was the case in Figure 5-8, it should be obvious that the VHG needs to know which PE to use when a subscriber connects.

The fact that VPN integrity is preserved is important. VPNs need to guarantee traffic separation from start to finish, so the VHG also needs to enforce this. This is true for both the device itself and the link between R1 and PE in Figure 5-8. Several models come to mind for this VHG-PE connection:

- Point-to-point Layer 2 connection, such as ATM, Frame Relay, or Ethernet 802.1q trunks
- Point-to-point Layer 3 tunnel, such as GRE
- Layer 2 Tunneling Protocol (L2TP)

L2TP works very well here, as shown in Figure 5-9, because there is a very well defined way to forward traffic based on the subscribers' domain names. When using L2TP, R1 operates as an L2TP Access Concentrator (LAC) and forwards PPP to the PE, which now becomes an L2TP Network Server (LNS)/PE.

Figure 5-9   *L2TP VHG*

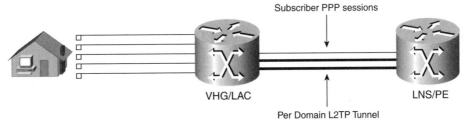

This solution has many useful advantages:

- VPN integrity is preserved on the VHG because PPP is not terminated till the LNS/PE, where it is immediately placed in a VRF.
- The VHG can find the right PE dynamically, thanks to standard L2TP provisioning, which maps an LNS IP address to a VPDN domain name.
- Host routes are created automatically on the LNS.
- There is extensive instrumentation for control.

The disadvantage to this solution is that the PE still needs to process PPP—as well as L2TP, which can be expensive in terms of CPU requirements. This extra processing was one of the reasons for introducing a VHG in the first place, so there is a definite trade-off here between avoiding the need for VRF preinstantiation, the flexibility of the L2TP solution, and the processing requirements of the LNS/PE.

Could one of the other protocols, such as 802.1q or ATM PVCs, provide a simpler alternative? The scenario certainly sounds straightforward. The operation is as follows:

1. Terminate PPP traffic on the VHG.

2. Use policy routing to direct traffic to the right 802.1q subinterface.

3. The PE maps the 802.1q traffic to the right VRF.

This scenario works, but VPN integrity is lost because the IP address spaces on the VHG are no longer private. At the very least, this means that addresses cannot overlap, but it also means that there is a routed path between different VPN subscribers on the VHG. You would have to use ACLs very carefully to make sure that there are no security issues with such a design. Policy map provisioning is less flexible than L2TP because it is applied to a range of source addresses on an interface, not a name, both of which can be hard to know in advance for a given subscriber. Also, with policy routing there is no easy way to failover between links, again unlike L2TP. Finally, there is no easy way to update the VRF routes automatically when subscribers connect or disconnect. Routing and failover are often overlooked issues with two-box solutions, but one that L2TP solves very nicely.

VHG for Cable or Ethernet

A two-box solution is by no means mandatory. Sometimes it makes sense, sometimes it doesn't. In general, if there is a large number of dynamic VRFs, then some level of divide and conquer can be beneficial.

What about bridged architectures? If there is no PPP in the picture, then the problem of dynamic instantiation does not arise. Subscribers are statically mapped to a VRF. This really reduces the need for a separate VHG router.

For cable, CMTS/PE configuration is simple, and the SFID-based solution allows for multiple VPNs per cable modem. Given the provisioning complexity, this is probably a more appropriate solution for application VPNs, with a small number of VRFs, such as one for voice or video. The number of VRFs per PE is also small, and preinstantiation is not an issue.

Is there any need for a two-box VHG in Ethernet-based topologies? Not really. The VPN mappings are static and are configured per port on the CE and per subinterface on the PE. Unlike DSL, the subscriber densities per device are relatively low, limited as they are by the physical ports on the CE. (Ethernet CPE has tens, not hundreds, of ports, and upstream routers aggregate thousands, not tens of thousands, of subscribers.) However, as Ethernet becomes more widely deployed for residential access, this demarcation between DSL and Ethernet densities will start to blur.

Examples of the Basic Architectures

After a discussion of basic architectures, it is a good time to look at basic configuration and encapsulation details for scenarios with and without two-box VHG as well as with and without PPP.

Direct PPP Termination Configuration

This section gives sample configurations of PPP clients and PEs for when PPP sessions are terminated directly into a VRF. As already discussed, this does mean that the VRF is already instantiated on the PE.

Figure 5-10 shows the protocol stack from client through to PE. PPPoE and PPP are terminated on the aggregation router. Figure 5-11 shows the sample network topology used for Example 5-1. RAMPLS1 is the PPPoE test client. RAMPLS2 terminates PPP and is a PE router. RAMPLS3 is a remote PE router. All the interfaces are Fast Ethernet.

Figure 5-10   *Protocol Stack for Direct PPP Termination*

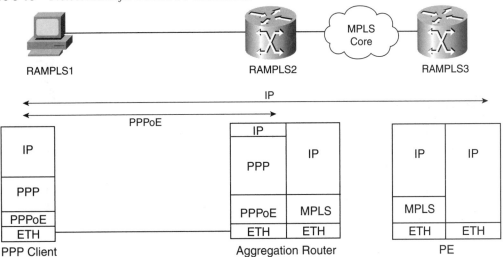

Figure 5-11 *Topology of Direct PPP Termination Example*

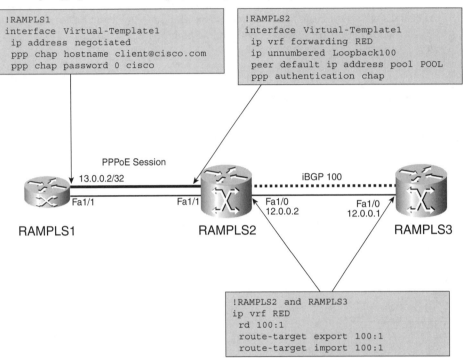

RAMPLS1 is the PPPoE client. (For the detail oriented, it is a PPPoEoE client.) In a real deployment, the client might be either a router or a software stack on a PC. The configuration is given in Example 5-1 through Example 5-3.

Example 5-1 shows how to enable PPPoE on the client router. This device still uses vpdn-groups to configure PPPoE, but the others use the newer bba-groups. Both methods are included for the sake of completeness. You will continue to see the vpdn-group in many operational networks for some time to come. Even though RAMPLS1 is a client, the vpdn-group is identical to what you would see on a PPPoE server. The details of PPPoE configuration were covered in Chapter 2.

NOTE   Only partial configurations are provided in this book. You can find the complete configurations on the Cisco Press website, at http://www.ciscopress.com/1587051362.

Example 5-1   *RAMPLS1 VPDN-group Configuration*

```
hostname RAMPLS1
vpdn enable
vpdn-group 1
 accept-dialin
  protocol pppoe
  virtual-template 1
 pppoe limit per-mac 10
 pppoe limit per-vlan 10
 !
 !
```

The next step is to enable PPPoE on the interface that connects to the aggregator, which is shown in Example 5-2. The IP address of 11.0.0.1 is not necessary for PPPoE connection. It is useful, however, for troubleshooting, because it lets you ping the client interface to test connectivity.

Example 5-2   *RAMPLS1 Fast Ethernet Enabled for PPPoE*

```
interface FastEthernet1/1
 description connection to RAMPLS2
 ip address 11.0.0.1 255.255.255.252
pppoe enable
 !
```

Finally, because this is a Cisco IOS PPPoE client, you need a virtual-template that uses a PPP session to get an IP address. This is also where you configure the client name, in this case client@cisco.com. The default route points to RAMPLS2's virtual-access interface. In production, this would be downloaded dynamically as part of PPP negotiation.

Example 5-3   *RAMPLS1 virtual-template Configuration*

```
interface Virtual-Template1
 ip address negotiated
 ppp chap hostname client@cisco.com
 ppp chap password 0 cisco
 !
ip route 0.0.0.0 0.0.0.0 13.0.2.1
```

| NOTE | I used the **test pppoe** command on RAMPLS1 to initiate PPPoE sessions. This command is exceedingly useful in lab situations. It is a single-line command that can bring up thousands of calls, with a defined setup rate. The simplest way to use it is as follows: |

```
RAMPLS1#test pppoe 1 1 fa1/1
RAMPLS1#
```

The first parameter indicates the number of sessions, the second is the call setup rate (not really important with just a single call) and the egress interface. The router needs to be correctly configured to do PPPoE on the selected interface. (**pppoe enable** is required on Ethernet interfaces, for example.)

This **test** command does require that **lcp renegotiation** always be configured on the LNS (which is not necessary on an LAC, of course).

RAMPLS2 is the interesting part of this network. There are two main sections:

- MPLS-VPN configuration in Example 5-5 with a single VRF, called RED, and associated MP-BGP configuration (RAMPLS2 peers with RAMPLS3).

- PPPoE server configuration in Example 5-6 with **bba-group 100** , which terminates the PPPoE session from RAMPLS1 and places it into the RED VRF.

Note that the major change from the PPPoE configurations shown in Chapter 3, "VPNs in Broadband Networks," is that **virtual-template 1** and the unnumbered interface are both in the RED VRF. This is a deliberately simple configuration. As you read further, you will see how to deal with addressing pools, RADIUS servers, and so on. RAMPLS2 also uses **bba-groups** instead of vpdn-groups to configure the Cisco IOS PPPoE server.

Example 5-4 lists the different usernames configured on RAMPLS2. These must match the name used by the PPP client, because the router authenticates locally.

Example 5-4 *RAMPLS2 Usernames*

```
!
version 12.2

!
hostname RAMPLS2
username client password 0 cisco
username client@cisco.com password 0 cisco
```

Example 5-5 is an extract of all the MPLS VPN–related configuration, with the exception of the interface used for the PPP sessions. RAMPLS2 peers with RAMPLS3, and the configuration to do this is very standard. RAMPLS announces connected routes to RAMPLS3. As each PPPoE client connects, a virtual-access interface is created with a directly connected host route in the

VRF RED routing table. BGP picks this up and thus the routes to clients are announced to other PEs. Letting host routes be announced in this way is not a best practice, but it is done here so that you can follow how client reachability is provided to the RAMPLS3 PE. In an operational network, RAMPLS2 could have, for example, a static Null0 route for the 13.0.0.*x* address pool and announce that with a **redistribute static** BGP command and avoid the use of **redistribute connected**. The end of this section shows how to configure this.

Example 5-5   *RAMPLS2 MPLS VPN–Related Configuration*

```
ip cef!
mpls label protocol ldp
!
ip vrf RED
 rd 100:1
 route-target export 100:1
 route-target import 100:1
!
! interface used for BGP peering
interface Loopback1
 ip address 10.0.0.2 255.255.255.255
!
! interface in VRF RED
! also used as the default route
! on the pppoe client
interface Loopback100
 ip vrf forwarding RED
 ip address 13.0.2.1 255.255.255.255
!
! interface that connects across MPLS core
interface FastEthernet1/0
 description Interface to RAMPLS3
 ip address 12.0.0.2 255.255.255.252
tag-switching ip
!
! IGP protocol used across core! announces loopback address used for BGP
! runs on Fa1/0 interface
router ospf 100
 log-adjacency-changes
 network 10.0.0.2 0.0.0.0 area 0
 network 12.0.0.0 0.0.0.3 area 0
!
! MP-BGP configuration that peers
! with RAMPLS3
router bgp 100
 no synchronization
 bgp log-neighbor-changes
 neighbor 10.0.0.3 remote-as 100
 neighbor 10.0.0.3 update-source Loopback1
 no auto-summary
 !
 address-family vpnv4
 neighbor 10.0.0.3 activate
 neighbor 10.0.0.3 send-community extended
```

Example 5-5   *RAMPLS2 MPLS VPN–Related Configuration (Continued)*

```
no auto-summary
exit-address-family
!
address-family ipv4 vrf RED
redistribute connected
no auto-summary
no synchronization
exit-address-family
!
```

Example 5-6 is the other half of RAMPLS2's role and lists all the commands needed to terminate PPPoE and place the virtual-interfaces created for each session in VRF RED. The main point here is that the virtual-template interface is in the RED VRF and is unnumbered to interface loopback 100, which is also in the RED VRF. The virtual-template is the link between the PPPoE and MPLS-VPN worlds. The **bba-group** definition and use and VRF use are highlighted in Example 5-6.

Example 5-6   *RAMPLS2 PPPoE-Related Configuration*

```
vpdn enable
!
bba-group pppoe 100
 virtual-template 1
 sessions per-vc limit 10
 sessions per-mac limit 10
!
! client-facing interface running PPPoE protocol
! links to group bba-group 100
interface FastEthernet1/1
 description Interface to RAMPLS1
 ip address 11.0.0.2 255.255.255.252
pppoe enable group 100
!
! user virtual-interfaces are cloned from this
! template in VRF RED. Unnumbered interface is
! also VRF RED.
interface Virtual-Template1
 ip vrf forwarding RED
 ip unnumbered Loopback100
 peer default ip address pool POOL
 ppp authentication chap!
```

Example 5-7 shows the address pool used for the PPPoE clients, 13.0.0.2 to 13.0.0.10.

Example 5-7   *RAMPLS2 Address Pool for PPPoE Clients*

```
ip local pool POOL 13.0.0.2 13.0.0.10
```

RAMPLS3 is the remote PE device and is used to test the end-to-end configuration. Once connected, RAMPLS1 should be able to ping through to RAMPLS3, across the MPLS cloud. RAMPLS3's configuration is really that of a standard PE, and the highlights are given in Example 5-8. (Remember that the full configurations are provided online at Ciscopress.com.)

Example 5-8   *RAMPLS3 Configuration*

```
!
hostname RAMPLS3
!
ip vrf RED
 rd 100:1
 route-target export 100:1
 route-target import 100:1
!
ip cef
mpls label protocol ldp

!
interface Loopback1
 ip address 10.0.0.3 255.255.255.255
!
interface Loopback100
 ip vrf forwarding RED
 ip address 13.0.3.1 255.255.255.255
!
interface FastEthernet0/0
 ip address 2.1.50.61 255.0.0.0
!
interface FastEthernet1/0
 description Interface to RAMPLS2
 ip address 12.0.0.1 255.255.255.252
 tag-switching ip

!
router ospf 100
 log-adjacency-changes
 network 10.0.0.3 0.0.0.0 area 0
 network 12.0.0.0 0.0.0.3 area 0
!
router bgp 100
 no synchronization
 bgp log-neighbor-changes
 neighbor 10.0.0.2 remote-as 100
 neighbor 10.0.0.2 update-source Loopback1
```

Example 5-8   *RAMPLS3 Configuration (Continued)*

```
no auto-summary
!
address-family vpnv4
neighbor 10.0.0.2 activate
neighbor 10.0.0.2 send-community extended
no auto-summary
exit-address-family
!
address-family ipv4 vrf RED
redistribute connected
no auto-summary
no synchronization
exit-address-family
!
```

Monitoring Direct PPP Termination

The topology of this example is deliberately simple so that you can set this up and test it. The first step should be to check connectivity between each router. To do so, a simple ping of the 11.0.0.*x* and 12.0.0.*x* interfaces does the job just fine. Next, check the MPLS portion of the network. LDP (in this case, TDP works just as well) should be up on the 12.0.0.x interfaces and each label-switching router (only two PEs here) should announce labels for all of its interfaces. Example 5-9 shows the LDP session.

Example 5-9   *LDP Peers on RAMPLS3 Configuration*

```
RAMPLS3#show mpls ldp neighbor
    Peer LDP Ident: 10.0.0.2:0; Local LDP Ident 10.0.0.3:0
        TCP connection: 10.0.0.2.646 - 10.0.0.3.11208
        State: Oper; Msgs sent/rcvd: 6456/6459; Downstream
        Up time: 3d22h
        LDP discovery sources:
          FastEthernet1/0, Src IP addr: 12.0.0.2
          Targeted Hello 10.0.0.3 -> 10.0.0.2, active, passive
        Addresses bound to peer LDP Ident:
          2.1.50.60       12.0.0.2       10.0.0.2       11.0.0.2
```

The BGP session should be running between the two PEs, as shown in Example 5-10.

Example 5-10   *BGP Session on RAMPLS3 Configuration*

```
RAMPLS3#show ip bgp neighbor
BGP neighbor is 10.0.0.2,  remote AS 100, internal link
  BGP version 4, remote router ID 10.0.0.2
  BGP state = Established, up for 3d21h
  ...
```

It is very important that the correct routes are announced between the PEs. In this case, on RAMPLS3 you should see routes to the Loopback100 interface on RAMPLS2, as shown in Example 5-11.

Example 5-11 *BGP Route Table on RAMPLS3 Before PPPoE Client Connection*

```
RAMPLS3#show ip bgp vpn vrf RED
BGP table version is 10, local router ID is 10.0.0.3
Status codes: s suppressed, d damped, h history, * valid, > best, i - internal,
              r RIB-failure, S Stale
Origin codes: i - IGP, e - EGP, ? - incomplete

   Network          Next Hop          Metric LocPrf Weight Path
Route Distinguisher: 100:1 (default for vrf RED)
*>i13.0.2.1/32      10.0.0.2               0    100      0 ?
*> 13.0.3.1/32      0.0.0.0                0         32768 ?
```

You should be able to ping the Loopback100 interfaces from either PE. Example 5-12 shows RAMPLS2 pinging 13.0.3.1 on RAMPLS3. Once this works, you can be pretty confident that the MPLS VPN is working (at least in this simple topology). If, for some reason, the ping fails, you should check the contents of the VRF routing tables, the BGP tables, route-target and route-distinguisher values, and LFIB and FIB tables. Appendix A lists some useful documents that cover MPLS-VPN troubleshooting.

Example 5-12 *Ping Between Loopback Addresses in VRF RED*

```
RAMPLS2#ping vrf RED 13.0.3.1
Type escape sequence to abort.
Sending 5, 100-byte ICMP Echos to 13.0.3.1, timeout is 2 seconds:
!!!!!
Success rate is 100 percent (5/5), round-trip min/avg/max = 1/1/1 ms
```

Once you are happy with the MPLS-VPN setup, it is time to connect the client. Use the **test pppoe** command on RAMPLS1. Once again, check that the session connects with **show pppoe session** [**all** | **packets**] or with the **show ip vrf** command used in Example 5-13. By the way, the (traditional) **show vpdn** command still displays PPPoE information, even though the configuration uses bba-groups.

Example 5-13 *VRF RED on RAMPLS2 Showing Virtual-Access Interface After PPPoE Connection*

```
RAMPLS2#show ip vrf RED
  Name                         Default RD        Interfaces
  RED                          100:1             Virtual-Access1.1
                                                 Virtual-Template1
                                                 Loopback100
```

If you have problems getting the session to connect, remove all the VRF information from the virtual-templates and debug that first using the **debug pppoe** command. This is a general recommendation when debugging VPN solutions: Try to get the individual components to work before putting everything together. The next section, "Two-Box Virtual Home Gateway Example," gives more details on how to check PPPoE connectivity.

Interesting things happen when the client connects to RAMPLS2. Because this router is configured to announce /32 routes, you should see in the RAMPLS3 BGP table a new route, shown highlighted in Example 5-14, and a label for the same address, highlighted in Example 5-15.

Example 5-14 *BGP Route Table on RAMPLS3 After PPPoE Client Connection*

```
RAMPLS3#show ip bgp vpn vrf RED
BGP table version is 10, local router ID is 10.0.0.3
Status codes: s suppressed, d damped, h history, * valid, > best, i - internal,
              r RIB-failure, S Stale
Origin codes: i - IGP, e - EGP, ? - incomplete

   Network          Next Hop          Metric LocPrf Weight Path
Route Distinguisher: 100:1 (default for vrf RED)
*>i13.0.0.2/32      10.0.0.2               0    100      0 ?
*>i13.0.2.1/32      10.0.0.2               0    100      0 ?
*>  13.0.3.1/32     0.0.0.0                0         32768 ?
```

Example 5-15 *Labels on RAMPLS3, with Entry for PPPoE Client at 13.0.0.2*

```
RAMPLS3#show ip cef vrf RED detail
IP CEF with switching (Table Version 7), flags=0x0
  7 routes, 0 reresolve, 0 unresolved (0 old, 0 new), peak 1
  27 leaves, 36 nodes, 38712 bytes, 57 inserts, 30 invalidations
  0 load sharing elements, 0 bytes, 0 references
  universal per-destination load sharing algorithm, id 34A91F93
  3(0) CEF resets, 0 revisions of existing leaves
  Resolution Timer: Exponential (currently 1s, peak 1s)
  0 in-place/0 aborted modifications
  refcounts:  9744 leaf, 9728 node

  Table epoch: 0 (7 entries at this epoch)

Adjacency Table has 6 adjacencies
0.0.0.0/0, version 0, epoch 0, attached, default route handler
0 packets, 0 bytes
  via 0.0.0.0, 0 dependencies
    valid null adjacency
0.0.0.0/32, version 1, epoch 0, receive
13.0.0.2/32, version 6, epoch 0, cached adjacency 12.0.0.2
0 packets, 0 bytes
  tag information set
    local tag: VPN-route-head
    fast tag rewrite with Fa1/0, 12.0.0.2, tags imposed: {17}
  via 10.0.0.2, 0 dependencies, recursive
    next hop 12.0.0.2, FastEthernet1/0 via 10.0.0.2/32
    valid cached adjacency
    tag rewrite with Fa1/0, 12.0.0.2, tags imposed: {17}
13.0.2.1/32, version 5, epoch 0, cached adjacency 12.0.0.2
0 packets, 0 bytes
```

Example 5-15 *Labels on RAMPLS3, with Entry for PPPoE Client at 13.0.0.2 (Continued)*

```
 tag information set
   local tag: VPN-route-head
   fast tag rewrite with Fa1/0, 12.0.0.2, tags imposed: {18}
 via 10.0.0.2, 0 dependencies, recursive
   next hop 12.0.0.2, FastEthernet1/0 via 10.0.0.2/32
   valid cached adjacency
   tag rewrite with Fa1/0, 12.0.0.2, tags imposed: {18}
13.0.3.1/32, version 4, epoch 0, connected, receive
 tag information set
   local tag: 16
224.0.0.0/24, version 3, epoch 0, receive
255.255.255.255/32, version 2, epoch 0, receive
```

Of course, the true test of connectivity is for the client to be able to ping the VRF interface on RAMPLS3, as shown in Example 5-16. The ping traverses the entire network of Figure 5-11: across broadband session and MPLS network.

Example 5-16 *Ping from RAMPLS3 to PPPoE Client at 13.0.0.2*

```
RAMPLS3#ping vrf RED 13.0.0.2

Type escape sequence to abort.
Sending 5, 100-byte ICMP Echos to 13.0.0.2, timeout is 2 seconds:
!!!!!
Success rate is 100 percent (5/5), round-trip min/avg/max = 1/1/4 ms
```

Earlier in this section, you read that you should avoid redistributing connected routes on RAMPLS2. For the sake of completeness, Example 5-17 shows a modified configuration for RAMPLS2 that redistributes static routes in BGP and has a **Null0** route that matches the addresses used in the pool. The changes from the previous BGP configuration are highlighted in Example 5-17. Don't forget to make the static route part of VRF RED, and make sure the /32 addresses used to reach the PEs are reachable!

Example 5-17 *BGP Configuration with Static **Null0***

```
router bgp 100
 no synchronization
 bgp log-neighbor-changes
 neighbor 10.0.0.3 remote-as 100
 neighbor 10.0.0.3 update-source Loopback1
 no auto-summary
 !
 address-family vpnv4
 neighbor 10.0.0.3 activate
 neighbor 10.0.0.3 send-community extended
 no auto-summary
 exit-address-family
 !
 address-family ipv4 vrf RED
 redistribute static
```

Example 5-17 *BGP Configuration with Static* **Null0** *(Continued)*

```
 no auto-summary
 no synchronization
 exit-address-family
!
ip local pool POOL 13.0.0.2 13.0.0.10
ip classless
ip route vrf RED 13.0.0.0 255.255.255.240 Null0
```

Example 5-18 shows the new BGP route table for VRF RED on RAMPLS3 after the PPP client has connected. Note that no /32 route exists for the client. Instead, you see an iBGP route for 13.0.0.0/28. You will see the same thing in the RED VRF routing table on RAMPLS3.

Example 5-18 *BGP Table on RAMPLS3 with Aggregate Route*

```
RAMPLS3#show ip bgp vpn all
BGP table version is 8, local router ID is 10.0.0.3
Status codes: s suppressed, d damped, h history, * valid, > best, i - internal,
              r RIB-failure, S Stale
Origin codes: i - IGP, e - EGP, ? - incomplete

   Network          Next Hop            Metric LocPrf Weight Path
Route Distinguisher: 100:1 (default for vrf RED)
*>i13.0.0.0/28      10.0.0.2                 0    100      0 ?
*> 13.0.3.1/32      0.0.0.0                  0          32768 ?
```

Finally, just to be really thorough, Example 5-19 shows the labels announced by RAMPLS2 to RAMPLS3, and Example 5-20 shows the labels on RAMPLS3. Once again, there is only a label for the aggregate route, and none for 13.0.0.2/32. This is a good thing. Compare this to the output in Example 5-15.

Example 5-19 *Labels Announced by RAMPLS2*

```
RAMPLS2#show tag forwarding vrf RED detail
Local   Outgoing    Prefix           Bytes tag  Outgoing    Next Hop
tag     tag or VC   or Tunnel Id     switched   interface
18      Aggregate   13.0.0.0/28[V]   0
        MAC/Encaps=0/0, MRU=0, Tag Stack{}
        VPN route: RED
        No output feature configured
    Per-packet load-sharing
```

Example 5-20 *Labels Received by RAMPLS3215*

```
RAMPLS3#show ip cef vrf RED detail
IP CEF with switching (Table Version 9), flags=0x0
  6 routes, 0 reresolve, 0 unresolved (0 old, 0 new), peak 1
  25 leaves, 34 nodes, 36480 bytes, 72 inserts, 47 invalidations
  0 load sharing elements, 0 bytes, 0 references
  universal per-destination load sharing algorithm, id 34A91F93
  3(0) CEF resets, 0 revisions of existing leaves
```

Example 5-20 *Labels Received by RAMPLS3215 (Continued)*

```
   Resolution Timer: Exponential (currently 1s, peak 1s)
   0 in-place/0 aborted modifications
   refcounts:  9230 leaf, 9216 node

   Table epoch: 0 (6 entries at this epoch)

Adjacency Table has 5 adjacencies
0.0.0.0/0, version 0, epoch 0, attached, default route handler
0 packets, 0 bytes
  via 0.0.0.0, 0 dependencies
    valid null adjacency
0.0.0.0/32, version 1, epoch 0, receive
13.0.0.0/28, version 8, epoch 0, cached adjacency 12.0.0.2
0 packets, 0 bytes
  tag information set
    local tag: VPN-route-head
    fast tag rewrite with
        Recursive rewrite via 10.0.0.2/32, tags imposed {18}
  via 10.0.0.2, 0 dependencies, recursive
    next hop 12.0.0.2, FastEthernet1/0 via 10.0.0.2/32
    valid cached adjacency
    tag rewrite with
        Recursive rewrite via 10.0.0.2/32, tags imposed {18}
13.0.3.1/32, version 4, epoch 0, connected, receive
  tag information set
    local tag: 18
224.0.0.0/24, version 3, epoch 0, receive
255.255.255.255/32, version 2, epoch 0, receive
```

Of course, the ping still has to work! Example 5-21 shows the RED VRF routing table followed by a ping from RAMPLS3 through to RAMPLS1.

Example 5-21 *Ping from RAMPLS3 to 13.0.0.2, Using Aggregate Routes in VRF RED*

```
RAMPLS3#show ip route vrf RED
Routing Table: RED
Codes: C - connected, S - static, R - RIP, M - mobile, B - BGP
       D - EIGRP, EX - EIGRP external, O - OSPF, IA - OSPF inter area
       N1 - OSPF NSSA external type 1, N2 - OSPF NSSA external type 2
       E1 - OSPF external type 1, E2 - OSPF external type 2
       i - IS-IS, L1 - IS-IS level-1, L2 - IS-IS level-2, ia - IS-IS inter area
       * - candidate default, U - per-user static route, o - ODR
       P - periodic downloaded static route

Gateway of last resort is not set

     13.0.0.0/8 is variably subnetted, 3 subnets, 2 masks
B       13.0.0.0/28 [200/0] via 10.0.0.2, 00:00:09
B       13.0.2.1/32 [200/0] via 10.0.0.2, 00:00:09
C       13.0.3.1/32 is directly connected, Loopback100
RAMPLS3#
```

Example 5-21 *Ping from RAMPLS3 to 13.0.0.2, Using Aggregate Routes in VRF RED (Continued)*

```
RAMPLS3#
RAMPLS3#ping vrf RED 13.0.0.2

Type escape sequence to abort.
Sending 5, 100-byte ICMP Echos to 13.0.0.2, timeout is 2 seconds:
!!!!!
Success rate is 100 percent (5/5), round-trip min/avg/max = 1/1/4 ms
```

If you get this far, take a break. You deserve it.

Two-Box Virtual Home Gateway Example

This section gives sample configurations of PPP clients and VHG/LAC, LNS/PE, and PE for a VHG topology.

Figure 5-12 shows the protocol stack from the client right through to the PE. You can see how the VHG/LAC terminates PPPoE and tunnels the PPP session onwards and how the LNS/PE terminates L2TP and PPP, and maps the IP packets into an MPLS VPN.

Figure 5-13 shows the sample network topology used for the two-box VHG example. The difference with the direct PPP termination example is simple: RAMPLS2 is an LAC and RAMPLS3 becomes the LNS/PE. RAMPLS1 is again the PPPoE client. All the underlying IP addresses are the same, making it easy for you to follow what is going on. The rest of this section follows the same flow as the previous example, covering the different configurations. The next section goes through useful **show** commands for monitoring and troubleshooting.

Figure 5-12 *Protocol Stack for VHG*

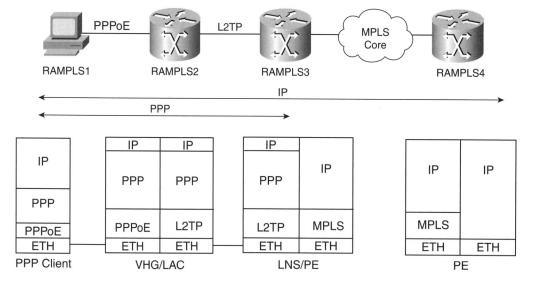

Figure 5-13   *Topology of VHG Example*

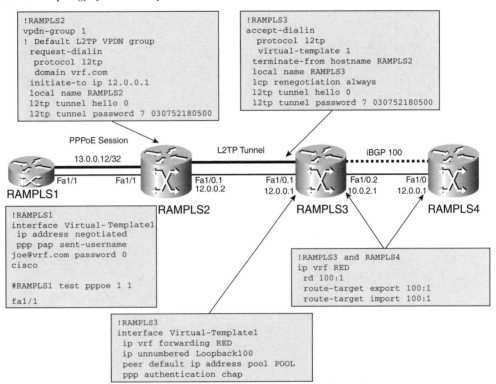

RAMPLS1 is again the PPPoE client, with an almost identical configuration to the previous case, but with a different username, in this case joe@vrf.com, which the RAMPLS2 will map to an L2TP tunnel. The LCP setup can be tricky, so the virtual-template configuration is shown in Example 5-22.

Example 5-22   *RAMPLS1 Configuration*

```
!
interface Virtual-Template1
 ip address negotiated
 no keepalive
 ppp authentication pap chap
 ppp pap sent-username joe@vrf.com password 0 cisco
 ppp timeout authentication 100
!
```

In a VHG architecture, RAMPLS2 is no longer a PE. The PPPoE and VPDN configuration portion is shown in Example 5-23. Note that the username joe@vrf.com, used by the client in Example 5-22, is *not* configured on the LAC. (User authentication is always on the LNS in an

L2TP scenario.) Another difference with the direct PPP termination example is that the network connection across interface FastEthernet1/0.1, between LAC and LNS, does not use label switching; it is pure IP.

Example 5-23 *RAMPLS2 LAC Configuration*

```
!
hostname RAMPLS2
!
username RAMPLS2 password 0 cisco
username RAMPLS3 password 0 cisco
ip cef
vpdn enable
!
! definition of tunnel to RAMPLS3
! for vrf.com domain
vpdn-group 1
! Default L2TP VPDN group
 request-dialin
  protocol l2tp
  domain vrf.com
 initiate-to ip 12.0.0.1
 local name RAMPLS2
 l2tp tunnel hello 0
 l2tp tunnel password 7 030752180500
!
! bba-group to terminate pppoe sessions
! on virtual-template 1
bba-group pppoe 100
 virtual-template 1
 sessions per-vc limit 10
 sessions per-mac limit 10
!!
interface Loopback1
 ip address 10.0.0.2 255.255.255.255
!
!
! interface used for L2TP tunnel
! to LNS
interface FastEthernet1/0.1
 description Interface to RAMPLS3
 encapsulation dot1Q 120
 ip address 12.0.0.2 255.255.255.252
!
interface FastEthernet1/1
 description Interface to RAMPLS1
 ip address 11.0.0.2 255.255.255.252


pppoe enable group 100
!
interface Virtual-Template1
 no ip address
 no peer default ip address
 ppp authentication pap chap
!
```

If you download the full configuration from the Cisco Press website, you will see a second virtual-template on RAMPLS2. This is also shown in Example 5-24.

Example 5-24 *RAMPLS2 Second virtual-template for* **test vpdn** *Command*

```
interface Virtual-Template2
 ip address negotiated
 no keepalive
 ppp authentication chap
 ppp chap hostname joe@vrf.com
 ppp chap password 0 cisco
 !
```

RAMPLS22 is an LAC and the bba-group on this device uses **virtual-template 1** , so what is going on? This second virtual-template is there for another very useful **test** command, which allows you to initiate an L2TP tunnel, with a PPP session, directly from a Cisco IOS LAC (i.e., you do not need a separate PPP client). This is a huge timesaver when you are configuring or troubleshooting L2TP.

The **test** command syntax is as follows:

```
test vpdn scalability domain vrf.com session 40
```

This command would initiate 40 PPP sessions in an L2TP tunnel for domain vrf.com. There must be a **vpdn-group** with such a domain name already on the LAC (which is a normal part of the L2TP configuration anyway). In this case, it is **vpdn-group 1** in Example 5-23. The virtual-template in Example 5-24 looks somewhat like the one used on the PPPoE client in Example 5-22.

Getting back to the VHG example, this time, RAMPLS3 has the most interesting configuration. It has an LNS component to terminate the tunnel from RAMPLS2, as well as the PE component. The PE component is really just like what you already saw in the direct PPP termination example, so it is not included here. (It is in the online configuration.) The same design considerations apply for routing, both to be able to reach the BGP and LDP source-identifier address, and to control the distribution of routes and labels by avoiding announcements of connected routes in BGP.

Example 5-25 gives the VPDN portion of RAMPLS3's configuration. The link between L2TP and MPLS comes from **virtual-template 1** , which is part of the RED VRF. Any PPP sessions that are terminated using this template are part of the RED VRF, and **vpdn-group 1** configures the LNS to use **virtual-template 1** for any sessions that come from RAMPLS2. The operation is as follows:

1. An L2TP tunnel from the LAC called RAMPLS2 matches is terminated using **vpdn-group 1** .

2. All PPP sessions in this tunnel are terminated using **virtual-template 1** .

3. **Virtual-template 1** is in VRF RED, so all PPP virtual-access interfaces are also in VRF RED.

4. The host routes for each PPP client are created in the RED VRF. Depending on how routing is configured, these may be announced to peer routers.

Example 5-25 *RAMPLS3 VPDN Configuration*

```
! VHG/LNS
hostname RAMPLS3
!
username joe@vrf.com password 0 cisco
username RAMPLS3 password 0 cisco
username RAMPLS2 password 0 cisco
!

vpdn enable
!
vpdn-group 1
 accept-dialin
  protocol l2tp
  virtual-template 1
 terminate-from hostname RAMPLS2
 local name RAMPLS3
 lcp renegotiation always
 l2tp tunnel hello 0
 l2tp tunnel password 7 030752180500
!

!!
!

interface Loopback100
 ip vrf forwarding RED
 ip address 13.0.3.1 255.255.255.255
!
!
! interface used to terminate L2TP
interface FastEthernet1/0.1
 description Interface to RAMPLS3
 encapsulation dot1Q 120
 ip address 12.0.0.1 255.255.255.252interface Virtual-Template1
 ip vrf forwarding RED
 ip unnumbered Loopback100
 peer default ip address pool POOL
 ppp authentication chap
!

ip local pool POOL 13.0.0.12 13.0.0.30
```

Finally, RAMPLS4 is the egress PE in Figure 5-13. The configuration is shown in Example 5-26.

Example 5-26 *RAMPLS4 Configuration*

```
! PE for LNS/PE
version 12.2
!
hostname RAMPLS4
ip vrf RED
 rd 100:1
 route-target export 100:1
 route-target import 100:1
!
ip cef
!
interface Loopback1
 ip address 10.0.0.4 255.255.255.255
!
interface Loopback100
 ip vrf forwarding RED
 ip address 13.0.2.2 255.255.255.255
!
!
interface FastEthernet1/0
 no ip address
!
interface FastEthernet1/0.2
 description Interface from LNS/PE (RAMPLS3)
 encapsulation dot1Q 130
 ip address 10.0.2.2 255.255.255.252
 tag-switching ip
!
router bgp 100
 no synchronization
 bgp log-neighbor-changes
 neighbor 10.0.2.1 remote-as 100
 no auto-summary
 !
 address-family vpnv4
 neighbor 10.0.2.1 activate
 neighbor 10.0.2.1 send-community extended
 no auto-summary
 exit-address-family
 !
 address-family ipv4 vrf RED
 redistribute connected
 no auto-summary
 no synchronization
 exit-address-family
 !
```

Monitoring the Two-Box VHG Solution

When you configure a VHG environment for the first time, you might consider checking each component separately before trying to make them all work together. For example, first check that PPPoE can terminate on RAMPLS2. Then, check that the L2TP portion between RAMPLS2 and RAMPLS3 works using **test pppoe** and **test vpdn**. Next, without using any remote-access sessions, make sure the MPLS-VPN portion is working. (This was reviewed previously in this chapter.) Finally, ensure that you can connect from the client to the remote PE.

This section shows useful **show** commands that you can use to check that the PPP session terminates in the right place on the LNS/PE and that traffic can pass between the client and the remote PE, right across the MPLS core. The assumption is that the PPPoE session has been already established. You may also assume that the network is correctly configured; the purpose here is to prove that everything works, as opposed to finding a hidden error.

First, follow the PPP session from the client, across the LAC, to the LNS. Example 5-27 shows a normal PPP/L2TP tunnel on the VHG/LAC, RAMPLS2, after RAMPLS1 connects.

Example 5-27 **show vpdn** *on RAMPLS2*

```
RAMPLS2#show vpdn

L2TP Tunnel and Session Information Total tunnels 1 sessions 1

LocID RemID Remote Name    State   Remote Address  Port  Sessions VPDN Group
10404 9780  RAMPLS3        est     12.0.0.1        1701  1        1

LocID RemID TunID Intf          Username             State  Last Chg Uniq ID
13    13    10404 SSS Circuit    joe@vrf.com          est    00:06:25 13

%No active L2F tunnels

%No active PPTP tunnels

PPPoE Tunnel and Session Information Total tunnels 1 sessions 1

PPPoE Session Information
Uniq ID  PPPoE  RemMAC          Port                VT  VA          State
         SID    LocMAC                                  VA-st
    13    11    0050.e2e7.601d  Fa1/1               1   N/A         FWDED
                0008.e261.841d
```

Moving across to the LNS/PE, this tunnel is terminated on the 12.0.0.1 address on RAMPLS3, as shown in Example 5-28. The tunnel's remote name, RAMPLS2, in Example 5-28 matches the **terminate-from** parameter in the **vpdn-group** on the LNS/PE, which you saw earlier, in Example 5-25.

Example 5-28 show vpdn *on RAMPLS3*

```
RAMPLS3#show vpdn

L2TP Tunnel and Session Information Total tunnels 1 sessions 1

LocID RemID Remote Name   State  Remote Address  Port  Sessions VPDN Group
9780  10404 RAMPLS2       est    12.0.0.2        1701  1        1

LocID RemID TunID Intf         Username            State  Last Chg Uniq ID
13    13    9780  Vi3.1        RAMPLS1             est    00:11:04 6

%No active L2F tunnels

%No active PPTP tunnels

%No active PPPoE tunnels
```

There is now a new virtual-access interface in the RED VRF on RAMPLS3, shown in Example 5-29, and the address pool has a used entry, which, as you can see in Example 5-30, is 13.0.0.12. This is the address allocated to the PPP session. By the way, you don't see this address in Example 5-29. 13.0.3.1 is the address of the loopback interface used on **virtual-template1** (as unnumbered).

Example 5-29 *RED VRF Interfaces*

```
RAMPLS3#show ip vrf interface
Interface           IP-Address      VRF                        Protocol
Virtual-Template1   13.0.3.1        RED                        down
Virtual-Access3.1   13.0.3.1        RED                        up
Loopback100         13.0.3.1        RED                        up
```

Example 5-30 ip pool *on RAMPLS3*

```
RAMPLS3#show ip local pool POOL
Pool                    Begin           End             Free  In use
POOL                    13.0.0.12       13.0.0.30       18    1
Available addresses:
   13.0.0.13
   13.0.0.14
   13.0.0.15
   13.0.0.16
   13.0.0.17
   13.0.0.18
   13.0.0.19
   13.0.0.20
   13.0.0.21
   13.0.0.22
   13.0.0.23
```

Example 5-30 ip pool *on RAMPLS3 (Continued)*

```
    13.0.0.24
    13.0.0.25
    13.0.0.26
    13.0.0.27
    13.0.0.28
    13.0.0.29
    13.0.0.30
Inuse addresses:
    13.0.0.12            Vi3.1                      RAMPLS1
RAMPLS3#
```

Now that you know that the PPP session is terminated on the LNS/PE, you should also check that the virtual-access is in the right VRF. Example 5-31 shows the VRF RED route table on RAMPLS3, with a directly connected interface, corresponding to the PPP session from RAMPLS1. You can see that the address of the highlighted line in Example 5-31 matches the address used in the local pool, shown in Example 5-25.

Example 5-31 *RAMPLS3 Routing Information in RED VRF*

```
RAMPLS3#show ip route vrf RED

Routing Table: RED
Codes: C - connected, S - static, R - RIP, M - mobile, B - BGP
       D - EIGRP, EX - EIGRP external, O - OSPF, IA - OSPF inter area
       N1 - OSPF NSSA external type 1, N2 - OSPF NSSA external type 2
       E1 - OSPF external type 1, E2 - OSPF external type 2
       i - IS-IS, L1 - IS-IS level-1, L2 - IS-IS level-2, ia - IS-IS inter area
       * - candidate default, U - per-user static route, o - ODR
       P - periodic downloaded static route

Gateway of last resort is not set

     13.0.0.0/32 is subnetted, 2 subnets
C       13.0.0.12 is directly connected, Virtual-Access3.1
C       13.0.3.1 is directly connected, Loopback100
```

The real test is to ping the client from RAMPLS4, which is on the far side of the MPLS cloud. As was the case for the directly terminated PPP solution, the VPN routing table on RAMPLS4 should have an entry for the virtual-access interface created on the VHG/LNS (RAMPLS2). Look for a BGP imported route to 13.0.0.2 in Example 5-32. Note that the /32 addresses are not aggregated in this example, to make it easier to follow what is going on.

Example 5-32 *RAMPLS4 Routing Information in RED VRF*

```
RAMPLS4#show ip route vrf RED

Routing Table: RED
Codes: C - connected, S - static, R - RIP, M - mobile, B - BGP
       D - EIGRP, EX - EIGRP external, O - OSPF, IA - OSPF inter area
```

Example 5-32 *RAMPLS4 Routing Information in RED VRF (Continued)*

```
            N1 - OSPF NSSA external type 1, N2 - OSPF NSSA external type 2
            E1 - OSPF external type 1, E2 - OSPF external type 2
            i - IS-IS, L1 - IS-IS level-1, L2 - IS-IS level-2, ia - IS-IS inter area
            * - candidate default, U - per-user static route, o - ODR
            P - periodic downloaded static route

Gateway of last resort is not set

       13.0.0.0/32 is subnetted, 3 subnets
B         13.0.0.12 [200/0] via 10.0.2.1, 00:16:49
C         13.0.4.4 is directly connected, Loopback100
B         13.0.3.1 [200/0] via 10.0.2.1, 00:18:34
```

Sure enough, the ping works, as you can see in Example 5-33.

Example 5-33 *Ping from RAMPLS4*

```
RAMPLS4#ping vrf RED 13.0.0.12

Type escape sequence to abort.
Sending 5, 100-byte ICMP Echos to 13.0.0.12, timeout is 2 seconds:
!!!!!
Success rate is 100 percent (5/5), round-trip min/avg/max = 1/1/4 ms
```

What does the client see? Example 5-34 shows the client routing table on RAMPLS1.

Example 5-34 *RAMPLS1 Routing Information*

```
RAMPLS1#show ip route
Codes: C - connected, S - static, R - RIP, M - mobile, B - BGP
       D - EIGRP, EX - EIGRP external, O - OSPF, IA - OSPF inter area
       N1 - OSPF NSSA external type 1, N2 - OSPF NSSA external type 2
       E1 - OSPF external type 1, E2 - OSPF external type 2
       i - IS-IS, L1 - IS-IS level-1, L2 - IS-IS level-2, ia - IS-IS inter area
       * - candidate default, U - per-user static route, o - ODR
       P - periodic downloaded static route

Gateway of last resort is 13.0.3.1 to network 0.0.0.0

C    2.0.0.0/8 is directly connected, FastEthernet0/0
     10.0.0.0/32 is subnetted, 1 subnets
C       10.0.0.1 is directly connected, Loopback1
     11.0.0.0/30 is subnetted, 1 subnets
C       11.0.0.0 is directly connected, FastEthernet1/1
     13.0.0.0/32 is subnetted, 2 subnets
C       13.0.0.12 is directly connected, Virtual-Access1.1
C       13.0.3.1 is directly connected, Virtual-Access1.1
S*   0.0.0.0/0 [1/0] via 13.0.3.1
```

The client has a default route, which is highlighted in Example 5-34. This route points to the **virtual-template** address of the VHG/LNS. This is usually downloaded to the client during PPP negotiation.

From the client, you can ping the LNS/PE loopback address, which is in VRF RED. This is shown in Example 5-35.

Example 5-35 *Ping from RAMPLS1 to RAMPLS3*

```
RAMPLS1#ping 13.0.3.1

Type escape sequence to abort.
Sending 5, 100-byte ICMP Echos to 13.0.3.1, timeout is 2 seconds:
!!!!!
Success rate is 100 percent (5/5), round-trip min/avg/max = 1/1/4 ms
```

You can also ping the remote PE, RAMPLS4, as shown in Example 5-36.

Example 5-36 *Ping from RAMPLS1 to RAMPLS4*

```
RAMPLS1#ping 13.0.4.4

Type escape sequence to abort.
Sending 5, 100-byte ICMP Echos to 13.0.2.2, timeout is 2 seconds:
!!!!!
Success rate is 100 percent (5/5), round-trip min/avg/max = 1/1/4 ms
```

There are no specific debug commands for VHG scenarios. Useful commands concern **PPP authentication** and **negotiation**, as well as **VPDN L2X events**, **error**, and **packet**. However, all the commands BGP- and MPLS-related commands you saw in the earlier section "Direct PPP Termination Configuration" are equally valid here and you should use them to check that the PEs are correctly announcing routes and labels.

Multi-VRF CE Configuration

The final example gives extracts of configuration files for a Multi-VRF CE and associated PE.

Figure 5-14 shows the protocol stack from the client right through to the PE, and the network topology was shown back in Figure 5-4, which appeared in the first discussion of Multi-VRF CE.

Figure 5-14 *Protocol Stack for Multi-VRF CE*

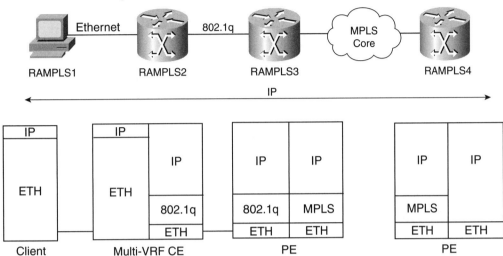

The Multi-VRF CE runs on an Ethernet switch, not a router, so the configuration is a little different. The following are the three major sections of the configuration:

- **The VRF definitions for each VPN** —Just as on a PE, these have route-descriptor and route-target values, as shown in Example 5-37.

- **The physical port connections** —On an Ethernet switch, you need to configure access/trunk mode, as shown in Example 5-38.

- **The VLAN subinterfaces** —Map trunk interfaces to VRFs, as shown in Example 5-39, with the IP addresses and VRF names.

Example 5-37 *Multi-VRF CE VRF Definitions*

```
!
ip vrf PINK
 rd 200:1
 route-target export 200:1
 route-target import 200:1
!
ip vrf RED
 rd 300:1
 route-target export 300:1
 route-target import 300:1
!
ip vrf BLUE
 rd 400:1
 route-target export 400:1
 route-target import 400:1
!
```

Example 5-38 *Multi-VRF CE Switch Port Configuration*

```
!
interface FastEthernet0/8

switchport access vlan 300
!
interface FastEthernet0/9

switchport access vlan 200
!
interface FastEthernet0/10

switchport access vlan 400

interface FastEthernet0/11
switchport trunk encapsulation dot1q
switchport mode trunk Switch
no ip address
```

Example 5-39 *Multi-VRF CE VLAN Configuration*

```
!
interface Vlan200
 ip vrf forwarding PINK
 ip address 10.0.0.2 255.255.255.0
!
interface Vlan300
 encapsulation dot1Q 300
 ip vrf forwarding RED
 ip address 10.0.0.2 255.255.255.0
!
interface Vlan400
 encapsulation dot1Q 400
 ip vrf forwarding BLUE
 ip address 10.0.0.2 255.255.255.0
!
```

Finally, Example 5-40 shows a PE configuration.

Example 5-40 *PE for Multi-VRF CE*

```
ip vrf PINK
 rd 200:1
 route-target export 200:1
 route-target import 200:1
!
ip vrf RED
 rd 300:1
 route-target export 300:1
 route-target import 300:1
!
ip vrf BLUE
```

Example 5-40 *PE for Multi-VRF CE (Continued)*

```
 rd 400:1
 route-target export 400:1
 route-target import 400:1
 !
 !
 interface FastEthernet0/0.1
  encapsulation dot1Q 200
  ip vrf forwarding PINK
  ip address 10.0.0.2 255.255.255.0
 !
 interface FastEthernet0/0.2
  encapsulation dot1Q 300
  ip vrf forwarding RED
  ip address 10.0.0.2 255.255.255.0
 !
 interface FastEthernet0/0.3
  encapsulation dot1Q 400
  ip vrf forwarding BLUE
  ip address 10.0.0.2 255.255.255.0
 !
 !
 interface FastEthernet1/1
  description Interface to core
  ip address 10.0.2.2 255.255.255.252
  tag-switching ip
```

As you can see in Example 5-40, the PE configuration is very straightforward. There is only IP traffic on the CE-PE link, no labels. The VRF construct is used only as a local private routing table and that there is no special requirement to use the same **RD** and **route-targets** on the Multi-VRF CE as the PE. However, because there are these private tables, you still need to use the **/vrf** option to ping or telnet across the cloud.

Comparison Using the Broadband VPN Framework

You have seen that GRE, IPSec, and L2TP VPNs all have their strengths and weaknesses when used with broadband access. Now it is time to look at how well MPLS VPNs perform. For the sake of consistency, the evaluation is done using the broadband VPN framework introduced in Chapter 1, "Introduction: Broadband Access and Virtual Private Networks."

MPLS is not some sort of magic technology that makes all the earlier problems go away. It solves some elegantly, others approximately, and still others not at all. When it comes to making the choice, you should balance the relative advantages of each solution against one another.

Recall that the broadband framework was defined by a list of 12 elements, reviewed next.

Site VPNs need the following:

- Data confidentiality
- Efficient operation (including ease of provisioning)
- Efficient routing
- High availability and resiliency
- Multicast
- Quality of service
- Fragmentation

Telecommuter VPNs need the following, in addition to those mentioned previously:

- Authentication, authorization, and accounting
- Service selection

Wholesale VPNs need the following beyond the requirements of telecommuter VPNs:

- Support for any IP addressing plan
- Efficient address management
- Additional L3 services

Each of the items in the preceding lists is discussed in detail in the following sections.

Data Confidentiality

Interestingly enough, there have been more questions about data confidentiality than you might think are warranted. An MPLS VPN is just as secure as a Frame Relay or ATM VPN. That is to say, traffic from one VPN is never mixed with that of another. The MPLS core is in a completely different routing domain from that of the VPNs. Customer traffic cannot leak into the core. The only difference with a traditional Layer 2 core is that the core and customer networks use the same control plane. In theory, a misconfigured PE could let customer traffic leak into the core. But a misconfigured Frame Relay network could switch the wrong data-link connection identifier (DLCI) to a customer site. A good NMS/OSS system would mitigate against either eventuality, and it is fair to say that Frame Relay, being a more mature solution, has much better OSS support.

Efficient Operation

This is a big advantage for the MPLS-based solution. Setting aside the number of steps on the CLI, the MPLS-VPN solution is the only one that allows you to add new sites to a VPN without updating all the PEs connected to the other sites. DMVPN trys to do the same thing for IPSec tunnels, but MPLS VPN has a lot more deployment behind it.

MPLS VPN is also known to scale extremely well, and the control protocol, BGP, is used on the largest network of them all, the Internet.

MPLS VPNs also have the option of using BGP route reflectors (RRs), as shown in Figure 5-15, whereby all PEs peer-establish their BGP sessions with a central route reflector, not with each other. Route reflectors are a well-known feature of large-scale BGP networks and they also allow MPLS-VPN networks to scale very well because different RRs can be used for different VRFs.

Figure 5-15   *PEs and Route Reflector*

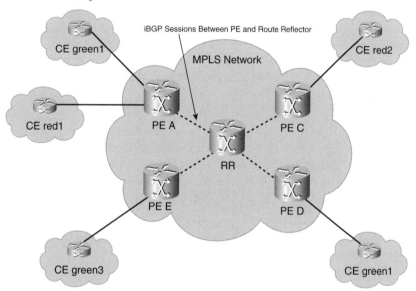

Efficient Routing

Efficient routing is probably the biggest gain for a customer who uses any IP VPN. Intersite routing is outsourced to the service provider, and CE routing becomes very simple to do. The biggest headache encountered is if the service provider does not support the routing protocol used across the previous WAN.

Compare this with the complexity of routing in a tunnel environment, where sites have the responsibility for knowing which hub to send traffic to, and hubs have the heavier burden of correctly forwarding traffic between sites. With an MPLS-VPN solution, this problem is transferred to the service provider, who typically offers full-mesh connectivity or other, more constrained topologies. Recall that with MPLS VPN, other service provider core routers do not carry the customers' routes.

High Availability and Resiliency

MPLS availability is now very sophisticated and entirely comparable to the Layer 2 VPN solutions it is steadily displacing. It is probably fair to say that MPLS is in a class of its own when compared to GRE, IPSec, or L2TP.

There are several layers to consider. First, there is an IP control plane across the VPN. CE-PE link failure, for example, can be detected by the IP routing protocol on that interface. If a site, or CE or PE, is no longer available, BGP withdraws the relevant routing entries automatically. When the site or device comes back up, BGP again updates the VPN routing tables to reflect the change in topology. There is no need for any tricks to detect remote tunnels going down.

You can also deploy redundancy between CE and PE. As you can see in Figure 5-16, several scenarios are available. You can install secondary routes to backup CEs, as shown in scenario a, with higher costs to make sure they are only used if the primary fails. You can have more than one service provider and load-balance routes across them, as shown in scenario b. CEs can even peer with redundant PEs, as shown in scenario c. (Be careful of routing loops.)

In the core network, the service provider can use MPLS OAM (Operation, Administration, and Maintenance) to check LSP continuity either segment to segment or right across the network. Refer to Appendix A for additional documents that explain the details of MPLS OAM, including mechanisms such as **mpls ping** and **traceroute** , VCCV, and so on. Another option for the service provider is to use MPLS Fast Reroute in the core. This subject was touched upon in Chapter 4, "Introduction to MPLS," and it greatly reduces convergence time in case of a link or node failure in the core.

All in all, an MPLS-based solution has a rich set of availability mechanisms, both at the service and transport layers.

Multicast

For the longest time, IP multicast was something of a challenge because MPLS VPN supported only unicast IP. This is no longer the case, even if there are several alternative implementations, each of which with its own advantages and disadvantages. The difference with the other solutions is really about where multicast replication takes place for residential subscribers. In an L2TP network, IP stops (or starts, depending on your perspective) on the LNS. This device would have to be responsible for replicating streams to subscribers as they joined multicast groups. The whole service provider core network must then carry multiple instances of the same stream, driving up bandwidth requirements considerably. In an MPLS-VPN scenario, replication can be done closer to the subscriber on the PE that "replaces" the LAC in the network architecture.

As a general rule, it is better to do replication as close to the subscriber as possible, especially if the underlying network supports it, as is the case with Ethernet.

Figure 5-16   *CE-PE Backup Scenarios*

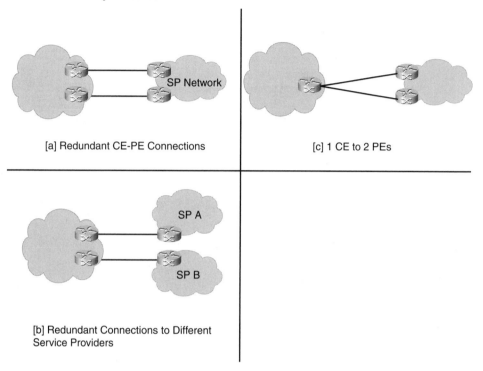

[a] Redundant CE-PE Connections

[c] 1 CE to 2 PEs

[b] Redundant Connections to Different
Service Providers

Quality of Service

QoS is a huge advantage for the MPLS-based VPN solution. As described more fully in Chapter 4, IP QoS to MPLS QoS mapping is very well defined and there are clear mechanisms to allow subscriber policy to be mapped to service provider classes of service. The CPE-based solutions discussed in Chapter 3 are, of course, IP based and also have the ability of mapping subscriber traffic QoS settings to the IP header used to carry the packet across the service provider core. A point in favor of MPLS is the ability to use traffic engineering in the core network to better utilize bandwidth. L2TP is the least flexible solution from a QoS perspective. The IP core between LAC and LNS basically has no way of knowing what QoS is required by the subscriber traffic buried deep in a PPP frame.

In a VHG context, as long as the underlying Layer 2 infrastructure supports the required QoS, then MPLS VPN fully supports IP multiservice applications. With the possible exception of GRE, MPLS has the best-developed Cisco IOS QoS implementation of all the VPN technologies you have studied so far.

Fragmentation

All the broadband PE solutions terminate subscriber encapsulations before routing IP packets over the MPLS core network, as was shown in Figures 5-10, 5-11, and 5-12. This means that the fragmentation equation really does not change. The MTU is shorter on the access interface than on the core interface.

Be careful of the VHG architecture, especially if the VHG and LNS/PE connect over Ethernet, because additional L2TP and UDP headers are added, which can reduce the MTU. Anyway, both of these devices are under the control of the service provider, so it is easy to correct the settings.

So far, everything has been very positive for the MPLS-VPN approach. Routing is easier, operations are more efficient, IP QoS just works: How could life get any better?

Unfortunately, not all of the remaining requirements are satisfied with what you have seen so far.

Authentication, Authorization, and Accounting

MPLS VPN doesn't add any new controls specific to broadband access. So, any VPN solution must use the mechanisms that come with the Layer 2 encapsulations, such as RADIUS or DHCP.

For example, AAA messages are originated on the SP edge device, but need to reach to the customer network for authentication, because that is where the customer database is. This poses a real problem: How do you get non-VPN traffic into the VPN? The answer, as will be the case for much of the rest of these features, is to make the Cisco IOS AAA subsystem *VRF aware*. In essence, that means that AAA traffic can be configured to look up destination server addresses in the correct VRF, instead of in the global routing table.

Don't confuse the need for VRF-aware DHCP with the case in which the DHCP relay is on the CE. In this instance, the DHCP request is just an IP packet to the PE. You need the VRF-aware version only when either the relay agent or the DHCP server is run on the PE.

Service Selection

PPP allows VPN selection by mapping VPDN domain names to VRF names. This is not possible with the other access encapsulation methods. In this regard, MPLS is equivalent to the other VPN solutions that support service selection.

Support Any IP Addressing Plan

MPLS VPN supports overlapping IP address spaces just perfectly. In Cisco IOS, VRFs were introduced to provide private routing tables on PE devices. VRFs can in fact be deployed in other places in the network, an example of which you saw with Multi-VRF CE in this chapter.

The voluntary exception to the classic MPLS-VPN model is the cable SFID to VRF mapping model, where the cable modem has a single address space (and routing table), even though traffic can be mapped to different VPNs on the CMTS, using different RD values.

Efficient Address Management

Unlike IPSec and L2TP, an MPLS-VPN wholesaler is in the IP address-management business. Subscribers need IP addresses before they can send traffic through the PE. Because the wholesaler terminates the subscriber access protocols, it has the responsibility for providing addresses. The wholesaler can use the same control protocols, namely DHCP and RADIUS, that an ISP would usually use. Once again, protocols must be VRF aware. This is the downside of being able to offer IP services.

Additional L3 Services

The tunnel solutions require the wholesale provider to do just one thing: transport packets. Because an MPLS-VPN wholesale provider terminates the access protocols, it can insert additional value-added services such as firewalls into the data path and offer these to end users. This is a significant benefit to the wholesale provider.

Services can include multicast, NAT, firewall, packet inspection, and subscriber self care. At the risk of being repetitive, the underlying Cisco IOS features need to be VRF aware.

Summary

This chapter introduced basic concepts of MPLS-VPN architectures for broadband networks and looked at the impact of connecting broadband subscribers to an MPLS VPN.

The new architectural concepts for broadband are Virtual Home Gateways and VRF extension to the CE, with Multi-VRF CE. These are conceptually quite simple, and you saw examples of each in this chapter. The difficulty is in the details.

VRF awareness is an important concept, and specific Cisco IOS features or subsystems need to be modified before they can work on a PE. Chapter 6 looks at these more closely.

In this chapter, you learn about the following topics:

- Dynamic VRF Selection Using PPP, DHCP, and Other Methods
- Deploying Proxy RADIUS for MPLS-VPN Architectures, Using Per-VRF AAA and Per-VRF Phase II
- Managing Dynamic Address Assignment for VRFs, Using Local Pools and ODAP

Wholesale MPLS-VPN Related Service Features

Wholesale VPN providers have a specific set of operational requirements. They must be able to apply policy to subscribers with whom they cannot explicitly interact, and they must respect the private nature of VPN traffic. Many sophisticated features have evolved over the years to serve the needs of this particular category of providers. This chapter deals with the implementation of the most significant of the features in the context of MPLS and looks at them as comprising a toolkit that gives you a variety of ways to deploy the features in your network.

The chapter starts by reviewing the whole issue of binding: how to dynamically put a subscriber in the right VPN and how to know which VPN subscriber belongs to which VPN. RADIUS is a good, widely deployed option for PPP architectures that can be used to map subscribers to VRFs. Dynamic Host Configuration Protocol (DHCP) offers another way to assign VRFs but is more limited than RADIUS. Finally, there are some point solutions that can be useful, depending on the application, such as policy-based routing.

The next topic is address management in a VRF context, first using RADIUS architectures, then at the DHCP equivalents that allow wholesale VPN providers to allocate addresses to their subscribers. Wholesale VPN providers all have some method for doing this today, so an MPLS-based solution should, as much as possible, use the same methods.

Bindings Again—Dynamic VRF Allocation

In an MPLS-VPN environment, getting a subscriber into a VPN becomes a matter of knowing which VRF to use for their traffic (once the subscriber is suitably authenticated, of course).

All the examples in Chapter 5, "Introduction to MPLS-Based Access VPN Architectures," showed static bindings for interfaces to their relevant VRFs, using the **ip vrf forwarding <VRF NAME>** command.

However, in residential access scenarios, the wholesale provider might not know which VPN a subscriber is going to use until the subscriber connects. For example, you may use the foo.com ISP over your DSL line today, but you might switch to the bar.com ISP tomorrow. When you do this, you have to tell the ISPs, so that each one updates its records accordingly. But the wholesale DSL provider never even knows that you switched. One day, you connect with a foo.com suffix, the next with a bar.com suffix, and so on. To have an efficient network operation, the wholesaler needs to be able to forward your session just as well in either case, without any manual intervention. Since you use PPP, the wholesaler does this by looking at your domain name when you connect.

NOTE   There are features in Cisco IOS that prevent a subscriber from changing his domain. No matter which virtual private dial-up network (VPDN) he connects with, he is always forwarded to a preconfigured destination ISP. Obviously, I am assuming that my wholesale provider is not hardwiring its customers like this.

The process of mapping a subscriber interface to a VRF is called *binding,* and there are four basic mechanisms available for dynamic VRF binding:

- AAA
- DHCP
- Two-box solutions: policy-based routing and Service Selection Gateway (SSG)
- VRF Select

The following sections look at each of these mechanisms in turn.

AAA Again—VRF Name and the AAA Attribute

The discussion of Virtual Home Gateways in Chapter 5 deliberately sidestepped the issue of how to integrate AAA with PPP and MPLS. Now, it is time to look at that issue in some detail, by revisiting PTA and VHG architectures, but this time with the focus on AAA.

In PPP environments, recall that every subscriber has a dedicated **virtual-access** interface on the router. The commands applied to a subscriber **virtual-access** interface are cloned from a template, called, imaginatively, a **virtual-template** . So far, my examples have shown PPP sessions mapped to a VPN using a VRF name that is statically defined on a **virtual-template** interface. Any **virtual-access** interfaces cloned from that template are in the same VRF.

Static mapping is useful, but there are many cases in which you have to be able to map a subscriber to an MPLS VPN using a domain name, just as with L2TP. Cisco IOS Virtual Profiles allow you to apply any interface configuration commands to a subscriber that you would normally execute on the CLI, but using RADIUS. The final, complete configuration of the subscriber **virtual-access** interface is the "sum" of what is in RADIUS and what is local to the router's **virtual-template** interface. Figure 6-1 shows how this works.

Figure 6-1   virtual profile, virtual-template, virtual-access

RADIUS Server

Virtual Profile
joe@green.com Password = "cisco"
Framed-IP-Address = 2.254.1.4

Virtual Template Configuration
Int virtual-template 1
Ip vrf forwarding green

Virtual Access Interface
Int virtual-access
Ip address 2.254.1.4
Ip vrf forwarding green

Subscriber interface configuration
combines virtual profile and virtual-template.

There is nothing new here: **virtual-profiles** , **virtual-template** , and so on were first implemented on Cisco dial platforms and, because PPP is involved in both places, were subsequently carried over to broadband access. The next two sections cover how to download subscriber VRF configuration information from RADIUS in both PTA and VHG architectures.

Direct PPP Termination and Aggregation with AAA

Consider the case in which the PPP session is directly terminated in a VRF. This architecture, shown in Figure 6-2, is also called PPP Termination and Aggregation (PTA).

The call flow is as follows:

1. A subscriber connects as joe@green.com.

2. The aggregation router, RAMPLS2, sends a RADIUS ACCESS-REQUEST to the AAA server.

3. The AAA server at 2.254.1.2 finds a subscriber profile for joe@green.com and returns an ACCESS-ACCEPT, which includes the VRF name.

4. RAMPLS2 terminates the PPP session and the new virtual access interface is created and placed in the VRF GREEN.

5. A new directly connected route is created in the GREEN VRF.

Traffic can pass to and from joe@green.com and the rest of the GREEN VPN.

Figure 6-2 *PTA Architecture Using AAA*

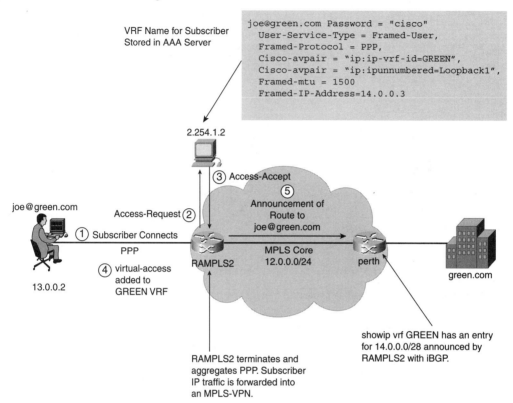

The subscriber profile is the all-important piece here. It is given in Example 6-1.

Example 6-1 *Subscriber's RADIUS Profile for VRF Download*

```
joe@green.com Password = "cisco"
  User-Service-Type = Framed-User,
  Framed-Protocol = PPP,
  Cisco-avpair = "ip:ip-vrf-id=GREEN",
  Cisco-avpair = "ip:ipunnumbered=Loopback1",
  Framed-mtu = 1500
  Framed-IP-Address=14.0.0.3
```

Initially, there was no specific **av-pair** for VRF or names, so the Cisco LCP attribute was used. This attribute is used in many other different cases, and basically allows you to send a text string to the router with interface-level configuration commands. It is not very elegant, but it works.

As you can see in Example 6-1, there are now specific RADIUS attributes to configure a subscriber's VRF and unnumbered interface names, and you should prefer this to LCP.

Nevertheless, Example 6-2 shows how to configure the LCP method. The concept is the same either way, and that is the important concept to grasp in the discussion about dynamic VRF selection using AAA. As a side note, you must have an unnumbered interface added to the LCP string; use **av-pair = "lcp:interface-config = ip vrf forwarding vpn1\nip unnumbered loopback 1"** . Configure the **vpdn-profile aaa** command on the router if you use the LCP attribute—you will not need it with the IP av-pair. Irrespective of whether you use the LCP or the IP av-pair, remember to configure the unnumbered interface *after* the VRF name (just like on the CLI: The VRF name must come first).

Example 6-2   *Subscriber's RADIUS Profile Using LCP Attribute*

```
joe@green.com    Password = "cisco"
        Service-Type = Framed-User,
        Framed-Protocol=PPP,
        av-pair = "lcp:interface-config= ip vrf forwarding GREEN",
        Framed-IP-Address=14.0.0.3
```

The joe@green.com profile is used throughout this chapter.

The partial configuration of router RAMPLS2 from Figure 6-2 is given in Example 6-3. This is the matching router configuration to use the AAA profile from Example 6-1.

NOTE   Full configurations are posted on the ciscopress.com website at http://www.ciscopress.com/1587051362.

The configuration in Example 6-3 uses virtual-template1, which has no VRF configured. VRF information is downloaded from RADIUS. VRF FOO must be defined on the router before joe@green.com connects: Remember that a user is added to an existing VRF here. The router is not creating a VRF dynamically.

All the MPLS, routing (MP-BGP and OSPF) configuration and design considerations are exactly the same as in the examples in Chapter 5, so they are not reproduced here. The interface addressing is also identical.

Example 6-3   *PTA with AAA—RAMPLS2 Configuration*

```
!
hostname RAMPLS2
username RAMPLS2 password 0 cisco
aaa new-model
!
!
aaa authentication login default local
```

continues

Example 6-3 *PTA with AAA—RAMPLS2 Configuration (Continued)*

```
aaa authentication ppp default group radius local
aaa authorization network default group radius if-authenticated
aaa session-id common
!
ip vrf GREEN
 rd 100:1
 route-target export 100:1
 route-target import 100:1
!
ip cef
vpdn enable
!
bba-group pppoe 100
 virtual-template 1
 sessions per-vc limit 10
 sessions per-mac limit 10!
!
interface Loopback1
 ip vrf forwarding GREEN
 ip address 10.0.0.2 255.255.255.255
!
! Interface to AAA server
interface FastEthernet0/0
 ip address 2.1.50.60 255.0.0.0
load-interval 30
no keepalive
!
! Client facing interface
interface FastEthernet1/1
 description Interface to RAMPLS1
 ip address 11.0.0.2 255.255.255.252
pppoe enable group 100
!
! virtual-template used for PPPoE subscribers
! Note: no VRF name
interface Virtual-Template1
 no ip address
 peer default ip address pool POOL
 ppp authentication chap pap
!
ip local pool POOL 13.0.0.2 13.0.0.10
!
ip RADIUS source-interface FastEthernet0/0
!
! 2.254.1.2 is the address of the radius server for this router
radius-server host 2.254.1.2 auth-port 1645 acct-port 1646
radius-server key cisco
```

Example 6-4 has debug output for user joe@green.com connecting and being mapped to the GREEN VRF. The highlighted line shows RAMPLS2 downloading the VRF name.

Example 6-4   *Debug Output for joe@green.com Connection*

```
01:37:29: RADIUS:   authenticator 95 C7 D3 5B E7 ED 0E 16 - 94 13 C0 53 A9 56 6D 6D
01:37:29: RADIUS:   Framed-Protocol    [7]   6    PPP                          [1]
01:37:29: RADIUS:   User-Name          [1]   15   "joe@green.com"
01:37:29: RADIUS:   CHAP-Password      [3]   19   *
01:37:29: RADIUS:   NAS-Port-Type      [61]  6    Virtual                      [5]
01:37:29: RADIUS:   NAS-Port           [5]   6    0
01:37:29: RADIUS:   Service-Type       [6]   6    Framed                       [2]
01:37:29: RADIUS:   NAS-IP-Address     [4]   6    2.1.50.60
01:37:29: RADIUS: Received from id 21645/41 2.254.1.2:1645, Access-Accept, len 91
01:37:29: RADIUS:   authenticator A0 A1 7C 45 82 CB 14 12 - EE DF F9 42 EB 0F D3 BB
01:37:29: RADIUS:   Service-Type       [6]   6    Framed                       [2]
01:37:29: RADIUS:   Framed-Protocol    [7]   6    PPP                          [1]
01:37:29: RADIUS:   Vendor, Cisco      [26]  53
01:37:29: RADIUS:   Cisco AVpair       [1]   47   "lcp:interface-config= ip vrf forwarding
GREEN"
01:37:29: RADIUS:   Framed-IP-Address  [8]   6    14.0.0.3
```

NOTE   The debugs that were used are as follows:

```
RAMPLS2#show debug
General OS:
  AAA Authentication debugging is on
  AAA Authorization debugging is on
  AAA Administrative debugging is on
  AAA Subsystem debugs debugging is on
  AAA Unique Id debugs debugging is on
  AAA Local debugs debugging is on
  AAA RADIUS debugs debugging is on
PPP:
  PPP detailed event debugging is on
  PPP authentication debugging is on
  PPP protocol errors debugging is on
  PPP protocol negotiation debugging is on
RADIUS protocol debugging is on
RADIUS protocol verbose debugging is on
RADIUS packet protocol (authentication) debugging is on
RADIUS packet retransmission debugging is on
RADIUS server fail-over debugging is on
```

With the customary test in Example 6-5, you can see that the interface is in the correct VRF.

Example 6-5   **show ip vrf** *After PPP Session Establishment*

```
RAMPLS2#show ip vrf
  Name                        Default RD          Interfaces
  GREEN                       100:1                 Virtual-Access3
                                                    Loopback1
```

The Cisco IOS PPP client configuration in Example 6-6 is also handy to have.

Example 6-6   *PPP Client Configuration*

```
interface Virtual-Template1
 ip address negotiated
 no keepalive
 ppp authentication chap pap
 ppp chap hostname joe@green.com
 ppp chap password 0 cisco
 ppp timeout authentication 100
end
```

Once again, the **test pppoe 1 1 <interface>** command was used to set up connections and **clear vpdn tunnel pppoe** was used to tear them down.

Example 6-3 had all PPPoE subscribers using the same **virtual-template** but different customers could have different VRF names in their RADIUS profiles and hence be connected to different VPNs.

One of the headaches with early deployments of PPPoE-based MPLS-VPN architectures came from an implementation limitation, whereby all PPPoE sessions shared the same VPDN group, which in turn referred to a single **virtual-template** which in turn referred to a a single VRF name. In other words, all PPPoE subscribers had to be in the same VRF! Of course, RADIUS downloads using the **ip:vrf-id** command solves this problem. Another approach is to use multiple **bba-group** commands, as shown in Example 6-7. The different **virtual-templates** and their VRFs are highlighted in the example.

Example 6-7   *Using Multiple* **bba-group** *Commands*

```
!
!
bba-group pppoe FOO
virtual-template 1
sessions per-vc limit 2
sessions per-mac limit 1
!
bba-group pppoe BAR
virtual-template 2
sessions per-vc limit 2
sessions per-mac limit 1
!
...
! Used for FOO VPN
```

Example 6-7   *Using Multiple* **bba-group** *Commands (Continued)*

```
interface Virtual-Template1
 ip unnumbered loopback 1
 ip vrf forwarding FOO
 no ip directed-broadcast
peer default ip address pool FOO_POOL
 ppp authentication pap chap
!
! Used for BAR VPN
interface Virtual-Template2
 ip unnumbered loopback 2
 ip vrf forwarding BAR
 no ip directed-broadcast
peer default ip address pool BAR_POOL ppp authentication pap chap
!
```

In Example 6-7, **bba-group FOO** uses **virtual-template 1** and **bba-group BAR** uses **virtual-template 2**. These **bba-group** commands must be applied to the subscriber interfaces. Example 6-8 shows how.

Example 6-8   *Applying Multiple* **bba-group** *Commands to Subscriber Lines*

```
! Subscribers will use VRF FOO
interface FastEthernet0/1
no ip route-cache
 no ip mroute-cache
pppoe enable group FOO

! Subscribers will use VRF BAR
interface FastEthernet1/1
 no ip route-cache
 no ip mroute-cache
pppoe enable group BAR
```

In Example 6-8, subscribers on FastEthernet0/1 will be placed in VRF FOO. Those on FastEthernet1/1 will go in to VRF BAR. You can see that bba-groups still have a limitation, because you indirectly "hardwire" the VRF name to subscriber interfaces, but at least you can have more than one VRF to choose from for all the PPPoE subscribers. Non-PPPoE sessions never had this implementation limitation and you could always map different PPPoA interfaces to different virtual-templates with different VRFs. Still, using AAA is the most flexible option because you can use the domain name to map any subscriber to any VRF without having to worry about which interface they connect on.

VHG with AAA

Recall that Virtual Home Gateways (VHGs) use L2TP to select the PE router in situations where a particular VRF is already instantiated. There are two devices involved: a VHG/LAC, which terminates any existing PPPoE-level protocol, and maps PPP sessions into a L2TP tunnel using the VPDN domain name, and an LNS/PE, which terminates both tunnel and PPP sessions and maps the IP traffic into the subscriber's VRF.

Both VHG/LAC and LNS/PE can use AAA to store tunnel configuration in the form of RADIUS profiles. Figure 6-3 shows the new topology, and the sequence of steps during PPP session establishment is as follows. (Note that some of the steps are the same as for PTA, previously described.)

Figure 6-3   *VHG with AAA*

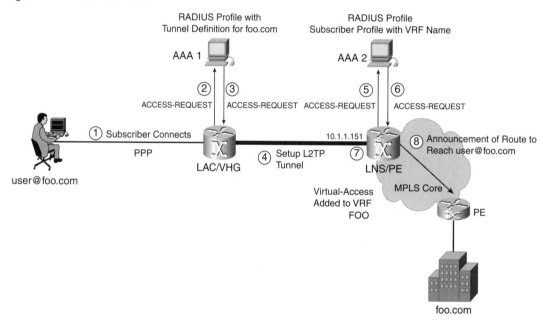

1. A subscriber connects as user@foo.com.

2. The LAC/VHG router sends a RADIUS ACCESS-REQUEST to server AAA1.

3. AAA1 server finds a subscriber profile for foo.com, shown in Example 6-9, and returns an ACCESS-ACCEPT.

4. The LAC/VHG builds a tunnel (if none exists) to the LNS/PE for domain foo.com.

5. The LNS/PE sends an ACCESS-REQUEST to server AAA2 to authenticate subscriber user@foo.com.

6. If the password is correct, server AAA2 returns an ACCESS-ACCEPT with the profile given in Example 6-10. This profile is the same as for the PTA case.

7. The LNS/PE creates a virtual-access interface for user@foo.com and places it in VRF FOO. A /32 route is added to the VRF FOO routing table.

8. If there is no aggregate route for the subnet, the LNS/PE announces the route and label to peer routers in the VPN.

9. The data from the PPP frame is forwarded to its destination.

The only difference with previous VHG/LAC configurations is that information about how to reach the LNS is stored in RADIUS. Example 6-9 shows the AAA profile for the bar.com tunnel, which is kept in server AAA1.

Example 6-9   *VHG/LAC Profile from AAA1*

```
foo.com Password = "cisco"
          av-pair = "vpdn:l2tp-tunnel-password=cisco",
          av-pair = "vpdn:ip-addresses=10.1.1.151",
          av-pair = "vpdn:tunnel-type=l2tp",
          av-pair = "vpdn:tunnel-id=FOO"
```

The LNS/PE at 10.1.1.151 has a standard VHG configuration, with a VPDN group that terminates a tunnel with a FOO ID. The subscriber profile for user@foo.com, shown in Example 6-10 and found on RADIUS server AAA2, uses the **ip:vrf-id** command to assign the subscriber to VRF FOO.

Example 6-10   *LNS/PE Subscriber Profile from AAA2*

```
joe@foo.com Password = "changeme"
  User-Service-Type = Framed-User,
  Framed-Protocol = PPP,
  Cisco-avpair = "ip:ip-vrf-id=FOO",
  Cisco-avpair = "ip:ipunnumbered=Loopback1",
  Framed-mtu = 1500
```

In summary, using PPP with AAA allows you to dynamically map a subscriber to the correct VPN based on the domain name. Both the PTA and VHG architectures use the same type of user profile, which has a RADIUS attribute that indicates the VRF name. With VHG, the L2TP endpoint definitions can also go into AAA.

DHCP—Life Without AAA

Of course, PPP is not the only protocol used in broadband architectures, and you need to consider how DHCP is used for residential bridged and Ethernet networks. There are a couple of scenarios to consider with DHCP.

The first and most common is the case in which all the DHCP servers are on the ISP network and the wholesaler plays no role in address allocation or management. In this case, there is no change if the wholesaler deploys an MPLS environment. Each ISP has dedicated servers, as shown in Figure 6-4.

Figure 6-4 *Dedicated DHCP Servers per VPN*

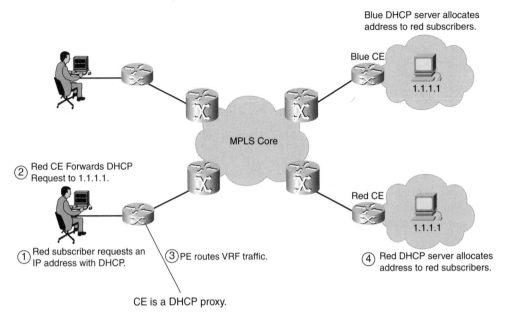

Blue DHCP server allocates
address to red subscribers.

Blue CE

1.1.1.1

MPLS Core

(2) Red CE Forwards DHCP
Request to 1.1.1.1.

Red CE

1.1.1.1

(1) Red subscriber requests an
IP address with DHCP.

(3) PE routes VRF traffic.

(4) Red DHCP server allocates
address to red subscribers.

CE is a DHCP proxy.

Now, an astute network operator might see an opportunity to sell an additional service by managing its customers' address allocation for them, as shown in Figure 6-5. In this case, you want to keep costs down by sharing a DHCP server between multiple VPNs.

Figure 6-5 *Shared DHCP Servers Across VPNs*

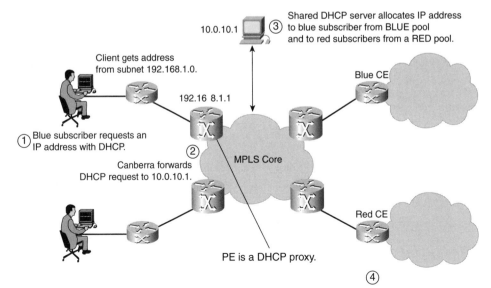

10.0.10.1

(3) Shared DHCP server allocates IP address
to blue subscriber from BLUE pool
and to red subscribers from a RED pool.

Client gets address
from subnet 192.168.1.0.

Blue CE

192.16 8.1.1

(1) Blue subscriber requests an
IP address with DHCP.

(2)

Canberra forwards
DHCP request to 10.0.10.1.

MPLS Core

Red CE

PE is a DHCP proxy.

(4)

Now, for the DHCP server to allocate the correct address, it has to know which VPN the client belongs to, and so the DHCP relay agent, which is router Canberra in Figure 6-5, inserts the VRF name into the Option 82 field of the DHCP request.

The flow of events is as follows:

1. A client issues a DHCP request.

2. Router Canberra forwards the request to the DHCP server, after inserting the Option 82 field indicating the VRF name, as well as its own IP address 192.168.1.1, in the giaddr field.

3. The DHCP server at 10.0.10.1 uses the VRF name to find the right address pool and selects one for this client (other policy mechanisms can be applied too) from the BLUE pool.

4. DHCP server 10.0.10.1 sends a DHCP reply back to Canberra.

5. Canberra forwards the DHCP reply containing the IP address to the client.

Note that in Figure 6-5, the DHCP server is not in any VPN. As a result, it can never communicate directly with the client.

The router configuration of a shared DHCP service is very straightforward. First, turn on VRF-aware Option 82 globally using **ip dhcp relay information option vpn** . Next, on each subinterface, add **ip helper-address vrf red 10.0.10.10** . (The IP address is that of the DHCP server.)

Referring again to Figure 6-5, when the relay agent receives a DHCPDISCOVER message, it unicasts the following information to the server 10.0.10.10:

```
giaddr = 10.0.0.1
circuit-id = e0/1/2
remote-id = 00:0a:95:66:d3:be
subnet selection option = 192.168.1.0
vpn-id = blue
server selection override = 192.168.1.1
```

The giaddr is the IP address the relay agent uses to reach the DHCP server.

The classic Option 82 fields are as follows:

- **circuit-id** —The subinterface the DHCPDISCOVER message was received on. Different Cisco devices use different formats for this field. For example, Catalyst switches use the SNMP ifIndex value, whereas a Cisco IOS router would use the IP address concatenated with a numeric encoding of the slot/card/port. For readability reasons, this is transcribed into the actual port name in the preceding example.

- **remote-id** —The client MAC address.

NOTE   The next three fields are added with the **option vpn** command only.

- **subnet selection option** —The subnet address of the client facing interface on the relay.
- **vpn-id** —The actual VRF name, or the numeric VPN ID.
- **server selection override** —The address of the client-facing interface on the relay agent. In cable environments, you might need to communicate the secondary interface address to the DHCP server. In this case, use the global **dhcp smart-relay** command.

Unfortunately, Cisco IOS will *not* include the classic Option 82 parameters (**circuit-id**), unless you configure both **ip dhcp relay information option** and **ip dhcp relay information option vpn** .

In a display of true cleverness, the router adds the VPN parameters only if the DHCP packets were received on an interface that is itself in a VRF (or is unnumbered to an interface in one).

Obviously, the DHCP server has to expect all this and must explicitly support the extra option fields, such as **vpn-id** .

The scenario in Figure 6-5 shows how to correctly allocate addresses once VRF information has been configured on the router. Unlike the AAA-based solutions, the incoming subscriber-facing interface must already be placed in the BLUE VRF before an address can be allocated from the right pool on the right server. In sum, this is an address allocation solution, but not a way to dynamically bind subscribers to their VRF.

Dynamic VPN binding is straightforward with PPP because the subscriber gives you a unique name, and Cisco IOS creates a distinct interface for each session. Per-interface features, such as VRF name, can be configured on a per-subscriber basis.

As anyone who is trying to offer subscriber services in a bridged environment can tell you, bridged interfaces do not work this way. An interface is either shared between many subscribers or statically provisioned for each subscriber (RBE, for example). Furthermore, recall that there is no protocol-level mechanism to identify subscriber identity in DHCP-based architectures. The following list looks at the different possible ways that might be used to uniquely identify a DHCP client for the purposes of dynamic VRF selection—they are not all suitable for wide-scale deployment and only one of these options is used today:

- **MAC address** —Of course, a MAC address–based scheme is possible (in theory at any rate), whereby a VPN is provisioned for each MAC address in the DHCP database. When a client requests an address, the server would look up the VRF and IP address name configured for the MAC address. Scalability would be a concern.
- **Relay agent information** —DHCP relay agents insert information about the client using Option 82, but information about the relay agent itself (its IP address for example) is not granular enough to serve as a subscriber identifier, because subscribers from many different networks can be attached to the same router. The server could not tell the difference between them if the relay address were all there was to work with.
- **Subscriber interface** —As long as different VPNs are not configured on the same interface, the subscriber interface can be a unique identifier. But, as previously stated, this is not often the case in bridged environments.

Residential metro data/video/voice deployment is a nice, clean exception to this generalization. In such networks, the CPE is an Ethernet switch with dedicated ports for different traffic types: set-top box on one port; phone on another; computer(s) on a third. In this case, VPN membership can be happily bound to the subscriber interface.

In conclusion, DHCP has extensions that allow it to recognize a subscriber's VPN and to allocate addresses from different pools based on the VPN. Dynamic VRF binding in bridged and switched networks is hard to do using VRF. Most commercial deployments use an external mechanism, such as a web-based server that can trigger subscriber VRF assignment on PEs.

Sometimes, a switching environment does lend itself to a simple, static scheme, such as dedicating switch ports to different VPNs that transport different applications.

PBR—A Two-Box Solution

RADIUS and DHCP are the most flexible solutions for dynamic binding, but there are some other methods available that might make sense in some networks. This section covers policy-based routing; the next two sections discuss SSG and VRF Select.

Policy-based routing (PBR) refers to the process of forwarding packets using rules that override the criteria established by routing protocols. The specifics of Cisco IOS PBR involve defining an **access-list** (ACL) to match interesting traffic and a **route-map** that says what do with packets that match the ACL. Typical decisions are to change the TOS bit settings and to forward the packet on a particular interface.

PBR does not let you set the VRF directly, but you can do it in two stages, as shown in Figure 6-6.

Figure 6-6   *Two-Box Solution Using PBR*

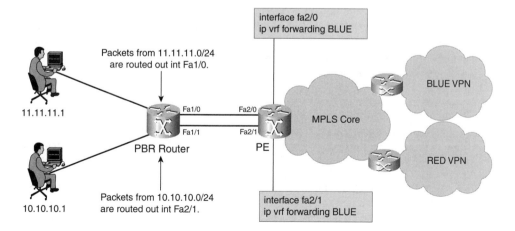

On the PBR router, you route traffic from different subscriber groups (for example, different floors in a building) to different egress interfaces. The next upstream device is a PE router, with different VRFs on its ingress ports. The net result of the scenario in Figure 6-6 is that traffic from subnet 10.10.10.0/24 goes into VRF BLUE and traffic from subnet 11.11.11.0/24 goes to VRF RED.

The PBR solution does not work in all cases. You need to have separate subnets for each VPN for the match condition shown in Figure 6-6 to work. Customer registration is one case in which this approach can work. For example, when a subscriber first connects to a public wireless network, he gets an internal address. In this case, you can use PBR to force all traffic, irrespective of its destination, to a registration server, whereupon the subscriber must often reach for his credit card before he can go anywhere interesting. Paid-up customers receive globally routable addresses (from the provider's DHCP infrastructure) and are allowed into the rest of the network. A variation on this example involves free basic Internet access (subscribers are in the public pool), but premium subscribers, who are part of a different IP subnet, have access to local high-bandwidth content.

Service Selection Gateway—Another Two-Box Solution

The Cisco IOS Service Selection Gateway (SSG) is a separate data path that forwards user traffic to services, based on group membership. The services are network destinations, and an external policy server contains all the information about which services a particular subscriber belongs to.

SSG has a somewhat complex relationship with the global routing table. When user traffic is first received, SSG forces authentication by rerouting traffic to a portal web server login screen. Once the subscriber is authenticated, SSG retrieves the set of services to which they have access. Traffic can be forwarded to any one of these services but nowhere else. Services are basically IP subnet destinations, but they can overlap. To allow this, SSG forwards without reference to the IP routing table. (Incidentally, SSG does not use VRFs.) In other words, SSG builds its own forwarding table, independently of the dynamic routing protocols running on the device. For return traffic in the service-to-subscriber direction, however, SSG does use the standard routing table to choose the correct subscriber interface. So, traffic is policy forwarded in one direction and routed in the other.

The high-level takeaway of SSG is that it allows subscriber identity (a name) to be mapped to a Layer 3 traffic stream. This is hugely valuable because you might want to do all sorts of different things for a particular person, but you could never identify them a priori by looking at their packets.

SSG is another tool to map subscriber traffic to VRFs. The architecture is basically the same as that of Figure 6-7. The first router runs SSG and, based on the service selection (this can be based on the PPP domain name too), subscriber traffic is forwarded out a particular interface. The next-hop router is a PE and maps this interface to a VRF. If the subscriber changes service, their packets are forwarded out a different dedicated interface on the first box and so find their way into a different VRF.

SSG is more flexible than PBR because there is a subscriber-level control of what goes where. You are not limited to trying to map different ranges of IP addresses to different groups; instead, you can use a domain name or even a button on a web page.

The biggest headache with both of these two-box solutions is that you cannot extend the private routing domain to the first device. If any changes occur to the routes in the VPN, there is no way to propagate this between the components of the two-box solution.

VRF Select

VRF Select uses the IP packet source address to select a VRF and does not require a second device for VPN assignment, as do PBR and SSG. The feature works by building a table that maps IP addresses to a VRF name. When a packet arrives, the router looks up the packet's source address in this table and so finds the VRF name. The router then looks up the packet's destination address in the designated VRF routing table to find the next hop and labels. There is no need to do anything special on the return path. Example 6-11 shows the configuration. The VRF selection subnets must not overlap—the source IP address is the VPN selector, so it must map uniquely to every VRF.

Example 6-11   *Example of VRF Select*

```
vrf selection source 192.168.1.0 255.255.255.0 vrf RED
vrf selection source 192.168.2.0 255.255.255.0 vrf GREEN

...

interface POS1/0
description Link to the unknown CE
ip vrf select source
```

In Example 6-11, traffic arriving on interface POS1/0 can be in either subnet 192.168.1.0 or subnet 192.168.2.0. The PE does not know till a packet arrives. Note that VRF selection is done on every packet received on the interface, so you could have CEs belonging to different VPNs on the POS1/0 interface.

If the packet does not match any VRF, it is routed using the global routing table.

The astute reader will have picked up on that VRF Select is a simple form of PBR with direct mapping to VRFs. As long as you work with source address selection, you can dispense with the two-box PBR scenario and go with VRF Select.

Proxy RADIUS and Per-VRF AAA

Proxy RADIUS is a common VPN service found on dial and broadband networks, and is used in cases in which a wholesale provider terminates all subscriber PPP sessions and forwards IP packets to the end customer ISP. So that the ISP does not lose control over who is coming onto its network and what they are allowed to do, the wholesale provider forwards all the AAA messages to the customer network too. The win for the ISP is that it is able to outsource all the complex session termination but still retain full control of its network. For the wholesale provider, this is yet another value-added service to sell.

Figure 6-7 gives an idea of how the different pieces interact. The proxy RADIUS server dispatches RADIUS messages to the ISP using the subscriber's domain name to find the right server. In this way, joe@foo.com is authenticated against the foo domain AAA database. A subscriber from a different domain, say joe@bar.com, would be authenticated against the bar domain AAA database.

Figure 6-7   *Proxy AAA with Sequence of Events for Authentication*

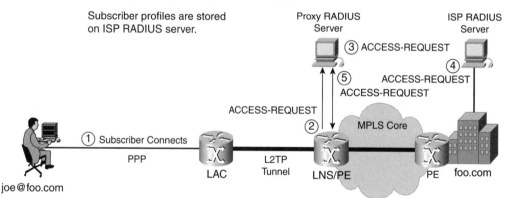

MPLS creates a simple problem for proxy RADIUS solutions. Each customer RADIUS server is in a private domain and is reachable only within a VRF. However, the wholesale provider's proxy server is not in any VRF. Therefore, there is no routed path from the proxy server to the ISP RADIUS servers, so the scenario in Figure 6-7 cannot, in fact, work.

There are two solutions to having proxy RADIUS with MPLS. The first way is to create a path between AAA servers so that they can talk to each other. Figure 6-8 shows how to do this by putting all the servers into the SP's global routing space.

Figure 6-8 *AAA Extranet VPN*

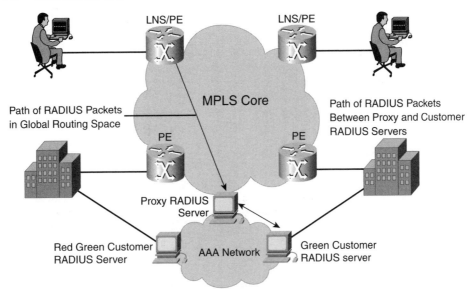

There is a path between all the radius servers, which are all in global routing space.

Security is obviously an issue. In Figure 6-8, each ISP is essentially on an extranet with all its competitors! You can tie things down with access lists, firewalls, and so forth at the edge of the wholesale network to make sure that only RADIUS packets (often udp/1845 and 1846) from the proxy server can pass between the wholesale and retail networks and forbid all traffic flow between the ISPs themselves. The advantage is the great simplicity of the solution and the fact that it is not unheard of in practice.

However, many carriers might prefer an approach that avoids a separate VPN. The alternative is to force the proxy RADIUS packets into the customer's VPN. In Cisco jargon, this is called Per-VRF AAA and it involves the PE router taking over the role of the proxy server, as shown in Figure 6-9. This is in contrast to the classic proxy architecture, in which the wholesale and retail AAA servers communicate directly.

Figure 6-9 *Per-VRF AAA Architecture*

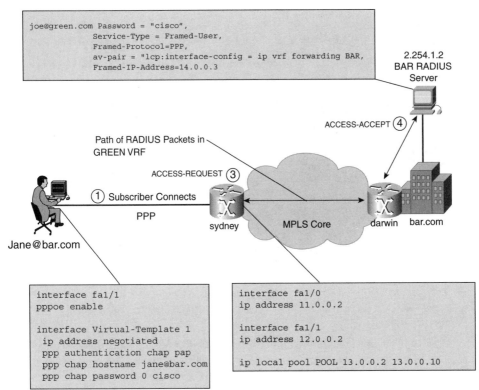

The per-VRF call setup process is a little different:

1. Subscriber jane@bar.com connects.

2. Sydney authorizes access for jane@bar.com to the bar.com domain.

3. Sydney authenticates the user by sending an ACCESS-REQUEST directly to the BAR AAA server. The RADIUS packet is routed into the BAR VRF, so traffic exits the MPLS network at darwin, the PE router connected to the site where the BAR AAA server sits.

4. Assuming the subscriber is valid, the BAR AAA server replies with an ACCESS-ACCEPT, which is sent back to sydney, the RADIUS client, across the MPLS network. Now, jane@bar.com joins the VPN and a new **virtual-access** interface is added to the BAR VRF as usual.

The difference with standard proxy RADIUS is that there is no intermediate server between sydney and the BAR AAA server.

Per-VRF AAA is transparent to the ISP AAA servers. (Of course, the client's file on BAR's RADIUS server in Figure 6-9 will need an entry for sydney.) Per-VRF AAA applies equally well to any PPP architecture—VHG as well as PTA. It is always activated on the device where the subscriber sessions are terminated, which is the LNS/PE in a VHG scenario.

Per-VRF AAA Configuration

From an implementation perspective, Per-VRF AAA has a surprising number of details to pay attention to. You have probably already guessed that, at the very least, the Cisco IOS RADIUS configuration needs some form of VRF option. There is more to it, though. Cisco IOS allows you to specify all sorts of things that determine what gets sent to the AAA server, such as accounting records. All of this must be made VRF aware, too.

There are two ways to accomplish this in Cisco IOS. The first uses standard AAA method_lists with a new VRF option. The second uses a structure created specifically for this application, called simply templates. Method_lists are covered first.

Example 6-3 is the "before" PTA configuration that will be migrated to use Per-VRF AAA in Example 6-12. There is a single AAA server, with subscriber profiles that use the **lcp:** option to configure per-user VRF.

A main requirement of Per-VRF AAA is to move from using the shared AAA server at 2.254.1.2 to using a private one for each customer domain. Step one, shown in Example 6-12, is to create an **AAA group server** for each VRF, here called GREEN_AAA. The group has a 2.254.1.2 server address and the VRF to which the server belongs. If you specify a source address for the RADIUS packets, as is the case in Example 6-12, make sure the interface you choose is in the same VRF as the RADIUS server.

Example 6-12 *AAA Group Server for GREEN VPN*

```
aaa group server RADIUS GREEN_AAA
 server-private 2.254.1.2 auth-port 1645 acct-port 1646 key cisco
 ip vrf forwarding GREEN
 ip RADIUS source-interface FastEthernet0/0
```

Example 6-13 threads the RADIUS group name throughout all the AAA configuration using a method_list. Any references to the green_method_list, such as in Example 6-14, tell Cisco IOS to use the GREEN_AAA server just defined for authentication and authorization.

Example 6-13 *AAA Method Lists for GREEN VPN*

```
aaa authentication ppp green_method_list group GREEN_AAA local
aaa authorization network green_method_list group GREEN_AAA local
```

Example 6-14 **virtual-template** *Referencing Method Lists*

```
interface Virtual-Template1
 ip unnumbered Loopback1
 peer default ip address pool POOL
 ppp authentication chap callin green_method_list
 ppp authorization green_method_list
```

Example 6-15 gives the final, complete Per-VRF AAA router configuration, with use of the method_list highlighted. Just to keep things simple, there is no AAA accounting yet. You can compare this to the original PTA configuration in Example 6-3.

Example 6-15 *Per-VRF AAA Router Configuration*

```
RAMPLS2#show run

!
hostname RAMPLS2
!
!
username RAMPLS2 password 0 cisco
username joe@green.com password 0 cisco
aaa new-model
!
! Define AAA server for GREEN VRF
aaa group server RADIUS GREEN_AAA
 server-private 2.254.1.2 auth-port 1645 acct-port 1646 key cisco
 ip vrf forwarding GREEN
 ip RADIUS source-interface FastEthernet0/0
!
aaa authentication login default local
aaa authentication ppp green_method_list group GREEN_AAA local
aaa authorization network green_method_list group GREEN_AAA local
aaa session-id common
ip subnet-zero
!
ip vrf GREEN
 rd 100:1
 route-target export 100:1
 route-target import 100:1
!
ip cef
vpdn enable
!
bba-group pppoe 100
 virtual-template 1
 sessions per-vc limit 10
 sessions per-mac limit 10
!
interface Loopback1
 ip vrf forwarding GREEN
 ip address 10.0.0.2 255.255.255.255
!
```

Example 6-15 *Per-VRF AAA Router Configuration (Continued)*

```
! Source address for RADIUS packets
interface FastEthernet0/0
 ip vrf forwarding GREEN
 ip address 2.1.50.60 255.0.0.0
load-interval 30
!!
! Client facing interface
interface FastEthernet1/1
 description Interface to RAMPLS1
 ip address 11.0.0.2 255.255.255.252
pppoe enable group 100


!
! template used by bba-group 100
! which refers to green method list
! for PPP sessions
interface Virtual-Template1
 ip unnumbered Loopback1
 peer default ip address pool POOL
 ppp authentication chap callin green_method_list
 ppp authorization green_method_list
!
ip local pool POOL 13.0.0.2 13.0.0.10
```

Example 6-15 shows that there is no longer a global RADIUS server configured. All AAA messages are now sent directly to the server in the GREEN VRF, as intended. The debug output in Example 6-16 shows that authentication does use the green_method_list. Thereafter, everything continues as before. The highlighting shows references to the method lists introduced in Example 6-15.

Example 6-16 *Debug Output of Per-VRF AAA Session Establishment*

```
RAMPLS2#

05:35:03: ppp31 PPP: Phase is AUTHENTICATING, Unauthenticated User
05:35:03: AAA/AUTHEN/PPP (00000022): Pick method list 'green_method_list'
05:35:03: ppp31 PPP: Sent CHAP LOGIN Request
05:35:03: AAA SRV(00000022): process authen req
05:35:03: AAA SRV(00000022): Authen method=SERVER_GROUP GREEN_AAA
05:35:03: RADIUS:   AAA Unsupported     [150] 7
05:35:03: RADIUS:    31 2F 30 2F 31                                [1/0/1]
05:35:03: RADIUS(00000022): Storing nasport 0 in rad_db
05:35:03: RADIUS(00000022): Config NAS IP: 2.1.50.60
05:35:03: RADIUS/ENCODE(00000022): acct_session_id: 41
05:35:03: RADIUS(00000022): sending
05:35:03: RADIUS(00000022): Send Access-Request to 2.254.1.2:1645 id 21645/47, len 84
05:35:03: RADIUS:   authenticator 2D 6F 45 C3 35 03 E0 03 - 94 13 C0 53 C3 10 15 E0
05:35:03: RADIUS:   Framed-Protocol    [7]  6   PPP                     [1]
05:35:03: RADIUS:   User-Name          [1]  15  "joe@green.com"
05:35:03: RADIUS:   CHAP-Password      [3]  19  *
05:35:03: RADIUS:   NAS-Port-Type      [61] 6   Virtual                 [5]
```

continues

Example 6-16 *Debug Output of Per-VRF AAA Session Establishment (Continued)*

```
05:35:03: RADIUS:    NAS-Port              [5]   6    0
05:35:03: RADIUS:    Service-Type          [6]   6    Framed              [2]
05:35:03: RADIUS:    NAS-IP-Address        [4]   6    2.1.50.60
05:35:03: ppp31 EVT: Auth Packet 0 0x635700DC
05:35:03: ppp31 CHAP: I SUCCESS id 1 len 4
05:35:03: RADIUS: Received from id 21645/47 2.254.1.2:1645, Access-Accept, len 91
05:35:03: RADIUS:    authenticator BD 64 4D 77 C0 5A 02 82 - 8C 1A 29 FF 0A 5F 6B 19
05:35:03: RADIUS:    Service-Type          [6]   6    Framed              [2]
05:35:03: RADIUS:    Framed-Protocol       [7]   6    PPP                 [1]
05:35:03: RADIUS:    Vendor, Cisco         [26]  53
05:35:03: RADIUS:    Cisco AVpair          [1]   47   "lcp:interface-config= ip vrf forwarding
GREEN"
05:35:03: RADIUS:    Framed-IP-Address     [8]   6    14.0.0.3
```

Somewhat strangely, even though the RADIUS server used is in a VRF, the global RADIUS statistics counters are incremented when the PE communicates with the Per-VRF AAA servers, which is shown in Example 6-17.

Example 6-17 **show radius statistics** *Output*

```
RAMPLS2#show radius statistic
                                 Auth.      Acct.      Both
          Maximum inQ length:     NA         NA          1
        Maximum waitQ length:     NA         NA          1
        Maximum doneQ length:     NA         NA          1
         Total responses seen:     1          0          1
      Packets with responses:      1          0          1
   Packets without responses:      0          0          0
   Average response delay(ms):     4          0          4
   Maximum response delay(ms):     4          0          4
    Number of RADIUS timeouts:     0          0          0
          Duplicate ID detects:    0          0          0
Source Port Range: (full range)
21645 - 21844
Last used Source Port/Identifier:
21645/47
```

NOTE If this is the first time that you are using named method lists—and a lot of Cisco IOS examples always use defaults—try getting things to work without the VRFs. For reference, the relevant parts of the configuration are as follows:

```
aaa group server RADIUS GREEN_AAA
 server 2.254.1.2 auth-port 1645 acct-port 1646
!
aaa authentication login default local
aaa authentication ppp green_method_list group GREEN_AAA local
aaa authorization network green_method_list group GREEN_AAA local
aaa session-id common

...
```

```
                interface Virtual-Template1
                 ip unnumbered Loopback1
                 peer default ip address pool POOL
                 ppp authentication chap callin green_method_list
                 ppp authorization green_method_list
                ...

                !
                ip RADIUS source-interface FastEthernet0/0
                !
                !
                RADIUS-server host 2.254.1.2 auth-port 1645 acct-port 1646 key cisco
```

Per-VRF AAA Templates

The link between the VRF AAA server and the subscriber relies on having the right method list on the right **virtual-template** . It is easy to imagine a situation with different subscribers on the same physical interface wanting to go to different VPNs, but all being authenticated using whatever method_list is configured for the **virtual-template** for their protocol or circuit.

For that reason, a construct called *templates* was added to Cisco IOS. Templates help improve AAA selection, but also, and just as importantly, allow you to move large chunks of the per-VRF configuration into a central, shared AAA server. Before templates, all the information about customers' RADIUS servers (in AAA server group) was configured on the device. There was no other choice. Templates give you the choice of local configuration on the router or central configuration on an AAA server. Cisco documentation sometimes refers to templates as *Per-VRF Phase II*.

Example 6-18 reworks Example 6-15 to use local templates. None of the underlying concepts changes; this is just another, more flexible way of configuring private RADIUS servers for each VRF. Example 6-18 contains only the chunks of configuration related to templates.

Example 6-18 *Per-VRF AAA Configuration Using Templates*

```
!
hostname RAMPLS2
aaa new-model
!
!
aaa group server RADIUS GREEN_AAA
 server 2.254.1.2 auth-port 1645 acct-port 1646
 ip vrf forwarding GREEN
 ip RADIUS source-interface FastEthernet0/0
!
aaa authentication login default local
aaa authentication ppp green_method_list group GREEN_AAA
aaa authentication ppp chap_method_list local
aaa authorization template
aaa authorization network green_method_list group GREEN_AAA
aaa session-id common
```

continues

Example 6-18 *Per-VRF AAA Configuration Using Templates (Continued)*

```
ip subnet-zero
!
!
template green.com
 peer default ip address pool POOL
 ppp authentication chap callin green_method_list
 ppp authorization green_method_list
!
!
interface Virtual-Template1
 ip vrf forwarding GREEN
 ip unnumbered Loopback1
 no peer default ip address
 ppp authentication chap callin chap_method_list
!
```

NOTE   The Cisco IOS images that are used here are big and you can't use TFTP to download them anymore. RCP or FTP both work. The syntax follows:

```
copy ftp://user:password@1.1.1.1//tftpboot/book/c7200-g4js-mz.123-4.T
disk0:c7200-g4js-mz.123-4.T
```

At a high level, the template in Example 6-18 points to a method_list, which in turn points to an AAA group server.

Take a look at Example 6-18 in more detail. The first change is that local templates are enabled by the **aaa authorization template** command. The PPP client uses the same name for both CHAP handshake and for LCP authentication, but the router terminating the PPP session needs to treat each of these differently. Example 6-18 does this with two different method lists. The **chap_method_list** on virtual-template 1 is used to authenticate the CHAP session between PPP client and server, and the joe@green.com **username** is defined locally for this. The green_method_list in the **template** is used to authenticate the GREEN VPN users against the private AAA server in that domain. In the previous examples in this section, the green_method_list supported both RADIUS and local methods, so only one list is needed.

The template name matches the subscriber's domain name. This is a big change over the pure method list approach. In this case, the domain is green.com. As you can see from the debug output in Example 6-19, once Cisco IOS gets the username during LCP authentication, it looks for a template with a name that matches that of the caller (just like an LAC does when trying to bring up an L2TP tunnel). If it finds a match, then all the configuration defined under the template is applied to the subscriber's connection. Thus, green.com users once again have their

AAA requests redirected to the RADIUS server associated with the green_method_list. Highlighting in Example 6-19 shows references to the green.com template and method_list.

Example 6-19 *Debug Output for Per-VRF AAA Session Establishment Using Templates (**debug template** Also Used)*

```
RAMPLS2#
[section using chap_method_list removed]
00:26:50: AAA/LOCAL/AUTHEN: starting
00:26:50: AAA/LOCAL/AUTHEN(8): authorizing vpn green.com
00:26:50: TEMPLATE/AUTHOR:(00000008) Found local template "green.com"
00:26:50: AAA SRV(00000008): protocol reply PASS for Authorization
00:26:50: AAA SRV(00000008): Return Authorization status=PASS
00:26:50: TEMPLATE/AUTHOR:(00000008) Successful processing template attributes
00:26:50: ppp7 PPP: Setting new auth type 'CHAP' (at index=0)
00:26:50: AAA/BIND(00000008) : Bind template "green.com"
00:26:50: ppp7 EVT: Hook 1 0x00000000
00:26:50: ppp7 EVT: Forwarded 0 0x00000000
00:26:50: ppp7 PPP: Phase is AUTHENTICATING, Unauthenticated User
00:26:50: AAA/AUTHEN/PPP (00000008): Pick method list 'green_method_list'
00:26:50: ppp7 PPP: Sent CHAP LOGIN Request
00:26:50: AAA SRV(00000008): process authen req
00:26:50: AAA SRV(00000008): Authen method=SERVER_GROUP GREEN_AAA
00:26:50: RADIUS:   AAA Unsupported     [150] 7
00:26:50: RADIUS:    31 2F 30 2F 31                              [1/0/1]
00:26:50: RADIUS(00000008): Storing nasport 0 in rad_db
00:26:50: RADIUS(00000008): Config NAS IP: 2.1.50.60
00:26:50: RADIUS/ENCODE(00000008): acct_session_id: 8
00:26:50: RADIUS(00000008): sending
00:26:50: ppp7 EVT: Auth Packet 0 0x63A4C8A4
00:26:50: ppp7 CHAP: I SUCCESS id 1 len 4
00:26:50: RADIUS(00000008): Send Access-Request to 2.254.1.2:1645 id 21645/4, len 84
00:26:50: RADIUS:   authenticator EB 4B D5 CC 83 A6 0E 13 - 94 13 C0 53 B3 91 6B FF
00:26:50: RADIUS:   Framed-Protocol   [7]   6   PPP                      [1]
00:26:50: RADIUS:   User-Name         [1]   15  "joe@green.com"
00:26:50: RADIUS:   CHAP-Password     [3]   19  *
00:26:50: RADIUS:   NAS-Port-Type     [61]  6   Virtual                  [5]
00:26:50: RADIUS:   NAS-Port          [5]   6   0
00:26:50: RADIUS:   Service-Type      [6]   6   Framed                   [2]
00:26:50: RADIUS:   NAS-IP-Address    [4]   6   2.1.50.60
00:26:55: RADIUS: Retransmit to (2.254.1.2:1645,1646) for id 21645/4
00:26:55: RADIUS: Received from id 21645/4 2.254.1.2:1645, Access-Accept, len 91
00:26:55: RADIUS:   authenticator 14 09 5E 4B C9 E0 36 3E - C8 BE C6 14 13 E0 42 6E
00:26:55: RADIUS:   Service-Type      [6]   6   Framed                   [2]
00:26:55: RADIUS:   Framed-Protocol   [7]   6   PPP                      [1]
00:26:55: RADIUS:   Vendor, Cisco     [26]  53
00:26:55: RADIUS:   Cisco AVpair    [1]   47  "lcp:interface-config= ip vrf forwarding
GREEN"
00:26:55: RADIUS:   Framed-IP-Address [8]   6   14.0.0.3
```

Example 6-20 shows how to use templates with multiple VPNs. Note that the IP addresses of the AAA servers for green and red domains are identical. This is deliberate. The servers are in different VPNs and thus can have overlapping IP addresses. Example 6-20 just proves that particular point.

Example 6-20 *Multiple Templates for Multiple VPNs*

```
aaa group server RADIUS GREEN_AAA
 server 2.254.1.2 auth-port 1645 acct-port 1646
 ip vrf forwarding GREEN
 ip RADIUS source-interface FastEthernet0/0
!
aaa group server RADIUS RED_AAA
 server 2.254.1.2 auth-port 1645 acct-port 1646
 ip vrf forwarding GREEN
 ip RADIUS source-interface FastEthernet1/0
!
aaa authentication login default local
aaa authentication ppp green_method_list group GREEN_AAA
aaa authentication ppp chap_method_list local
aaa authentication ppp red_method_list group RED_AAA
aaa authorization template
aaa authorization network green_method_list group GREEN_AAA
aaa authorization network red_method_list group RED_AAA

template green.com
 peer default ip address pool POOL
 ppp authentication chap green_method_list
 ppp authorization green_method_list
!
template red.com
 peer default ip address pool POOL
 ppp authentication chap red_method_list
 ppp authorization red_method_list
```

The final permutation when deploying Per-VRF AAA is to centralize the information about customer ISP servers on the wholesale provider's own RADIUS server and have all the PTA or LNS/PE routers dynamically retrieve the profile that matches a subscriber's domain name when they connect. This approach makes a lot of sense because all the PE routers that terminate broadband subscribers need access to the data in the templates in Example-20. It is much more efficient to configure this once and let routers access it as needed using AAA. Figure 6-10 shows the architecture and call setup.

You can configure Per-VRF AAA in RADIUS by using a combination of Cisco **av-pairs** for method_list names, VRF names as well as the details of the customer AAA server, such as IP address and UDP ports.

Figure 6-10   *Per-VRF AAA Architecture with Remote Templates*

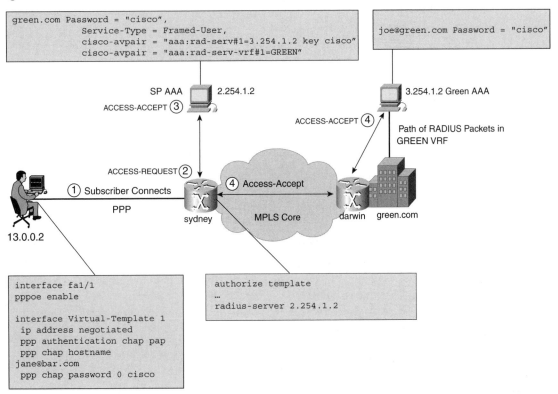

The call flow for the example shown in Figure 6-10 is as follows:

1. Subscriber connects with a username of joe@green.com.

2. Sydney sends an ACCESS-REQUEST to SP AAA at 2.254.1.2 for green.com user.

3. The SP AAA server returns a RADIUS profile for green.com, which gives the AAA server data for this VPN, as well as other information, such as the local address pool.

4. Sydney sends another ACCESS-REQUEST to the GREEN AAA server at 3.254.1.2. This request is sent in the GREEN VRF and request authentication for user joe@green.com.

5. The GREEN AAA server returns an ACCESS-ACCEPT with the VRF name and other attributes for the user.

Next, sydney negotiates an IP address with the PPP client and creates a **virtual-access** interface for the subscriber, places it in the GREEN VRF, and adds the /32 route for the interface to the GREEN routing table.

Example 6-21 gives the RADIUS profile on the 2.254.1.2 server. The joe@green.com profile is the same profile that has been used all along.

Example 6-21 *green.com Profile in SP AAA Server*

```
green.com   Password = "cisco"
cisco-avpair = "aaa:rad-serv#1=3.254.1.2 key cisco"
cisco-avpair = "aaa:rad-serv-vrf#1=GREEN"
cisco-avpair = "aaa:rad-serv-source-if#1=FastEthernet 0/0"
cisco-avpair = "template:ppp-authen-list=group 1"
cisco-avpair = "template:ppp-author-list=group 1
cisco-avpair = "ip: addr-pool=POOL"
cisco-avpair = "ip:ip-vrf-id=GREEN"
cisco-avpair = "ip:ip-unnumbered=Loopback 100"
framed-protocol = ppp
service-type = framed
```

Source: adapted by author from PER VRF AAA Phase II (CP-1519) document.

What do each of the av-pair attributes in Example 6-21 do?

The AAA attributes define the IP address, the VRF name, and the source interface for the customer VPN AAA server. The commands are exactly analogous to **aaa server group** in the previous examples. Notice how the AAA portion has a numeric label on every line that replaces the CLI group name. In Example 6-21, the AAA group is **1**, which corresponds to the GREEN_AAA label used before.

The IP attributes define the VRF name, unnumbered interface name, and IP address pool name to use for all subscribers in the green.com domain.

The template attributes basically list the method_list name. In RADIUS, template attributes reference the AAA attributes using the numeric label of the AAA block you want to use for the subscriber—for example, in the **ppp-authen-list=group 1** attribute. If you wanted to use a different customer server for accounting, for example, then the av-pair would use a different number–for example: **template:ppp-acct-list=start-stop group 2** . Finally, the template password is hardwired to be "cisco".

In summary, templates add to the palette of configuration options for Per-VRF AAA. The method_list approach still works. You could even mix and match: a template here, a method_list there. It is probably safer to choose one approach and stick with that consistently.

Per-VRF AAA Accounting

Accounting is interesting in a proxy RADIUS environment. Unlike subscriber authentication, the wholesaler cares deeply about accounting records because that is the source information that lets it bill its ISP customer. The ISP cares just as deeply because the same records are needed to bill its customers and to keep an eye on what the wholesaler is charging.

To keep all parties happy, the Per-VRF AAA router sends a copy of accounting records to both the service provider and customer servers. The feature used to do this is called *broadcast accounting*. It is a way of telling a router to send the same ACCOUNTING-START and ACCOUNTING-STOP records to multiple Cisco IOS **aaa server groups** .

Adding basic accounting to Per-VRF AAA is pretty straightforward. Just add an **aaa accounting** method list and reference it in the template, as highlighted in Example 6-22 and Example 6-23.

Example 6-22 *Accounting Method List*

```
aaa authentication login default local
aaa authentication ppp green_method_list group GREEN_AAA
aaa authorization template
aaa authorization network green_method_list group GREEN_AAA
aaa accounting network green_method_list start-stop group GREEN_AAA
aaa session-id common
```

Example 6-23 *Accounting Method List Reference in Template*

```
template green.com
 peer default ip address pool POOL
 ppp authentication chap callin green_method_list
 ppp authorization green_method_list
 ppp accounting green_method_list
```

Examples 6-22 and 6-23 send all the accounting streams directly to the server in the GREEN VPN. True broadcast accounting needs an extra detail: There is at least one additional group in the accounting method list, as shown in Example 6-24. This command instructs the router to send accounting records to the RADIUS servers defined for groups GREEN_AAA and WHOLESALE_AAA, which are also shown in Example 6-24. The net effect is that all ACCOUNTING-START and ACCOUNTING-STOP records are sent to port 1646 on 2.254.1.2 and port 1846 on 3.254.1.2.

Example 6-24 *Per-VRF* **broadcast accounting** *Command*

```
! enable broadcast accounting
aaa accounting network green_method_list start-stop broadcast group GREEN_AAA group
WHOLESALE_AAA
!
! Multiple AAA groups for broadcast accounting
! AAA server for client using Green VPN
aaa group server RADIUS GREEN_AAA
 server 3.254.1.2 auth-port 1845 acct-port 1846
 ip vrf forwarding GREEN
 ip RADIUS source-interface FastEthernet0/0
!
! AAA server for SP's own records
```

continues

Example 6-24 *Per-VRF* **broadcast accounting** *Command (Continued)*

```
aaa group server WHOLESALE_AAA
 server 2.254.1.2 auth-port 1645 acct-port 1646
 ip RADIUS source-interface Loopback0
```

Assigning and Managing Overlapping Addresses

Probably the biggest change for an operator who adopts MPLS VPN for broadband access (instead of, say, L2TP) is that she must manage customer addresses. In a way, this is the price to pay for being on the customer's data path.

In an L2TP architecture, the LNS has all the subscriber addresses and routes. In an MPLS scenario, these move to the PE. This creates a very complex problem, namely how to allocate addresses without waste. Before looking at the gory details, let's take a quick detour and cover probably the most widely used address assignment mechanism: address pools.

Overlapping Device-Local Pools

Local address pools are useful. They offer an easy alternative to AAA- or DHCP-based addressing. To function properly with VRFs, local address pools have to support overlapping addresses.

To support overlap, configure local address pools to be part of a group. Multiple pools can belong to a group, and addresses between groups can overlap. Addresses within the same group must be unique, however.

Example 6-25 shows a very simple example. There are two groups: GREEN_POOL_GROUP and RED_POOL_GROUP. The 13.0.0.0 subnet is configured in each pool and the addresses overlap.

Example 6-25 *Overlapping Address Pools Configuration*

```
ip local pool green 13.0.0.2 13.0.0.10 group GREEN_POOL_GROUP
ip local pool green 14.0.0.2 14.0.0.10 GREEN_POOL_GROUP
ip local pool red 13.0.0.2 13.0.0.10 group RED_POOL_GROUP
ip local pool red 14.0.0.2 14.0.0.10 group RED_POOL_GROUP
```

It is not widely known, but the on-board Cisco IOS DHCP service also supports overlapping pools of addresses.

On-Demand Address Pools

In classic VPN architectures, a large number of users connect to a single point of aggregation, where they join a private IP network. Both aggregators and users belong to the same network. Any networks that connect the subscribers to their destination are in essence transparent. This is just as true for IPSec tunnels as for dial-up connections with L2TP. Figure 6-11 gives a pictorial representation of this statement.

Figure 6-11   *Subscriber Concentration at Aggregation Point*

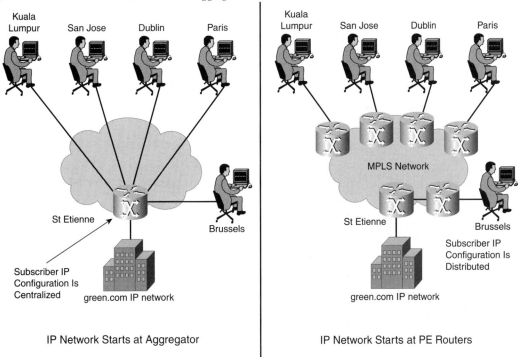

In an access MPLS VPN, the VPN aggregator function is spread across many different PEs — it is not centralized anymore. Furthermore, the subscriber joins an IP network as soon as he connects to a PE, before the eventual destination. Figure 6-11 shows this change, whereby all the IP configuration, specifically the subscriber address pools that had been concentrated on the aggregator in St. Etienne, must now be split across all the PE routers in the POPs in Kuala Lumpur, Brussels, San Jose, Dublin, and Paris.

The MPLS wholesale operator running the network shown in Figure 6-11 has the responsibility of assigning addresses to the retail subscribers that connect to its PE routers. A direct result of this structural difference is that the previously centralized subscriber address space must be shared across all the different PEs.

The retail customer deals with this very easily by handing over a block of addresses to the wholesaler, saying "Use these for my users." The wholesaler simply has to carve this block into appropriately sized chunks for each PE.

Unfortunately, managing addresses in this way is very hard to do intelligently. A wholesaler has no way to know which subscriber will connect to a given PE (this is the same reason that prompted the development of VHG), so there is no predictable way to know how much IP address space to put where. Figure 6-12 shows why this is so. At one time, PE1 has 100 subscribers from network foo.com and just 1 subscriber from bar.com. At some later time, the situation is reversed. There is just 1 foo.com customer, but a 100 from bar.com. PE2, however, now has 100 foo.com customers, whereas it had none before. What should the wholesaler do? Configure a pool for 100 subscribers for each VPN on every PE? PE3 in Figure 6-12 has no subscribers from bar.com, so this wastes addresses. What if bar.com continues its expansion? How many foo.com or bar.com addresses are enough?

Figure 6-12 *VPN Membership Changes with Time*

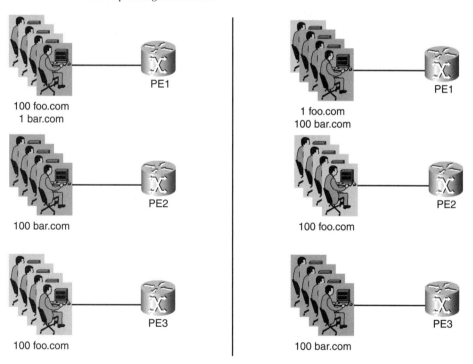

NOTE	Virtual Home Gateways are an artifice to scale PPP termination in VRFs. They neither change the fact that subscriber aggregation is geographically distributed nor help with address assignment.

The Host Route Solution

The problem shown in Figure 6-12 exists because all the PEs use statically defined pools of addresses. Why not use DHCP or RADIUS and assign the addresses dynamically to individual subscribers rather than indulge in wasteful preallocation? As the set of connected subscribers on a PE evolves over time, as it did in Figure 6-12, the address pools on the routers can change and no address space is wasted.

As you have seen many times in the examples, when a router issues addresses to clients, it adds /32 routes to its routing tables. But the addresses are allocated and routes are created without regard for network topology. Consider the following scenario, which refers back to Figure 6-11:

1. Network foo.com uses the 10.1.1.0/24 pool for all broadband subscribers, and a central DHCP server manages address allocation.

2. In Paris, subscriber emma@foo.com connects to the PE and requests an address.

3. The foo.com DHCP server returns 10.1.1.1 and the VPN routing tables are updated with the information that 10.1.1.1 is reachable at PE1.

4. Now, in a completely different city, chloe@foo.com connects and, using the same procedure, gets address 10.1.1.2.

The server did not take into account that the new subscriber is connected to a different PE. Pushed to extremes, the 10.1.1.0 subnet can be completely fragmented across all the PEs in the network and the 10.1.1.0 routes can only ever be advertised as /32s.

It is a good design principal to avoid fragmentation such as this. Announcing large numbers of small routes across your network not only uses router memory but, in the case of broadband, can also create instability in the routing domain because subscribers constantly connect and disconnect. Two makes PEs flood these changes to all other parts of the VPN. Routes could actually move from PE to PE as addresses are reused on different PEs, in the following way:

- Subscriber chloe@foo.com disconnects and address 10.1.1.2 is freed up again.

- A new subscriber in Tokyo, julia@foo.com, connects to the network and requests an address.

- The DHCP could allocate a previously used address, for example 10.1.1.2, which had been assigned to a subscriber in Dublin.

- Now all routes to 10.1.1.2/32 have to be updated with a new next-hop address.

Yes, it is correct that the DHCP server in the city example could use different scopes for each PE, but that is another way of configuring static pools per PE, which is a return to square one, because the service provider did not know how big or small to make the pools in the first place.

All of a sudden, local static pools are looking good again, because they let the service provider control address space fragmentation. One of the nice things about static pools is that they represent an aggregate unit for route announcements. The PE hands out addresses to subscribers as necessary, but the entire range of addresses in a pool is advertised to peer routers, which is the equivalent of saying, "If at any time you need to reach an address in this range, it is one of my subscribers." Remember that you can download pools using PPP, so they can be centrally provisioned.

The ideal solution to the address-assignment complexity would allow you to allocate single addresses dynamically but announce routes aggregately.

ODAP and Address Assignments

On-Demand Address Pools (ODAP) is a solution to the address-assignment problem. The idea is very simple indeed. Addresses are stored on a central server and chunks of address space are allocated to PEs on an as-needed basis (hence the name). If a PE needs more addresses, it just asks. If it has too many, it returns some. Thus, ODAP enables you to avoid wasting IP addresses. The cost is that you have to deploy a new mechanism.

An ODAP server maintains a pool of addresses. Each ODAP client (a router) requests a pool using either standard DHCP or RADIUS requests. Once a pool is downloaded, the client installs a summary route into the routing table. In MPLS situations, the route would be installed into the relevant VRF. As long as you have configured BGP to include **redistribute static** in the appropriate **address-family ipv4 <vrf name>**, the ODAP pools will be announced to all the peer routers.

When a subscriber connects, the router grants an address from the downloaded pool. When the total amount of address space in use exceeds a configurable threshold, the router sends another request to the ODAP server for a new pool. The new pools can be bigger or smaller than the initial pool (or the same size, of course). If the total amount of used addresses goes below another configurable threshold, the router returns a pool. It is better to be conservative with this threshold because if you return addresses too quickly, you just create needless churn.

From an implementation perspective, the Cisco IOS ODAP client operates like a DHCP *server*. Therefore, you use the same instructions as you would if you were using the PE as a regular DHCP server. For example, if you want to use ODAP with PPP, you would first configure PPP to retrieve addresses from a DHCP server, using either the highlighted command in Example 6-26 or the global **ip address-pool** command.

Example 6-26 *DHCP Proxy Configuration*

```
interface Virtual-Template1
ip vrf forwarding green
ip unnumbered loopback1
ppp authentication chap pap
peer default ip address dhcp
```

Before continuing, it is a good idea to look at all the different address-retrieval options in Cisco IOS. It can be a little overwhelming.

- **Static local pool** —A static, locally configured range of addresses. They may overlap.
- **Pool download** —Router uses AAA to download static pool definitions from server.
- **AAA**—Static address allocation either by using **framed-IP-address** or by naming a pool on the router from which an address is taken.
- **DHCP client** —The router learns an interface address from a DHCP server. Uses the **ip address dhcp** interface command.
- **DHCP relay** —The router forwards client DHCP requests to a server. The relay agent function is VRF aware and can include the VPN ID to help identify the scope to service the client request. For a relay agent to make sense, a client must originate the DHCP requests.
- **Cisco IOS DHCP server** —The router is a fully fledged DHCP server and replies to DHCPDISCOVER messages. The DHCP server is also VRF aware.
- **PPP with DHCP**—The router is a DHCP proxy client and originates a DHCPDISCOVER message on behalf of the PPP client to request a single address, which is what the router in Example 6-26 would do. You can implement this in conjunction with the Cisco IOS DHCP Server feature.
- **AAA and DHCP** —The reserved **framed-IP-address** 255.255.255.254 instructs the router to use DHCP proxy to get an address for the PPP client. It does the same thing as putting a **peer default ip address dhcp** statement on the **virtual-template** interface.

ODAP is basically an alternative to all of these choices.

The ODAP configuration has several components. First, enable it as shown in Example 6-27. Alternatively, you can use **peer default ip address dhcp-pool red_odap_pool** on the **virtual-templates** if you do not want to enable ODAP globally.

Example 6-27 *Enabling ODAP Globally*

```
! Make router an ODAP client
ip address-pool dhcp-pool

! Create RED ODAP pool using DHCP
```

continues

Example 6-27   *Enabling ODAP Globally (Continued)*

```
ip dhcp pool red_odap_pool
   vrf RED
utilization mark high 80
utilization mark low 40
origin dhcp subnet size initial /27 autogrow /27


! Create GREEN ODAP pool using AAA
ip dhcp pool green_odap_pool
vrf Green
utilization mark high 80
utilization mark low 10
origin aaa subnet size initial /27 autogrow /27
```

Source: Adapted by author from http://www.cisco.com/en/US/products/hw/routers/ps133/ products_configuration_guide_chapter09186a0080174a85.html

Then, define ODAP pools for each VRF. Example 6-27 has two such pools. The **green_odap_pool** uses DHCP to "fill up." The **red_odap_pool** uses AAA. Both clients request a /27-sized subnet when they first ask for a pool, as well as a /27 mask for all subsequent requests.

The **origin** command can take three different options: **dhcp** and **aaa**, which you see in Example 6-27, and **ipcp**, which is in fact a variant of **aaa**. An ODAP client can therefore use either DHCP or AAA to retrieve address pools from the ODAP server.

The **autogrow** option makes the pools dynamic. If it is missing, the router will not request new addresses when it runs out.

You obviously need a server to fulfill all these requests. There is a limited choice of ODAP servers today:

- **AAA origin** —Cisco Access Registrar
- **DHCP origin** —Cisco Network Registrar or Cisco IOS DHCP Server

When using the AAA origin, the ODAP client uses either the VPN ID, if there is one, or the VRF name as the RADIUS username with password "cisco" when asking for new addresses. The RADIUS server replies with special cisco av-pair attributes that give the pool start address and subnet mask. The client uses accounting STOP records to release pools, so you must configure the router with all the standard RADIUS accounting information.

Summary

This chapter looked at different feature sets required to efficiently deploy a wholesale VPN over MPLS. First, the chapter described how dynamic VRF selection is a way to map subscribers to their VRF by using their domain name, their source IP address, or their name.

Then the chapter looked at how to provide a proxy RADIUS service in an MPLS-VPN environment. Existing architectures do not work because wholesale and retail AAA servers are in different address spaces. There are two different solutions available: Either create a separate VRF for all the AAA servers or use Per-VRF AAA. Per-VRF has several different possible configuration options: using AAA method_lists or the **template** command. Also, you can centralize part of the Per-VRF AAA server information in RADIUS.

Finally, this chapter looked at the challenge of efficient address assignment and route summarization. ODAP was developed specifically for access VPN situations and provides a way to assign IP pools to client routers. The routers can request additional address space or return addresses, depending on the situation. ODAP pools are automatically added to the routing tables, which allow subscriber subnet summarization.

In this chapter, you learn about the following topics:

- Introduction to Virtual Routers
- Implementing Virtual Routing with Cisco IOS
- Using Tunnels to Build Network-Based IP VPN
- Using GRE for IP VPN
- Using IPSec for IP VPN
- Routing Between VRF-Lite PEs

CHAPTER 7

Implementing Network-Based Access VPNs Without MPLS

Up to this point in the book, only MPLS has been offered as a way to run network-based VPN services from provider edge (as opposed to customer premises) routers. However, not all networks in the world run MPLS. The IPSec and GRE VPNs discussed in Chapter 3, "VPNs in Broadband Networks," are all initiated from the customer premises. (Thus, they are CPE VPNs according to the taxonomy.) Using CPE VPNs is a perfectly valid and heavily deployed solution, but it is not the only option.

From a purely implementation perspective, a fundamental requirement of IP VPNs is to support overlapping IP addresses, but Cisco IOS crypto maps and tunnel subinterfaces did not allow this by themselves. By combining IP tunnels with the private routing tables added to Cisco IOS for MPLS-VPN services, you can have a network-based VPN service over an IP core, which is the subject of this chapter.

The chapter starts by introducing the concept of virtual routers (VRs) as a vehicle to provide services to end users. Virtual routers were first implemented on specialized broadband devices, on which they are still used. There is some work being done at the standards bodies regarding building IP VPNs using VR architectures. Although Cisco IOS does not support true VRs, VRF-Lite covers most, but not all, of what you can do with VRs.

Chapter 1, "Introduction: Broadband Access and Virtual Private Networks," discussed several VPN frameworks, such as RFC 2547bis and RFC 2764. In Chapter 5, "Introduction to MPLS-Based Access VPN Architectures," you looked at the peer-to-peer model and how it is applied to broadband networks. Now it is time to revisit the overlay model so that you understand more about this alternative topology and how it applies to broadband access. This chapter covers how to interconnect VRFs (and VRs) using tunnels. It does not introduce any new architecture concepts.

Although point-to-point tunnels have their disadvantages (but also advantages), they are certainly used in operational networks. So, you look at some implementations of point-to-point tunnels. First, you look at a GRE solution, with some detailed examples of routing across IP tunnels in an overlay network. Then, you look at an IPSec approach for both remote-access and site-to-site topologies.

The examples throughout the book are extracts from the complete configurations. The full configurations I used are posted on the Cisco Press website and are available for download on http://www.ciscopress.com/1587051362.

Introduction to Virtual Routers

What is a virtual router? For what is it used? There is no standard definition of a VR, but one that describes it adequately is as follows:

> A Virtual Router is a logical router process. Like a "real" router, it forwards packets between dedicated interfaces using routing protocols. Each Virtual Router has dedicated interfaces, routing tables, routing processes, radius servers, and even administrative accesses (telnet). Virtual Routers are isolated from each other.

Another way to think about this is to draw an analogy with processes on a multiprocessor operating system. Just as a UNIX process has its own logical memory space, instruction space, and so forth, each VR has its own address space, routing table, interfaces, and so forth.

Multiple VRs can run on a single physical device, as shown in Figure 7-1.

Figure 7-1   *Multiple Virtual Routers on a Single Device*

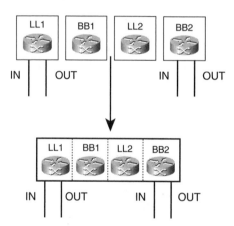

Figure 7-1 shows how a physical router running multiple VR instances can imitate multiple separate physical routers. The routers at the top of the figure are dedicated to different services: broadband (BB) services and leased-line (LL) services.

Bear in mind that this is a conceptual representation. Real VR implementations do not have the same separation as physical devices do—for example, they share the same underlying hardware.

Virtual routers all share the same hardware and run the same version of operating system image (although you could imagine a system in which different VRs run different versions of code).

Every VR runs its own services and network protocols, such as DHCP, access lists, IP address space, routing protocol and table, forwarding table, DHCP Relay, AAA Server, SNMP agent, Telnet interface, and so on.

To the rest of the network, VRs look exactly like multiple physical routers. Each can run a routing protocol and forward traffic over dedicated interfaces and subinterfaces. This means that VRs must be connected in such a way as to preserve their independent address space. Typically, this would require an overlay of point-to-point connections, such as tunnel, PVC, and VLAN connections.

VRs were first developed as a new, revenue-generating service model for service providers. The thought was that wholesale providers could use VRs to sublet router "real estate" to their customers: Every VPN would run in its own VR. These customers could in turn fully administer their own domain, right down to the hardware. However, a couple of design issues got in the way of this idea becoming widespread:

- **OAM and security, or the trust domain**   — Letting customers configure their devices is problematic for service providers because, just like everyone, customers can make mistakes that impact everyone else who is sharing the same hardware, even if they can operate only inside a VR. For example, if a customer were to start a **debug ip packet** command, it would have a big impact on the other processes running on the same machine. More pragmatically, it becomes very hard to determine who is responsible for mistakes or failures complying with an SLA — the service provider or the customer, if both parties can change device configurations. In practice, therefore, it is less contentious if SLA data is taken from the router in the time-honored fashion using SNMP polling or bulk statistics export, then presented to the customer in graphical reports.

- **Interconnection, or the superiority of the peer-to-peer model**   — Even if the router function is virtualized, the network between VRs is not. To keep VPN traffic separate, you must provide a private path between each VR across the network. Data forwarding and routing protocols need dedicated interfaces on each router. These interfaces can be either Layer 2 WAN links or IP tunnels. The net effect, so to speak, is to create a mesh of point-to-point connections between each VR, as shown in Figure 7-2. The RFC 2547 service model proved itself easier to operate and deploy than the tunnel-based VR model for VPN services, which was never widely used in this way. Since then, VRs have been combined with MPLS VPN to provide an RFC 2547 service, as shown in Figure 7-3.

Figure 7-2 *Connecting Virtual Routers*

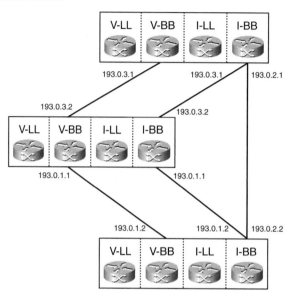

Figure 7-3 *VR and MPLS VPN*

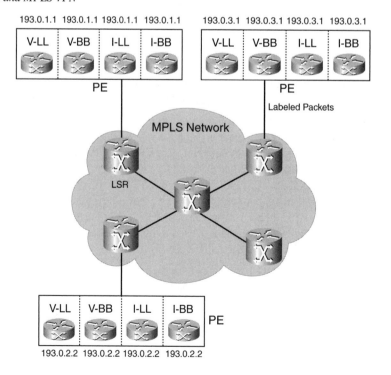

In spite of the previously discussed issues, VRs are still deployed, especially in broadband aggregation networks. They are used as follows:

- The main scenario is to use VRs to tidy up large configurations. As you will see in the examples that follow later in this chapter, Cisco IOS has the different services attached to the same VRF scattered around the configuration file. For example, the VRF definitions are at the start of the file, the interfaces are more or less in the middle, and the routing protocols are at the end.

  By using different VRs for different services, VRs offer the advantage of having all these bits and pieces in the same place. A common way to deploy this is to have the configuration for Internet access users separate from the configuration for business service subscribers, for example. This form of operational neatness is very simply represented in Figure 7-4. Note, however, that this is a presentation advantage only. It doesn't alter what you can or can't do from a functional perspective. However, despite all the many ongoing improvements in the Cisco IOS CLI, this is not something you can do on a Cisco router.

- Outside the broadband environment, multiple, separate routing processes are sometimes used to provide ISPs equal access: A wholesale provider uses IP data and a control interface, including routing protocol, as the open interface with third parties. The requirement here is to be able to peer with different routing peers, which is something BGP has been used to do for a long time. However, some designs might need to use IGPs between the wholesaler and its customer. Having multiple processes for each customer-facing routing instance just gives a sense of security: If one process fails, other customers are not affected. This is where VRs come into the picture: Each customer has its own VR, running its own IGP process. Again, Cisco IOS goes about this slightly differently, with per-VRF routing instances, which may or may not require multiple routing processes (OSPF does, BGP doesn't, for example).

  Like many of the VR usage scenarios, the VRs are not so much mandatory for a wonderfully efficient solution as they are useful if you already happen to have them.

- Running different services in different VRs allows a service provider to have service differentiation for its subscribers: one VR with basic Internet access, another with firewall service, and so forth. Again, Cisco IOS uses VRF-aware features to provide virtualized services.

  Remember that VRs share underlying hardware resources. There is nothing about them that allows you to control how much CPU each one receives, for example—that is a function of the operating system scheduler.

Figure 7-4 *Operational Neatness with Virtual Routers*

VR for VPN
Subscribers

VR for Internet Access
Subscribers

Implementing Virtual Routing with Cisco IOS

How close can you come to running a full VR in Cisco IOS? Let's start by saying that you cannot run multiple instances of Cisco IOS on the same physical hardware. The Cisco approach is a little different and involves virtualized services (in the largest sense of the word) attached to VRFs, using per-VRF features.

In the Cisco IOS lexicon, using VRFs without MPLS is called, alternatively, VRF-Lite and Multi-VRF CE. They are really one and the same thing. VRF-Lite is not specific to broadband access, and you could just as easily find it on an L3/L2 switch in a campus environment as you could on a broadband aggregator.

NOTE   There is a very reasonable argument that says that the term *VRF-Lite* is a misnomer. No features are actually removed from VRFs—*Lite* is in homage to the symbiotic relationship between VRF and MPLS and alludes to the lack of labels. That said, the name VRF-Lite will be widely used until someone comes up with a better name.

Because Cisco IOS uses VRFs, you can emulate a VR to the extent that the underlying features you need are VRF aware. For example, it is perfectly possible to have the following:

- Completely separate infrastructure for broadband: Using per-VRF AAA, you can emulate the separate VR for Internet access and business subscribers, with each category of subscribers using its own AAA server. This means you can implement the model shown in Figure 7-4.
- VPN "interworking," which takes subscriber traffic from, say, an IPSec tunnel and maps it to an MPLS VPN.

- Virtualized services. We will return to this topic in Chapter 8, "Case Studies for Using MPLS with Broadband VPNs."

In summary, the basics of VRs are simple enough to grasp. The tricky piece is making sure that all the "other stuff" you find on a router also works in the virtualized case.

Using Tunnels to Build Network-Based IP VPN

A network-based VPN is a VPN service provided entirely by the service provider network. If the service provider runs an IP core network, it must use some form of tunneling to transport private customer data.

Figure 7-5 *Site VPN Architecture with Tunnels*

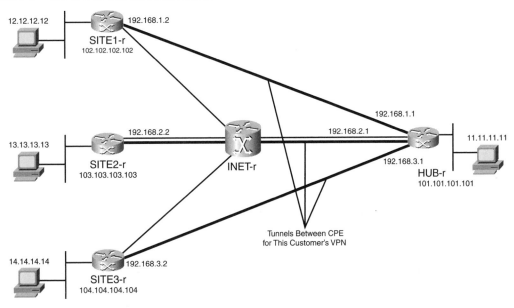

All Addresses Shown Are Private

Figure 7-6 *Network VPN Architecture with Tunnels*

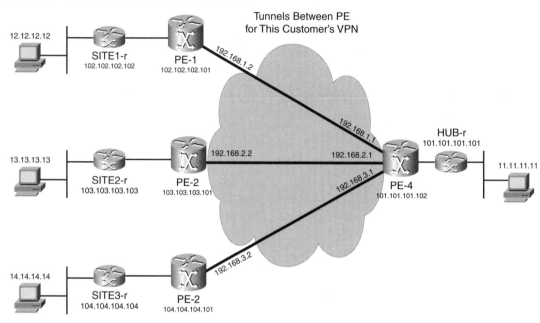

10.0.0.0/16 network Is public
Other addresses are private to VPN.

Compared with a CPE VPN of Figure 7-5, a network-based VPN of Figure 7-6 has the following characteristics: The tunnels move into the network and start and end on provider edge routers. Each VPN has its own VRF on the PE router, as well as its own set of tunnels, as shown in Figure 7-5. How Cisco IOS configurations do this is given later.

It is important to understand that these are still point-to-point architectures. Figure 7-6 shows a network-based version of the CPE-based VPN shown in Figure 7-5. The topology is hub and spoke. The PE connects to the CE router at each site over a different physical link and initiates a tunnel to other PEs. Some other differences between CPE and network-based VPNs are as follows:

- **Addressing** —The PE tunnel interfaces (192.168.3.0 network) are part of the VPN. Data forwarding and PE-to-PE routing go over the tunnels. The CE-PE links are new, compared to the CPE-based VPN topology, and so need new addresses.

- **VRFs**—PE-4 has a single VRF with all the tunnel interfaces, as well as the CE-PE link. PE-1 through PE-3 have a VRF with just two interfaces: the tunnel to PE-4 and the CE-PE link. In other words, a PE router can have a VRF with both tunnel and PE-CE interfaces. Figure 7-6 is an example of this.

- **Routing** — The CE and PE are routing peers. At the very least, each CE has a default route to its PE. The PEs have routing entries for all the customer networks. PE-1 through PE-3 will show these addresses as being reachable via the hub, PE-4. Example 7-1 shows a pseudo route table listing for the hub and one of the spoke PEs of Figure 7-6, with the simplifying assumptions that all the networks use a /24 bit subnet mask and that all networks are announced to all peers. When traffic goes from one spoke to another, it is routed through PE-4, not the HUB-r CE anymore.

- **Encapsulation** — All the tunnels carry IP packets and nothing but IP packets.

Example 7-1   *Pseudo Routing Entries for Network VPN*

```
PE-1 routing entries in VRF green
11.11.11.0, 13.13.13.0, 14.14.14.14, 101.101.101.0, 103.103.103.0, 104.104.104.0,
192.168.2.0, 192.168.3.0 through next-hop PE-4
12.12.12.0 through next-hop Site1-r

PE-4 routing entries in VRF green
12.12.12.0, 102.102.102.0 and 192.168.1.2 through next-hop PE-1
13.13.13.0, 103.103.103.0 and 192.168.2.2 through next-hop PE-2
14.14.14.0, 104.104.104.0 and 192.168.3.2 through next-hop PE-3
11.11.11.0 through next-hop HUB-4
```

If the CE and PE are routing peers, is this still an overlay network or is it a peer-to-peer network? It has characteristics of both, as discussed in the following list:

- **Peer to peer** — Just as in an MPLS-VPN environment, the service provider manages the VPN customer routing.

- **Overlay** — Every PE has core-facing tunnel interfaces for each VPN. As with any type of VPN, to guarantee both distinct address spaces and security, data from one VPN can never be mixed on the same tunnel as that of another VPN. With MPLS VPNs, labels allow traffic from different VPNs to be multiplexed on the same links. With tunnels, each VPN needs its own independent mesh. (Figure 7-2 showed this for a VR implementation, but the same picture applies for VRFs connected by tunnels.) Also, there is no form of auto-discovery or provisioning with the tunnels. When a new VPN is configured, the operator must manually configure the tunnels on each PE.

   The tunnel topology shown in Figure 7-6 is deliberately simple. A customer might want several hubs in the network, with spokes having a primary connection to different hubs, for reliability reasons. Now, each spoke PE needs multiple tunnels to the hub PEs, requiring additional configuration by the operator. You could argue that complex routing topologies require just as much work in an MPLS VPN, because you need to configure route-targets differently on spokes and hubs. This is correct, but whereas with an MPLS VPN you need to configure *only* the control plane (i.e., the routing protocol is doing all the work), with the tunnel topology, you have to work with both the control plane *and* the data plane (all the new tunnels). It is more work and there is more to go wrong.

The comments made earlier about VRF interconnection and network-based VPNs should be taken in this context. It is true that CE-PE routers are peers, but the customer routing topology is provided by using both the PE control plane *and* the data plane.

For tunnels across IP core networks, the choice of protocol today is either GRE or IPSec (or both). Service provider architectures require separate customer and provider networks, so the tunnels are overlaid across the core. However, campus networks or LANs might well need to run VRFs throughout the routing hierarchy (core, distribution, and possibly access), so tunnels could be configured hop to hop between each router in the network.

Using GRE for IP VPN

One of the main ways to connect VRFs is to use GRE tunnels. For broadband access, this is a good solution for site and wholesale VPNs, but not for remote-access or telecommuter because GRE is not much used as a client protocol. If you can live with the level of security, GRE is always an excellent choice, because it is simple to understand and operate. Another major factor when designing such a network is to understand the number of tunnels supported per platform. High-end routers have hardware support for GRE, which is an important consideration when choosing PEs.

GRE is straightforward to configure. Because the Cisco IOS implementation uses full subinterfaces, you only have to add the VRF name to the interface configuration to add the GRE tunnel to a VRF. GRE is not VRF aware. Therefore, the tunnel source and destination addresses are part of the global routing table. Remember, there are no labels. The data inside the tunnels is all IP, as are the tunnel packets themselves, as you can see in Figure 7-7, which shows the encapsulation stack from client to customer network. The CE-PE link is plain IP over a dedicated Layer 2 link.

GRE is sometimes used to transport MPLS. Why on earth would anyone want to carry labeled packets over an IP core? Well, consider either a very large enterprise or an ISP that is using MPLS (for whatever reason) throughout its network. If it needs to connect two remote sites, then it has basically three choices, as follows:

- Find an IXC offering MPLS transport service to another MPLS provider (called CsC). This is not yet widespread.

- Use a standard IXC IP service offering, terminate all the labels on the CE equipment, and use plain IP between sites. This requires a lot of configuration and monitoring.

- Send labeled packets over the IXC's IP core by encapsulating them in a tunnel. GRE is the natural choice because it is not limited to Layer 3 packet transport. This is what MPLS over GRE lets you do.

Figure 7-7 *GRE-PE Encapsulation Stack*

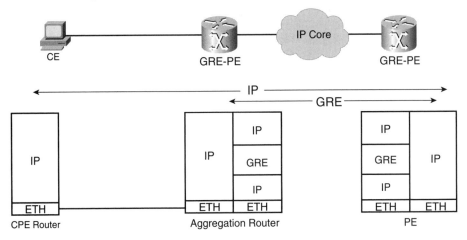

Using IPSec for IP VPN

If you are going to deploy network-based VPN over an IP core, IPSec is another good choice of protocol. Unlike GRE, it provides support for both site- and residential-VPN access over broadband connections.

Note that moving IPSec termination into the service provider cloud does not alter the main drawbacks, which are as follows:

- It is processor intensive.
- It has no native multicast support.

For example, if you want to run routing protocols between IPSec endpoints, you still need to use GRE first (as described in Chapter 3). Note, this limitation only applies to the IPSec PE.

With IPSec, there are two VPN scenarios to consider:

- **Site-to-site VPN**—The IPSec PE terminates at least one IPSec tunnel in every VRF. The architecture is identical to the GRE case, with sets of tunnels for each VPN. Each tunnel carries IP traffic, as shown in Figure 7-8.
- **Remote-access VPN** —Just as with DSL, you cannot know in advance which VPN a subscriber belongs to. Therefore, the IPSec PE terminates the tunnels on a subscriber-facing interface that is in the global routing space, so that anyone can connect as long as he has IP reachability, and then put the IP session into the correct VRF. The IPSec PE can be connected to other PEs using other tunnels across the IP core.

As you can see in Figure 7-8, which shows the protocol stacks used at different points in an IPSec-VRF network, the IPSec solution is really the same architecture as the GRE case, but with a different tunneling technology. Remember, Figure 7-8 shows a network-based VPN solution, where the CE-PE link uses IP over a dedicated Layer 2 link.

Figure 7-8 *IPSec-PE Encapsulation Stack*

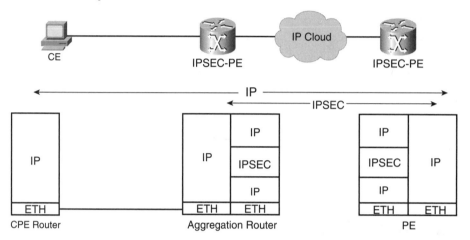

In a scenario where the IPSec sessions are terminated in VRFs, you must use the **keyring** command. This is shown in Example 7-2, where VPN1 is mapped into the YOSEMITE VRF.

Example 7-2 *IPSec Hub Configuration Modified for VRF Awareness*[1]

```
!
crypto keyring YOSEMITE
 pre-shared-key address 192.168.2.2 key secret
!
crypto isakmp policy 1
 encr esp-des
 authentication pre-share

crypto isakmp profile YOSEMITE
 vrf YOSEMITE
 keyring YOSEMITE
 match identity address 192.168.2.2 255.255.255.255
!
crypto ipsec transform-set ONE ah-md5-hmac esp-des
!
crypto map YOSEMITE 1 ipsec-isakmp
 set peer 192.168.2.2
 set transform-set ONE
 set isakmp-profile YOSEMITE
 match address 101
!
interface Serial0/0
```

Example 7-2   *IPSec Hub Configuration Modified for VRF Awareness[1] (Continued)*

```
description VPN to Site1
ip address 192.168.1.1 255.255.255.252
crypto map YOSEMITE
!
ip route 192.168.2.2 255.255.255.255 192.168.1.2
ip route vrf YOSEMITE 11.11.11.11 255.255.255.255 192.168.1.2 global
```

The configuration in Example 7-2 also has a profile for the IKE **isakmp** session. IKE must terminate in the same VRF as the IPSec session. If there were another VPN on the hub, instead of the single YOSEMITE VPN, there would be another **crypto isakmp profile**, with a different VRF. Also notice that the hub configuration now specifies the remote-peer addresses. The routing entries are also important: there are static VRF routes to the customer subnets on Site1 and a global route that tells the hub that these VRF addresses are reachable through a next hop that is in the global routing table. The reference to the global routing table is included because the IPSec sessions in this example terminate on public interfaces, not on an interface in a VRF.

IPSec is also used with remote-access clients, which is very common across broadband networks. This can also be transformed into an IPSec-to-VRF scenario. Example 7-3 shows part of such a per-VRF IPSec remote-access configuration.

Example 7-3   *Remote-Access IPSec to VRF[2]*

```
aaa new-model
!
aaa group server radius YOSEMITE-AAA
 server-private 2.0.0.12 auth-port 1645 acct-port 1646 timeout 5 retransmit 3 key cisco
!
aaa authorization network aaa-list group radius
!
crypto isakmp profile REMOTE-YOSEMITE
 vrf YOSEMITE
 match identify group YOSEMITE.COM
 client authentication list YOSEMITE-AAA
 isakmp authorization list YOSEMITE-AAA
 client configuration address initiate
 client configuration address respond
!
crypto ipsec transform-set YOSEMITE-SET esp-des
!
crypto dynamic-map YOSEMITE1 1
 set transform-set YOSEMITE-SET
 set isakmp profile REMOTE-YOSEMITE
 reverse-route
!
crypto map YOSEMITE-MAP 1 ipsec-isakmp dynamic YOSEMITE1
!
```

In Example 7-3, the **YOSEMITE-MAP crypto map** is applied to the subscriber-facing interfaces. The **REMOTE-YOSEMITE profile** configures the router to negotiate IP addresses with the client, regardless of whether the remote end initiates such a request. Clients are authenticated and authorized using the 2.0.0.12 server. The **match identity group** command matches the organizational unit field of the distinguished name sent by the remote IKE peer. The assumption here is that the client is configured to send this information correctly. Other, similar alternatives are to match against host or user domain name.

Note the many similarities with the per-VRF AAA solution:

- The RADIUS servers are in the VRF, not the global routing space.
- IP address pools can also have overlapping address spaces for each VRF.
- Subscribers are first authenticated using AAA, then connected directly to the correct VRF.
- The tunnel terminates on a public, not VRF, interface, but the sessions within them are placed in a VRF.

The concepts behind per-VRF remote-access solutions really are very similar regardless of the access protocol.

The architectures discussed in Chapter 5 were in fact quite generic. Once you are comfortable with them, you can apply them to other forms of broadband access. For example, the L2TP-MPLS solution discussed in Chapter 5 can be applied to the complete IPSec-to-MPLS–VPN solution. As shown in Figure 7-9, in an IPSec-MPLS solution, the client runs IPSec, instead of PPP. There is no L2TP Access Concentrator (LAC), obviously, and the virtual home gateway (VHG) terminates IPSec on the client-facing side and is an MPLS PE. Just like in the L2TP solution, the PE runs a control session (IKE instead of the L2TP control channel) with the clients and maps IP traffic from a tunnel (IPSec instead of the L2TP data channel) into a VRF.

Figure 7-9 *IPSec-to-MPLS VPN*

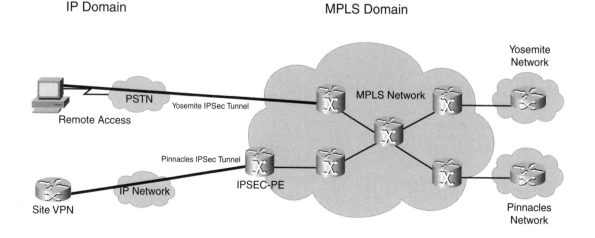

Because of the need for encryption, IPSec needs more CPU horsepower than L2TP, so you can also separate the IPSec-PE function across two separate devices. This is optional. Using an IPSec VHG also addresses the issue of VRF preinstantiation, which is just as relevant here as it is for L2TP.

Routing Between VRF-Lite PEs

Building tunnels is not the end of the story. For the VPN to work properly, you need some form of routing protocol to announce the routes between sites. Any routing protocol that can run on an MPLS CE-PE interface and is VRF aware can also be used across tunnels in a VRF-Lite environment. These routing protocols are OSPF, BGP, and RIPv2.

OSPF has some constraints both in terms of the number of distinct processes (each VRF has its own process) and how areas are handled. RIP is easy, of course, but it is, well, RIP. BGP is always a good choice for route distribution across a core network, even if this is often perceived as being too complex for simpler networks. By the way, BGP with VRFs does not automatically an RFC 2547 architecture make! It is still a point-to-point overlay.

Finally, if the network topology is simple enough, there is nothing wrong with using static routes. As you will see in the examples presented in this section, the core routing protocol domain can be completely separate from the VPN one. Furthermore, you can run different protocols between PEs, or one protocol between CE and PE and another between PE and PE.

Three scenarios are presented in the following subsections, each using a different routing protocol:

- A campus-oriented example, with three devices connected by 802.1q trunks over a Layer 2 network. Each device has two VRFs and each runs OSPF between them.

- A PE-to-PE scenario, in which each PE uses GRE tunnels to connect the VRFs and runs RIP. The core is an IP network.

- Another PE-to-PE scenario, in which one pair of PEs runs RIP, and the other pair runs BGP. This example shows both route redistribution in a VRF and how to use iBGP for VRF route distribution without labels. Once again, the core is an IP network.

The proof point to look for here is correct route distribution. You should be able to understand why each and every route appears where it does. Not only should a ping work from one VRF to the next, but pings must fail between different VRFs. When trying this, be sure that the features you are using are truly VRF aware.

The examples are deliberately simple. The idea is to be able to understand how routing between VRFs works without wading through ever more elaborate and esoteric configurations. Note that there are no specific monitoring or troubleshooting commands for VRF-Lite.

Campus Hop-to-Hop Topology

The first example involves three routers, each with a YOSEMITE VRF and a PINNACLES VRF. Each router has the same VRF definitions, which are shown in Example 7-4. The VRFs are connected using 802.1q trunks over standard Ethernet links. Each router has loopback addresses in the different VRFs—these represent customer networks and are very useful ways to test. The topology is shown in Figure 7-10.

Example 7-4   *Common VRF Definitions*

```
!
ip vrf PINNACLES
 rd 102:1
 route-target export 102:1
 route-target import 102:1
!
ip vrf YOSEMITE
 rd 101:1
 route-target export 101:1
 route-target import 101:1
!
```

Figure 7-10   *Campus Hop-to-Hop Topology*

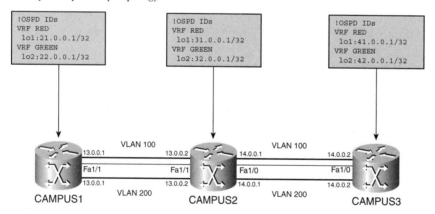

The scenario shown in Figure 7-10 involves running OSPF between VRFs with overlapping addresses. Each router has a static VRF route to reach the loopback address of its OSPF peer. When working, CAMPUS1 can ping 14.0.0.2 on CAMPUS3.

Example 7-5 lists the partial configuration file for router CAMPUS1.

Example 7-5   *CAMPUS1 Configuration*

```
!
interface Loopback1
 ip vrf forwarding YOSEMITE
 ip address 21.0.0.1 255.255.255.255
```

Example 7-5   *CAMPUS1 Configuration (Continued)*

```
 no ip directed-broadcast
!
interface Loopback2
 ip vrf forwarding PINNACLES
 ip address 22.0.0.1 255.255.255.255
 no ip directed-broadcast
!
interface Loopback100
 description BAD test for VRF reachability
 ip address 21.0.0.2 255.255.255.255
 no ip directed-broadcast
!
interface FastEthernet1/1.100
 encapsulation dot1Q 100
 ip vrf forwarding YOSEMITE
 ip address 13.0.0.1 255.255.255.252
 no ip directed-broadcast
!
interface FastEthernet1/1.200
 encapsulation dot1Q 200
 ip vrf forwarding PINNACLES
 ip address 13.0.0.1 255.255.255.252
 no ip directed-broadcast
!
router ospf 100 vrf YOSEMITE
 log-adjacency-changes
 network 13.0.0.0 0.0.0.255 area 0
 network 21.0.0.0 0.0.0.0 area 0
 network 21.0.0.2 0.0.0.0 area 0
!
router ospf 200 vrf PINNACLES
 log-adjacency-changes
 network 13.0.0.0 0.0.0.255 area 0
 network 21.0.0.0 0.0.0.0 area 0
 network 22.0.0.1 0.0.0.0 area 0
!
ip classless
ip route vrf YOSEMITE 31.0.0.1 255.255.255.255 13.0.0.2
ip route vrf PINNACLES 32.0.0.1 255.255.255.255 13.0.0.2
!
```

Apart from the per-VRF OSPF configuration, you have already seen all the other components of Example 7-5. Router CAMPUS1 runs two different OSPF processes: one in each VRF.

The OSPF process in Example 7-6 will choose its **router-id** using the same rules as usual.

The static route in each VRF (for 31.0.0.1 and 32.0.0.1, respectively) is there so that the remote loopback IDs used by the OSPF neighbor are reachable. The FastEthernet1.1 addresses overlap deliberately. One of the points of this entire exercise is to be able to have separate address spaces, so we might as well test it.

Each OSPF process announces the 13.0.0.0/24 and 21.0.0.0/24 networks and a host route to the loopback interfaces.

Loopback100 is not in any VRF and is used to check that there is no route leakage from the global address space to any VRF. Note how the address on Loopback100 falls in the network announced by the YOSEMITE VRF routing processes (highlighted in Example 7-5). Despite this, the interface should not be reachable from inside a VRF on a remote router.

Example 7-6 shows that Router CAMPUS1 has two interfaces in each VRF.

Example 7-6   *Interfaces in Each VRF on CAMPUS1*

```
CAMPUS1#show ip vrf interface
Interface            IP-Address    VRF                       Protocol
FastEthernet1/1.200  13.0.0.1      PINNACLES                   up
Loopback2            22.0.0.1      PINNACLES                   up
FastEthernet1/1.100  13.0.0.1      YOSEMITE                    up
Loopback1            21.0.0.1      YOSEMITE                    up
```

CAMPUS2 is the middle router, which peers with both CAMPUS1 and CAMPUS3. Example 7-7 gives the configuration.

Example 7-7   *CAMPUS2 Configuration*

```
!
interface Loopback1
 ip vrf forwarding YOSEMITE
 ip address 31.0.0.1 255.255.255.255
!
interface Loopback2
 ip vrf forwarding PINNACLES
 ip address 32.0.0.1 255.255.255.255
!
!
interface FastEthernet1/0.100
 encapsulation dot1Q 100
 ip vrf forwarding YOSEMITE
 ip address 14.0.0.1 255.255.255.252
!
interface FastEthernet1/0.200
 encapsulation dot1Q 200
 ip vrf forwarding PINNACLES
 ip address 14.0.0.1 255.255.255.252
!
!
interface FastEthernet1/1.100
 encapsulation dot1Q 100
 ip vrf forwarding YOSEMITE
 ip address 13.0.0.2 255.255.255.252
!
interface FastEthernet1/1.200
 encapsulation dot1Q 200
 ip vrf forwarding PINNACLES
```

Example 7-7   *CAMPUS2 Configuration (Continued)*

```
 ip address 13.0.0.2 255.255.255.252
!
router ospf 100 vrf YOSEMITE
 log-adjacency-changes
 network 13.0.0.0 0.0.0.255 area 0
 network 14.0.0.0 0.0.0.255 area 0
 network 31.0.0.0 0.0.0.0 area 0
!
router ospf 200 vrf PINNACLES
 log-adjacency-changes
 network 13.0.0.0 0.0.0.255 area 0
 network 14.0.0.0 0.0.0.255 area 0
 network 32.0.0.1 0.0.0.0 area 0
!
ip route 10.0.0.3 255.255.255.255 2.1.50.61
ip route vrf PINNACLES 22.0.0.1 255.255.255.255 13.0.0.1
ip route vrf PINNACLES 42.0.0.1 255.255.255.255 14.0.0.2
ip route vrf YOSEMITE 21.0.0.1 255.255.255.255 13.0.0.1
ip route vrf YOSEMITE 41.0.0.1 255.255.255.255 14.0.0.2
!
```

CAMPUS2 has basically the same configuration as CAMPUS1, only it has more interfaces in each VRF, because it peers with two routers. Example 7-8 shows the interfaces in each VRF on router CAMPUS2.

Example 7-8   *Interfaces in Each VRF on CAMPUS2*

```
CAMPUS2#show ip vrf interface
Interface              IP-Address      VRF                          Protocol
FastEthernet1/0.200    14.0.0.1        PINNACLES                       up
FastEthernet1/1.200    13.0.0.2        PINNACLES                       up
Loopback2              32.0.0.1        PINNACLES                       up
FastEthernet1/0.100    14.0.0.1        YOSEMITE                        up
FastEthernet1/1.100    13.0.0.2        YOSEMITE                        up
Loopback1              31.0.0.1        YOSEMITE                        up
```

Example 7-7 shows that the OSPF processes on CAMPUS2 again announce the /24 supernets for the interfaces that belong to each VRF, as well as the /32 for each loopback. Similar host routes exist as do on CAMPUS1, for similar reasons. Obviously, each VRF maps to a different VLAN to keep traffic separate on the interfaces.

Example 7-9 shows the configuration for the final router, CAMPUS3.

Example 7-9   *CAMPUS3 Configuration*

```
!
interface Loopback1
 ip vrf forwarding YOSEMITE
 ip address 41.0.0.1 255.255.255.255
!
```

continues

Example 7-9 *CAMPUS3 Configuration (Continued)*

```
interface Loopback2
 ip vrf forwarding PINNACLES
 ip address 42.0.0.1 255.255.255.255
!
interface Loopback100
 description GOOD test for VRF YOSEMITE reachability
 ip vrf forwarding YOSEMITE
 ip address 41.0.0.2 255.255.255.255
!
interface Loopback200
 description GOOD test for VRF PINNACLES reachability
 ip vrf forwarding PINNACLES
 ip address 42.0.0.2 255.255.255.255
!
!
interface FastEthernet1/0.100
 encapsulation dot1Q 100
 ip vrf forwarding YOSEMITE
 ip address 14.0.0.2 255.255.255.252
!
interface FastEthernet1/0.200
 encapsulation dot1Q 200
 ip vrf forwarding PINNACLES
 ip address 14.0.0.2 255.255.255.252
!
router ospf 100 vrf YOSEMITE
 log-adjacency-changes
 network 14.0.0.0 0.0.0.255 area 0
 network 41.0.0.1 0.0.0.0 area 0
 network 41.0.0.2 0.0.0.0 area 0
!
router ospf 200 vrf PINNACLES
 log-adjacency-changes
 network 14.0.0.0 0.0.0.255 area 0
 network 42.0.0.1 0.0.0.0 area 0
 network 42.0.0.2 0.0.0.0 area 0
!
ip route 10.0.0.2 255.255.255.255 2.1.50.60
ip route vrf PINNACLES 32.0.0.1 255.255.255.255 14.0.0.1
ip route vrf YOSEMITE 31.0.0.1 255.255.255.255 14.0.0.1
```

CAMPUS3 is almost a mirror image of CAMPUS1. The interfaces in each VRF are shown in Example 7-10.

Example 7-10 *Interfaces Per-VRF on CAMPUS3*

```
CAMPUS3#show ip vrf interface
Interface            IP-Address      VRF              Protocol
FastEthernet1/0.200  14.0.0.2        PINNACLES        up
Loopback2            42.0.0.1        PINNACLES        up
Loopback200          42.0.0.2        PINNACLES        up
```

Example 7-10 *Interfaces Per-VRF on CAMPUS3 (Continued)*

```
FastEthernet1/0.100    14.0.0.2       YOSEMITE                          up
Loopback1              41.0.0.1       YOSEMITE                          up
Loopback100            41.0.0.2       YOSEMITE                          up
```

Loopback100 and Loopback200 are again test interfaces. This time, they are in a VRF (YOSEMITE and PINNACLES, respectively), but there is no /32 announcement for them (unlike Loopback1 and Loopback2).

Example 7-11 shows the routing tables for each VRF on CAMPUS1. Look for the routes learned via OSPF (which are highlighted). In the YOSEMITE VRF, the test route to Loopback100 on CAMPUS3 (41.0.0.2) appears correctly. As you would expect, there is no route here to any of the 42.0.0.0 interfaces that are in the PINNACLES VRF on CAMPUS3. In turn, the PINNACLES routing table has all the correct routes to the networks on CAMPUS3. In each case, the next hop is CAMPUS2. Even though the same IP address shows up in the VRFs, the paths go over two different subinterfaces, with two different VLAN tags, so the traffic is never mixed.

Example 7-11 *YOSEMITE and PINNACLES VPN Routing Tables on CAMPUS1*

```
CAMPUS1#show ip route vrf YOSEMITE

Routing Table: YOSEMITE
Codes: C - connected, S - static, I - IGRP, R - RIP, M - mobile, B - BGP
       D - EIGRP, EX - EIGRP external, O - OSPF, IA - OSPF inter area
       N1 - OSPF NSSA external type 1, N2 - OSPF NSSA external type 2
       E1 - OSPF external type 1, E2 - OSPF external type 2, E - EGP
       i - IS-IS, L1 - IS-IS level-1, L2 - IS-IS level-2, ia - IS-IS inter area
       * - candidate default, U - per-user static route, o - ODR

Gateway of last resort is not set

     21.0.0.0/32 is subnetted, 1 subnets
C       21.0.0.1 is directly connected, Loopback1
     41.0.0.0/32 is subnetted, 2 subnets
O       41.0.0.1 [110/3] via 13.0.0.2, 00:18:44, FastEthernet1/1.100
O       41.0.0.2 [110/3] via 13.0.0.2, 00:18:44, FastEthernet1/1.100
     13.0.0.0/30 is subnetted, 1 subnets
C       13.0.0.0 is directly connected, FastEthernet1/1.100
     14.0.0.0/30 is subnetted, 1 subnets
O       14.0.0.0 [110/2] via 13.0.0.2, 00:18:44, FastEthernet1/1.100
     31.0.0.0/32 is subnetted, 1 subnets
S       31.0.0.1 [1/0] via 13.0.0.2

CAMPUS1#show ip route vrf PINNACLES

Routing Table: PINNACLES
Codes: C - connected, S - static, I - IGRP, R - RIP, M - mobile, B - BGP
       D - EIGRP, EX - EIGRP external, O - OSPF, IA - OSPF inter area
       N1 - OSPF NSSA external type 1, N2 - OSPF NSSA external type 2
       E1 - OSPF external type 1, E2 - OSPF external type 2, E - EGP
```

continues

Example 7-11 *YOSEMITE and PINNACLES VPN Routing Tables on CAMPUS1 (Continued)*

```
              i - IS-IS, L1 - IS-IS level-1, L2 - IS-IS level-2, ia - IS-IS inter area
              * - candidate default, U - per-user static route, o - ODR

Gateway of last resort is not set

     32.0.0.0/32 is subnetted, 1 subnets
S       32.0.0.1 [1/0] via 13.0.0.2
     22.0.0.0/32 is subnetted, 1 subnets
C       22.0.0.1 is directly connected, Loopback2
     42.0.0.0/32 is subnetted, 2 subnets
O       42.0.0.2 [110/3] via 13.0.0.2, 00:21:53, FastEthernet1/1.200
O       42.0.0.1 [110/3] via 13.0.0.2, 00:21:53, FastEthernet1/1.200
     13.0.0.0/30 is subnetted, 1 subnets
C       13.0.0.0 is directly connected, FastEthernet1/1.200
     14.0.0.0/30 is subnetted, 1 subnets
PINNACLES
```

The interesting routes are those carried by OSPF. For the sake of completeness, Example 7-12 gives the routing information on CAMPUS3 so that you have the full picture of which routes are distributed where.

Example 7-12 *YOSEMITE and PINNACLES VPN Routing Tables on CAMPUS3*

```
CAMPUS3#show ip route vrf YOSEMITE

Routing Table: YOSEMITE
Codes: C - connected, S - static, R - RIP, M - mobile, B - BGP
       D - EIGRP, EX - EIGRP external, O - OSPF, IA - OSPF inter area
       N1 - OSPF NSSA external type 1, N2 - OSPF NSSA external type 2
       E1 - OSPF external type 1, E2 - OSPF external type 2
       i - IS-IS, L1 - IS-IS level-1, L2 - IS-IS level-2, ia - IS-IS inter area
       * - candidate default, U - per-user static route, o - ODR
       P - periodic downloaded static route

Gateway of last resort is not set

     41.0.0.0/32 is subnetted, 2 subnets
C       41.0.0.1 is directly connected, Loopback1
C       41.0.0.2 is directly connected, Loopback100
     13.0.0.0/30 is subnetted, 1 subnets
O       13.0.0.0 [110/2] via 14.0.0.1, 00:19:14, FastEthernet1/0.100
     14.0.0.0/30 is subnetted, 1 subnets
C       14.0.0.0 is directly connected, FastEthernet1/0.100
     31.0.0.0/32 is subnetted, 1 subnets
S       31.0.0.1 [1/0] via 14.0.0.1


CAMPUS3#show ip route vrf PINNACLES

Routing Table: PINNACLES
Codes: C - connected, S - static, R - RIP, M - mobile, B - BGP
```

Example 7-12 *YOSEMITE and PINNACLES VPN Routing Tables on CAMPUS3 (Continued)*

```
         D - EIGRP, EX - EIGRP external, O - OSPF, IA - OSPF inter area
         N1 - OSPF NSSA external type 1, N2 - OSPF NSSA external type 2
         E1 - OSPF external type 1, E2 - OSPF external type 2
         i - IS-IS, L1 - IS-IS level-1, L2 - IS-IS level-2, ia - IS-IS inter area
         * - candidate default, U - per-user static route, o - ODR
         P - periodic downloaded static route

Gateway of last resort is not set

     32.0.0.0/32 is subnetted, 1 subnets
S       32.0.0.1 [1/0] via 14.0.0.1
     22.0.0.0/32 is subnetted, 1 subnets
O       22.0.0.1 [110/3] via 14.0.0.1, 00:22:20, FastEthernet1/0.200
     42.0.0.0/32 is subnetted, 2 subnets
C       42.0.0.2 is directly connected, Loopback200
C       42.0.0.1 is directly connected, Loopback2
     13.0.0.0/30 is subnetted, 1 subnets
O       13.0.0.0 [110/2] via 14.0.0.1, 00:22:20, FastEthernet1/0.200
     14.0.0.0/30 is subnetted, 1 subnets
C       14.0.0.0 is directly connected, FastEthernet1/0.200
```

Now for the connectivity tests, which are shown in Example 7-13. CAMPUS1 can ping the CAMPUS3 Loopback100 interface in VRF YOSEMITE and the Loopback200 interface in VRF PINNACLES.

Example 7-13 *Series of Pings from CAMPUS1 to CAMPUS3 in YOSEMITE and PINNACLES VPNs*

```
CAMPUS1#ping vrf YOSEMITE 41.0.0.2

Type escape sequence to abort.
Sending 5, 100-byte ICMP Echos to 41.0.0.2, timeout is 2 seconds:
!!!!!
Success rate is 100 percent (5/5), round-trip min/avg/max = 1/1/4 ms

CAMPUS1#ping vrf YOSEMITE 42.0.0.2

Type escape sequence to abort.
Sending 5, 100-byte ICMP Echos to 42.0.0.2, timeout is 2 seconds:
.....
Success rate is 0 percent (0/5)

CAMPUS1#ping vrf PINNACLES 42.0.0.2

Type escape sequence to abort.
Sending 5, 100-byte ICMP Echos to 42.0.0.2, timeout is 2 seconds:
!!!!!
Success rate is 100 percent (5/5), round-trip min/avg/max = 1/1/4 ms
```

Now it is time to run a simple test for route leakage between CAMPUS2 and CAMPUS1. Example 7-14 shows the routing tables for the YOSEMITE and PINNACLES VRFs on

CAMPUS2. Recall that this has static routes to the **router-id** addresses for each OSPF peer, so there are fewer routes marked as learned by OSPF than on the other two machines. (These are, again, highlighted.)

Example 7-14 *YOSEMITE and PINNACLES VPN Routing Tables on CAMPUS2*

```
CAMPUS2#show ip route vrf YOSEMITE

Routing Table: YOSEMITE
Codes: C - connected, S - static, R - RIP, M - mobile, B - BGP
       D - EIGRP, EX - EIGRP external, O - OSPF, IA - OSPF inter area
       N1 - OSPF NSSA external type 1, N2 - OSPF NSSA external type 2
       E1 - OSPF external type 1, E2 - OSPF external type 2
       i - IS-IS, L1 - IS-IS level-1, L2 - IS-IS level-2, ia - IS-IS inter area
       * - candidate default, U - per-user static route, o - ODR
       P - periodic downloaded static route

Gateway of last resort is not set

     21.0.0.0/32 is subnetted, 1 subnets
S       21.0.0.1 [1/0] via 13.0.0.1
     41.0.0.0/32 is subnetted, 2 subnets
S       41.0.0.1 [1/0] via 14.0.0.2
O       41.0.0.2 [110/2] via 14.0.0.2, 00:22:08, FastEthernet1/0.100
     13.0.0.0/30 is subnetted, 1 subnets
C       13.0.0.0 is directly connected, FastEthernet1/1.100
     14.0.0.0/30 is subnetted, 1 subnets
C       14.0.0.0 is directly connected, FastEthernet1/0.100
     31.0.0.0/32 is subnetted, 1 subnets
C       31.0.0.1 is directly connected, Loopback1

CAMPUS2#show ip ro vrf PINNACLES

Routing Table: PINNACLES
Codes: C - connected, S - static, R - RIP, M - mobile, B - BGP
       D - EIGRP, EX - EIGRP external, O - OSPF, IA - OSPF inter area
       N1 - OSPF NSSA external type 1, N2 - OSPF NSSA external type 2
       E1 - OSPF external type 1, E2 - OSPF external type 2
       i - IS-IS, L1 - IS-IS level-1, L2 - IS-IS level-2, ia - IS-IS inter area
       * - candidate default, U - per-user static route, o - ODR
       P - periodic downloaded static route

Gateway of last resort is not set

     32.0.0.0/32 is subnetted, 1 subnets
C       32.0.0.1 is directly connected, Loopback2
     22.0.0.0/32 is subnetted, 1 subnets
S       22.0.0.1 [1/0] via 13.0.0.1
     42.0.0.0/32 is subnetted, 2 subnets
O       42.0.0.2 [110/2] via 14.0.0.2, 00:25:07, FastEthernet1/0.200
S       42.0.0.1 [1/0] via 14.0.0.2
     13.0.0.0/30 is subnetted, 1 subnets
C       13.0.0.0 is directly connected, FastEthernet1/1.200
     14.0.0.0/30 is subnetted, 1 subnets
C       14.0.0.0 is directly connected, FastEthernet1/0.200
```

Example 7-15 shows the pings. The first, to Loopback1 on CAMPUS1, succeeds. The second, to Loopback100, fails.

Example 7-15 *Good Ping and Bad Ping Between CAMPUS2 and CAMPUS3*

```
CAMPUS2#ping vrf YOSEMITE 21.0.0.1

Type escape sequence to abort.
Sending 5, 100-byte ICMP Echos to 21.0.0.1, timeout is 2 seconds:
!!!!!
Success rate is 100 percent (5/5), round-trip min/avg/max = 1/1/4 ms

CAMPUS2#ping vrf YOSEMITE 21.0.0.2

Type escape sequence to abort.
Sending 5, 100-byte ICMP Echos to 21.0.0.2, timeout is 2 seconds:
.....
Success rate is 0 percent (0/5)
```

Actually, you could predict this result just by looking at the routing table on CAMPUS2, as shown in Example 7-13. There is no route to 21.0.0.2 announced by CAMPUS1.

RIP Between VRF-LITE

The next example shows how to build a network-based VPN by connecting two VRFs across an IP core using GRE tunnels. The core does not have any VRFs, so this is a pure overlay model. The edge routers, called VRFLITE1 and VRFLITE3, each have two VRFs with a separate GRE tunnel between each. The topology is shown in Figure 7-11. Notice how the tunnels go from edge router to edge router, instead of going hop to hop as in Example 7-16. For variety's sake, the network uses RIP instead of OSPF.

Figure 7-11 *RIP and VRF-Lite*

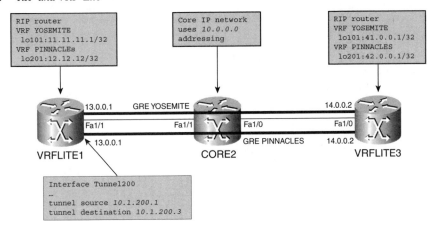

Example 7-16 gives the configuration files for the VRFLITE1 edge router.

Example 7-16 *VRFLITE1 Configuration*

```
!
interface Loopback0
 ip address 10.1.0.1 255.255.255.255
 no ip directed-broadcast
!
interface Loopback1
 ip vrf forwarding YOSEMITE
 ip address 21.0.0.1 255.255.255.255
 no ip directed-broadcast
!
interface Loopback2
 description BAD test for VRF reachability
 ip vrf forwarding PINNACLES
 ip address 21.0.0.2 255.255.255.255
 no ip directed-broadcast
!
interface Loopback3
 description YOSEMITE tunnel end-point
 ip address 10.1.100.1 255.255.255.255
 no ip directed-broadcast
!
interface Loopback4
 description PINNACLES tunnel end-point
 ip address 10.1.200.1 255.255.255.255
 no ip directed-broadcast
!
interface Loopback101
 ip vrf forwarding YOSEMITE
 ip address 11.11.11.1 255.255.255.255
 no ip directed-broadcast
!
interface Loopback201
 ip vrf forwarding PINNACLES
 ip address 12.12.12.1 255.255.255.255
 no ip directed-broadcast
!
! tunnel source and destination are in
! global routing table
! tunnel interface and IP address
! are in VRF YOSEMITE
interface Tunnel100
 description YOSEMITE tunnel to VRFLITE3
 ip vrf forwarding YOSEMITE
 ip address 13.0.0.1 255.255.255.252
 no ip directed-broadcast
 tunnel source Loopback3
 tunnel destination 10.1.100.3
!
interface Tunnel200
 description PINNACLES tunnel to VRFLITE3
```

Example 7-16 *VRFLITE1 Configuration (Continued)*

```
 ip vrf forwarding PINNACLES
 ip address 13.0.0.1 255.255.255.252
 no ip directed-broadcast
 tunnel source Loopback4
 tunnel destination 10.1.200.3
!
interface FastEthernet1/1
 description connection to CORE2
 ip address 10.0.0.1 255.255.255.252
 no ip directed-broadcast
!
! core routing protocol
! provides reachability to tunnel destination
router ospf 1
 router-id 10.1.0.1
 log-adjacency-changes
 network 10.0.0.0 0.255.255.255 area 0
!
! VRF routing protocol
! provides reachability to remote loopback
! addresses in VRFs
router rip
 version 2
 !
 address-family ipv4 vrf YOSEMITE
 version 2
 network 11.0.0.0
 network 13.0.0.0
 no auto-summary
 exit-address-family
 !
 address-family ipv4 vrf PINNACLES
 version 2
 network 12.0.0.0
 network 13.0.0.0
 no auto-summary
 exit-address-family
!
ip classless
!
```

First, note that OSPF is running. Unlike Example 7-9, this is the global routing process. The core network uses 10.0.0.0/24 addresses and each router advertises the loopback interfaces used as tunnel source addresses, which allows the tunnels to be built. In addition, Loopback0 on each router is also in the global routing table for the OSPF **router-id** . The routing table and configuration on the core devices are shown in Example 7-17. You can see the routes to the Loopback0 addresses on VRFLITE1 and VRFLITE2.

Example 7-17 *Core Router OSPF Configuration and Routing Table*

```
CORE2#show run ¦ begin router
router ospf 1
 router-id 10.1.0.2
 log-adjacency-changes
 network 10.0.0.0 0.255.255.255 area 0
!

CORE2#show ip route
Codes: C - connected, S - static, R - RIP, M - mobile, B - BGP
       D - EIGRP, EX - EIGRP external, O - OSPF, IA - OSPF inter area
       N1 - OSPF NSSA external type 1, N2 - OSPF NSSA external type 2
       E1 - OSPF external type 1, E2 - OSPF external type 2
       i - IS-IS, L1 - IS-IS level-1, L2 - IS-IS level-2, ia - IS-IS inter area
       * - candidate default, U - per-user static route, o - ODR
       P - periodic downloaded static route

Gateway of last resort is not set

C    2.0.0.0/8 is directly connected, FastEthernet0/0
     10.0.0.0/8 is variably subnetted, 8 subnets, 2 masks
O       10.1.0.3/32 [110/2] via 10.0.1.2, 00:33:57, FastEthernet1/0
O       10.1.0.1/32 [110/2] via 10.0.0.1, 00:33:57, FastEthernet1/1
C       10.0.0.0/30 is directly connected, FastEthernet1/1
C       10.0.1.0/30 is directly connected, FastEthernet1/0
O       10.1.100.3/32 [110/2] via 10.0.1.2, 00:33:57, FastEthernet1/0
O       10.1.100.1/32 [110/2] via 10.0.0.1, 00:33:57, FastEthernet1/1
O       10.1.200.3/32 [110/2] via 10.0.1.2, 00:33:58, FastEthernet1/0
O       10.1.200.1/32 [110/2] via 10.0.0.1, 00:33:58, FastEthernet1/1
```

Routers VRFLITE1 and VRFLITE3 use RIP to exchange routes for each VRF. The following is the sequence of events that must complete before VPN addresses are reachable:

5. VRFLITE1, VRFLITE3, and CORE2 exchange routes using OSPF. This provides reachability. The output shown in Example 7-17 was obtained once OSPF had converged.

6. VRFLITE1 and VRFLITE3 build the two GRE tunnels, whose endpoints are in the YOSEMITE and PINNACLES VRFs.

7. When the tunnel interfaces are up, VRFLITE1 and VRFLITE3 RIP processes exchange routes for the two VRFs. Example 7-18 and onward were run during or after this stage.

8. VRF routes are reachable between VRFLITE1 and VRFLITE3.

Example 7-16 shows that per-VRF RIP configuration looks somewhat similar to BGP! There are **address-family ipv4** subsections for each VRF, under which you need to configure the networks you want RIP to announce.

You can use the standard RIP **debug** commands to see how routes are exported. This is shown in Example 7-18, with VRFLITE1 sending, and in Example 7-19, with VRFLITE3 receiving. The example shows how the RIP process announces addresses using the tunnel interface addresses.

Example 7-18 *RIP* **Debug** *Output on VRFLITE1*

```
VRFLITE1#debug ip rip
RIP protocol debugging is on
VRFLITE1#debug ip rip event
RIP event debugging is on
VRFLITE1#
00:33:51: RIP: sending v2 update to 224.0.0.9 via Loopback201 (12.12.12.1)
00:33:51:      13.0.0.0/30 -> 0.0.0.0, metric 1, tag 0
00:33:51: RIP: Update contains 1 routes
00:33:51: RIP: Update queued
00:33:51: RIP: sending v2 update to 224.0.0.9 via Tunnel200 (13.0.0.1)
00:33:51: RIP: Update sent via Loopback201
00:33:51:      12.12.12.1/32 -> 0.0.0.0, metric 1, tag 0
00:33:51: RIP: Update contains 1 routes
00:33:51: RIP: Update queued
00:33:51: RIP: sending v2 update to 224.0.0.9 via Loopback101 (11.11.11.1)
00:33:51: RIP: Update sent via Tunnel200
00:33:51:      13.0.0.0/30 -> 0.0.0.0, metric 1, tag 0
00:33:51: RIP: Update contains 1 routes
00:33:51: RIP: Update queued
00:33:51: RIP: sending v2 update to 224.0.0.9 via Tunnel100 (13.0.0.1)
00:33:51: RIP: Update sent via Loopback101
00:33:51:      11.11.11.1/32 -> 0.0.0.0, metric 1, tag 0
00:33:51: RIP: Update contains 1 routes
00:33:51: RIP: Update queued
00:33:51: RIP: Update sent via Tunnel100
00:33:51: RIP: ignored v2 packet from 12.12.12.1 (sourced from one of our addresses)
00:33:51: RIP: ignored v2 packet from 11.11.11.1 (sourced from one of our addresses)
```

Example 7-19 *RIP* **Debug** *Output on VRFLITE3*

```
VRFLITE3#debug ip rip event
RIP event debugging is on
VRFLITE3#debug ip rip
RIP protocol debugging is on
VRFLITE3#
00:31:21: RIP: received v2 update from 13.0.0.1 on Tunnel200
00:31:21:      12.12.12.1/32 via 0.0.0.0 in 1 hops
00:31:21: RIP: Update contains 1 routes
00:31:21: RIP: received v2 update from 13.0.0.1 on Tunnel100
00:31:21:      11.11.11.1/32 via 0.0.0.0 in 1 hops
00:31:21: RIP: Update contains 1 routes
00:31:25: RIP: sending v2 update to 224.0.0.9 via Tunnel200 (13.0.0.2)
00:31:25: RIP: build update entries - suppressing null update
00:31:25: RIP: sending v2 update to 224.0.0.9 via Tunnel100 (13.0.0.2)
00:31:25: RIP: build update entries - suppressing null update
```

There is a logic behind which routes are announced in which VRF. Each RIP peer advertises both a unique route (the address is used only once on the router) and a duplicate route (the same address is used in both VRFs). For example, VRFLITE1 advertises the unique address 11.11.11.1 in VRF YOSEMITE and the unique address 12.12.12.1 in VRF PINNACLES.

Additionally, VRFLITE1 runs RIP on interfaces with the overlapping IP addresses—look for the **network 13.0.0.0** statement in each VRF in the **router rip** command block, which is highlighted in Example 7-16.

The unique addresses let you check connectivity quite easily. If you ping 11.11.11.1 from VRF YOSEMITE on VRFLITE3, it should work, and a ping to 12.12.12.1 in VRF RED must fail. If you use duplicate addresses only, it can be hard to know whether things are working as they should.

VRFLITE3's configuration is given in Example 7-20. VRFLITE3 does not advertise unique routes per VRF—just the 13.0.0.0 network.

Example 7-20 *VRFLITE3 Configuration*

```
interface Loopback0
 ip address 10.1.0.3 255.255.255.255
!
interface Loopback1
 ip vrf forwarding YOSEMITE
 ip address 41.0.0.1 255.255.255.255
!
interface Loopback2
 ip vrf forwarding PINNACLES
 ip address 42.0.0.1 255.255.255.255
!
interface Loopback3
 description YOSEMITE tunnel end-point
 ip address 10.1.100.3 255.255.255.255
!
interface Loopback4
 description PINNACLES tunnel end-point
 ip address 10.1.200.3 255.255.255.255
!
interface Loopback100
 description GOOD test for VRF YOSEMITE reachability
 ip vrf forwarding YOSEMITE
 ip address 41.0.0.2 255.255.255.255
!
interface Loopback200
 description GOOD test for VRF PINNACLES reachability
 ip vrf forwarding PINNACLES
 ip address 42.0.0.2 255.255.255.255
!
! tunnel Source/Destination in global routing table
! tunnel Address 13.0.0.2 is in VRF
interface Tunnel100
 description YOSEMITE tunnel to VRFLITE1
```

Example 7-20 *VRFLITE3 Configuration (Continued)*

```
 ip vrf forwarding YOSEMITE
 ip address 13.0.0.2 255.255.255.252
 tunnel source Loopback3
 tunnel destination 10.1.100.1
!
interface Tunnel200
 description PINNACLES tunnel to VRFLITE1
 ip vrf forwarding PINNACLES
 ip address 13.0.0.2 255.255.255.252
 tunnel source Loopback4
 tunnel destination 10.1.200.1
!
interface FastEthernet1/0
 description Interface to CORE2
 ip address 10.0.1.2 255.255.255.252
 duplex half
!
! Core IGP protocol
router ospf 1
 router-id 10.1.0.3
 log-adjacency-changes
 network 10.0.0.0 0.255.255.255 area 0
!
! VRF routing protocol
router rip
 version 2
 !
 address-family ipv4 vrf YOSEMITE
 version 2
 network 13.0.0.0
 no auto-summary
 exit-address-family
 !
 address-family ipv4 vrf PINNACLES
 version 2
 network 13.0.0.0
 no auto-summary
 exit-address-family
!
!
```

On both VRFLITE1 and VRFLITE3, each VRF has two loopback interfaces and the tunnel IP address, as shown in Example 7-21. It is important to note that the tunnel source and tunnel destination in all the GRE examples that follow are *not* in the VRF, but are global. This means that the router looks in the global routing table to find the path to the address specified by the **tunnel destination** command. Now, as Example 7-22 shows very clearly, the GRE interfaces *are* in a VRF. Once there is a path to the tunnel destination in VRFLITE3's routing table, for example, Tunnel100 and Tunnel200 are marked as up, whereupon RIP will run over each tunnel (in different VRFs, of course) and VRFLITE3 will discover the interfaces advertised by VRFLITE1.

GRE is VRF aware and there is the option to use a VRF table to resolve tunnel destination. (This requires the **tunnel vrf <VRFNAME>** command to be configured on a tunnel interface.) If you use this command, be careful unresolved routes. For example, if you configured **tunnel vrf YOSEMITE** on interface Tunnel100 of Example 7-20, the tunnel would go down, because there is no route to address 10.1.100.1 in the YOSEMITE VRF routing table. (Remember that a GRE tunnel is marked as down if there is no route to its destination.)

Example 7-21 *Interfaces Per-VRF on VRFLITE3*

```
VRFLITE3#show ip vrf interface
Interface            IP-Address     VRF                          Protocol
Loopback2            42.0.0.1       PINNACLES                       up
Loopback200          42.0.0.2       PINNACLES                       up
Tunnel200            13.0.0.2       PINNACLES                       up
Loopback1            41.0.0.1       YOSEMITE                        up
Loopback100          41.0.0.2       YOSEMITE                        up
Tunnel100            13.0.0.2       YOSEMITE                        up
```

Example 7-22 shows the VRF and global routing tables on VRFLITE3. Check to make sure that no addresses announced by RIP appear in the global table, and that no addresses announced by OSPF routes appear in the VRF tables. (They don't.)

Example 7-22 *YOSEMITE VPN and Global Routing Tables on VRFLITE3*

```
VRFLITE3#show ip route vrf YOSEMITE

Routing Table: YOSEMITE
Codes: C - connected, S - static, R - RIP, M - mobile, B - BGP
       D - EIGRP, EX - EIGRP external, O - OSPF, IA - OSPF inter area
       N1 - OSPF NSSA external type 1, N2 - OSPF NSSA external type 2
       E1 - OSPF external type 1, E2 - OSPF external type 2
       i - IS-IS, L1 - IS-IS level-1, L2 - IS-IS level-2, ia - IS-IS inter area
       * - candidate default, U - per-user static route, o - ODR
       P - periodic downloaded static route

Gateway of last resort is not set

     41.0.0.0/32 is subnetted, 2 subnets
C       41.0.0.1 is directly connected, Loopback1
C       41.0.0.2 is directly connected, Loopback100
     11.0.0.0/32 is subnetted, 1 subnets
R       11.11.11.1 [120/1] via 13.0.0.1, 00:00:18, Tunnel100
     13.0.0.0/30 is subnetted, 1 subnets
C       13.0.0.0 is directly connected, Tunnel100

VRFLITE3#show ip route
Codes: C - connected, S - static, R - RIP, M - mobile, B - BGP
       D - EIGRP, EX - EIGRP external, O - OSPF, IA - OSPF inter area
       N1 - OSPF NSSA external type 1, N2 - OSPF NSSA external type 2
```

Example 7-22 *YOSEMITE VPN and Global Routing Tables on VRFLITE3 (Continued)*

```
            E1 - OSPF external type 1, E2 - OSPF external type 2
            i - IS-IS, L1 - IS-IS level-1, L2 - IS-IS level-2, ia - IS-IS inter area
            * - candidate default, U - per-user static route, o - ODR
            P - periodic downloaded static route

Gateway of last resort is not set

C    2.0.0.0/8 is directly connected, FastEthernet0/0
     10.0.0.0/8 is variably subnetted, 9 subnets, 2 masks
C       10.1.0.3/32 is directly connected, Loopback0
S       10.0.0.2/32 [1/0] via 2.1.50.60
O       10.1.0.1/32 [110/3] via 10.0.1.1, 00:32:08, FastEthernet1/0
O       10.0.0.0/30 [110/2] via 10.0.1.1, 00:32:08, FastEthernet1/0
C       10.0.1.0/30 is directly connected, FastEthernet1/0
C       10.1.100.3/32 is directly connected, Loopback3
O       10.1.100.1/32 [110/3] via 10.0.1.1, 00:32:08, FastEthernet1/0
C       10.1.200.3/32 is directly connected, Loopback4
O       10.1.200.1/32 [110/3] via 10.0.1.1, 00:32:09, FastEthernet1/0
```

Finally, Example 7-23 shows a ping from VRFLITE3 to VRFLITE1.

Example 7-23 *Ping from VRFLITE3 to VRFLITE1*

```
VRFLITE3#ping vrf YOSEMITE 11.11.11.1

Type escape sequence to abort.
Sending 5, 100-byte ICMP Echos to 11.11.11.1, timeout is 2 seconds:
!!!!!
Success rate is 100 percent (5/5), round-trip min/avg/max = 1/1/4 ms
```

The command in Example 7-23 uses an address that is advertised only in VRF YOSEMITE. The ICMP packets are routed to 11.11.11.1 using VRF YOSEMITE, which gives the next-hop address to be 13.0.0.1. (The relevant line is highlighted in Example 7-22.) Address 13.0.0.1 is a directly connected interface for router VRFLITE3 through interface Tunnel100. Interface Tunnel100 is a GRE tunnel, so the ICMP ECHO request for 11.11.11.1 is encapsulated in a GRE header with a destination address 10.1.100.1. The tunnel destination is resolved using VRFLITE3's global routing table (because there is no **tunnel vrf** command, as explained previously), which gives a next-hop address, learned through OSPF, of 10.0.1.1 (also highlighted in Example 7-22).

When VRFLITE1 receives the packet, the GRE packet destination matches interface Tunnel100. The IP payload has a destination address of 11.11.11.1, which is resolved using VRF YOSEMITE, because Tunnel100 is configured to be in that VRF. Interface Loopback101 in VRF YOSEMITE has an address that matches, so the router correctly receives the packet. VRFLITE1 then sends an ICMP reply back to the sender. You should be able to work out the details of the return path.

RIP to BGP

The final example introduces BGP between VRFs. Remember, there is no MPLS used in the core, so the BGP next hop is to be found in the global routing table (which is a nice way of reinforcing the fact that MPLS is an additional forwarding plane, not a replacement for IP). The network topology is given in Figure 7-12.

Figure 7-12 *RIP to BGP Topology*

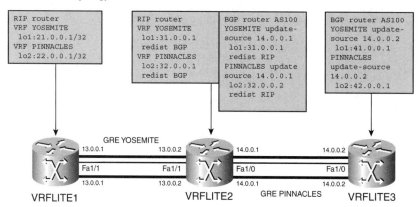

Having RIP and BGP configured in this way simulates a scenario in which the CE-PE interface uses a different routing protocol from the PE-PE one. (In any case, it is always fun to do route redistribution.) The example uses RIP between VRFLITE1 and VRFLITE2 and BGP between VRFLITE2 and VRFLITE3. Remember to specify the metric for the routes redistributed from BGP to RIP. This is not a book about routing, so here it is just one hop.

The VPN is built of GRE tunnels, one set per VPN. Unlike the previous example, there are three peer routers and each uses overlapping addresses for both the tunnels and the customer address spaces.

The VRFLITE1 configuration is unchanged from Example 7-16, so it is not shown. Example 7-24 gives the configuration for VRFLITE2, which is where all the interesting work is done.

Example 7-24 *VRFLITE2 Configuration*

```
interface Loopback0
 ip address 10.1.0.2 255.255.255.255
!
! the next two loopbacks are
! announced by BGP
interface Loopback1
 ip vrf forwarding YOSEMITE
 ip address 31.0.0.1 255.255.255.255
!
interface Loopback2
 ip vrf forwarding PINNACLES
 ip address 32.0.0.1 255.255.255.255
```

Example 7-24 *VRFLITE2 Configuration (Continued)*

```
!
! The next two loopbacks are for tunnel
! source
interface Loopback30
 ip address 10.1.100.2 255.255.255.255
!
interface Loopback40
 ip address 10.1.200.2 255.255.255.255
!
interface Tunnel100
 ip vrf forwarding YOSEMITE
 ip address 13.0.0.2 255.255.255.252
 tunnel source Loopback30
 tunnel destination 10.1.100.1
!
interface Tunnel101
 ip vrf forwarding YOSEMITE
 ip address 14.0.0.1 255.255.255.252
 tunnel source Loopback30
 tunnel destination 10.1.100.3
!
interface Tunnel200
 ip vrf forwarding PINNACLES
 ip address 13.0.0.2 255.255.255.252
 tunnel source Loopback40
 tunnel destination 10.1.200.1
!
interface Tunnel201
 ip vrf forwarding PINNACLES
 ip address 14.0.0.1 255.255.255.252
 tunnel source Loopback40
 tunnel destination 10.1.200.3
!
interface FastEthernet1/0
 description Interface to CORE3
 ip address 10.0.1.1 255.255.255.252
 duplex half
!
interface FastEthernet1/1
 description Interface to CORE1
 ip address 10.0.0.2 255.255.255.252
 duplex half
!
! Core IGP for tunnel source/destination
! reachability
router ospf 1
 router-id 10.1.0.2
 log-adjacency-changes
 network 10.0.0.0 0.255.255.255 area 0
!
router rip
```

continues

Example 7-24 *VRFLITE2 Configuration (Continued)*

```
version 2
!
address-family ipv4 vrf YOSEMITE
version 2
redistribute connected metric 1
redistribute bgp 100 metric 1
network 13.0.0.0
no auto-summary
exit-address-family
!
address-family ipv4 vrf YOSEMITE
version 2
redistribute connected metric 1
redistribute bgp 100 metric 1
network 13.0.0.0
no auto-summary
exit-address-family
!
router bgp 100
no synchronization
bgp log-neighbor-changes
no auto-summary
!
address-family ipv4 vrf YOSEMITE
redistribute connected
redistribute rip
neighbor 14.0.0.2 remote-as 100
neighbor 14.0.0.2 update-source Tunnel101
neighbor 14.0.0.2 activate
no auto-summary
no synchronization
exit-address-family
!
address-family ipv4 vrf PINNACLES
redistribute connected
redistribute rip
neighbor 14.0.0.2 remote-as 100
neighbor 14.0.0.2 update-source Tunnel201
neighbor 14.0.0.2 activate
no auto-summary
no synchronization
exit-address-family
```

VRFLITE2 connects to two others, so there are two tunnels in each direction, one for each VRF.

VRFLITE2 (and the other routers) also uses OSPF as the core routing protocol. OSPF advertises the addresses used by the GRE tunnels. After OSPF converges, traffic can flow between the VRFs across the tunnels, and the RIP and BGP routing protocols start to exchange routes with their peers, which in turn builds connectivity for the VPNs. VRFLITE2 runs RIP to exchange VRF routes with VRFLITE1 and runs BGP to exchange routes with VRFLITE3. The

RIP process has a **redistribute BGP** statement for each VRF (with the metric that will be used for the network announcement) and is enabled for network 13.0.0.0 (which matches Tunnel100 and Tunnel200). In turn, the BGP process redistributes both the RIP and directly connected routes. You can also see that BGP uses the Tunnel101 and Tunnel201 interfaces as its source address in VRFs YOSEMITE and PINNACLES, respectively. Of course, the 14.0.0.2 addresses must be reachable for VRFLITE2 BGP to establish a BGP session with VRFLITE3.

Example 7-25 shows the routing tables for each VRF on VRFLITE2. So that you can follow the distribution thread, the output from **show ip route vrf commands** are also included for VRFLITE1 in Example 7-26. You can see that VRFLITE2 has routes learned from both RIP and BGP, but that Example 7-26 has all the routes learned from RIP. The highlighted routes in Example 7-25 show up in Example 7-26.

Example 7-25 *YOSEMITE and VPN Routing Tables on VRFLITE2*

```
VRFLITE2#show ip route vrf YOSEMITE

Routing Table: YOSEMITE
Codes: C - connected, S - static, R - RIP, M - mobile, B - BGP
       D - EIGRP, EX - EIGRP external, O - OSPF, IA - OSPF inter area
       N1 - OSPF NSSA external type 1, N2 - OSPF NSSA external type 2
       E1 - OSPF external type 1, E2 - OSPF external type 2
       i - IS-IS, L1 - IS-IS level-1, L2 - IS-IS level-2, ia - IS-IS inter area
       * - candidate default, U - per-user static route, o - ODR
       P - periodic downloaded static route

Gateway of last resort is not set

     41.0.0.0/32 is subnetted, 2 subnets
B       41.0.0.1 [200/0] via 14.0.0.2, 00:18:40
B       41.0.0.2 [200/0] via 14.0.0.2, 00:18:40
     11.0.0.0/32 is subnetted, 1 subnets
R       11.11.11.1 [120/1] via 13.0.0.1, 00:00:17, Tunnel100
     13.0.0.0/30 is subnetted, 1 subnets
C       13.0.0.0 is directly connected, Tunnel100
     14.0.0.0/30 is subnetted, 1 subnets
C       14.0.0.0 is directly connected, Tunnel101
     31.0.0.0/32 is subnetted, 1 subnets
C       31.0.0.1 is directly connected, Loopback1
```

Example 7-26 *YOSEMITE VPN Routing Tables on VRFLITE1*

```
VRFLITE1#show ip route vrf YOSEMITE

Routing Table: YOSEMITE
Codes: C - connected, S - static, I - IGRP, R - RIP, M - mobile, B - BGP
       D - EIGRP, EX - EIGRP external, O - OSPF, IA - OSPF inter area
       N1 - OSPF NSSA external type 1, N2 - OSPF NSSA external type 2
       E1 - OSPF external type 1, E2 - OSPF external type 2, E - EGP
       i - IS-IS, L1 - IS-IS level-1, L2 - IS-IS level-2, ia - IS-IS inter area
       * - candidate default, U - per-user static route, o - ODR
```

continues

Example 7-26 *YOSEMITE VPN Routing Tables on VRFLITE1 (Continued)*

```
Gateway of last resort is not set

     21.0.0.0/32 is subnetted, 1 subnets
C       21.0.0.1 is directly connected, Loopback1
     41.0.0.0/32 is subnetted, 2 subnets
R       41.0.0.1 [120/1] via 13.0.0.2, 00:00:16, Tunnel100
R       41.0.0.2 [120/1] via 13.0.0.2, 00:00:16, Tunnel100
     11.0.0.0/32 is subnetted, 1 subnets
C       11.11.11.1 is directly connected, Loopback101
     13.0.0.0/30 is subnetted, 1 subnets
C       13.0.0.0 is directly connected, Tunnel100
     14.0.0.0/30 is subnetted, 1 subnets
R       14.0.0.0 [120/1] via 13.0.0.2, 00:00:16, Tunnel100
     31.0.0.0/32 is subnetted, 1 subnets
R       31.0.0.1 [120/1] via 13.0.0.2, 00:00:18, Tunnel100
```

Example 7-27 shows VRFLITE3's configuration file, which now uses BGP for VPN routes, but still uses OSPF for core network connectivity.

Example 7-27 *VRFLITE3 Configuration File*

```
!
interface Loopback0
 ip address 10.1.0.3 255.255.255.255
!
interface Loopback1
 ip vrf forwarding YOSEMITE
 ip address 41.0.0.1 255.255.255.255
!
interface Loopback2
 ip vrf forwarding PINNACLES
 ip address 42.0.0.1 255.255.255.255
!
interface Loopback3
 description YOSEMITE tunnel end-point
 ip address 10.1.100.3 255.255.255.255
!
interface Loopback4
 description PINNACLES tunnel end-point
 ip address 10.1.200.3 255.255.255.255
!
interface Loopback100
 description GOOD test for VRF YOSEMITE reachability
 ip vrf forwarding YOSEMITE
 ip address 41.0.0.2 255.255.255.255
!
interface Loopback200
 description GOOD test for VRF PINNACLES reachability
 ip vrf forwarding PINNACLES
 ip address 42.0.0.2 255.255.255.255
!
```

Example 7-27 *VRFLITE3 Configuration File (Continued)*

```
interface Tunnel100
 description YOSEMITE tunnel to VRFLITE2
 ip vrf forwarding YOSEMITE
 ip address 14.0.0.2 255.255.255.252
 tunnel source Loopback3
 tunnel destination 10.1.100.2
!
interface Tunnel200
 description PINNACLES tunnel to VRFLITE2
 ip vrf forwarding PINNACLES
 ip address 14.0.0.2 255.255.255.252
 tunnel source Loopback4
 tunnel destination 10.1.200.2
!
interface FastEthernet1/0
 description Interface to CORE
 ip address 10.0.1.2 255.255.255.252
 duplex half
!
router ospf 1
 router-id 10.1.0.3
 log-adjacency-changes
 network 10.0.0.0 0.255.255.255 area 0
!
router bgp 100
 no synchronization
 bgp log-neighbor-changes
 no auto-summary
 !
 address-family ipv4 vrf YOSEMITE
 redistribute connected
 neighbor 14.0.0.1 remote-as 100
 neighbor 14.0.0.1 update-source Tunnel100
 neighbor 14.0.0.1 activate
 no auto-summary
 no synchronization
 exit-address-family
 !
 address-family ipv4 vrf PINNACLES
 redistribute connected
 neighbor 14.0.0.1 remote-as 100
 neighbor 14.0.0.1 update-source Tunnel200
 neighbor 14.0.0.1 activate
 no auto-summary
 no synchronization
 exit-address-family
!
```

VRFLITE3's configuration is, to all intents and purposes, that of a PE router without any label switching.

Example 7-28 shows the routing tables for each VRF on VRFLITE3. You can see that the highlighted 13.0.0.0, 12.12.12.1, and 11.11.11.1 networks, originally announced by RIP from VRFLITE1, are correctly imported by BGP here into the appropriate VRF. The other route learned via BGP was announced as a connected route by VRFLITE2 (and corresponds to Loopback1 and Loopback2 in Example 7-24). Of course, there are no routes from the global routing table in either of the VRFs, even though the address spaces overlap.

Example 7-28 *YOSEMITE and PINNACLES VPN Routing Tables on VRFLITE3*

```
VRFLITE3#show ip route vrf YOSEMITE

Routing Table: YOSEMITE
Codes: C - connected, S - static, R - RIP, M - mobile, B - BGP
       D - EIGRP, EX - EIGRP external, O - OSPF, IA - OSPF inter area
       N1 - OSPF NSSA external type 1, N2 - OSPF NSSA external type 2
       E1 - OSPF external type 1, E2 - OSPF external type 2
       i - IS-IS, L1 - IS-IS level-1, L2 - IS-IS level-2, ia - IS-IS inter area
       * - candidate default, U - per-user static route, o - ODR
       P - periodic downloaded static route

Gateway of last resort is not set

     41.0.0.0/32 is subnetted, 2 subnets
C       41.0.0.1 is directly connected, Loopback1
C       41.0.0.2 is directly connected, Loopback100
     11.0.0.0/32 is subnetted, 1 subnets
B       11.11.11.1 [200/1] via 14.0.0.1, 00:19:14
     13.0.0.0/30 is subnetted, 1 subnets
B       13.0.0.0 [200/0] via 14.0.0.1, 00:19:14
     14.0.0.0/30 is subnetted, 1 subnets
C       14.0.0.0 is directly connected, Tunnel100
     31.0.0.0/32 is subnetted, 1 subnets
B       31.0.0.1 [200/0] via 14.0.0.1, 00:19:15

VRFLITE3#show ip ro vrf PINNACLES

Routing Table: PINNACLES
Codes: C - connected, S - static, R - RIP, M - mobile, B - BGP
       D - EIGRP, EX - EIGRP external, O - OSPF, IA - OSPF inter area
       N1 - OSPF NSSA external type 1, N2 - OSPF NSSA external type 2
       E1 - OSPF external type 1, E2 - OSPF external type 2
       i - IS-IS, L1 - IS-IS level-1, L2 - IS-IS level-2, ia - IS-IS inter area
       * - candidate default, U - per-user static route, o - ODR
       P - periodic downloaded static route

Gateway of last resort is not set

     32.0.0.0/32 is subnetted, 1 subnets
B       32.0.0.1 [200/0] via 14.0.0.1, 00:01:59
     42.0.0.0/32 is subnetted, 2 subnets
C       42.0.0.2 is directly connected, Loopback200
C       42.0.0.1 is directly connected, Loopback2
     12.0.0.0/32 is subnetted, 1 subnets
```

Example 7-28 *YOSEMITE and PINNACLES VPN Routing Tables on VRFLITE3 (Continued)*

```
B        12.12.12.1 [200/1] via 14.0.0.1, 00:01:59
         13.0.0.0/30 is subnetted, 1 subnets
B        13.0.0.0 [200/0] via 14.0.0.1, 00:01:59
         14.0.0.0/30 is subnetted, 1 subnets
C        14.0.0.0 is directly connected, Tunnel200
```

Finally, Example 7-29 shows a ping right across the network, from VRFLITE3 to VRFLITE1.

Example 7-29 *Ping from VRFLITE3 to VRFLITE1*

```
VRFLITE3#ping vrf YOSEMITE 11.11.11.1

Type escape sequence to abort.
Sending 5, 100-byte ICMP Echos to 11.11.11.1, timeout is 2 seconds:
!!!!!
Success rate is 100 percent (5/5), round-trip min/avg/max = 1/1/4 ms
```

For this ping to work, the following steps must have all successfully taken place:

1. The core network routing, which uses OSPF, has converged.

2. Each router has built the GRE tunnels for each VRF to its neighbors. Route VRFLITE2 has two neighbors, so it terminates four tunnels.

3. VRFLITE1 uses RIP to advertise routes to networks 13.0.0.0 and 11.11.11.1 in VRF YOSEMITE and networks 13.0.0.0 and 12.12.12.1 in VRF PINNACLES.

4. VRFLITE2 redistributes these routes into BGP and announces them to VRFLITE3.

5. VRFLITE3 installs the routes learned by BGP into its routing tables for VRF YOSEMITE and VRF PINNACLES.

6. The **ping vrf YOSEMITE** command in Example 7-29 results in a lookup of address 11.11.11.1 in the VRF routing table. Example 7-28 shows that the next hop, 14.0.0.1, was learned by BGP.

7. Address 14.0.0.1 is directly connected, using GRE Tunnel100, so the router encapsulates the IP packet in a GRE packet, with destination 10.1.100.2 (from the configuration in Example 7-27).

8. The next hop for 10.1.100.2 is resolved using VRFLITE3's global routing table and the packet is forwarded through interface FastEthernet1/0 to VRFLITE2.

9. VRFLITE2 has a GRE tunnel interface in VRF YOSEMITE with a source address that matches the packet's destination, so the GRE header is stripped off.

10. VRFLITE2 then sees that the packet is intended for 11.11.11.1, so it looks for a match in the routing table for VRF YOSEMITE. Example 7-25 shows that the next hop—learned through RIP—is address 13.0.0l using interface Tunnel100.

11. The ICMP packet is encapsulated in a GRE header and sent to destination address 10.1.100.3 (which you can see in VRFLITE2's configuration file). This address is resolved through the global routing table to be on VRFLITE1.

12. VRFLITE1 receives the GRE packet on an interface in VRF YOSEMITE, removes the header, and finds that the destination matches one of its loopback addresses. VRFLITE1 then returns an ICMP REPLY to the packet source. Once again, you should be able to figure out the details of the return path.

Summary

The central point in this chapter is that the concepts and solutions of broadband access to MPLS VPN are, in fact, relatively generic and apply for other forms of IP VPN. To show this, the chapter introduced network-based VPNs using GRE and IPSec tunnels, with passing reference to the topic of virtual routers and how they can be emulated using per-VRF functions. You could just as easily substitute another tunneling protocol that transports IP, for example L2TPv3.

The examples in this chapter illustrated how to use different routing protocols between VRFs connected by either 802.1q or GRE tunnels. The first design simulated a simple campus environment with route distribution to every router. Using VRFs in this way is gaining popularity as a way to segment campus environments without running VLANs across the network. The second design showed a service provider deploying network-based IP VPNs over an IP core. The example used RIP between PEs, more for simplicity than as an actual endorsement of this protocol in live networks. The third case study added BGP and touched on route redistribution in VRF-Lite scenarios, which is useful when the CE-PE routing protocol is different from the PE-PE routing protocol.

In this chapter, you learn about the following topics:

- Applying Broadband VPN Design Principles in Two Case Studies

- Migrating an L2TP-Based Wholesale Service to a Managed-LNS Offering Using VRF-Lite, and to a Full MPLS-Based Offering, and a Comparison Between the Two

- Deploying a Residential Ethernet Service for Data, Voice, and Video Services with and Without MPLS in the Access Layer

CHAPTER 8

Case Studies for Using MPLS with Broadband VPNs

This chapter looks at how to combine all the different building blocks introduced in the previous chapters to make a working solution. The chapter also introduces some ideas to help you choose products, with the understanding that evolution and natural selection make product characteristics a fast-moving target. To help reinforce how MPLS-based solutions compare to other choices of technology, migration scenarios are included as part of the case studies.

There is also a large component of review in the case studies, with reference to previous chapters for background information or more detailed discussion of the implementation details or alternatives.

The two case studies presented in this chapter are an amalgam of different network designs, based on answers to some fundamental design checks that you can ask yourself pretty much regardless of the network service model:

- **Static versus dynamic binding**—How are subscriber interfaces bound to VRFs? Are the mappings (or bindings) always the same for a particular interface, or is this a kind of run-time decision made only when the subscriber connects?

- **Scale and numbers**—How many VRFs are in the network? How many subscribers exist per VRF? The answers have an impact on both how route tables are managed and the type of PE used.

- **VRF compatibility**—Are the features you need VRF compatible? As discussed in Chapter 7, you cannot just assume that they are VRF compatible, you have to check, sometimes at a very detailed level.

- **Isolation of changes across administrative domains**—Do changes in one customer's network have an impact on another network? Obviously, you should try to design things so that such impact is minimal.

- **Review of routing, addressing, and security design**—Does the end result comply with the best practices of IP network design? You will be surprised to find out how many white board ideas do not comply.

Case Study 1: Managed LNS

A regional DSL wholesale provider, Etiolles Networks, wants to sell additional services and decides to try a managed L2TP Network Server (LNS) offering. Etiolles Networks currently has 20 ISP customers and operates in 30 different districts. Each ISP has between 1000 and 20,000 subscribers to whom Etiolles Networks provides high-speed Internet access. Table 8-1 gives the number of subscribers for each ISP. Table 8-2 shows the actual distribution of subscribers per ISP. The average subscriber count per ISP is 6100, and there are 122,000 subscribers on the wholesale network.

NOTE	For the more inquisitive reader, Etiolles is a small town on the outskirts of Paris. I'm not aware of any regional network provider located there.

Table 8-1 *Subscriber Count per ISP*

ISP	Number of Subscribers
ISP_A	20,000
ISP_B	5000
ISP_C	10,000
ISP_D	20,000
ISP_E	3000
ISP_F	3000
ISP_G	2000
ISP_H	10,000
ISP_I	10,000
ISP_J	3000
ISP_K	10,000
ISP_L	5000
ISP_M	3000
ISP_N	1000
ISP_O	2000
ISP_P	1000
ISP_Q	2000
ISP_R	2000
ISP_S	5000
ISP_T	5000

Table 8-2   *Subscriber Distribution per ISP*

Subscriber Count	Number of ISPs
20,000	2
10,000	4
5000	4
3000	4
2000	4
1000	2

Etiolles Networks provides the following high-speed access rates that each ISP can offer to its customers:

- 128 Kbps upstream/384 Kbps downstream
- 128 Kbps upstream/768 Kbps downstream
- 256 Kbps upstream/1.5 Mbps downstream
- 384 Kbps upstream/1.5 Mbps downstream

Etiolles Networks also has a standard set of hand-off interfaces to carry IP packets between its network and the ISP networks, as follows:

- ATM VC: 64 Kbps, 256 Kbps, and 512 Kbps
- Ethernet port: 1 Mbps, 1.5 Mbps, 2 Mbps, 8 Mbps, 10 Mbps, and 34 Mbps

Etiolles Networks' marketing department has projected an annual end-user increase of 200 percent, to 480,000 subscribers, starting next year. Based on long experience of marketing forecasts, the engineering department considers that it needs to plan for less than that, so it wants a network that scales to 240,000 subscribers. Etiolles Networks also hopes to sign 10 new ISPs.

Etiolles Networks is currently using a classic L2TP solution. Each ISP has its own LNS and maintains its subscriber database in a RADIUS server. To be able to make money as quickly as possible with the new service, Etiolles Networks wants to share the same LNS device between many different VPN customers. On the other hand, the network operations department is very wary of doing anything new that might disrupt existing services and wants a solution that causes the least amount of disruption.

To summarize the requirements of Etiolles Networks' design team:

- Each ISP retains control over authentication
- ISP data must remain private
- The network design allows future growth
- The LNS device is shared between multiple customers

Service Definitions

Like any ISP, Etiolles Networks' advertised data rates refer to nominal bandwidth. In practice, the amount of bandwidth given to each subscriber is oversubscribed. The degree to which this is done varies, but for residential services, you may see ratios from 10:1 to 50:1, even 100:1. If you interpret the first ratio, it means that for a 10-bps service, the ISP engineers the network to carry only 1 bit per second.

The oversubscription ratio also determines what product mix the ISP can offer. Applying an oversubscription ratio of 20:1 to a 384-Kbps service means that an ISP needs to provision 20 Kbps/subscriber. A higher oversubscription ratio means that the effective throughput per subscriber is lower, so a lower-performance router might be sufficient.

In addition, Etiolles Networks wants to enforce the traffic contracts that it has with each ISP (trust is a wonderful thing, but it does not run a network) and make sure that no one subscriber is trying to draw more data than it has paid for.

Consider the following scenario, which refers to Figure 8-1, to understand the problem. Note that the data in Figure 8-1 goes from the MP3 servers on the right side, across ISP_A's network, and then to Etiolles Networks' high-speed core. The arrow denotes the flow of data from server to LNS without intermediate hops.

- It is 3 a.m. on New Year's Eve. Everyone is partying except for a single, lonely engineer (left side of Figure 8-1), who is downloading every MP3 on the Internet.

- The subscriber's DSL service is rated at 384 Kbps downstream. His DSL line has trained at a higher speed, but the ATM PVC between Etiolles Networks' DSLAM and LAC is configured for an effective peak rate of 384 Kbps.

- Etiolles Networks' core network uses 2G links.

- The link between the LNS and our lonely subscriber's ISP is an E1 connection of 34 Mbps. (The connections from there to the MP3 servers are not important.)

- By sending a sufficient number of requests, the subscriber can pull a large amount of traffic from the Internet. Because this rather extreme scenario has only one active subscriber on the DSL network, in theory, the LNS will forward 34 Mbps of data to the LAC.

- Of course, the subscriber has only paid for a 384-Kbps connection, but this is not actually enforced anywhere before the LAC.

- TCP would make sure that any single MP3 fetch never uses more than the end-to-end bandwidth, but UDP offers no such guarantee.

Figure 8-1 *Unpaid Bandwidth Consumption Scenario*

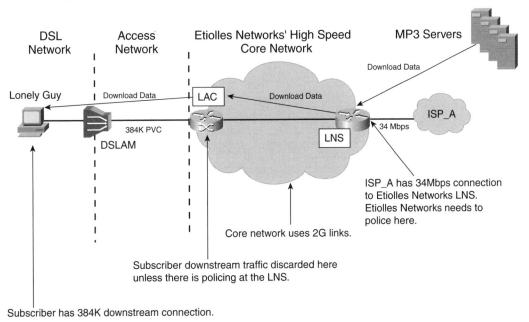

Per-subscriber policing at the LNS would solve the problem shown in Figure 8-1 because traffic would be dropped at the ISP interface of Etiolles Networks' core.

Per-subscriber policing in the wholesale network can also be useful if there is any differentiation between classes of services, such as a premium service, with a lower drop probability than services. Etiolles Networks can actually police subscriber flows more easily than any ISP can. The ISP can use only IP header information to identify subscribers. Subscriber addresses change, however, so this is not easy. Etiolles Networks, on the other hand, has a (virtual-access) interface for each subscriber on which it is easy to police traffic.

L2TP-Based Wholesale Service: Managed LNS

The first option chosen by the design team was to retain L2TP as the transport mechanism, but to modify the LNS to be hosted by the wholesale provider and shared amongst multiple ISPs (called a *managed LNS service*).

Figure 8-2 shows a reference architecture of Etiolles Networks' managed LNS architecture. The following sections look at the design layer by layer.

Figure 8-2 *Managed LNS Service Reference Architecture*

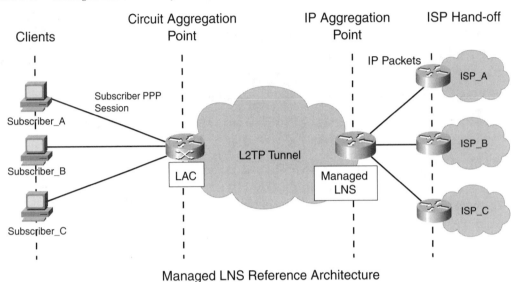

Managed LNS Reference Architecture

Clients

The network in this scenario is a DSL network and thus has a fairly standard choice of protocols on the client side, which were covered in Chapter 2, "Delivering Broadband Access Today: An Access Technologies Primer." Etiolles Networks decided to use PPPoE for two reasons: because it is available on all the operating system platforms, and, most of all, because of its tight integration with a full-service control plane (i.e., RADIUS). As previous chapters have discussed at length, PPPoE has all the hooks necessary for authentication, network selection, and so forth. Etiolles Networks does not use PPPoE service selection; the VPDN domain name is enough to choose the correct destination ISP.

Circuit Aggregation: LAC

Etiolles Networks serves a subscriber base that extends over 30 different cities and towns. This means that there are at least 30 LACs, with an average of 4000 users now, and an expected 6000 subscribers per device as the network grows. (Real deployments are never so uncomplicated as to have the same number of people at each site, but this is a good place to start.) Assuming also that the average downstream subscriber traffic stream is 56 Kbps (which is the midpoint of actual bit rates required for Etiolles Networks' subscriber access rates, using a 20:1 oversubscription), a Fast Ethernet trunk interface is easily adequate to transport subscriber traffic. (A T3 is not adequate, by the way, once you factor in overhead and the upstream traffic.) Note that given the density and throughput requirements, a modern midrange router can handle this amount of traffic quite well.

IP Aggregation: LNS

As stated previously, Etiolles Networks specifically does not want to have a different LNS for every customer. To calculate the absolute minimum number of devices, divide the number of subscribers by the maximum session capacity of the LNS; for example, 240,000 sessions and 32,000 L2TP tunnels works out to be 8 LNSs.

The global network tunnel count is 1 per VPN per LAC, for a total of 600 (20×30) L2TP tunnels. If, for some reason, this is perceived to be too high (and it is comfortably within the capacity of what even a small router can handle), the operator could use tunnel sharing to share a tunnel between different VPNs, thus potentially getting down to 30 tunnels. (You always need at least one per LAC.)

Returning to the issue of tunnel count, there are 20 ISPs and 8 LNSs, which means each LNS needs to support between 2 and 3 VPNs and therefore terminate up to 90 tunnels. (For any given VPN, there are 30 tunnels, 1 per LAC, so for 3 VPNs, the LNS terminates 90 tunnels.) Figure 8-3 summarizes the tunnel counts per LAC and LNS.

Figure 8-3   *LAC and LNS Tunnel Counts in Etiolles's Network*

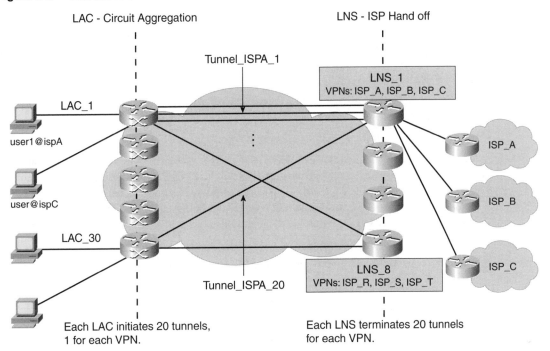

This is a managed LNS service, so the router needs address space separation for the subscriber sessions. At this point, you can use VRF-Lite, which was introduced in Chapter 7, "Implementing Network-Based Access VPNs without MPLS." Each ISP has its own VRF, and

Etiolles Networks can run Per-VRF dynamic routing protocols with the different ISPs. The L2TP tunnels themselves are terminated in global routing, but individual sessions are terminated into the appropriate VRF, as discussed in depth in Chapter 5, "Introduction to MPLS-Based Access VPN Architectures." If you decide to use Per-VRF L2TP tunnels, which involve terminating L2TP tunnels into VRFs instead of the global routing table, you cannot use tunnel sharing. This is quite intuitive: One feature uses private address space for tunnels, the other shares a tunnel between multiple sessions belonging to different VPNs. Chapter 7 covers this territory in more depth.

Using an example of just 3 VPNs to manage, with 6100 subscribers on average per VPN (see Figure 8-3), each LNS has about 18,300 VPNv4 routes in total, because there is 1 route per subscriber (and probably only a default route to the ISP). The biggest VRF is estimated to have 20,000 VPNv4 routes. These are easily manageable numbers.

Note how aggregation has proceeded at each layer. The design started with 120,000 different subscriber circuits, went to 30 LACs, and finished with 8 LNSs. The network is also designed to accommodate subscriber growth, to 240,000 users.

Control Plane: AAA

Etiolles Networks' design starts with 16,000 subscribers per LNS today and with a plan to double that next year. The time to set up all these calls is an important, if often overlooked, parameter to deal with in situations such as the following:

- Sudden increases in load (An earthquake hits San Jose and everyone in Silicon Valley checks the web.)

- After a power failure occurs and service is restored

A good LNS has a setup rate of 200–400 cps (calls per second). Not taking any AAA delays into account, this means that a fully loaded LNS will bring up 32,000 subscribers in 80 seconds, which is very acceptable. This will be slower in real-world situations because of RADIUS lookups and so forth. Indeed, you should try to avoid building an AAA infrastructure that reduces the calls per second by orders of magnitude.

A brute-force approach to Etiolles Networks' AAA architecture would be for each LNS to send RADIUS requests directly to the appropriate ISP server. This works perfectly well, except that

- Each ISP AAA server needs a client entry for every LNS. If the LNS address changes, the ISP has to update its database. This breaks the design requirement for limiting changes to a single administrative domain.

- There is no way for Etiolles Networks to check the attributes returned by the ISP, because they go directly to the LNS. (Although Cisco IOS supports RADIUS attribute inspection, Etiolles Networks decided not to deploy that feature.)

For the preceding reasons, Etiolles Networks' managed LNS design uses a proxy AAA server, as discussed in Chapter 6, "Wholesale MPLS-VPN Related Service Features." Thus, the LNSs send data to a single address. The proxy uses the domain name to select the correct ISP server to which to forward AAA packets.

The proxy server can also check, add, or remove attributes as needed. For example, Etiolles Networks might want to do VRF allocation itself, and add the appropriate av-pair to ACCESS-ACCEPT packets. (Assigning VRFs on the device itself is also an option. There are just a few VPDN domains per LNS and it is perfectly possible to have separate virtual templates for each. In this case, the proxy server would need to remove any VRF av-pair from customer records, because RADIUS overrides local configuration.)

Per-VRF AAA is the right way to deploy a proxy RADIUS architecture with VRFs. Note from the preceding discussion that all the LNSs are going to use the same proxy server, so this has to be in the global address space, which in turn means that all the ISP AAA servers are reachable from Etiolles' network. This design option was also covered in Chapter 6.

IP addresses are assigned using overlapping local pools: There is one pool per ISP, which are referenced with using the pool-name av-pair in the RADIUS ACCESS-ACCEPT packets. There is a small number of LNSs, probably all collocated at just a few physical locations, so address management is not a complex issue and deploying On Demand Address Pools (ODAP) is not worth the trouble.

Network and Service Availability

How robust is Etiolles Networks' design? Well, consider the following:

- There are limited options to improve availability on the LAC. You can have physical device redundancy with an appropriate choice of hardware platform. Etiolles Networks has not gone this route with its choice of a smaller platform and lower subscriber density per LAC, but it does have dual uplinks. There is no redundancy for the subscriber-facing ATM circuits.

- The LNS is fully redundant both from a line card and processor point of view. The subscriber densities are higher here, so this decision makes economic sense. Redundant uplinks between the ISP and Etiolles Networks are an optional extra in the service contract, but are recommended from a technical point of view. Because the subscriber density allows it, Etiolles Networks deploys L2TP failover mechanisms between pairs of LNSs; each LNS is a primary for some ISPs (and VRFs) and a backup for others. This provides extra security in case an LNS becomes unreachable.

MPLS-Based Wholesale Service

The L2TP solution for managed LNS service used a combination of L2TP for transport and VRF-Lite on the LNS itself. Now, this section looks at what would change in the design if Etiolles Networks decided to use MPLS instead of L2TP as the wholesale VPN technology.

The MPLS-based solution is shown Figure 8-4. Once again, the following sections go through each layer of the design, as well as address allocation, routing quality of service, and multicast considerations.

Figure 8-4   *Etiolles's MPLS-VPN Network*

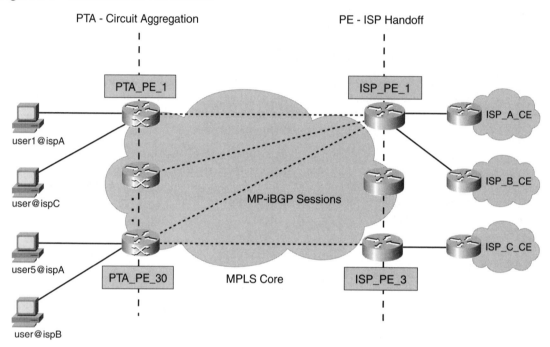

Clients

There is no change whatsoever to the clients, which continue to use PPPoE. The choice of L2TP or MPLS as the wholesale technology is completely transparent to the subscriber.

PTA PE

PPP is terminated at the entry of the Etiolles Networks' core on a PTA PE. There would be a total of 30 PTA PEs doing circuit and IP aggregation, which is unchanged from the number of LACs in the previous design.

The PTA-PE role is more processor intensive than that of a simple LAC, because the device is responsible for complete session termination and authentication.

Each PTA PE in Figure 8-4 needs 20 VRFs, 1 for each ISP. Based on Table 8-2, the number of routes per PTA PE will range from approximately 1000 to 20,000, because there is a route per subscriber. We earlier calculated an average of 6100 subscribers per VPN, which is approximately 120,000 VPNv4 routes per LNS (6000×20). This total number is again within the capacities of a decent PE, but it is climbing toward an upper bound. This number and the number of AAA servers are probably going to be the key determinants in the timing of the decision to use a virtual home gateway, instead of a regular PTA PE, at least for the biggest VPNs. For now, Etiolles Networks does not need to.

ISP PE

The ISP-facing router, called ISP_PE_1 and ISP_PE_3 in Figure 8-4, is completely transformed from a session-terminating device into a straightforward PE router. Each ISP PE peers with every PTA PE, as shown in Figure 8-5 later in the chapter, during the discussion of the second scenario.

The number of routes at this layer of the design has been reduced from the tens of thousands to the tens of hundreds, because the PTA PEs aggregate all the subscriber routes. Session and tunnel counts had been the factors that most influenced the number of LNSs in the network, but now the number of PEs is determined by route table size, interface speed, redundancy considerations, and other very traditional router-sizing considerations.

Etiolles Networks has decided to deploy three ISP PEs, but it is free to increase the number of ISPs connected to each ISP-PE router. Or, Etiolles Networks can decide on simpler devices, either for reasons of scalability or if it is cheaper to have many such routers in different locations closer to the ISP customers, which saves on WAN links.

Address Allocation and Routing

With the MPLS design, the number of points at which addresses need to be managed has grown from 8 LNSs to 30 PTA PEs. Etiolles Networks should at least consider ODAP as a tool to simplify management of address pools, but in all cases, the PTA PEs must be configured to announce summarized pools of addresses and not individual host routes.

Routing is not complex in this network, but Etiolles Networks should use an MPLS hub-and-spoke architecture (which is what Figure 8-4 shows).

It is interesting to imagine what happens if this does not happen: Etiolles Networks gives away free bandwidth. Why? Well, look at Figure 8-4 again. With a full mesh of BGP sessions, all the PTA PEs also peer with one another. This allows traffic from user1@ispA on PTA_PE_1 to go directly to user5@ispA on PTA_PE_30, without ever crossing the ISP network. This path across Etiolles Networks' core is high bandwidth but is not billed to the ISP. A hub-and-spoke design would correctly route this traffic first through ISP_PE_1 then on to ISP_A_CE.

Control Plane: AAA

The LT2P-based design used Per-VRF AAA, with all RADIUS packets going through Etiolles Networks' own proxy server. There is no technical reason to change that architecture with an MPLS-based solution. However, Etiolles Networks now also has the option of using the second Per-VRF AAA model covered in Chapter 6, where the PTA PE sends requests directly to ISP RADIUS servers. Be careful about how many AAA servers would be involved in this case. Each ISP will have at least one AAA server, and there are 20 ISPs. Once again, this is a reasonable number, but is also something for Etiolles Networks to monitor as the number of ISPs increases.

QoS and Multicast

Unlike the L2TP-based solution, quality of service can be applied to subscriber packets on Etiolles Networks' core. For example, discard is much more efficient because Etiolles can drop or shape excess packets at the PTA PE and throughout its core network, not just at the LNS. (remember the case for per-user policing in Figure 8-1.) The QoS options for MPLS are covered in Chapter 4, "Introduction to MPLS."

The choice of MPLS also means that Etiolles Networks' network is much more efficient at transporting multicast. In the L2TP-based solution, all the multicast replication takes place on LNS, which means the core carries more traffic than it has to. With the MPLS solution at the edge, multicast data is replicated much later, on the PTA PEs.

Finally, the following list answers whether the original design requirements are satisfied with either solution:

- **The customer retains control over authentication**—Proxy AAA is the answer with both L2TP and MPLS, but with an additional design option in MPLS.

- **Customer data must remain private**—The L2TP-based managed LNS uses VRF-Lite and dedicated Layer 2 links to the ISP routers. The full MPLS-VPN solution uses, obviously, MPLS VPN!

- **The network design allows future growth**—The network is dimensioned to accommodate twice the number of subscribers, but PEs are less bound by the number of subscribers than LNSs are.

- **The LNS device is shared between multiple customers**—VRF-Lite allows this sharing, to reduce the number of LNSs to eight devices in the L2TP case. With the MPLS solution, there were three ISP PEs.

Although this case study showed and somewhat contrasted two different approaches to solving the same design problem, and although the MPLS-based solution had some distinct advantages over the L2TP-based one, this is not a one-size-fits-all endorsement of MPLS solutions. The next case study shows that other approaches may work better, depending on the problem you need to solve.

Case Study 2: D/V/V Over Ethernet

This case study is of a residential Ethernet service in a European city. The provider, Rengstorff Networks, owns both the access infrastructure and the service component. There is no open access–style breakdown of wholesale/retail that is required in the world of DSL. However, Rengstorff Networks would like to be able to offer other providers access to its network, for a fee of course. The service mix is high-speed Internet, voice, and, above all, video. Rengstorff Networks has partnered with local media firms to be able to provide Video-On-Demand (VOD) service and wants to compete with local telephone carriers (called PTTs or ILECs) by selling cheap voice calls and compete with cable operators by selling competitive video services.

With its current buildout, Rengstorff Networks has an immediately addressable market of 64,000 subscribers and wants to build its network to accommodate half that number of customers. It projects a 20 percent adoption rate of its video service, and a 100 percent use of voice, which is bundled with the data service.

Rengstorff Networks' requirements are as follows:

- **Secure operation**—Subscribers must be protected from attacks by other subscribers that exploit holes in Rengstorff Networks' local equipment. What goes and comes over the Internet is a completely different matter!

- **Support of the cheapest possible CPE**—Rengstorff is launching a service and wants to keep its costs per subscriber and per building as low as possible. A cheap, simple CPE is very central to its business plan.

- **Multiservice network, supporting video and voice traffic**—As described in the introduction to this section, Rengstorff Networks needs to offer voice and video services to entice customers away from competing offerings.

- **Future support of open access**—Rengstorff Networks currently partners with a single ISP for its Internet access service. There is a possibility that regulators may decide to force Ethernet wholesale operators to offer their customers a free choice of ISPs, which is common in DSL.

Service Definitions

Subscribers each get a 10-Mbps connection spread across three different services (video, voice, and data).

The video service is on demand, which uses unicast streams, with 2-Mbps MPEG2 channels. The service comes with a set-top box. Each subscriber can receive up to two different channels simultaneously, so 4 Mbps is dedicated to each video subscriber. Video has very strict QoS requirements, as follows:

- Latency $< 0.5 - 1$ s
- Bit Error Rate (BER) $< 10^{-7}$
- Jitter < 50 ms

All layers of the network have to be carefully designed to support these requirements and so guarantee an acceptable viewing experience. The network core supports standard IP QoS mechanisms, and the access and aggregation layers support Ethernet TOS mechanisms. The full details of the QoS design are beyond the scope of this book. Interested readers will find suggested reference works in Appendix A.

The VOD infrastructure consists of several servers, a subscriber database, a set-top box application server, a content server, and a VOD server, which actually transmits the streams to the clients. All these servers are in a regional point of presence (POP). Video traffic does not need to go across the core network. The video traffic is carried in a dedicated VLAN.

The voice service is VoIP-based at the subscriber premises, with a voice gateway in the regional POP to a traditional circuit-based PTT network for off-network calls. Voice traffic is also carried in a dedicated VLAN. VoIP QoS requirements are well studied and documented. The major impact to Rengstorff's design is support of low-latency queuing on all the platforms.

Network Design

Rengstorff's network is shown in Figure 8-5. The rest of this section discusses each layer in turn.

NOTE   I am indebted to my colleague and reviewer, Steve Phillips of Cisco Systems, for many hours of conversation about alternative designs for wholesale Ethernet access, as well as subscriber numbers.

Clients

The situation for the clients is every bit as complex as the previous case study was straightforward. First, this is not a PC-centric solution. Set-top boxes (STBs) and IP phones are part of the mix. Given the wide variety of clients to accommodate and the current lack of any requirement to open the network to other providers, the most straightforward option it to use static service provisioning and assign a different physical port to each service. Every customer, therefore, would have three Ethernet ports if they subscribe to the full offering of voice, video, and data. The CPE aggregates the ports to VLANs, one per service. This is the situation shown in Figure 8-5.

All the STBs, PCs, and phones need to do is churn out IP in an Ethernet frame. Voice and video clients each have signaling protocols that interact directly with application servers, and registration and service subscription is also run on dedicated servers, so there is no need for network-based service selection.

Figure 8-5   *Rengstorff's Ethernet Network*

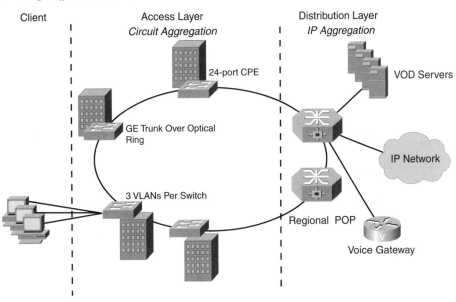

3 Ethernet Ports per Customer for
Voice, Video and Data.

Internet access is basic, with no requirement for ISP selection, or usage-based billing.
(Rengstorff's Internet access is a flat-fee service.) Because this is an Ethernet-based network,
simple bridged access works fine, but security is an obvious concern, because all subscribers on
a single switch can be in the same broadcast domain. Thankfully, this is a well-researched
problem and there is a considerable arsenal of tools available to stop people from trying to harm
their neighbors:

- Private VLAN
- Spanning Tree protection: BPDU and Root Guard
- DHCP Option 82
- VACL

It is beyond the scope of this book to go into these tools in detail, but the goal of all of them is
the same: to secure a switched Ethernet environment.

Access Layer: Circuit Aggregation

Referring to Figure 8-5, the first level of aggregation consolidates traffic from 10-Mbps
subscriber ports onto a Gigabit Ethernet (GE) trunk, with VLANs.

Making some very crude calculations (and heroic, if unrealistic, assumptions about a total
absence of Layer 2 payload overhead), you can see that the aggregation trunks are not filled to

capacity—1 Gbps is enough to carry 100 10-Mbps ports' worth of traffic. In Rengstorff's case, the most a subscriber can consume is 10 Mbps, but split over three ports (one for each service), so each CPE switch serves 16 different customers. The peak load per CPE trunk port is 160 Mbps.

The CPE sits on a GE ring, and Rengstorff typically tries to have 10 premises on a single ring, so there is oversubscription (of the data service), which has to be correctly managed on the CPE and aggregation devices so as not to interfere with video and voice traffic. Rengstorff has predicted a fairly conservative 20 percent adoption of video. On a per-switch basis, this represents 3 subscribers who have guaranteed bandwidth for their 4-Mbps video stream, for a total of 12 Mbps.

Of course, 10 CPE per ring represents 120 Mbps of video. Fortunately, voice is not bandwidth intensive. Assuming 64 Kbps per household, there is a total of 1 Mbps of voice traffic per switch and 10 Mbps per ring.

Of the 160 Mbps per CPE, less than 10 percent is reserved for voice or video. Referring again to the aggregation ring in Figure 8-5 and again making rough estimates, 900 Mbps is available to the data service. The oversubscription ratio is less than 2:1; therefore, Rengstorff has a lot of scope to sell more video, or to put more premises on its rings.

Distribution Layer: IP Aggregation

The next level of aggregation is at the regional POP level. Rengstorff has five regional POPs, in different parts of the city. Each one has pairs of Ethernet switches that aggregate the GE traffic and route or switch VLAN traffic to its proper destination. There are 160 subscribers per GE ring (see Figure 8-5 again) and 10 rings per switch, for a total of 1600 subscribers per distribution switch. Processing speed is no issue; high-end LAN switches can easily process 40 Gbps of traffic.

Remember, the network buildout is for 32,000 subscribers, with a total of 20 switches in all, or 4 per POP. Again, there is spare capacity here, both in terms of empty slots (there are 8- or 16-port GE cards, so you could use just one slot), network bandwidth, and switch processing horsepower. This extra horsepower is fairly typical of initial residential Ethernet buildouts, where the number of subscribers (as on any new network) starts small and where the capacity of the network can rise very quickly.

At each POP, there is a voice VLAN with a voice gateway for off-network voice calls, and a video VLAN with the VOD infrastructure. You can see in Figure 8-5 how each POP switch connects the VLANs. Internet traffic is routed across a simple 2.5-Gbps IP network to a tier 1 ISP.

Where is the VPN in all this? Rengstorff's entire network is built using a Layer 2 VPN solution, also known as VLANs. There are three different VPNs in the network, one for each service.

Adding Open Access

One of the design goals is to move to open access and allow subscribers to choose their own ISP for Internet access. (Rengstorff is not about to let go of video and voice traffic.) Rengstorff wants to move to an MPLS core and use an MPLS-VPN solution as the vehicle to provide open access. Its new network is shown in Figure 8-6.

Figure 8-6   *Rengstorff's Open Access Network*

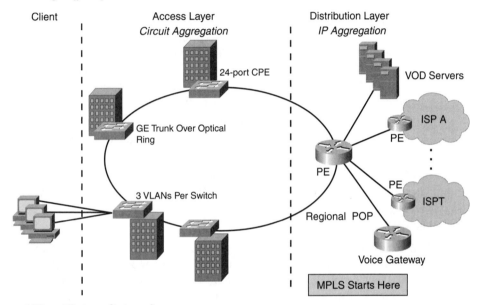

Note the following about Rengstorff's new network:

- There are now PE routers in the place of regional POP switches.

- Because of the way Rengstorff's metro network was engineered, there is no need to change anything at either the client or aggregation layers, which is still a purely Layer 2 affair (and is very analogous to a DSL access network with DSLAMs and ATM switches).

- In the new POP, traffic from the data VLAN is mapped to VRFs for the different ISPs. All voice and video traffic goes into separate VPNs.

The move to open access is a straightforward operation and when additional IP network destinations are added to the network.

Compare the networks in Figure 8-5 and Figure 8-6 and you will see that the POP "switches" already-routed IP traffic; now, they need to do so into several different IP VPN networks. Of course, there has to be a way for the PE to know which VPN to use for any given IP packet (referred to as *service selection* in previous chapters). Which is the best option for service (ISP) selection depends on address management requirements, as follows:

- If there is no overlapping IP address space, then VRF Select, introduced in Chapter 6, on the PE is a good choice. To have overlapping IP addresses, you must use a different subnet for each ISP. In a slight variation on this approach, Rengstorff could use VRF Select with an egress NAT router to map private client addresses to public ISP addresses.

- If there is a need for overlapping addresses in the access network, Rengstorff can stay with its current Layer 2 approach and dedicate a VLAN to each ISP. On each CPE switch, subscriber ports would be mapped to the correct VLAN, so the address space would be private throughout the access network. The change on the PE would simply involve having additional VLAN interfaces mapped to VRFs for every ISP, with no need for VRF Select. This is obviously static service selection. Alternatively, Rengstorff could move to IP in the aggregation network. This second option is discussed in more detail later in this section.

- The total number of routes does not change because that is a function of the number of subscribers, but the routers now have to handle VPNv4 routes instead of standard IPv4 routes.

Address assignment and routing are straightforward. Each PE is a DHCP relay agent and uses Option 82 to help the DHCP server sitting in the ISP network select the appropriate scope for the client. Ideally, the PE can be configured to announce summarized subnets and not host routes (as discussed in detail in Chapter 6). Finally, like the L2TP example, the PEs are configured in a hub-and-spoke topology.

In the general enthusiasm to put MPLS everywhere, you might be confronted (or tempted) with the idea of moving the PE function as close to the subscriber as possible. The architectural analogy with DSL is moving the PE function to the DSLAM. The most significant change if you do this is in the number of PEs, which can increase dramatically, but there is a knock-on effect on the rest of the design. Figure 8-7 shows Rengstorff's network with MPLS in the access layer.

You can see in Figure 8-7 that the access switches now become PE devices and the POP switches become LSRs for data service and PEs for video and voice traffic. The POP devices continue in their role of doing physical aggregation.

Here are some advantages to this solution:

- All the IP functionality moves out to the network edge and the VLANs disappear from the aggregation layer. This can be useful if a design is hitting a VLAN scalability limit, but it is not the case for Rengstorff's network.

- In Rengstorff's Ethernet environment, security considerations do improve because the CPE transforms from a Layer 2 device into a Layer 3 device. For example, the broadcast domains are now much smaller, essentially limited to an individual subscriber's line (like RBE). This prevents a lot of the simpler attacks, such as ARP spoofing, that a Layer 2 CPE must otherwise deal with.

- The QoS tools are richer for IP than for Layer 2, so Rengstorff can use DSCP-based policies instead of the simpler per-port or per-VLAN mechanisms it had used previously.

Figure 8-7   *Rengstorff's Network with MPLS Everywhere*

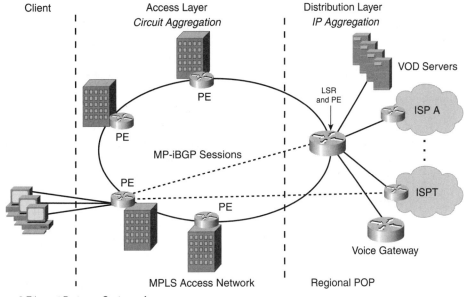

Here are some disadvantages to having MPLS in the access layer:

- Additional operational complexity is introduced into what had been a simple network, which is very bad. The number of PEs goes from approximately 20 to over 600. Straightaway, this complicates peering, address assignment, and announcements. Yes, route reflectors can help, but there is still a lot more to manage.

- The economic effect is probably as consequential as the functional one. Cost is an overriding factor in choosing CPE and adding MP BGP, LDP, and so on turns a low-cost switch into a midcost router (even if it still has switched Ethernet ports—such things exist).

Nothing else really changes in the move to MPLS to the edge: It is the same architecture after all. For example, Ethernet networks are effective at multicast transport, so the move to IP in the access network does not make a big difference. This is very much unlike the case of ATM that you saw in the L2TP design.

An Alternative Open Access Design

Is bridging the only option for an Ethernet network? What about using PPPoE on the clients? Actually, PPPoE is certainly a possibility, as shown in Figure 8-8.

There are two issues that could prevent Rengstorff from going that route:

- Ethernet switches are not designed for PPP termination, so, if they support it at all, they would not have the sort of density that you are used to with broadband routers. Of course, there is a way to design around almost anything, and the POP device could switch the data VLAN frames to a dedicated aggregation router, as shown in Figure 8-8. The router terminates both PPPoE (actually PPPoEo8021q) and PPP protocols, because the downstream network is entirely bridged.

- One of the major design goals is to have simple clients. PPPoE breaks this requirement and, furthermore, there is no guarantee that non-PC— based clients, such as set-top boxes or IP phones, will include a PPPoE stack at all! If Rengstorff really wanted PPPoE for just the data service, that would represent a compromise solution. All the usual possibilities apply for the VPN solution: PPP to L2TP, PPP to VLAN or, of course, PPP to MPLS VPN.

Figure 8-8   *Using a PPPoE Server*

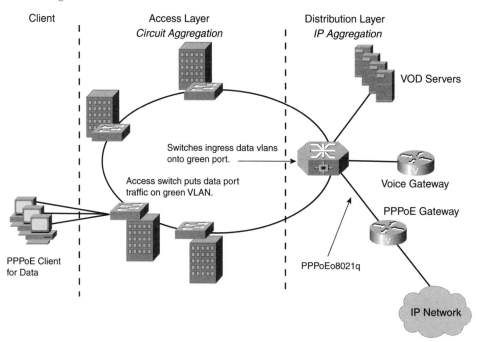

To conclude, the following list reviews how the main design requirements were satisfied:

- **Secure operation**—Advanced Layer 2 security features on the CPE device prevent attacks on the network and on other subscribers.

- **Support of the cheapest possible hosts**—Rengstorff uses bridged Ethernet for all subscriber hosts. PPPoE for data only is an alternative, and one that is used in operational networks.

- **Multiservice network, supporting video and voice traffic**—Use Ethernet TOS and IP QoS processing throughout the network.

- **Future support of open access**—There is an easy migration to open access using MPLS VPN. The simplest scenario involves keeping a single address space for the access network, but overlapping address spaces are also possible.

Summary

This chapter looked at two different network designs and discussed how to arrive at complete working solutions. Each case started with an alternative VPN technology—L2TP in the first case and VLANs in the second—and migrated to MPLS VPN.

The move for Etiolles Networks was quite beneficial. Not only was it able to sell a new managed service, but its multicast and QoS operation also improved considerably. For Rengstorff Networks, the case for using MPLS VPN as a solution for open access was pretty clear. It was much less obvious that there would be any comprehensive reason to migrate its entire access network, though.

This chapter also tried to make the case that you can have too much of a good thing: Some of the gains you realize by opting for an MPLS-based solution may be outweighed by operational complexity if you greatly increase the number of PEs, such as by pushing MPLS to the furthest edge of the network. There may be cases in which this is the right thing to do, but you should look at all the details before making a decision.

Because the implementation-related details of the design issues have already been covered in prior chapters, this chapter did not go into all the details, but instead provided references where appropriate.

In this chapter, you learn about the following topics:

- Introduction to IPv6 Protocol
- VPN Migration Scenarios from IPv4 to IPv6
- Introduction to L2VPN Technology and Pseudo-wires Using MPLS and L2TPv3
- Implications of L2VPN for Broadband Access Providers

CHAPTER 9

Future Developments in Broadband Access

This chapter looks out into the future a little at some protocol-level changes that might be coming soon to a network near you. Even though the protocols discussed here, IPv6 and L2VPN, are new and different, the architectural issues and requirements for broadband VPNs stay the same.

IPv6 has been sitting on the shelf for almost 10 years now, waiting to play the role it was designed for: namely, to replace IPv4 as the standard Layer 3 protocol. Although IPv6 is still often found in trial and research networks, it is also turning up in production networks, especially in Asia, and is mandatory for U.S. federal environments. Interestingly enough, all the major host and router vendors support IPv6, so that is not the gating factor to deployment.

The second topic of discussion, Layer 2 VPN (L2VPN), is getting a lot of air time at the standards bodies, so it is worthwhile to spend a little time understanding the service models, the technical details, and the potential impact on broadband access.

Introduction to IPv6

IPv6 was developed by the IETF during the mid-1990s to prepare for the next wave of Internet growth. The challenges were to determine how to provide connectivity for extremely large sets of devices, not just computers, and to learn from experiences with IPv4. The goal was to simplify and clarify as much as possible. Many of the objectives and decisions of the various working groups are well documented and are part of IPv6 lore.

IPv6 has the following properties (as discussed in RFC 2460):

- **Expanded addressing capabilities**—IPv6 increases the IP address size from 32 bits to 128 bits, to support more levels of addressing hierarchy, a much greater number of addressable nodes, and simpler autoconfiguration of addresses. The scalability of multicast routing is improved by adding a Scope field to multicast addresses. A new type of address, called an *anycast address*, is defined, which is used to send a packet to any one of a group of nodes.

- **Header format simplification**—Some IPv4 header fields have been dropped or made optional, to reduce the common-case processing cost of packet handling and to limit the bandwidth cost of the IPv6 header.

- **Improved support for extensions and options**—Changes in the way IP header options are encoded allows for more efficient forwarding, less stringent limits on the length of options, and greater flexibility for introducing new options in the future.
- **Flow labeling capability**—A new capability is added to enable the labeling of packets belonging to particular traffic flows for which the sender requests special handling, such as nondefault QoS or real-time service.
- **Authentication and privacy capabilities**—Extensions to support authentication, data integrity, and (optional) data confidentiality are specified for IPv6.

Figure 9-1 illustrates the IPv6 header, which is where the differences between IPv4 and IPv6 begin.

Figure 9-1   *IPv6 Header (Source: RFC 2460)*

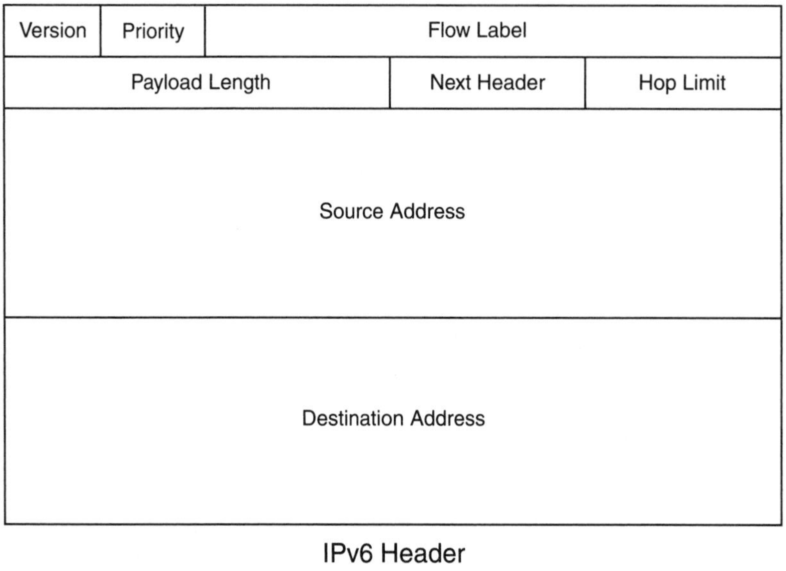

Version	Priority	Flow Label		
Payload Length			Next Header	Hop Limit
Source Address				
Destination Address				

IPv6 Header

Table 9-1 defines the fields in the IPv6 header. (Table 9-1 and the following discussion are from RFC 2460.)

Table 9-1   *IPv6 Header Fields*

Field	Description
Version	4-bit IP version number = 6.
Priority	8-bit priority, or traffic class, field.
Flow Label	20-bit flow label.

Table 9-1   *IPv6 Header Fields*

Payload Length	16-bit unsigned integer. Length of the IPv6 payload; i.e., the rest of the packet following this IPv6 header, in octets. Note that any extension headers (section 4) present are considered part of the payload; i.e., included in the length count.
Next Header	8-bit selector. Identifies the type of header immediately following the IPv6 header. Uses the same values as the IPv4 Protocol field (RFC 1700 et seq.).
Hop Limit	8-bit unsigned integer. Decremented by 1 by each node that forwards the packet. The packet is discarded if Hop Limit is decremented to 0.
Source Address	128-bit address of the originator of the packet.
Destination Address	128-bit address of the intended recipient of the packet (possibly not the ultimate recipient, if a Routing header is present).

The IPv6 header has fewer fields than the IPv4 header. You may read that IPv6 improves QoS processing in some way. This is not true. IPv6 by itself does absolutely nothing that changes how QoS is processed on a router. Yes, there is a 20-bit Flow ID, but the specification states that this field may be used by a source to label only packets for which it requires some special processing. How to do this is still an open question.

The rest of the discussion in this section focuses on the major changes introduced with IPv6, namely:

- Address space size
- Extensions
- Autoconfiguration

Address Space Size

Lack of address space is consistently held up as the single most important reason to switch to IPv6, but the fact is that IPv4 also has a large address space. Doing a very crude calculation reveals that 2^{32} (the size of an IPv4 address space) gives more than eight addresses for every square kilometer of the earth's surface (all 510,100,000 square kilometers of it, not just the dry parts—this leaves addresses for submarines too).

Of course, far fewer addresses than this are used in practice, because of the way the address space is organized. But, despite what is sometimes claimed, there is no imminent danger of running out, even if, for historical reasons, a disproportionate number of addresses are assigned to U.S. institutions. Some studies suggest that 37 percent of the IPv4 address space is as yet unassigned. (The *Internet Packet Journal* [http://www.cisco.com/ipj] carried an opinion piece called "The Myth of IP Version 6" in its June 2003 edition, which referred to the 37 percent free space.)

The designers of IPv6 tried to imagine a world in which everything and anything could be on the Internet: refrigerators, portable music devices, televisions, light bulbs, oil refinery process control systems, and so on. With all these new devices, the 32 bits of IPv4 addressing would not be enough to make the leap from the computer-driven Internet of its origins to a future of permanent and pervasive connectivity. Any exponential growth in Internet connection is likely to be driven by anything but computers, and the IETF wanted to make sure that the network could continue to evolve as needs changed.

IPv6 uses 128-bit addresses. There has been some interesting analysis that suggests, even in the very worst case, this provides 1564 addresses per square meter of the surface of the earth. The best case has many orders of magnitude more. Either way, this should be enough for quite a while. (See RFC 3194 for details on the calculation and a study of the efficiency of other addressing systems.)

NOTE   The very long addresses of IPv6 have caused headaches for hardware engineers. Every cache, table, and lookup algorithm used to process IP addresses now needs to be changed to cater to this four-fold increase. ASIC real estate costing what it does, high-performance IPv6 implementations were a long time coming. They are now available.

Addressing

It is pretty well accepted that classless interdomain routing (CIDR) in some way "saved" the Internet. Before its adoption, route table size was growing exponentially and threatened to overwhelm the capacity of backbone routers. CIDR introduced a hierarchy that the IPv6 designers wanted to retain and, if possible, enhance in the new protocol.

For that reason, the IETF introduced some pretty strict guidelines about address scopes and tried to take into account the needs of ISPs, inter-exchange carriers (IXCs), and enterprise network administrators. This last group must often use private addressing and NAT to manage networks that are larger than their allocation of public addresses would allow.

IPv6 uses an explicit topological hierarchy. The network portion of an address is formed from the public and, optionally, site prefixes. The host portion comes from the interface identifier (the typical identifier length being 48 bits, designed to match the Ethernet address format). The address architecture is defined in RFC 3513. Table 9-2 is an extract from that document and shows IPv6 address space allocation.

Table 9-2   *IPv6 Address Allocation*

Allocation	Prefix (Binary)	Fraction of Address Space
Reserved	0000 0000	1/256
Unassigned	0000 0001	1/256
Reserved for NSAP Allocation	0000 001	1/128

Table 9-2   *IPv6 Address Allocation (Continued)*

Allocation	Prefix (Binary)	Fraction of Address Space
Reserved for IPX Allocation	0000 010	1/128
Unassigned	0000 011	1/128
Unassigned	0000 1	1/32
Unassigned	0001	1/16
Unassigned	001	1/8
Provider-Based Unicast Address	010	1/8
Unassigned	011	1/8
Reserved for Neutral-Interconnect–Based Unicast Addresses	100	1/8
Unassigned	101	1/8
Unassigned	110	1/8
Unassigned	1110	1/16
Unassigned	1111 0	1/32
Unassigned	1111 10	1/64
Unassigned	1111 110	1/128
Unassigned	1111 1110 0	1/512
Link-Local Use Addresses	1111 1110 10	1/1024
Site-Local Use Addresses	1111 1110 11	1/1024
Multicast Addresses	1111 1111	1/256

The addressing structure is designed to support allocation of provider, private (site), and local addresses. Just 15 percent of the address space is assigned, as you can see from all the unassigned address ranges in Table 9-2.

Unlike the dotted-decimal representation used for IPv4, IPv6 uses colon-hexadecimal representation. You need to understand the notational conventions of IPv6 to correctly interpret the addresses:

- The basic representation involves colon-separated 16-bit hex strings, such as 2001:0DB8:1111:2222:3333:4444:5555:7777.

- Leading zeroes in a field are optional, so 2001:0DB8:0001:0002:3333:4444:5555:7777 can be written as 2001:0DB8:1:2:3333:4444:5555:7777.

- A series of zeros can be represented by a double colon (**::**). This may be used only once, so FE80::1 is legal, whereas FE80::1::1 is not.

- IPv4 addresses can still be written using dotted decimal, so ::192.168.1.1 is a legal address. You can also use the hex equivalent, which would be ::C0A8:0101.

IPv6 defines three types of addresses:

- **Unicast**—The packet is delivered to one interface.

- **Multicast**—The packet is delivered to many interfaces. Broadcast is just a special case of multicast (where the group includes everybody), so it does not get a special category.

- **Anycast**—The packet is delivered to one of many candidate interfaces.

There are different types of unicast and anycast address scopes, which basically define when to use the different prefixes defined in the address architecture. The types are as follows:

- **Link local**—The packet that is using a link-local address is destined for other interfaces on the same Layer 2 link. Routers do not forward link-local addresses.

- **Site local**—Think of this as an IPv6 version of the IPv4 10.0.0.0 network. A site-local prefix can be used only locally and routers must not forward any packet with a site-local source to a destination outside the network.

  Since the initial standard was published, there has been some debate about the validity of site-local addresses, and they are now deprecated. The central issue behind this decision comes from the ambiguity of what constitutes a "site." Is it a campus? A corporate network? A laptop? It is hard to say where a site begins or ends. Given that the definition of a site is difficult to pin down, it becomes even harder to make sure that such addresses are never advertised (stopping forwarding is pretty easy: the router junks the packet if a prefix match succeeds) by DNS or peer-to-peer applications (VoIP, for example). The current proposal is to use local addresses instead.

- **Global or public**—Fully routable Internet addresses. These addresses are usually allocated to ISPs by regional or national organizations, such as APNIC in Asia, ARIN in America and RIPE in Europe. The ISPs, in turn allocate blocks of addresses to their customers.

Extensions

IPv6 treats options very differently from IPv4. To start with, they are no longer part of the header but rather are appended as extensions between the header and the payload. If an extension is added to a packet, the IPv6 Next Header field must be modified to indicate this. Figure 9-2 shows how this works.

Figure 9-2   *IPv6 Extension Headers*

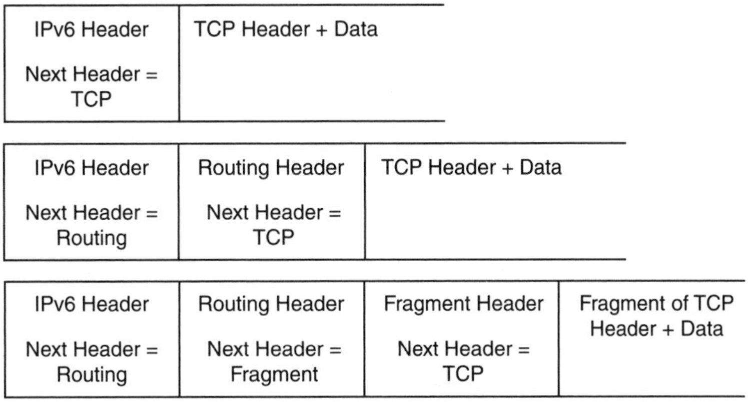

IPv6 Header Next Header = TCP	TCP Header + Data

IPv6 Header Next Header = Routing	Routing Header Next Header = TCP	TCP Header + Data

IPv6 Header Next Header = Routing	Routing Header Next Header = Fragment	Fragment Header Next Header = TCP	Fragment of TCP Header + Data

RFC 2460 defines the following extensions:

- **Hop-by-Hop options**—Options processed by intermediate systems along a routed path:
  - **Routing (Type 0)**—Similar to IPv4 loose source routing and record routing.
  - **Fragment**—Used by the source to send packets larger than would fit in the path MTU. Note, only the source fragments in IPv6—never the hops.
- **Destination options**—Options processed by end systems:
  - **Authentication**—Along with ESP, provides for IPSec protection of the packet.
  - **Encapsulating Security Payload**—Along with AH, provides for IPSec protection of the packet.

With the exception of Hop-by-Hop, extension headers are examined only by the host that matches the packet's destination address, not by any intermediate systems.

Autoconfiguration

IPv6 supports two types of automatic configuration:

- Stateful
- Stateless

DHCP is an example of stateful configuration: A server somewhere remembers things about the client, such as which IP address should be handed out. IPv4 also supports stateful autoconfiguration.

Stateless configuration is more novel. Each host creates its own unique link-local address by appending its interface MAC address to the well-known FE80::0 prefix. Once this happens, the host has IP connectivity on its local link(s). The host then waits for (or asks for) a Router

Advertisement, which contains prefix information for a global address. The host builds its unique global address by again combining this advertised network prefix with its interface MAC address. This is assumed to be unique on the interface, so the overall host address will also be unique. However, the RFC states that a host must check for conflicts by sending a Neighbor Solicitation message on the link before actually using any address. If another host is using the address, it replies with a Neighbor Advertisement. There is no automated mechanism for configuring the prefixes on the routers.

The beauty of the stateless approach is that no manual configuration is required. The downside is that no authentication was built into the process (though IETF drafts now exist that propose solutions for this), so, for example, any rogue laptop can gain access to a wireless IPv6 LAN running stateless autoconfiguration.

NOTE   Autoconfiguration is defined in RFC 2462. Neighbor discovery is specified in RFC 2461.

Deployment Scenarios of IPv6

IPv6 is at an interesting stage. Thanks to the general inventiveness of the Internet community, very few of the features originally thought to warrant full-scale rollout of IPv6 are now unique to this protocol. For example, host dynamic autoconfiguration can be adequately done with DHCP. Sure, this is another protocol, not part of Layer 3 itself, but it gets the job done. That leaves the vast 128-bit address space that will really come into its own as more and more nontraditional devices are connected to the Internet, such as mobile phones and gaming stations. It is unlikely (but not altogether impossible) that so many addresses will be required just for computers that IPv4 and NAT will no longer suffice.

Still, imagine that IPv6 does catch on. If it does, there are three scenarios that could apply to broadband networks. The following sections discuss those scenarios using the L2TP architecture as a framework for discussion.

Enterprise Deploys IPv6 Internally but Uses an IPv4 VPN Service

This is a very well-documented migration scenario and can be implemented in a variety of ways (using some form of tunnel that carries IPv6 packets over the IPv4 network, for example). RFCs and drafts of notes that discuss tunneling mechanisms include RFC 3046 (6to4), RFC 2529 (6over4), ISATAP, RFC 3053 (tunnel broker), RFC 2893 (IPv4-compatible tunneling), and Teredo. We will not go into more detail here because it is beyond the scope of this book.

A Retail ISP Moves to IPv6

In this scenario, all of the retail ISP's customers now require IPv6 addressing and all the common protocols need to adapt to the longer addresses. Figure 9-3 represents this scenario.

Figure 9-3   *IPv6 in ISP Network*

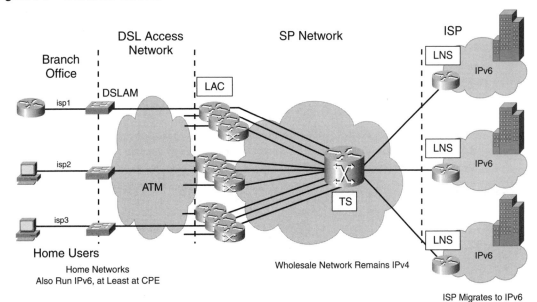

Although the ISP now runs IPv6, there is no change to the wholesale IPv4 core network. L2TP, for example, is carried over UDP/IP just as before. However, inside the tunnel, things are different. First, you need IP Control Protocol (IPCPv6) to transport the IPv6 packets in PPP. You also need to make sure that the control plane is IPv6 aware. For example, RADIUS attributes also have to accommodate IPv6 (the general guideline is that anything that touched an IPv4 address, or part thereof, needs to change), such as Framed-IPv6-Pool, Framed-IPv6-Prefix, and Framed-IPv6-Route. (See RFC 3162 for a more complete list.) The RADIUS server architecture is the same, though, as for IPv4 support, insofar as the wholesaler can deploy proxy AAA, perform server load balancing, and generally do all the other optimizations needed to run an efficient network using RADIUS.

On the CPE, things also change. Remember, a CPE might need its own address. It might also need a pool to hand out to client systems on its LAN interface, if it behaves as a local DHCP server.

In IPv4 environments, the address comes through PPP or DHCP requests, depending on the access architecture. With the IPCP subnet feature, if the CPE gets a pool of addresses, it keeps one of them and allocates the others to the clients by using DHCP. If the CPE gets just one public address, it typically allocates private addresses and translates these to the public address on its WAN interface by using NAT.

In the IPv6 world, the CPE can certainly continue to allocate addresses by using DHCPv6, or it can take advantage of stateless autoconfiguration á la RFC 2462 and get a prefix from the Broadband Remote Access Server (BRAS), which it in turn announces to local hosts in Router Advertisements. Mechanisms to do this are currently in draft form at the IETF, but one involves using DHCP between the BRAS and CPE to request and return prefixes. Some form of CLI-based configuration is, of course, another possibility.

In theory, broadband access is a good place to use stateless configuration because there is no need to impose structure on client addresses beyond a simple network prefix. For its own address, the CPE will either use PPP negotiation (IPCPv6 in particular) or issue a stateful address request using DHCPv6. Figure 9-4 summarizes some of the possible ways to allocate addresses in an IPv6 context. Addresses can be allocated to subscribers using DHCPv6 or RADIUSv6 directly at the LAC/PTA router. Or, in an L2TP scenario, addresses may be allocated to sessions at the LNS, using Server2 in Figure 9-4, for example.

Figure 9-4   *IPv6 Address Allocation Options*

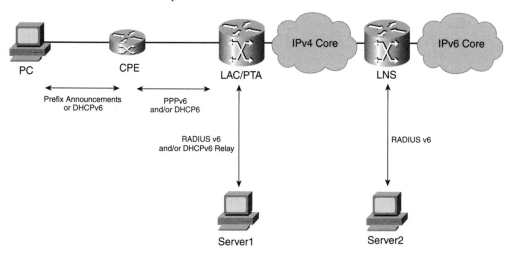

To summarize, this scenario can require an upgrade to both the LNS *and* the LAC, even though only the ISP wants to move to IPv6. So, a retail network cannot transparently upgrade to IPv6 without the cooperation of the wholesaler provider.

draft-allen-lap-ipv6-00.txt is an interesting discussion of the benefits of migrating to IPv6 for a broadband service provider, as well as a proposal to provide VPN services using IPv6.

Only the Wholesaler Moves to IPv6

This is a straightforward scenario in which only the wholesale provider migrates its network to IPv6. As shown in Figure 9-5, there are no changes to the PPPoE client, CPE, LAC, or LNS functions, which all touch the retail network.

Figure 9-5   *Wholesale IPv6 Network*

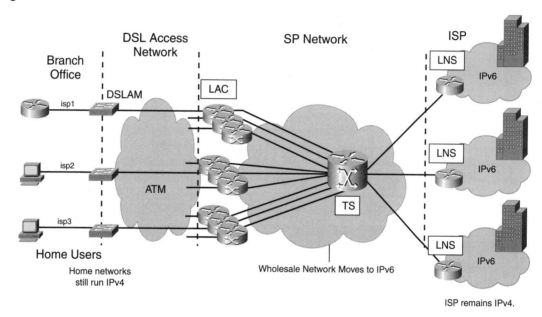

The L2TP packets are encapsulated in UDP, and then transported in IPv6. The major gotcha here is to check that the LAC and LNS devices have been updated so as to allow L2TP over IPv6. The wholesale core migration is transparent to ISPs and their customers.

It is generally true that a core migration from IPv4 to IPv6 does not impact the traffic transported in VPNs across that core, be it for L2TP or any other tunneling protocol. The bigger question is how to provide a VPN service using IPv6 and how to leverage operational experience from providers who have made the switch to IPv6. Today, most studies touch on how to migrate from IPv4 to IPv6 or, alternatively, how to run IPv6 over an IPv4 backbone.

L2 Transport and L2VPN

One of the most active areas of research right now is in the area of Layer 2 transport over IP or MPLS networks. The motivation is to arrive at the networking nirvana of convergence, where all traffic types can be carried by a single infrastructure. In its day, ATM also held out hope to become every service provider's single network, with voice, video, and data running happily across it. That did not happen and only time will tell whether transporting data link protocols such as Frame Relay or Ethernet over packet networks will be operationally viable. Technically, it works, but it sure is not always simple.

NOTE Harald Alverstand, the current IETF chair, has a wonderful web page about the fate of protocols that "just try to do a little bit more": http://www.alvestrand.no/ietf/complexity.php.

When looking at either the protocols or their application to broadband VPNs, it is very important to understand the distinction between Layer 2 transport and the VPN service built on top.

NOTE For those with long memories, L2 over MPLS is functionally reminiscent of FRF.5 Network Interworking.

The following section describes how to transport Layer 2 traffic over emulated point-to-point circuits, called *pseudo-wires*. That is followed by a short discussion of the implications for broadband access.

Pseudo-wires

The basic building block of packet-based Layer 2 service is an emulated point-to-point connection that carries protocol data across a packet network. Such circuits are known as pseudo-wires. To be slightly more formal, a pseudo-wire is a connection between two PEs, which connects two Pseudo Wire Emulation Edge-to-Edge (PWE3) of the same type. Link-layer data is forwarded across the pseudo-wire as variable-length PDUs. The pseudo-wire crosses the core packet network in an MPLS LSP or L2TP tunnel. As far as possible, pseudo-wires should preserve the essence of the Layer 2 protocol they carry, but the emulation is not necessarily perfect.

Pseudo-wire standardization work is the responsibility of the IETF PWE working group. Documents that you should read to know more details include draft-ietf-pwe3-requirements and draft-ietf-pwe3-arch-05.txt. Other PWE documents specify how to transport the different Layer 2 data-link protocols, which include Frame Relay, ATM AAL5, TDM, Ethernet, and 802.1q VLAN. Information in the documents involve details such as whether an LSP maps to individual circuits (for example, a Frame Relay DLCI) or to an ingress port (called *port mode*), which preserves LSP space if you are using MPLS.

The PWE architecture is quite agnostic about the means used to implement a pseudo-wire and in fact tries to unify two originally alternative tunneling solutions: one using MPLS, the other based on L2TP. The following sections cover each point-to-point solution in turn, first with MPLS, called AToM in Cisco jargon, and then with L2TPv3.

AToM

Any Transport over MPLS (AToM) is the Cisco terminology for tunneling Layer 2 over an MPLS network as defined in draft-ietf-pwe3-control-protocol-04.txt. In this case, labels are announced between PEs using directed LDP. Consider the network shown in Figure 9-6.

Figure 9-6   *AToM Example*

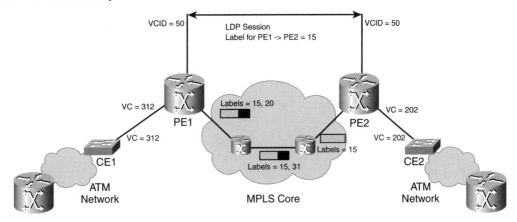

The goal in Figure 9-6 is to connect VC312 on CE1 to VC202 on CE2. PE1 sets up a directed LDP session with PE2 and negotiates a label for each direction. When configuring a Cisco router, you must create a logical VC ID on each PE. The VC ID must be the same on both ends of the connection, even if the ingress Layer 2 VC (or VLAN or DLCI) on PE1 and egress VC on PE2 are different, which is the case in Figure 9-6. This is how PE2 knows that packets with label 15 are for VC202.

How data is encapsulated varies from protocol to protocol. For Ethernet, for example, the entire frame minus preamble and FCS is transmitted along with a Control Word, which is used to transparently send signaling information associated with the payload protocol. There are two options for handling VLAN tags. In raw mode, the tags are stripped before the packet is transmitted. In tagged mode, every frame must have a VLAN tag, and the PE appends one if necessary. The different modes allow service providers more flexibility in identifying where the service stops. For example, VLANs could be used to identify customers. Alternatively, customers might request the ability to append their own VLAN tags so as to control to which site data is sent.

L2 Transport over L2TPv3

If you have read this far, hopefully you are quite comfortable with L2TP. L2TPv3 is an extension of regular L2TP that allows transport of data-link traffic other than PPP. The differences between the two versions are relatively minor and generally involve making the protocol less PPP specific.

The IETF draft defines three different models:

- **LAC/LNS**—Classic dial/DSL scenario. As a reminder, the LNS terminates the tunnel and processes IP on a virtual interface. The LAC performs an L2/PPP cross-connect and does no (user session) Layer 3 processing.

- **LAC/LAC**—Each L2TP endpoint performs an L2 cross-connect. This is the scenario for pseudo-wires.

- **LNS/LNS**—A PC is running an L2TP client and initiates an L3 tunnel to another LNS over IP.

When configuring L2 cross-connect using L2TPv3, as shown in Figure 9-7, you once again use the concept of VC ID to bind the attachment VC on the CE-PE link to a session in the tunnel. First, PE1 and PE2 use L2TP SCCRQ/SCCRP messages to set up a tunnel, if one does not already exist. Then, the PE routers set up a session for the VC ID using ICRQ/ICRP. During this phase, unique session and cookie IDs are allocated for the VC ID. Multiple VCs can be transported inside the same tunnel. Either PE can initiate tunnel or sessions within them.

Figure 9-7 *L2TPv3 Example*

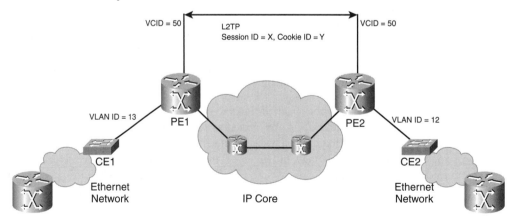

Like AToM, L2TPv3 supports Ethernet, 802.1q (VLAN), Frame Relay, HDLC, and PPP. (AToM also supports ATM AAL5.) Continuing with the example of Ethernet encapsulation, once again the entire frame minus preamble and payload is encapsulated in the L2TP tunnel. In port-to-port mode, VLAN tags are removed. In VLAN-to-VLAN mode, the tag is sent, but may be overwritten at the remote end.

Actually, L2TPv3 also supports so-called *static sessions*, which do not use a VC ID or any form of signaling, but match the attachment VC to L2TP session and cookie IDs (which must be identical on both ends of the traffic). Of course, without signaling, if the tunnel goes down for some reason, the L2TP endpoints have no way of knowing about it.

The L2TPv3 tunnel operation is similar to the classic LAC/LNS scenario, with L2TP hostname, authentication, and TOS rewrite rules.

Applications and Implications for Broadband Access

People often confuse using Ethernet transport for Layer 3 service with the Layer 2 variety. For example, a cable access subscriber has a bridged link up to a CMTS, but is paying for Internet access, which is, of course, a Layer 3 service. In fact, it is unlikely that a residential subscriber would need a true Layer 2 service, because it would "lock" them into a broadcast domain with a bunch of other people they hardly know. So, even as much of broadband migrates to some form of Ethernet encapsulation, either in the first mile or in the access network, the service offered will still be Layer 3.

For business subscribers, it is another story. In fact, L2 services are already offered over broadband links. The reasons to choose L2 over L3 vary from place to place, but they include the following:

- Amount of non-IP traffic on the LAN
- The willingness to peer with a service provider router (and so to essentially outsource the management of WAN routing tables)
- Issues with IGP routing (Does the service provider support the in-house IGP?)
- Price

NOTE *L2 services* refers to the transport of L2 frames over a packet core. Obviously, most VPN services are still Layer 2–based today, namely Frame Relay, ATM, and the venerable X.25. The distinction is in the type of core used. If and when carriers can offer Layer 2 service over their packet infrastructure, this should allow them to offer a more competitive price.

Summary

This chapter discussed recent and emerging technologies and their possible impact on broadband access.

IPv6 is in many ways quite mature from the standpoint of standards definition, but it has seen limited deployment. The chapter discussed three possible scenarios involving enterprise, retail, and wholesale network migration to IPv6. As a general rule, any protocol that processed IP addresses in some shape or form must be "upgraded" to work in an IPv6 network. This includes RADIUS AAA records and DHCP also.

L2VPN for packet networks is still in the discussion stage at the standards bodies, but commercial services are already available. Apart from discussing the distinction between L2 pseudo-wire and L2VPN service, the main conclusion here was that there will probably be a very limited impact on residential subscribers, who are primarily interested in Layer 3 service, unless it is for some very specific, closed user group scenario. L2 business services are currently and will continue to be offered over broadband access.

References and Bibliography

Because online content is a dynamically shifting media form, some of the URLs listed in this Appendix might have changed by the time the book was printed. If the URL cited yields no returning document, use your preferred search engine to find the document by its title. When available, website references are provided in conjunction with document titles. All Cisco Systems documents that are available online can be found by going to www.cisco.com and entering the document title in the Search box. Note that although many documents were used as source material for several different chapters, they are referenced only once, under the first chapter in which they are relevant.

Chapter 1

Cisco Systems Publications, Available Online at Cisco.com

Remote Access to MPLS VPN Solution for Service Providers:

- "Cisco Remote Access to MPLS VPN Business Overview." Brochure.
- "Cisco Cable Remote Access to MPLS VPN Technical Solution." Brochure.
- "VPN Architectures—Comparing MPLS and IPSec." White paper.

"Navigating the IP VPN Market: A Decision-Making Guide." Business case. *VPN Solutions for Service Providers*.

Bredin, Alice. "Telecommuting." Series of articles. Cisco Small/Medium Business Center, http://www.cisco.com/warp/public/779/smbiz/netsolutions/find/alice/telecommuting.

"Which VPN Solution Is Right for You?" Tech Note, Document ID: 14147, December 2002.

In-Stat/MDR Resources, Available Online at www.instat.com

"EFM Enables Cheap Broadband in Asia Pacific." Press release, August 27, 2003, http://www.instat.com/press.asp?ID=741&sku=IN030818RC.

Mantion, Eric M. "The Economics of Online Gaming." White paper, June 2003, http://www.instat.com/catalog/downloads/onlinegaming_download.htm.

"With End-User Migration Inevitable, IP VPN Services Market Poised to Grow." *Market Alert*, February 4, 2004, http://www.instat.com/newmk.asp?ID=874&SourceID=00000512000000000000.

Wolf, Mike. "The Top Ten Drivers of the Converged Home Network." White paper, April 2003, http://www.instat.com/catalog/downloads/homenetwork1_download.htm.

IETF Draft RFCs, Available Online at www.ietf.org

draft-ietf-l3vpn-applicability-guidelines-00.txt

draft-ietf-l3vpn-as-vr-01.txt

draft-ietf-l3vpn-as2547-06.txt

draft-ietf-l3vpn-bgpvpn-auto-03.txt

draft-ietf-l3vpn-ce-based-02.txt

draft-ietf-l3vpn-framework-00.txt

draft-ietf-l3vpn-ipsec-2547-02.txt

draft-ietf-l3vpn-requirements-xx.txt

draft-ietf-l3vpn-rfc2547bis-01.txt

draft-ietf-ppvpn-bgpvpn-auto-02.txt

draft-ouldbrahim-bgp-vpn-xx.txt

Miscellaneous Online Resources

EFMA Alliance. "Ethernet in the First Mile: Making Universal Broadband Access a Reality." White paper (revision 8), November 2003, http://www.efmalliance.org/technicallink.html.

IEEE 802.3 Study Group. "Ethernet in the First Mile Tutorial." IEEE 802 LMSC, Portland, Oregon, July 9, 2001, http://www.ieee802.org/3/efm/public/jul01/tutorial/.

"French City of Pau deploys Carrier-Class Optical Ethernet Services for 'Triple Play.'" Press release by the City of Pau.

Gorshe, Steve. "Ethernet Transport Services—The Current State of the Art." PMC-Sierra. White paper, May 2003, http://www.pmc-sierra.com/ cgi-bin/document.pl?docnum=2030897

Mendler, Camille and Amy Rodger. "Navigating the IP VPN Market: A Decision-Making Guide for European Businesses." The Yankee Group. Cisco Systems white paper, May 2003, http://www.cisco.com/en/US/netsol/ns341/ns121/ns193/ networking_solutions_packages_list.html.

Pappalardo, Denise. "DSL Oversubscription." Network World ISP Newsletter, Network World, Inc., May 22, 2000, http://www.nwfusion.com/newsletters/isp/0522isp1.html.

Yongsik Lim and Tae Sun Kim (NeoWave, Inc.). "Enabling Systems for KT's Residential Ethernet Solutions." Presented at ISSLS 2002, Seoul, Korea, http://www.issls-council.org/proc02/papers/S3A2m.pdf.

Useful Websites

Ethernet in the First Mile Alliance (EFMA): http://www.efmalliance.org/index.html.

IEEE 802.3ah Ethernet in the First Mile Task Force: http://www.ieee802.org/3/efm/public/ index.html.

Chapter 2

Cisco Systems Publications, Available Online at www.cisco.com

"Cisco Cable Modem Termination System Commands." Chapter 2 in *Cisco Broadband Cable Command Reference Guide*.

"DOCSIS and CMTS Architectural Overview," in *Cisco uBR100012 Universal Broadband Router Software Configuration Guide*.

"DOCSIS Specification Summary." Section in Appendix A, "DOCSIS and CMTS Architectural Overview," in *Cisco uBR10012 Universal Broadband Router Software Configuration Guide*.

"CMTS Configuration FAQ." Document ID: 12180.

"Configuring Basic Broadband Internet Access."

"Maximum CPE or Host Parameters for the Cisco Cable Modem Termination System." Chapter 7 in Cisco CMTS Feature Guide.

"Cable Access to MPLS VPN Integration." Chapter 5 in *Cisco Remote Access to MPLS VPN Integration Overview and Provisioning Guide 2.0*.

"Configuring GRE Tunnel over Cable." Sample Configuration, Document ID: 12084, December 2002.

"Deploying Metropolitan Ethernet Services: Features and Technologies Essentials." White paper.

"Release Notes for Cisco 7000 Family for Cisco IOS Release 12.2 B." Cisco IOS Software Releases 12.2 Special and Early Deployments.

"Configuring IP Unicast Routing." *Catalyst 3550 Multilayer Switch Software Configuration Guide, 12.1(8)EA1.*

"Understanding debug ppp negotiation Output." Point-to-Point Protocol Tech Note, Document ID: 25440.

"Configuring the DHCP Option 82 for Subscriber Identification." *Catalyst 3550 Multilayer Switch Software Configuration Guide, 12.1(12c)EA1.*

"DHCP Option 82 Support for Routed Bridge Encapsulation." *Cisco IOS Software Releases 12.2T Feature Guide.*

Cisco Technology Marketing. "Principles and Architecture for Ethernet over MPLS-based Layer 2 VPNs. Guidelines for Deploying Ethernet Virtual Circuit Service Networks." Cisco Systems white paper.

Cisco Metro Solution Team. "Metro Ethernet Switching Design and Implementation Guide." Cisco internal document.

"Extreme Networks Virtual Metropolitan Area Networks" Tech Brief, Extreme Networks, http://www.extremenetworks.com/common/asp/frameHandler.asp?go=/libraries/whitepapers/technology/vMAN.asp.

Garg, Subodh. "IP-Based VPNs on uBR." Cisco engineering document, ENG-55424.

Hranac, Ron. "Cable 101: How a Cable System Works." Cisco internal presentation.

McKelvey, Joel T. "End-to-End Quality of Service with DOCSIS 1.1." Presented at The Western Show, November 27-30, 2001.

McKelvey, Joel T. "Introduction to MPLS-VPNs for Cable." Cisco internal presentation, July 23, 2000. Version 1.0.

Mukai, Wesley. "Secure and Scalable Ethernet Services for Mixed Environments (ETTX)." Cisco internal presentation.

Phipps, Marcus. "Metro Ethernet Technology Decoder Ring." Cisco internal presentation.

Schubert, Steve. "Enterprise Solutions Engineering—MxU Solution Overview." Cisco engineering document, ENG-131473, July 2001.

Unattributed. "Cisco's Metro Ethernet Overview. Achieving Success with Ethernet Services." Cisco internal presentation, May 2002.

CableLabs Online Resources, Available Online at www.cablelabs.com

"DOCSIS Overview." Presentation by The DOCSIS Team CableLabs, January 2003.

"CableHome Overview." Presentation by The CableHome Team, CableLabs, January 2002.

"Introduction to OpenCable." Presentation, CableLabs, January 2002.

Lipoff, Stuart. "Data Over Cable Interface Specifications: Cable Modem Termination System—Network Side Interface Specification." July 2, 1996.

Miscellaneous Online Resources

Claes, Stan, Gert Marynissen, and Dirk Van Aken. "User Multiplexing in a single PPP/PPPoA Session vs. PPPoE Session Multiplexing." Alcatel white paper, SpeedTouch DSL, December 2000, http://www.speedtouch.com/pdf/510/st510_white.pdf.

Convery, Sean. "Hacking Layer 2: Fun with Ethernet Switches." Black Hat, Cisco Systems white paper, July 2002, http://www.cisco.com/security_services/ciag/initiatives/research/projectsummary.html.

Davies, Joseph. "Virtual Private Networking with Windows 2000: Deploying Router-to-Router VPNs." Microsoft Corporation white paper, October 2001, http://www.microsoft.com/windows2000/server/evaluation/features/deplyr2rvpn.asp.

RFCs, Available Online at www.ietf.org

RFC 2516: "A Method for Transmitting PPP Over Ethernet (PPPoE)"

RFC 2637: "Point-to-Point Tunneling Protocol"

RFC 2684: "Multiprotocol Encapsulation over ATM Adaptation Layer 5"

Chapter 3

Cisco Systems Publications, Available Online at www.cisco.com

"Configuring GRE Tunnel Over Cable." Sample Configuration, Document ID: 12084.

"Configuring Dynamic Multipoint VPN (DMVPN) Using GRE over IPSEC between Multiple Routers." Sample Configuration, Document ID: 29240.

"Dynamic Multipoint VPN (DMVPN)." Cisco IOS Software Releases 12.2 T.

"Dynamic Mulitpoint IPSec VPNs (Using Multipoint GRE/NHRP to Scale IPSec VPNs.)"

"Configuring GRE and IPSec with IPX Routing." Sample Configuration, Document ID: 14125.

"Deploying IPSec Virtual Private Networks." White paper.

"Dynamic Layer-3 VPNs (RFC 2547) Support Using Multipoint GRE (mGRE) Tunnels." Cisco IOS Software Releases 12.0 S.

"Why Can't I Browse the Internet When Using a GRE Tunnel?" Tech Note, Document ID: 13725.

"IPSec Configuration Examples."

"An Introduction to IP Security (IPSec) Encryption." Tech Note, Document ID: 16439.

"IP Fragmentation and PMTUD." White paper, Document ID: 25885.

"Configuring IKE Pre-Shared Keys Using a RADIUS Server for the Cisco Secure VPN Client." Sample configuration, Document ID: 5726.

"Mapping Service Flows to MPLS-VPN on the Cisco CMTS." Cisco uBR7200 Series Software Features.

"IPSec Configuring IPSec—Wild-card Pre-shared Keys with Cisco Secure VPN Client and No-mode Config." Sample configuration, Document ID: 14148.

"Network-Based IPSec VPN Solution for Service Providers Configuring IPSec to MPLS."

"MGRE+IPSec SW Unit Functional Spec." Cisco Engineering Document, ENG-168110.

RFCs, Available Online at www.ietf.org

RFC 1701: "Generic Routing Encapsulation (GRE)"

RFC 2401: "Security Architecture for the Internet Protocol"

RFC 2402: "IP Authentication Header"

RFC 2403: "The Use of HMAC-MD5-96 within ESP and AH"

RFC 2404: "The Use of HMAC-SHA-1-96 within ESP and AH"

RFC 2405: "The ESP DES-CBC Cipher Algorithm With Explicit IV"

RFC 2406: "IP Encapsulating Security Payload (ESP)"

RFC 2407: "The Internet IP Security Domain of Interpretation for ISAKMP"

RFC 2408: "Internet Security Association and Key Management Protocol (ISAKMP)"

RFC 2409: "The Internet Key Exchange (IKE)"

RFC 2661: "Layer Two Tunneling Protocol 'L2TP'"

RFC 2784: "Generic Routing Encapsulation (GRE)"

RFC 2868: "RADIUS Attributes for Tunnel Protocol Support"

RFC 2890: "Key and Sequence Number Extensions to GRE"

Chapter 4

Cisco Systems Internal Documents

Alverez, Santiago. "Service Provider Quality of Service Case Study." Cisco IOS Technical marketing. Internal publication.

Alverez, Santiago. "MPLS QoS." Cisco internal presentation. ITD Technical Marketing.

"ATM MPLS Quality of Service" Student Guide. Cisco MPLS Solutions.

Kumarasamy, Jay. "MPLS-QoS." Cisco internal training presentation.

Kumarasamy, Jay. "MPLS Architecture Overview." Cisco internal training presentation.

Osbourne, Eric. "MPLS TE TOI." Cisco internal training presentation.

"QoS Classification and Marking Reference Guide to Implementing Crypto and QoS." Cisco internal white paper.

Swallow, Greg. "MPLS Traffic Engineering." Cisco internal training presentation.

Cisco Systems Publications, Available Online at www.cisco.com

"Deploying Guaranteed-Bandwidth Services with MPLS." White paper.

"Quality of Service for Multi-Protocol Label Switching Networks." Q&A.

"Configuring Remote Access to MPLS VPN." Chapter 3 in *Cisco 10000 Series ESR Broadband Aggregation Configuration Guide*.

"Advanced MPLS VPN Solutions." Volume 1 and Volume 2, AMVS Student Guide.

Alverez, Santiago. "MPLS QoS FAQ." August 2001.

"Advanced Topics in MPLS-TE Deployment." White paper.

"Multicast Virtual Private Networks." White paper.

"Advanced Concepts and Developments in Quality of Service." Cisco Networkers Presentation, Session IPS-430.

Osbourne, Eric. "Deploying MPLS Traffic Engineering Session." Cisco Networkers Presentation, Session RST-231.

Miscellaneous Online Resources

Xial, Xipeng. "Providing Quality of Service in the Internet." Michigan State University, 2000, http://www.cse.msu.edu/~xiaoxipe/.

RFCs, Available Online at www.ietf.org

RFC 2547(bis): "BGP/MPLS VPN"

RFC 3031: "Multiprotocol Label Switching Architecture"

RFC 3032: "MPLS Label Stack Encoding"

RFC 3035: "PLS using LDP and ATM VC Switching"

RFC 3036: "LDP Specification"

RFC 3037: "LDP Applicability"

Chapters 5, 6, 7, and 8

Cisco Systems Internal Documents

Anthony, Tony et al. "Piccadilly—Solution Architectural Specification Metro Ethernet Switching System." Cisco Engineering Document, EDCS-238704.

Brockners, Frank and Wolfgang Fischer. "Ethernet DSL Considerations (EMEA Perspective)." Cisco internal presentation.

Brockners, Frank. "Service Driven Networks—Ethernet to the Consumer" Cisco internal presentations.

Cramer, Tom. "IOS PPP/MPLS-VPN Integration." Cisco engineering document, EDCS-41217.

Crumpton, Nick and Richard Licon. "Broadband Aggregation Phase II. Cisco 10000 Product Description Document." Cisco internal document.

Foltak, Rich. "AAA attributes for VRF name." Private e-mail correspondence with Rich Foltak.

Gagne, François. "EAN Concept Based on Service Gateway." Cisco internal presentation.

Gagne, François. "Valhala Solution, Transport Architecture." Cisco engineering presentation, ENG-104299.

"Integration of Network Address Translation and MPLS VPN." Cisco engineering document, EDCS-101501.

Junker, Martin and Peter Weinberger. "MPLS-VPN Customer Requirements." Cisco internal document.

Nguyen, Huw. "AAA Configuration Supports for NAIAD." Cisco Engineering Document, EDCS-122606.

Nguyen, Tram and Di Wu. "IOS DHCP Features in NAIAD." Cisco engineering document, ENG-114781.

Nguyen, Huw. "AAA Username Domain-Stripping Extensions." Cisco engineering document, CSCdy40332.

"PER VRF AAA Phase II." Cisco engineering document. CP-1519.

Pieters, Alain. "Chelmsford NAIAD TOI." Cisco internal presentation. NSITE Bruxelles.

Pieters, Alain. "IP VT—NSITE Naiad Program Update." Cisco internal presentation. NSITE Bruxelles.

"PPP User Authentication & Authorization: Per VRF AAA." Cisco internal presentation.

"Remote Access into MPLS/VPN Phase II: Solution Description." Cisco internal document.

Sadaka, Sam. "Technical Overview of the Cisco Video Solution." Cisco Partner Summit Presentation.

Voit, Eric. "Avoiding Dynamic Instantiation of VRFs." Private e-mail correspondence from Eric Voit.

VPN Solutions Engineering Team. "Application Note—L2TP Multihop in Remote Access to MPLS/VPN Deployments." Cisco Engineering Document, EDCS-293888.

VPN Solutions Engineering Team. "Application Note—Per-VRF AAA Implementation Options in L2TP Remote Access to MPLS/VPN." Cisco engineering document, ENG-291658.

VPN Solutions Engineering Team. "Remote Access to MPLS—DSL Architectures Design and Implementation Guide." Cisco engineering document, ENG-195514.

Wang, Jun. "Per VRF RADIUS Server Group." Cisco engineering document, ENG-282614.

Wang, Jun et al. "Per VRF AAA Feature" Cisco Engineering Document, ENG-282617.

Cisco Systems Publications, Available Online at www.cisco.com

"Using On-Demand Address Pools." Chapter 7 in *Cisco CNS Access Registrar Identity Cache Engine User's Guide*.

"Mapping Service Flows to MPLS-VPN on the Cisco uBR7100 Series and Cisco uBR7200 Series Routers." Cisco IOS Release 12.2 BC.

"A Comparison Between IPSec and Multiprotocol Label Switching Virtual Private Networks."

"Cisco IOS TFTP Client Cannot Transfer Files Larger than 16MB in Size." Cisco IOS Software Releases 12.1 Mainline Field Notice, December 14, 2000.

"Configuring DHCP." Cisco IOS Software Releases 12.2 T.

"DHCP Relay—MPLS VPN Support." Cisco IOS Software Releases 12.2 T.

"Configuring Address Pools." Cisco 10000 Series Routers.

"Using the Cisco IOS DHCP Server on Access Servers." Sample Configuration, Document ID: 10315.

"Per VRF AAA." Cisco IOS Software Releases 12.2 T.

"DHCP ODAP Server Support." Cisco IOS Software Releases 12.2 T.

"DHCP Server—On-Demand Address Pool Manager." Cisco IOS Software Releases 12.2 T.

"VRF-Aware VPDN Tunnels." Cisco IOS Software Releases 12.2 T.

"VRF-Aware IPSec." Cisco IOS Software Releases 12.2 T.

"Dynamic Multipoint VPN (DMVPN)." Cisco IOS Software Releases 12.2 T.

"IP Overlapping Address Pools." Cisco IOS Software Releases 12.2 T.

"NAT Integration with MPLS VPNs." Cisco IOS Software Releases 12.2 T.

"RADIUS Logical Line ID." Cisco IOS Software Releases 12.2 T.

"Session Limit Per-VRF." Cisco IOS Software Releases 12.2, Special and Early Deployments.

"RADIUS Attributes." Cisco Secure Access Control Server Solution Engine.

"PPPoE Profiles." Cisco IOS Software Releases 12.2 T.

"Generic Routing Encapsulation Tunnel IP Source and Destination VRF Membership." Cisco IOS Software Releases 12.0 S.

Remote Access to MPLS VPN Solution for Service Providers:

- "Cisco Remote Access to MPLS VPN Integration 2.0 FOA3 Release Notes." Design Guide.
- "Cisco Remote Access to MPLS VPN Solution Overview and Provisioning Guide 2.0." Design Guide.
- "Cisco DSL Remote Access to MPLS VPN Technical Solution." Brochure.

"DHCP Extension Dictionary." Cisco Access Registrar.

"VRF Selection Based on Source IP Address." Cisco IOS Software Releases 12.0 S MPLS VPN.

"Using On-Demand Address Pools." Cisco CNS Access Registrar.

"VRF Selection Based on Source IP Address for the Cisco 7304 Router." Cisco IOS Software Releases 12.2, Special and Early Deployments MPLS VPN.

"Deployments DHCP Relay Support for MPLS VPN Suboptions." Cisco IOS Software Releases 12.2, Special and Early Deployments.

"Using On-Demand Address Pools." Cisco CNS Access Registrar Identity Cache Engine.

"SNMP Support for VPNs." Cisco IOS Software Releases 12.0 S.

"Classification Overview."

Miscellaneous Online Resources

BOOTP and DHCP Extensions. The Internet Corporation for Assigned Names and Numbers. April 18, 2002, http://www.iana.org/assignments/bootp-dhcp-extensions.

RFCs, Available Online at www.ietf.org

RFC 2764: A Framework for IP Based Virtual Private Networks

IETF Draft, Available Online at www.ietf.org

draft-ietf-dhc-subnet-alloc-xx.txt

Chapter 9

Cisco Systems Internal Documents

Barozet, Jean-Marc. "Metro Ethernet Solutions."

Grossetete, Patrick. "IPv6 @ Cisco." Cisco internal presentation.

Lourdelet, Benoit. "Deploying an IPv6 Broadband Service."

Truitt, Todd. "IPv6—Solution Readiness." Cisco internal presentation. Enterprise Solutions Engineering

Cisco Systems Publications, Available Online at www.cisco.com

"Implementing ADSL and Deploying Dial Access for IPv6."

"IPv6 Deployment Strategies." Cisco IP Version 6 Solutions.

"IPv6 Access Services." White paper.

"IPv6 Access Services." Cisco IOS Software Releases 12.2 Mainline.

Unified VPN Suite Solution for Service Providers:

- "L2TPv3 Enables Layer 2 Services for IP Networks." White paper.
- "MPLS AToM. White paper."
- "MPLS AToM Application Brief." White paper.

"MPLS AToM: Configuring." Cisco IOS Software Releases 12.2 T, New Features.

"L2TPv3: Layer 2 Tunnel Protocol Version 3." Cisco IOS Software Releases 12.3 T.

"Cisco Service Adapters Overview."

Metro Ethernet Switching Solution for Service Providers:

- "Enterprise Connections to Layer 2 Ethernet Services Design." White paper.
- "Metro Ethernet WAN Services and Architectures." White paper.
- "Metro Ethernet Technology on Cisco Catalyst 6500 Series Switch." White paper.

"Using Dot1q Tunneling (1q in 1q) to Form Layer 2 VPNs." *Metro Ethernet Switching Solution for Service Providers*.

"Virtual Private LAN Service Architectures and Operation-Routing Solutions for Service Providers."

Miscellaneous Online Resources

"6WIND Solutions for Providing IP Services over DSL." 6WIND white paper, http://www.6wind.com/common/main.php?Rub=5&SRub=18#.

Austein, Rob. "Connected Site-Local Considered Harmful." 55th IETF, Atlanta, November 2002, http://www.ietf.org/proceedings/02nov/slides/ipv6-6.pdf.

"Frame Relay/ATM PVC Service Interworking Implementation Agreement." MPLS and Frame Relay Alliance Technical Committee. The Frame Relay Forum Document Number FRF 8.2, February 2002, http://www.mplsforum.org/tech/ia.shtml.

Fujisaki, Tomohiro. "Depreciation of Site Local Addresses." NTT Corporation. Presented at Apnic 16 IPv6 SIG, August 20, 2003, http://www.apnic.net/meetings/16/programme/sigs/ipv6.html.

Hinden, Robert M. "IP Next Generation Overview." May 14, 1995, http://playground.sun.com/ipv6/INET-IPng-Paper.html.

Hinden, Robert M. "IPv6 Site Local Usage." Nokia. 54th IETF, Yokohama, July 2002, http://playground.sun.com/pub/ipng/html/presentations/nov2002/site-local-usage.pdf.

Houston, Geoff. "The Myth of IPv6." The *Internet Protocol Journal*, Volume 6, Issue 2: 5 (June 2003). Cisco Systems. http://www.cisco.com/en/US/about/ac123/ac147/ac174/ac235/about_cisco_ipj_archive_article09186a00801a0cc3.html.

Houston, Geoff. "IPv4—How Long Have We Got?" *The ISP Column*, (July 2003),. http://www.potaroo.net/ispcolumn/2003-07-v4-address-lifetime/ale.html.

"IPv6 Configuration Methods." Microsoft Corporation. http://msdn.microsoft.com/library/default.asp?url=/library/en-us/wcetcpip/html/cmconipv6addressautoconfiguration.asp.

"IPv6 Features and Benefits." 6WIND white paper, May 3, 2003, http://www.6wind.com/common/main.php?Rub=5&SRub=18.

"The IPv4/IPv6 Access and Edge Routers Providing Enhanced Services to Enterprise Networks." 6WIND white paper.

"IPv6 Transition Mechanisms and Scenarios." 6WIND white paper, July 16, 2003, http://www.6wind.com/common/main.php?Rub=5&SRub=19&Year=2003.

"IPv6 Tutorial Notes." Massachusetts Institute of Technology, Department of Electrical Engineering and Computer Science. September 27, 2001, http://nms.lcs.mit.edu/6.829-f02/tutorials/T3-IPv6.ps.

Knight, Paul and Chris Lewis. "Layer 2 and 3 Virtual Private Networks: Taxonomy, Technology, and Standardization Efforts." Nortel Networks and Cisco Systems, respectively. *IEEE Communications Magazine, IEEE*, Volume 42, Issue 6: 124-131 (June 2004). http://www.comsoc.org/livepubs/ci1/public/2004/jun/current.html.

Lind, Mikael. "ISP Networks." Presentation of draft-lind-v6ops-isp-scenarios-00.txt. TeliaSonora. Presented at 57th IETF, Vienna, July 2003, www.ietf.org/proceedings/03jul/slides/v6ops-0.pdf.

Mauch, Charles P. "An Introduction to IPv6." Tacoma Linux User Group. http://www.taclug.org/documents/ipv6/t1.htm.

"Metro Ethernet Services for Enterprises." Metro Ethernet Forum Business Case white paper, October 2002, http://www.metroethernetforum.org/documents.htm.

Miyakawa, Shin. "IPv6/v4 Dual Stack Commercial ADSL Service Specification." NTT Communications. IETF v6OPS WG Interim Meeting, Sept. 18, 2002, http://6bone.net/v6ops/minutes/.

O'Leary, Doug. "Frame Relay/ATM PVC Network Interworking Implementation Agreement." The Frame Relay Forum Document Number FRF.5, December 1994, http://www.mplsforum.org/frame/frfia.shtml.

Palet, Jordi. "Outlooks on IPv6 Deployment: A European View." Consulintel. European IPv6 Task Force & Steering Comittee, Global IPv6 Summit, December 2002, http://www.jp.ipv6forum.com/2002/en/conference.html.

"Planning IPv6 Addressing." Microsoft Corporation. http://www.microsoft.com/technet/treeview/default.asp?url=/technet/prodtechnol/windowsserver2003/proddocs/deployguide/dnsbb_tcp_xmzh.asp.

"Private Line Frame Relay & ATM. Provide Support For Legacy Data Services on Consolidated IP/MPLS Infrastructure." Juniper Networks white paper, http://www.juniper.net/solutions/network_services/private_line.

Rao, Shankar. "IPv6: A Carrier's Perspective." Qwest. ARIN XI Tutorial, April 6, 2003, http://ww1.arin.net/library/minutes/ARIN_XI/tut.html.

"Remote Connectivity: DSL." University of California, San Francisco. http://www.ucsf.edu/its/remoteconnect/DSL.html.

RIPE NCC IPv6 Registration Services. http://www.ripe.net/ripencc/mem-services/registration/ipv6/ipv6.html.

Rosen, Eric. "Protocol Actions Required for BGP/MPLS VPNs (rfc2547bis)" Presented by Jeremy de Clerq, Alcatel. 54th IETF, Yohokama, July 2002, http://www.ietf.org/proceedings/02jul/slides/ppvpn-6.pdf.

Santitoro, Ralph. "Metro Ethernet Services—A Technical Overview." The Metro Ethernet Forum white paper, December 2003, http://www.metroethernetforum.org/documents.htm.

"Securing Network Autoconfiguration." IPv6Nordic.com. http://www.ipv6nordic.com/news/p/37.

Skarmeta, Antonio F. Gomez. "Security Services on IPv6 Networks: PKIv6 and IPv6-VPNs." University of Murcia, Spain. Joint 6NET/Euro6IX Workshop, June 5, 2002, http://www.6net.org/events/joint-workshop/.

"Transparent LAN Services...Seamless, Cost-effective Network Expansion Solutions." Hydro One Telecom white paper, January 1, 2003, http://www.hydroonetelecom.com/business_solutions/transparent_lan_services.php.

Useful Website

6bone: http://www.6bone.net/

IETF Drafts, Available Online at http://www.ietf.org

draft-ietf-l2tpext-l2tp-base-xx.txt

draft-ietf-l2vpn-l2-framework-00.txt

draft-ietf-l2vpn-requirements-00.txt

draft-ietf-l2vpn-vpls-bgp-00.txt

draft-ietf-l2vpn-vpls-ldp-00.txt

draft-ietf-l2vpn-vpls-requirements-00.txt

draft-ietf-pwe3-arch-05.txt

draft-ietf-pwe3-atm-encap-02.txt

draft-ietf-pwe3-control-protocol-03.txt

draft-ietf-pwe3-ethernet-encap-03.txt

draft-ietf-pwe3-hdlc-ppp-encap-mpls-00.txt

draft-ietf-pwe3-requirements-06.txt

draft-ietf-l3vpn-bgpvpn-auto-xx.txt

draft-ietf-l2vpn-signaling-01.txt

draft-allen-lap-ipv6-01.txt

draft-ietf-pwe3-requirements-03.txt

draft-ietf-pwe3-arch-00.txt

draft-ietf-pwe3-control-protocol-04.txt

draft-ietf-ppvpn-l2-framework-00.txt

draft-ietf-ppvpn-l2-terminology-xx.txt

draft-ietf-l3vpn-bgpvpn-auto-01.txt

draft-ieft-l2vpn-signaling-xx.txt

draft-martini-l2circuit-encap-mpls-03.txt

draft-martini-l2circuit-trans-mpls-07.txt

draft-kompella-l2vpn-l2vpn-01.txt

draft-lasserre-tls-mpls-02.txt

draft-raggarwa-mpls-bfd-00.txt

RFCs, Available Online at www.ietf.org

RFC 1700: "Assigned Numbers"

RFC 2080: "RIPng for IPv6"

RFC 2464: "Transmission of IPv6 Packets over Ethernet Networks"

RFC 2529: "Transmission of IPv6 over IPv4 Domains without Explicit Tunnels"

RFC 2545: "Use of BGP-4 Multiprotocol Extensions for IPv6 Inter-Domain Routing"

RFC 2640: "Internet Protocol, Version 6 (IPv6) Specification"

RFC 2641: "Neighbor Discovery for IP Version 6 (IPv6)"

RFC 2642: "IPv6 Stateless Address Autoconfiguration"

RFC 2740: "OSPF for IPv6"

RFC 2874: "DNS Extensions to Support IPv6 Address Aggregation and Renumbering"

RFC 2893: "Transition Mechanisms for IPv6 Hosts and Routers"

RFC 3046: "DHCP Relay Agent Information Option"

RFC 3053: "IPv6 Tunnel Broker"

RFC 3162: "RADIUS and IPv6"

RFC 3194: "The H-Density Ratio for Address Assignment Efficiency: An Update..."

RFC 3513: "Internet Protocol Version 6 (IPv6) Addressing Architecture"

INDEX

Numerics

802.1q headers, 44

A

AAA attribute
control planes, 308-309
MPLS-based wholesale services, 312
per-VRF AAA, 234–240
accounting, 246–247
templates, 241–246
VRFs, 218–225
VHG, 225–227
access cards, 18
access networks, DSL networks, 7–8
access requirements, VPNs, 74–75
accounting
bridged access networks, 53
MPLS-VPNs, 214
per-VRF AAA, 246–247
PPP, 64–65
address alignment, VPNs, 23
address allocation
IPv6, 326
MPLS-based wholesale services, 311
address assignments
DOCSIS networks, 40–41
ETTX, 47–49
PPPoA, 60–63
RBE networks, 35–37
address management, MPLS-VPNs, 215
address routing, MPLS-based wholesale
services, 311
address space size, IPv6, 325–326
address spoofing, bridged access networks, 49–50
addresses
IPv6, 323, 326-328
on-demand address pools, 249–251
address assignments, 252–254
host-route solution, 251–252
overlapping, assigning and managing, 248–254
single address, downloading with PPPoA, 60
"Advanced Topics in MPLS-TE Deployment", 139

aggregation routers, cost considerations, 72
AH header (IPSec), 93
Alverstand, Harald, 334
Any Transport over MPLS (AToM), 335–336
Anycast addresses (IPv6), 328
architectures
broadband access, bridged access networks,
28–53
centralized architectures, VPNs, 71–74
PPP networks, 54
accounting, 64–65
authentication, 64–65
PPPoA, 59–63
PPPoE, 54–58
QoS (qulaity of service), 63
security, 65
assigning overlapping addresses, 248–254
ATM (Asynchronous Transfer Mode)
MPLS, compared, 140
PPPoA, 59
address assignments, 60–63
configuration, 59
atm pppatm passive command, 59
AToM (Any Transport over MPLS), 335–336
attributes
AAA attribute
control planes, 308-309, 312
per-VRF AAA, 234–247
VRFs, 218–227
BPG, 156-157
iBGP, 156
MPLS-VPN reference architecture, 156–158
authentication
bridged access networks, 53
IPSec, 93
IPv6, 324
MPLS-VPNs, 214
PPP, 64–65
VPNs, 21–22
authorizations
MPLS-VPNs, 214
remote-access networks, 53
autoconfiguration, IPv6, 329–330
availability, MPLS-VPNs, 212–213

E

K-L

M

N

W

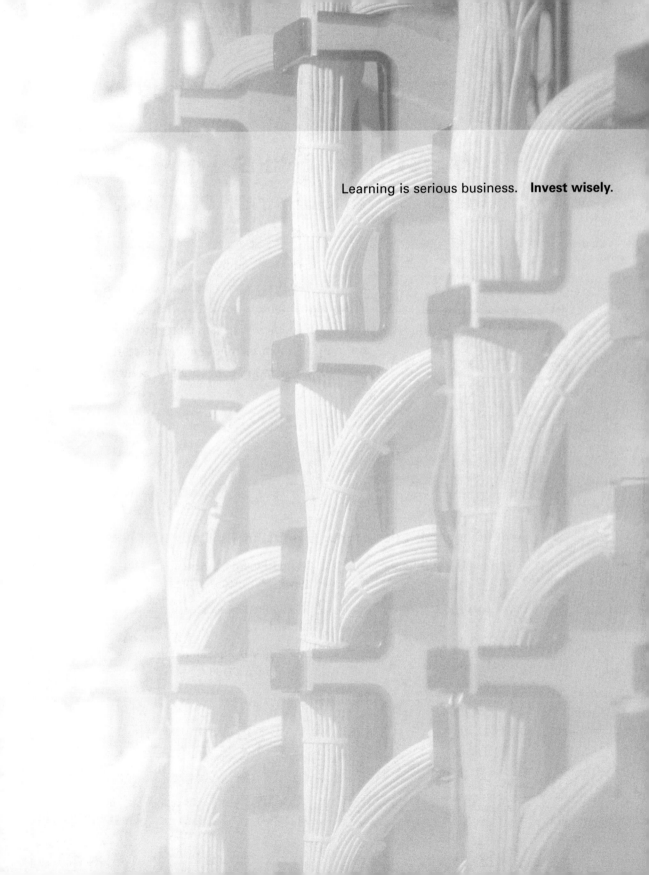
Learning is serious business. **Invest wisely.**

CISCO SYSTEMS

Cisco Press

Cisco Press

SEARCH THOUSANDS OF BOOKS FROM LEADING PUBLISHERS

Safari® Bookshelf is a searchable electronic reference library for IT professionals that features more than 2,000 titles from technical publishers, including Cisco Press.

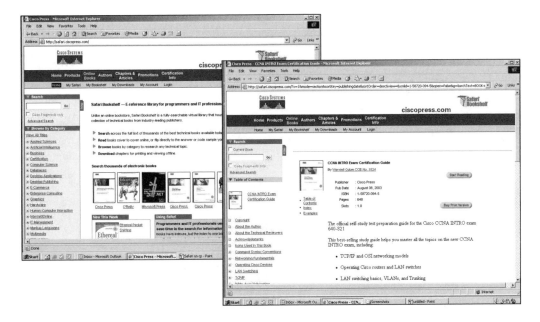

With Safari Bookshelf you can

- **Search** the full text of thousands of technical books, including more than 70 Cisco Press titles from authors such as Wendell Odom, Jeff Doyle, Bill Parkhurst, Sam Halabi, and Karl Solie.

- **Read** the books on My Bookshelf from cover to cover, or just flip to the information you need.

- **Browse** books by category to research any technical topic.

- **Download** chapters for printing and viewing offline.

With a customized library, you'll have access to your books when and where you need them—and all you need is a user name and password.

TRY SAFARI BOOKSHELF FREE FOR 14 DAYS!

You can sign up to get a 10-slot Bookshelf free for the first 14 days. Visit **http://safari.ciscopress.com** to register.

Cisco Press

Learning is serious business.

Invest wisely.

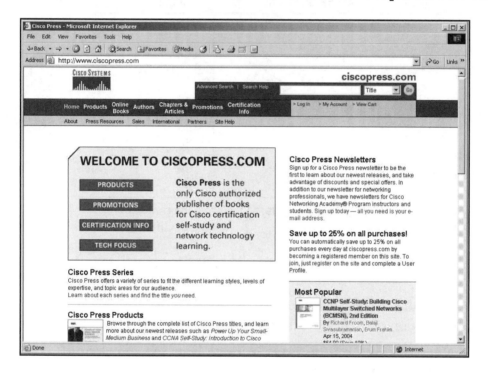

DISCUSS
NETWORKING PRODUCTS AND TECHNOLOGIES WITH CISCO EXPERTS AND NETWORKING PROFESSIONALS WORLDWIDE

VISIT NETWORKING PROFESSIONALS
A CISCO ONLINE COMMUNITY
WWW.CISCO.COM/GO/DISCUSS

THIS IS THE POWER OF THE NETWORK. now.

CISCO SYSTEMS